THE 9/11 TORONTO REPORT

INTERNATIONAL HEARINGS ON THE EVENTS OF SEPTEMBER 11, 2001

AUTHORIZED EDITION
Edited by James Gourley

INTERNATIONAL CENTER FOR 9/11 STUDIES
Dallas, Texas

THE 9/11 TORONTO REPORT

Published by:
International Center for 9/11 Studies
Dallas, Texas
www.ic911studies.org

Copyright © 2013 James Gourley
All rights reserved. This book may not be reproduced, in whole or part, in any form without permission of the copyright owner.

Cover design by Mark Dotzler
Interior design by Erin Stark; TLC Graphics, *www.TLCGraphics.com*

ISBN-10: 1478369205
EAN-13: 9781478369202

Printed in the United States of America

Table of Contents

Introduction vii

CHAPTER 1
Testimony of Lorie Van Auken
and Bob McIlvaine 1

CHAPTER 2
Anomalies in the 9/11 Commission Report
By David Ray Griffin.. 21

CHAPTER 3
Why the NIST World Trade Center Reports are False
By Kevin Ryan... 37

CHAPTER 4
Seeing 9/11 from Above: A Comparative Analysis of
State Crimes Against Democracy
By Lance deHaven-Smith.................................. 61

CHAPTER 5
9/11 as a Deep Event: How CIA Personnel Helped
Allow It to Happen
By Peter Dale Scott.. 107

CHAPTER 6
Evidence of Insider Trading before September 11th Re-examined
By Paul Zarembka 129

CHAPTER 7
Anomalies in the Official Accounts of American 77 and United 93
By David Ray Griffin 151

CHAPTER 8
Eyewitness Evidence of Explosions in the Twin Towers
By Graeme MacQueen 173

CHAPTER 9
WTC 7: A Refutation of NIST's Analysis
By David Chandler 197

CHAPTER 10
Evidence for Extreme Temperatures at the World Trade Center
By Kevin Ryan 215

CHAPTER 11
The Official Collapse Narrative and the Experimental Method
By Jon Cole 233

CHAPTER 12
Advanced Pyrotechnic or Explosive Material Discovered in WTC Dust
By Richard Gage, Gregg Roberts and Andrea Dreger 253

TABLE OF CONTENTS

CHAPTER 13
Evidence of Explosives at the Pentagon
By Barbara Honegger 257

CHAPTER 14
In Denial of Democracy: Social Psychological Implications for Public Discourse on State Crimes Against Democracy Post-9/11
By Laurie Manwell 285

CHAPTER 15
Reflections on the Toronto Hearings
By David Johnson 323

CHAPTER 16
Strengths and Weaknesses of the Toronto 9/11 Hearings in Advancing the Case for a New Investigation
By Herbert Jenkins 343

CHAPTER 17
Remarks on the Toronto Hearings
By Richard B. Lee 375

CHAPTER 18
Report on the Toronto Hearings
By Ferdinando Imposimato 383

Appendix 409

Introduction

BY JAMES GOURLEY

THIS REPORT IS ISSUED FROM THE INTERNATIONAL HEARings on the Events of September 11, 2001, which were held in Toronto, Canada over the Tenth Anniversary of the 9/11 attacks.[1]

The Toronto Hearings, held at Ryerson University, constituted a four-day event that ran from September 8-11, 2011. The mandate of the Toronto Hearings was to bring to light the most substantial evidence which has accumulated over the past ten years – evidence that the 9/11 Commission Report and the various reports issued by the National Institute of Standards and Technology failed to adequately address – demonstrating that there is the need for a new, independent and international investigation into the events of 9/11. The Hearings were not a new investigation in themselves, but provided a succinct summary of the strongest evidence that a new investigation is immediately warranted and that the international community cannot abdicate this responsibility any longer.

THE 9/11 TORONTO REPORT

The format and conduct of the Hearings was analogous to – though not exactly the same as – a legal proceeding that is known in the United States as a grand jury hearing. Other legal jurisdictions have similar mechanisms known as preliminary hearings or committal procedures. One common thread among all of these proceedings is that, after a crime has been investigated, a prosecutor presents his best evidence that the defendant or suspect committed the crime in question. Typically, the suspect or defendant does not have the opportunity to present counter-evidence to a grand jury, but sometimes is invited by the prosecutor to do so.

Indeed, neither the National Institute of Standards and Technology nor the 9/11 Commission – the U.S. government bodies that have promulgated what are referred to as the official government version of 9/11 – testified at the Toronto Hearings. These parties were invited several times to participate in the Hearings, but declined to do so. We cannot help but conclude that these entities will continue to hide behind their reports until a body with subpoena power, or sufficient political clout, forces them to appear and defend their work.

In a grand jury proceeding, the grand jury simply decides whether there is a *prima facie* case that can be made against the defendant. A prima facie case has been made when evidence has been presented that – unless rebutted – would be sufficient to prove a particular proposition or fact. If the grand jury does find that a prima facie case has been made, then, at a separate proceeding known as a trial, which the defendant is required to attend, the case is presented to an adjudicator, usually a judge or jury. At the trial, the defendant has the opportunity to rebut the case with counter-evidence.

INTRODUCTION

Again, the analogy between the Toronto Hearings and a grand jury proceeding is not perfect, because there are some differences in format and product of the Toronto Hearings.

The Hearings were not conducted according to any specific laws or legal procedures, and the outcome does not have the force of law. Also, unlike a grand jury, the evidence was not presented to citizens chosen at random, due to obvious logistical problems. Governments can force citizens to show up for jury duty, but the organizers of the Toronto Hearings did not have that ability.

Instead of convening a traditional jury panel, we decided to gather together an international panel of prominent individuals, who agreed to do what governments and major media outlets around the world have so far refused to do: look at the evidence objectively and decide whether it deserves wider consideration. In selecting panelists, we looked for two qualifications in an individual: someone who is (1) highly credible and (2) open to objectively assessing the evidence. We certainly found four such individuals, and we are grateful to have had such distinguished gentlemen participating in their important role in these Hearings.

Ferdinando Imposimato is the Honorary President of the Supreme Court of Italy. As a former Senior Investigative Judge, he presided over several major terrorism-related cases, including cases involving the kidnapping and assassination of President Aldo Moro, the attempted assassination of Pope John Paul II, and the Mafia assassination of Carabinieri General Carlo Alberto Della Chiesa. In 1984 the French journal Le Point named him "Man of the Year: Courageous Judge," and in 1985 the London Times devoted a full page to his work as "scourge of the Mafia," while a book published by the United Nations described him as "the symbol of Justice." Ferdinando Imposimato is also a former Senator who served on the Anti-Mafia Commission in three administrations, a former legal consultant to the United Nations on drug trafficking, the author or co-author of seven books on international terrorism, state corruption, and related matters, and a Grand Officer of the Order of Merit of the Republic of Italy.

Herbert Jenkins is a Professor Emeritus of Psychology at McMaster University. Educated at Oberlin College and Harvard University, he held positions at the Lincoln Laboratories in Massachusetts, at MIT, and at the Bell Telephone Laboratories before coming to McMaster in 1963. Herbert Jenkins helped create McMaster's interdisciplinary Arts and Science Program and its Engineering and Society Program, and served as Director of both. In 2009 Professor Jenkins was awarded an honorary doctorate by McMaster University in recognition of his influential contributions to the psychology of learning and judgment, as well as his leadership in developing models of inquiry-based, interdisciplinary, and socially responsible undergraduate education that have had a significant impact on current thinking about curriculum development in Canadian universities.

Richard B. Lee is University Professor Emeritus of Anthropology at the University of Toronto. Internationally recognized for his ethnographic studies, he has held academic appointments at Harvard, Rutgers, and Columbia University. The author of books that have had a major influence in the discipline, and of more than a hundred articles and book chapters, he is a Fellow of the Royal Society of Canada, a Foreign Honorary Member of the American Academy of Arts and Sciences, and a Foreign Associate of the National Academy of Sciences. Professor Lee has served as

INTRODUCTION

President of the Canadian Anthropological Society, and holds honorary doctorates from the University of Alaska Fairbanks and the University of Guelph. The journal *American Scientist* has listed his 1979 book on the !Kung San people as standing among the hundred greatest scientific works of the twentieth century.

David Johnson is a Professor Emeritus of Urban and Regional Planning at the University of Tennessee. He holds BA and Master's degrees in architecture and planning from Yale University, and a PhD in regional planning from Cornell University. A Fellow of the American Institute of Certified Planners, he served with the US Army Corps of Engineers, and was a planner on the staffs of the Boston Redevelopment Authority, the Washington National Capital Planning Commission and the Regional Plan Association of New York. David Johnson has been a Fulbright Scholar in India, Thailand, the Soviet Union, and Cyprus, and has served as Professor and Chair of the Planning Departments at Syracuse University and at Ball State University. A Past President of the Fulbright Association of the United States, he has directed educational projects in Brazil and Portugal, and helped to found the Fulbright Prize, whose recipients include Nelson Mandela and Jimmy Carter.

There is no question that the opinions of these four gentlemen on the evidence will carry significant influence in many quarters, as well they should.

Over the course of four days, these panelists listened to the best evidence that has been collected over the last 10 years that contradicts the official government version of events for 9/11. Each witness presented an opening statement, and then answered questions posed by the panel. The panel was given considerable latitude in the subject and nature of the questions they may ask, and witnesses answered every question to the best of their knowledge. After the Hearings adjourned on the fourth day, the panel reconvened over the following weeks and months, and made a decision on which aspects, if any, of the evidence presented deserves further investigation by governments with subpoena and political power. The panelists' conclusions and recommendations can be found in their respective contributions to this report.

The witnesses who testified at the Toronto Hearings included the following:

- **Lance DeHaven-Smith** – Professor in the Reubin O'D. Askew School of Public Administration and Policy at Florida State University
- **Peter Dale Scott** – Former English professor at the University of California, Berkeley; former diplomat and a poet; author of numerous books, including "The Road to 9/11"
- **David Ray Griffin** – retired professor of philosophy of religion and theology; co-founder of the Center for Process Studies, a research center of Claremont School of Theology which seeks to promote the common good by means of the relational approach found in process thought; author of a number of books on the subject of the September 11 attacks
- **Paul Zarembka** – Professor of Economics at the State University of New York at Buffalo
- **Jonathan Cole** – Professional Engineer licensed in New Hampshire and Florida, with 28 years of experience
- **David Chandler** – physics instructor; graduate of Harvey Mudd College, Claremont Graduate University, and Cal Poly in Pomona

INTRODUCTION

- **Laurie Manwell** – PhD candidate in Behavioral Neuroscience and Toxicology at the University of Guelph
- **Niels Harrit** – retired professor of Chemistry at the University of Copenhagen; lead author of peer-reviewed scientific paper titled "Active Thermitic Material Discovered in Dust from the 9/11 WTC Catastrophe"
- **Richard Gage, AIA** – San Francisco Bay Area architect and a member of the American Institute of Architects
- **Graeme MacQueen** – doctor of philosophy in comparative religion from Harvard University; professor in the Religious Studies department of McMaster University for 30 years; founding Director of the Centre for Peace Studies at McMaster University
- **Kevin Ryan** – former scientist at Underwriters Laboratories (UL), the company that certified the steel used in the World Trade Center; fired by UL in 2004 for publicly asking questions about the WTC investigation being conducted by the National Institute of Standards and Technology (NIST)
- **Barbara Honegger** – former White House Policy Analyst and Special Assistant to the Assistant to the President for Domestic Policy; former Senior Military Affairs Journalist at the Naval Postgraduate School, the science, technology and national security affairs graduate research university of the U.S. Department of Defense
- **Jay Kolar** – freelance writer; film studies instructor
- **Michel Chossudovsky** – Professor Emeritus of Economics at the University of Ottawa; Director of the Centre for Research on Globalization.

THE 9/11 TORONTO REPORT

- **Mike Gravel** – former U.S. Senator; 2008 Presidential Candidate
- **Cynthia McKinney** – former US Congresswoman; Green Party Presidential Candidate in 2008

All of the substantive chapters in this final report of the Toronto Hearings were prepared by the experts listed above, though not all were able to contribute to the report. All of the witness testimony presented at the Toronto Hearings is available on DVD at *www.pressfortruth.ca*. The panel considered the evidence presented at the hearings, and read pre-publication drafts of all of the chapters these experts wrote in preparing their own chapters. The panel's conclusions and recommendations follow the experts' chapters.

The Toronto Hearings were also supported by 9/11 family members Lorie Van Auken and Bob McIlvaine. That day, Lorie lost her husband and Bob lost his son. Both testified at the Hearings by video submission. The text of Lorie's and Bob's remarks to the Toronto Hearings is presented following this introduction.

September 11, 2001 was a horrific event, and we still mourn for those who lost their lives and those who lost loved ones. Our hope is that these Hearings will take us one step closer to achieving real justice and accountability for the damage that was caused. We certainly believe, and all of the panelists have agreed, that the evidence presented at the Toronto Hearings, if objectively evaluated, presents a *prima facie* case that the official government version of events is wrong and deserves further investigation.

CHAPTER ONE

Testimony of Lori Van Auken and Bob McIlvaine to the Toronto Hearings

Testimony of Lori Van Auken

THANK YOU FOR CONTINUING ON THE PATH TO SEEKING the truth on this tenth anniversary of 9/11 and for inviting me to speak to you.

My name is Lorie Van Auken. On September 11, 2001, my husband, Kenneth, went to work at Cantor Fitzgerald in the North Tower of the World Trade Center. Ken was on the 105th floor of Tower One when American Airlines flight 11 hit his building. He left a message that began with "I love you" and went on to let me know that he had felt the building get "hit by something." Ken didn't know if he would "get out" … essentially he was calling to say goodbye. I knew that my husband had survived the initial strike, but that's all I knew.

It was a harrowing day. As the planes were striking their targets, my mother called and said, "put the TV on." My sister called as she was heading into Manhattan to see if I knew what was happening in New York City. As we were speaking, the second hijacked plane, UA 175, flew over her head. I remember telling her to just turn around and get away from there.

My two kids were 12 and 14 years old, and were at school. I was in a panic, and didn't know what to do. I called their schools and was assured that my children were both safe and would not hear about the attacks at school. Of course that was absurd. My son watched the attacks in real time on a TV that a teacher was riveted to. The teacher was unaware that my son was watching from behind. My daughter heard about a plane crashing into her father's office building from another student.

While I sat in utter shock from what I was watching on television, I continued to hope for a glimpse of Ken, somewhere in the chaos of people running and jumping from the buildings.

At some point, President Bush was shown sitting in an elementary school class listening to a story about a Pet Goat – this footage was in a split screen with a video of the WTC that had smoke billowing from a plane-shaped hole. I clearly remember trying to will Mr. Bush to get up and do something, but even after Andrew Card whispered something to him, he just continued to sit there. That was my first clue that something was not quite right. Shouldn't the "Commander-in-Chief" have a more important job to do while planes are crashing into the WTC than listening to an elementary school class reading lesson? Wasn't the President of the United States, himself, a potential terrorist target? I thought of my own kids and worried that the children in that Florida classroom were in harm's way if President Bush was a target.

As I continued watching the most unbelievable drama I had ever seen, the WTC buildings started crumbling and crashing to

TESTIMONY OF LAURIE VAN AUKEN AND BOB MCILVAINE TO THE TORONTO HEARINGS

the ground. The building that was hit first, my husband's building, remained standing as the South Tower, which was hit second, fell. I thought, how did the South Tower get hit in the top corner of the building without that piece of the building falling away from the rest of the structure, as you would expect it to? Suddenly, Ken's building exploded into dust and I watched as people tried to run away from the gigantic wall of smoke and debris that seemed to follow them down the street. Really? Steel-framed skyscrapers could disintegrate just like that?

My next-door neighbor picked my kids up from school that day. My parents were up from Florida, and were supposed to head back home on 9/11. They ended up staying with us for a month attempting to help.

As the news spread, our friends and family members seemed to appear from nowhere to sit with us while we waited for news about Ken's whereabouts and condition.

That first night I got almost no sleep and made hundreds of phone calls to NYC and NJ hospitals as well as the Red Cross, hoping to find my husband alive somewhere. We didn't find out how much our lives would change until two days later when Howard Lutnick, the CEO of Cantor Fitzgerald, appeared on TV. That's when we learned that Ken didn't get out … that no one in the building above the impact of the airplane had gotten out alive.

The sadness and horror that shrouded my family after September 11th cannot possibly be conveyed to you. Before long the gnawing questions started overwhelming me. I wasn't eating or sleeping very much and instead I found myself hunched over my computer in my basement, reading and researching every 9/11 related article I could get my hands on. I read articles from all around the globe, trying to make sense of what had happened. I found that nothing made sense and I felt I could trust no one to tell me the truth. I started noticing that after September 14, 2001, the 9/11 stories in all of the newspapers began to look eerily the same. How could every writer be handling the emerging news in exactly the same way?

There would eventually be three different versions of NORAD's timeline of their 9/11 response, but on September 18, 2001, the first version was released to the public. Since it seemed that there was little, if any, military intervention during these attacks, the obvious question became: what was the military response on 9/11 supposed to look like? We learned that NORAD had certain protocols to follow for planes that have lost radio contact, and for planes that are off-course. There is a separate set of protocols for hijacked airliners. With all these protocols already in place, how could four hijacked commercial airliners fly around the skies of the U.S. for so long with no military response? How were the hijackers able to evade our country's elaborate defenses?

Mindy Kleinberg and I live in the same town, and our husbands worked for the same company, but we had never met prior to September 11, 2001. Right after the tragedy, a mutual friend introduced us. Mindy and I began attending a support group that the families affected by Pan Am 103/Lockerbie had set up for the 9/11 families. There we met Bob Monetti who had lost a child in the crash of Pan Am 103. At another meeting for 9/11 victims' family members, we became acquainted with Patty Casazza and Kristen Breitweiser, and we began emailing each other about questions we had.

Soon we would learn that there would be a Congressional investigation into ONLY the intelligence failures that led to 9/11.

TESTIMONY OF LAURIE VAN AUKEN AND BOB MCILVAINE TO THE TORONTO HEARINGS

But by then we knew that every governmental agency had failed us on September 11th: NORAD, the FAA, the DOJ, etc., in addition to the FBI, CIA and NSA. We wanted an investigation into ALL of the actions and failures that had led to the deaths of our loved ones and so many others on that horrible September day.

Many people couldn't, or more likely, didn't *want* to hear the difficult questions regarding 9/11 that were emerging, but Bob Monetti listened and encouraged us to go to Washington D.C. to ask for a comprehensive investigation. We learned that there was a stalled bill proposing a 9/11 commission and decided to go and see if we could light a fire under the lawmakers to push forward with the legislation for an inquiry.

Asking for an investigation into 9/11 became a full-time job. The four of us planned a rally in Washington D.C. for June 11, 2001, nine months after 9/11, to garner support for our cause. Other 9/11 family groups joined forces with us. The rally's attendance was less than we had hoped for, but the press was there, and our journey had begun.

When seeking meetings in Washington, you are asked for the name of your organization. Thus, the four of us, Mindy Kleinberg, Patty Casazza, Kristen Breitweiser and I, became the September 11th Advocates. Soon, other victims' family members from other states began referring to us as "The Jersey Girls." Before long, the press picked it up as well.

We came to learn that we had some allies and some detractors in Washington. Senator Toricelli (D-NJ) and his office helped us with the details of planning our rally. We needed chairs, water, a podium and a sound system. Representative Chris Smith (R-NJ) lent us his Chief of Staff, Mary Noonan, and she helped us navigate the complex and treacherous terrain of Washington D.C.

The four of us set up a meeting with Eleanor Hill, who led the Joint Intelligence Committee's investigation (the JICI), into intelligence failures. From her we got confirmation that we needed more than just a scant look at intelligence failures to find out what had gone wrong to allow 9/11 to happen.

Gail Sheehy wrote an article about us called "Four 9/11 Moms Battle Bush" that told our story and brought public attention to our plight.

The group of us that would later become the twelve members of the Family Steering Committee for the 9/11 Commission had now loosely formed, and we learned to split up in order to meet with as many Senators and Congressmen as we could, on a given visit to Washington. We also met a few times with the director of the FBI, Robert Mueller and his staff, where we were told about the FBI's ongoing PENTTBOM investigation – PENT for Pentagon, Pen for Pennsylvania, TT for the Twin Towers and Bom, B-o-m for the exploding planes. The reasons given for why we couldn't have any immediate answers often came from the FBI's "ongoing investigation" excuse. We were not at all reassured by those meetings.

Suffice it to say, raising kids alone while having to go to Washington was difficult. We didn't want to stay overnight so we would rise at 4:30 AM in order to be in D.C. on time for early meetings, remain all day, and get back on the road to be home by 11 PM.

As the final language for a bill that would give us the 9/11 Commission was almost agreed upon, we began to notice a lot of foot dragging. Vice President Dick Cheney had clearly been against having an inquiry from the start, and was working behind the scenes to keep things from moving forward. Cheney was often seen on TV with some *scary* reason for why we couldn't have an investigation into 9/11. One time, while we were all together in Rep. Porter Goss's office, Goss got a phone call from Cheney telling him to "keep negotiating" with us. Goss looked flustered by that phone call, and we were beginning to learn how Washington worked.

We finally got fed up with the intense run-around that we were getting with everyone blaming everyone else for the delay. We couldn't take it anymore and asked Senator Lieberman (D-CT) to organize a meeting with all of the involved parties in *one* room, and to our surprise, he obliged. During that gathering it became painfully apparent to everyone that it was the Bush/Cheney White House that was causing the stalemate. As the meeting wore on, and it appeared that once again there wouldn't be an agreement to the terms, all of the 9/11 family members that were in attendance stood up in solidarity saying that we would not leave without an agreement on the legislation. The press was outside waiting to hear about the outcome, and the White House knew it. That was a critical moment and a turning point for us.

Finally, the House passed a version of our legislation for an independent investigation. When the Senate voted on their version of the 9/11 Commission bill, we were invited to Washington to witness the event. As the Senate voted on the 9/11 Commission legislation, we were there cheering.

Then, we learned about conference committees, where the two houses of Congress would mesh the versions of the legislation that each had voted on. We wanted two years for the investigation, but got only 18 months. Initially, only three million dollars was allotted, compared with 50 million dollars allotted to investigating the Challenger explosion. We wanted subpoena power for each Commissioner, but with pressure from the Bush/Cheney White House, there was an agreement made that would allow subpoena power only if the Chair and Vice Chair OR at least six Commissioners voted for it. This was a political body, split between five democrats and five republicans. Getting six commissioners to agree to ask for a subpoena would have meant that one person had to jump over to the other side, which was highly unlikely.

The Commission legislation also gave guidance as to who would appoint the 9/11 Commissioners. As per the legislation, President Bush got to choose who would head the Commission. His first choice was Henry Kissinger. This news was getting some very negative press. Since Kissinger was informally known as the "king of cover-ups," and we had fought long and hard for the creation of an independent investigation into the events of 9/11, this was unacceptable to most of us. Since Kissinger was tapped to head our commission, the Family Steering Committee asked to meet with him in his NYC office. It was as hot as a sauna in his office, and we wondered about the heat as we looked at the photos he had hanging on his walls. We all started peeling off our coats and sweaters. I walked around looking for any photos of Kissinger with the bin Ladens. A lot of research was done in preparation for that meeting and we had learned that Kissinger and Associates had some of the bin Laden family members as their clients.

Henry Kissinger didn't want to publicly reveal his client list, but we knew that all of the commissioners were required to do so. After some polite conversation, I felt compelled to ask him

TESTIMONY OF LAURIE VAN AUKEN AND BOB MCILVAINE TO THE TORONTO HEARINGS

directly if he had any Saudi clients or any clients by the name of bin Laden. After I asked my questions he spilled his coffee and nearly fell off of his couch. We'll never know exactly why, but the next day Kissinger resigned.

President Bush then named Tom Kean, the former Governor of New Jersey, as Chairman of the 9/11 Commission, which was now taking shape. Various Congressional leaders picked the balance of the Commissioners. As we did our research it became clear that all of the members that had been chosen for the commission had some conflict of interest. It began to appear as if the choices had been made by those in power, more for the purpose of covering political backs than for the purpose of a comprehensive investigation. Our fight to establish the commission took 14 months.

The Family Steering Committee first met with Governor Kean in his office at Drew University in New Jersey, *and* after all ten of the commissioners were named, we met with them for the first time to lay out our concerns. At that meeting we asked them to *subpoena early and often*. At that meeting everyone seemed sympathetic.

The 9/11 Commission had been passed into law, however the work could not begin until all of the Commissioners and staff received their security clearances. This took far too long. They also needed to find and furnish office space in Washington D.C. and New York City. Meanwhile the clock was ticking on our investigation.

The first public Commission hearing was in March of 2003. Unbeknownst to us, our real work was just beginning. As "watchdogs" of the Commission, the next two years of our lives were exhausting and exasperating as we battled the White House, Congress, The Commission's executive director, Phillip Zelikow and at various times both with and against the 9/11 Commissioners themselves on the various issues that arose.

We fought along with the Commissioners to get more money for the Commission, to get an extension of time, to get access to important White House documents and to get Condoleeza Rice to testify. We battled against the Commissioners trying to get them to subpoena recalcitrant witnesses and agencies, and were outraged when we learned they were using "minders" in interviews. We tried in vain to get them to fire their conflict-laden executive director, Zelikow, and fought against allowing Bush and Cheney to testify together in a void, with no transcript and no press. We let them know when they fell short of asking hard-hitting questions.

We went to every open hearing hoping that the Commissioners would ask tough questions. I can recall only a few instances during the 12 public hearings that we were actually pleased with the vigor of questioning. For example, we gave Richard Ben-Veniste high marks for his questioning of Condi and the uncovering of the August 6th President's Daily Brief (PDB), which emerged as a key document.

As Executive Staff Director of the Commission, Phillip Zelikow really ran the show, deciding what topics would be covered at the hearings and who would be called to testify. After some cursory research we found that in 1995, he and Condoleezza Rice had co-authored a book called "Germany Unified and Europe Transformed: A Study in Statecraft". They had worked together in the first Bush White House, and had both been members of the second Bush's transition team, in 2000-2001.

TESTIMONY OF LAURIE VAN AUKEN AND BOB MCILVAINE TO THE TORONTO HEARINGS

As our intense monitoring of the 9/11 Commission continued, we found that there were even more insidious conflicts surrounding Dr. Zelikow. In his work for President Bush's Foreign Intelligence Advisory Board (PFIAB), Zelikow helped write the plans for the Iraq war.

The Family Steering Committee immediately put out a press release.

"It is apparent that Dr. Zelikow should never have been permitted to be Executive Staff Director of the Commission. As Executive Staff Director his job has been to steer the direction of the Commission's investigation, an investigation whose mandate includes understanding why the Bush Administration failed to prioritize the Al Qaeda threat. It is abundantly clear that Dr. Zelikow's conflicts go beyond just the transition period."

The press release went on to request Zelikow's resignation.

We also wrote a letter directly to the Commissioners reiterating this issue going even further by stating:

"It is now apparent why there has been so little effort to assign individual culpability. We now can see that trail would lead directly to the staff director himself."

Again we asked for his immediate resignation. Our urgent requests were denied.

This was not the ideal formula for an independent investigation. The 9/11 families, or at least some of us, were hoping for a real investigation with scholars and experts in the appropriate fields and evidence to back up the work. We had wanted true independence from politics. We had fought so hard to get this Commission and did not want someone who clearly had huge conflicts of interest to be running the investigation. But unfortunately, that was what we got.

Zelikow split the Commission into eight teams, with each one covering a specific topic. The Family Steering Committee set up conference calls with whichever team was in charge of the upcoming hearing. Zelikow, or his assistant, Chris Kojm monitored the calls. The FSC wrote questions that we felt needed to be asked and as we sat at the 9/11 Commission hearings, we prayed that our questions would be posed. Sometimes our questions and concerns were addressed, but more often they weren't. If one of our questions was asked, the follow-up was mostly non-existent which basically let the witness completely off the hook. If a witness didn't have the information that they were being asked about and said that they would send the information along at a later date, we never knew if they had kept their promise.

In the beginning, no witnesses were even sworn in. And the subpoena power that we had fought so hard for them to have, was not being used. The first time the Commissioners used their subpoena power was on the FAA in October 2003, almost a year after the formation of the commission. In November of 2003 they issued their second subpoena to NORAD with threats of more subpoenas to come. But no more were issued.

Soon we were told by Zelikow not to send our questions directly to the Commissioners. We didn't adhere to that rule, and continued to forward our questions along. We were appalled to learn that all the witnesses called before the 9/11 Commission were interviewed with "minders" in the room. This sounded to us more like tactics that would be used to control people's responses, not an open search for the truth.

TESTIMONY OF LAURIE VAN AUKEN AND BOB MCILVAINE TO THE TORONTO HEARINGS

The Commission finally got catapulted into the media spotlight after Richard Clarke's book "Against All Enemies" was released. The coverage really heated up when the families staged a walk out to protest the fact that Richard Armitage was called to testify in place of Condoleezza Rice. Ultimately, the White House capitulated and allowed Rice to testify. Under questioning from Richard Ben-Veniste, Condi revealed that the title of the August 6th, 2001 PDB was "bin Laden determined to strike in the United States." She claimed that the document was historical and did not speak of a domestic threat. I felt that her claims were patently ridiculous and color-coded the August 6th PDB to show where the threats highlighted were both domestic *and* current. In one of our appearances on Hardball with Chris Matthews, I showed and explained my version of the document.

In July of 2004, the 9/11 Commission released its final report. We wanted time to read it before commenting publicly, but it didn't take long for us to realize that the report was a huge disappointment. Many important topics weren't covered, and far too many of our questions remained unanswered. "Everyone was at fault, therefore no one was at fault" was the Commission's mantra. To us that just sounded like a hollow excuse for finding no one accountable.

With the passage of time, more evidence has come to light showing that the Commission's report was less than a complete investigation. The official 9/11 story is based on tortured confessions, and legal experts acknowledge that evidence based on torture is not reliable. Zelikow himself has even tacitly acknowledged this.

THE 9/11 TORONTO REPORT

In 2006, Kean and Hamilton released a book called *Without Precedent, The Inside Story of the 9/11 Commission*. In it they state that they knew that NORAD had lied to them, but never followed up to get the full story from them. They also catalogued their concerns about Phil Zelikow. Contrary to the assurances we had received from them regarding Zelikow during the Commission's tenure, in their book they admit to having had their own reservations about him. Slowly, other commissioners came out with similar comments and staff members, such as John Farmer, have written books that speak of issues within the commission.

Philip Shenon, a NY Times reporter wrote an in depth book about the Commission, which shows how Phillip Zelikow derailed the investigation. If information came up during an interview that did not fit with what he had decided the storyline would be, he would not allow the new information to be investigated. For example, documents from the NSA were never even looked at, even though they were a potential treasure trove of information.

Ten years after the 9/11 attacks, the old questions still linger and new ones have arisen. A real investigation into 9/11 has never been done. This is incredible considering the direction that we have taken as a country. The passing of the Patriot Act, entering two wars, and our entire foreign policy, has all been based on the official account of 9/11.

The proper place for the 9/11 proceedings would be a courtroom with subpoena power, rules for swearing in witnesses and established protocols for handling questioning, cross examination and evidence. And ultimately, one would hope, real accountability for the actions that led to the deaths of so many.

TESTIMONY OF LAURIE VAN AUKEN AND
BOB MCILVAINE TO THE TORONTO HEARINGS

A reporter recently asked me if there is anywhere at all that we can still take our unanswered questions. My answer, sadly, was no. Many of the events that occurred on 9/11 were caught on video, so it is still possible to see the evidence of the unfolding crime. Forums such as this one, set up to scrutinize the events of September 11th, are critical.

I want to thank you all for taking the time to gather together on this tenth anniversary in order to explore the issues and to continue asking the questions that have never been answered regarding the events of September 11th, 2001.

Testimony of Bob McIlvaine

Hello, my name is Bob McIlvaine. I live in the suburbs of Philadelphia.

My son Bobby, almost ten years ago, died right here on the site at the north tower. It's been a long ten years. Basically all I wanted to do was introduce how I've come to the point of doing what I'm doing now.

On September 11th 2001, Bobby lived on 66th between first and second and took the subway to Fulton Street and walked over from Fulton Street where he had just started a job at Merrill Lynch. We're standing on Vesey Street. If we go down the street and make a left on West, Merrill Lynch is across the street on West.

He had just started there two or three weeks before 9/11. So that day we had no idea what happened to Bobby but we came up to New York and we did find his body and we took Bobby home and buried him a week later on Tuesday the 18th.

For years and years I've been trying to find out what happened that day. But in the beginning things were so frantic. You spent almost a year just grieving because you just can't figure out what happened. But I questioned the story of 9/11 immediately. I just wasn't getting involved in it too much. I had chosen, at that time, to go into the anti-war movement or the peace movement. I joined a group called September 11th Families for Peaceful Tomorrows who were against the war, specifically a war because of 9/11. So I spent a lot of time doing that. I traveled around the world and it sort of culminated right before the Iraq War when I got arrested in front of the White House, which is one of the best things I've ever done in my life. It just felt good.

I traveled to Japan to walk from Nagasaki to Hiroshima to honor the civilians killed in wars, particularly the bombings of Nagasaki and Hiroshima. I've been to Bogota, Colombia talking about basically what I felt at that time – the blowback of American foreign policy had created this havoc that we have in the world.

And of course I went to 90% of the 9/11 Commission hearings. Well, my whole life changed after Condoleezza Rice testified. I don't call it testimony. As far as Condoleezza Rice, it was a filibuster. They were questioning her about this August 6th memo that said Osama Bin Laden was supposed to attack the United States. And of course, I assume everyone knows what a filibuster is but she just talked nonsense, and each commissioner only had five minutes to speak up or to ask questions. Well, anyway that ended and nothing was said, nothing was done. All the commissioners were surrounding Condoleezza Rice shaking her hand, everyone's smiling and that's when I lost my cool. It was after that that I did an interview. I was angry and I've been angry ever since. The investigation was a total sham and I think everyone in the

TESTIMONY OF LAURIE VAN AUKEN AND BOB MCILVAINE TO THE TORONTO HEARINGS

world knows the investigation was a total sham. Even some of the commissioners admit that it was a sham.

I've dedicated my life since then to just concentrating on 9/11 truth. Even at that time I felt strongly that there were people in the United States that were involved in this, but, who knew? Since 2004, I've dedicated my life to what happened that day. And I've been very global in that thinking. You talk about put options, you talk about NORAD, you talk about some of the other things that are so important to 9/11. But I've noticed that when I talk to people they get glassy eyed because there is so much information.

Now, all this time that I'm looking into 9/11, I'm also [realizing that] if anyone has lost a child, specifically murdered, you always want to know exactly what happened to your child. I know people that have lost a child in a car accident. They wanted to know – did that child suffer? And that's a big part. I could never figure out what happened so we took Bobby home that week and he was one of the first ten bodies found. I never viewed the body itself, and I'm glad I didn't because it was truly mangled. But his whole body was taken home.

Well, a few years ago I finally ran into the doctor who examined Bobby and he gave me an outline and he told me not to look at the pictures but he gave me an outline of all his injuries. And this was very revealing to me because there was over a hundred phone calls made to Bobby that morning and of course, not one of them was answered. Now if he was anywhere he would have immediately answered that phone. So what was happening, this is what I think, is that he came down Fulton Street and walked over here and decided to go to a seminar that was on the 106th floor of the old north tower. And we ruled out that he was on the 106th floor because he wouldn't have been one of the first ten bodies found.

We thought maybe he jumped but the thing is he had one small break on his leg and all his injuries were in his chest and in the face. The back of him – no problem. His skull was still intact but everything was blown off his face. He lost his arm, and there were severe lacerations of his chest. So from talking to the doctor, we knew that Bobby died instantly. He didn't have a chance to pick up his phone or answer it.

Through the years in my investigation, and I'll get to that real fast after we've done this, in talking to so many EMS workers, so many firemen, so many policemen, there were explosions that were taking place in the towers before and after the plane hit. And this is the most important point to me. The 9/11 Commission hearings talked about a fireball from the plane hitting from the 93rd up to the 98th floor. The plane went in at an angle, and the fuel was in the wings, and the 9/11 Commission report attributes the damage in the lobby [to the fireball]. Many firemen have told me it looked like a bomb went off in the lobby, and bombs went off in the subbasement. I've had reports that bombs went off before the plane hit.

My scenario is that, where the Commission said that a fireball created this damage, it was the explosions that were going off in the basement and in the lobby. I feel that Bobby walked into the lobby, or might not have even made it into the lobby, and there was a huge explosion. And what finally caught me onto what exactly happened to Bobby was that I was wondering why they said it was a fireball because he would have had severe burns.

TESTIMONY OF LAURIE VAN AUKEN AND BOB MCILVAINE TO THE TORONTO HEARINGS

Within the north tower you had people who were charred. People's bodies were cut in half, but everybody was charred.

So I asked, what happened to Bobby? I don't know exactly where they found him but, and this is a key point, in an explosion, in a detonation, the air that shoots out from that explosion is supersonic. It shoots out at supersonic speed and then the heat follows it. The fireball that supposedly came down does not have that energy. Remember, every window in the [lobby of the] north tower was blown out. You had an area of 208 feet by 208 feet. It's impossible that a fireball created that damage. Therefore, my thinking with Bobby was that he was walking into the tower, there was a huge explosion, it killed him instantly, hit him in the face and hit him in the chest, obviously took off his arm, and that's how he died.

I give presentations now and I ask – how in the world did those explosions take place? And my point is that there is no way in the world Muslims set those detonations. It was impossible that the planes created that havoc. So when I'm talking to you great people up in Toronto, I ask that, if you could, please spend time on these explosions. There is so much testimony.

Remember the 9/11 Commission Report refused to acknowledge the testimony they got from firemen, from policemen, from the EMS workers, of these explosions that were taking place in the subbasements. Both the 9/11 Commission Report and NIST lied about that. NIST said that there were no explosions so they didn't have to test the steel that came from the towers.

Do I want a new investigation? Quite frankly, I don't care if there's a new investigation. I know it's necessary but I can't believe an honest investigation will ever take place. You're having hearings up in Toronto. I just think it's such a wonderful thing because it's going to put this information out there, hopefully to the whole world and maybe from that we would have a non-partisan, objective investigation. But just for me, please spend the time on the explosions because that's a key, key point to me. If these explosions took place, I can't believe, I mean I know that the Muslims did not set those bombs within the towers. And I would rather exonerate, or let the Muslims off the hook. I'm getting to the point that I don't really care who murdered Bobby. The thing is that we're in constant war and it's based on what happened that day, what happened that morning, and there were explosions that took place.

I really wish you luck in Toronto. My spirit is with you but my family is here at Ground Zero every September 11th. I'll be thinking of you and I just want you all to stay strong and do your thing. Thank you.

CHAPTER TWO

Anomalies in the 9/11 Commission Report

BY DAVID RAY GIFFIN

IN THIS CHAPTER, I SPEAK OF "ANOMALIES IN THE 9/11 Commission Report." By anomalies, I mean features about and in this Report that would not be expected on the assumption that the official account of 9/11 is true and the Commission was a truth-seeking body. In the first part of this chapter, I discuss the background to, and some facts about, the 9/11 Commission. In the second part, I refer to some anomalous omissions in The 9/11 Commission Report.

I. Background to, and Facts about, the 9/11 Commission

After the 9/11 attacks, one might have expected the US Senate to have conducted an investigation, or hearings analogous to the Senate's Watergate Hearings, to determine who was responsible for the attacks. But Senate Majority Leader Tom Daschle acquiesced to an appeal by

THE 9/11 TORONTO REPORT

President Bush and Vice President Cheney "that only the House and Senate intelligence committees look into the potential breakdowns among federal agencies that could have allowed the terrorist attacks to occur, rather than a broader inquiry that some lawmakers have proposed." Bush and Cheney made this request, they said, because a broader inquiry would take resources and personnel "away from the war on terrorism."[2] So the resulting Joint Inquiry, authorized in February 2002, did not inquire as to who was responsible for the attacks, but simply presupposed the truth of the claims made by the Bush-Cheney administration.

Even with its limited scope, the Joint Inquiry was impeded by the Administration, which refused to give it access to many types of information.[3] But the Joint Inquiry was not in vain. It provided enough damaging revelations to leave President Bush little choice but to support the proposed creation of The National Commission on Terrorist Attacks upon the United States, which came to be called The 9/11 Commission. Nevertheless, there were continuing signs that the Bush administration did not want the truth about 9/11 to be discovered. I will cite five pieces of evidence.

1. Bush appointed Henry Kissinger to head the 9/11 Commission, leading the New York Times to ask whether this was not "a clever maneuver by the White House to contain an investigation it long opposed."[4]

2. When Kissinger had to resign, because he refused to name his clients, Bush appointed former New Jersey Governor Thomas Kean, who had no experience with Washington and national issues, and Representative Lee Hamilton, who had previously served as a Democrat covering up a Republican crime[5] and who had become friends with Cheney.[6] The Bush White House also

managed to get Philip Zelikow, a close friend of Condoleezza Rice, appointed as the executive director.

3. Bush promised only $3 million for the Commission (whereas Ken Starr's investigation of President Clinton's affair with Monica Lewinsky had cost almost $30 million).[7]

4. In March of 2003, the Commission asked for an additional $11 million, but the Bush administration turned the request down.[8] (Eventually, the Commission was given $15 million.)

5. Having declared that the Commission must finish its work by May 2004, the Bush administration delayed authority clearances for some of the Commissioners – Commissioner Max Cleland said, "The White House wants to run out the clock here"[9] – with the result that the Commission could not begin work until the middle of 2003, leaving it with less than a year to finish its work. (The Bush administration later did allow for a few more months.)

The most fateful of these impediments to a truth-seeking investigation proved to be the appointment of Philip Zelikow as executive director. Here are seven reasons.

First, Zelikow was essentially a member of the Bush-Cheney administration: He had worked with Condoleezza Rice on the National Security Council in the administration of George H. W. Bush; when the Republicans were out of office during the Clinton administration, Zelikow and Rice coauthored a book; then, after Rice was named National Security Advisor for President George W. Bush, she brought on Zelikow to help make the transition to the new National Security Council; and after that, Bush named him to the President's Foreign Intelligence Advisory Board, on which he served until he in 2003 became the 9/11 Commission's executive director.[10]

Second, when Rice needed to prepare the 2002 version of the *National Security Strategy of the United States* (generally known as *NSS 2002*) and wanted something "bolder" than the first draft, written by the State Department's Richard Haass, she turned to Zelikow.[11] The resulting document used 9/11 to justify a new doctrine of preemptive (technically, "preventive") warfare that had long been desired by Cheney and other neoconservatives for imperial purposes.[12] Whereas international law as articulated in the UN charter said that a country cannot launch a preemptive attack on another country unless it knows that an attack from that country is imminent – too imminent for the case to be taken to the UN Security Council – *NSS 2002* stated: "[T]he United States can no longer rely on a reactive posture.... [We must take] anticipatory action to defend ourselves, even if uncertainty remains as to the time and place of the enemy's attack. To forestall or prevent ... hostile acts by our adversaries, the United States will, if necessary, act preemptively."[13] This became known as the "Bush doctrine."[14] *NSS 2002* was used, as then-New York Times writer Philip Shenon stated in his 2008 book entitled *The Commission*, to "justify a preemptive strike on Iraq."[15]

Third, from watching the Commission's public hearings, one might have assumed that the Commission was under the guidance of the Commissioners, especially Kean and Hamilton. But none of the Commissioners, including Kean and Hamilton, were given offices in the K Street office building used by the Commission's staff. As a result, Shenon says, "most of the commissioners rarely visited K Street. Zelikow was in charge."[16] "Zelikow more than anyone else," Shenon says, "controlled what the final report of the 9/11 Commission would say."[17] He could exert this control because, although the first draft of each chapter was written by one of the investigative teams, Zelikow headed up a team in the front office that revised these drafts.[18] Indeed, Shenon says, "Zelikow rewrote virtually everything that was handed to him – usually top to bottom."[19] The 9/11 Commission's report could, therefore, be called "The Zelikow Report."

Fourth, insofar as the Commission was investigating the White House, the Commission was the White House investigating itself. Under Zelikow's guidance, the Commission simply assumed the truth of the Bush administration's account of 9/11, according to which the attacks were carried out by al-Qaeda terrorists. For example, when Zelikow divided the 80-some staff members into teams, "the subject of 'al Qaeda' [was assigned] to staff team 1" – explained Kean and Hamilton in their 2006 book giving the "inside story" of the Commission – and team 1A was told to "tell the story of al Qaeda's most successful operation – the 9/11 attacks."[20]

Fifth, before the staff even had its first meeting, Zelikow had written – along with his former professor, Ernest May – a detailed outline of the Commission's report, complete, as Shenon put it, with "chapter headings, subheadings, and sub-subheadings." When Kean and Hamilton were later shown this outline, they worried that it would be seen as evidence that the report's outcome had been predetermined, so the three of them decided to keep it a secret from the rest of the staff.[21] When the staff did finally learn about this outline a year later, they were alarmed, Shenon reported, and some of them circulated a parody entitled: "The Warren Commission Report – Preemptive Outline." One of its chapter headings read: "Single Bullet: We Haven't Seen the Evidence Yet. But Really. We're Sure."[22] The implication was that the crucial chapter of the Zelikow-May outline could have been headed: "Osama bin Laden and al-Qaeda: We Haven't Seen the Evidence yet. But Really. We're Sure."

Sixth, the Family Steering Committee, composed of 9/11 widows who had pressed for the creation of the 9/11 Commission, had by March 2004 learned many of the facts about Zelikow, and declared: "It is apparent that Dr. Zelikow should never have been permitted to be Executive Staff Director of the Commission.... The Family Steering Committee is calling for ... Dr. Zelikow's immediate resignation... [and for] [t]he Commission to apologize to the 9/11 families and America for this massive appearance of impropriety."[23] But Kean and Hamilton, as they had earlier, refused to dismiss Zelikow.

Seventh, Shenon revealed one more reason why Zelikow would not have been chosen for a 9/11 Commission seeking the truth: Although Zelikow promised that he would put his relationships with senior Bush administration officials on hold until the 9/11 Commission's report was completed, he continued, secretly, to have conversations not only with his good friend Rice but also with Karl Rove, who had been central to the appointments of Kissinger and Kean and who was, in general, the White House's "quarterback for dealing with the Commission."[24]

As the Commission's hearings were ending in May of 2004, an Associated Press story reported that "victims' families are now furious at the Sept. 11 commission for what they say is a failure to thoroughly investigate the disaster."[25]

ANOMALIES IN THE 9/11 COMMISSION REPORT

In October of that year, a story in *Harper's* magazine was entitled "Whitewash as Public Service: How The 9/11 Commission Report Defrauds the Nation." The author, Benjamin Demott, called the 9/11 Commission "a cheat and a fraud," adding that the Commission "stands as a series of evasive maneuvers that infantilize the audience, transform candor into iniquity, and conceal realities that demand immediate inspection and confrontation."[26]

A 2006 documentary film, *9/11: Press for Truth*, dealt with 9/11 family members who had worked with the Commission. One of them, Monica Gabrielle, said: "What we're left with after our journey are no answers.... I've wasted four years of my life." Another family member, Bob McIlvaine, said: "I'm so pissed off at this government, because of this cover-up."[27]

II. Anomalous Omissions in The 9/11 Commission Report

In 2004, an open letter, signed by 25 individuals "who have worked within various government agencies (FBI, CIA, FAA, DIA, Customs) responsible for national security and public safety," was sent to the US Congress. This letter said: "Omission is one of the major flaws in the Commission's report. We are aware of significant issues and cases that were duly reported to the commission by those of us with direct knowledge, but somehow escaped attention. Serious problems and shortcomings within government agencies likewise were reported to the Commission but were not included in the report."[28]

As that letter by professionals said, "Omission is one of the major flaws in the Commission's report." Indeed, in my 2005 book, *The 9/11 Commission Report: Omissions and Distortions*, I identified over a hundred significant omissions in the Report, and in the meantime I have become aware of dozens more. Below I will discuss, for illustrative purposes, a few of the anomalous omissions in *The 9/11 Commission Report* – omissions that would not have been present in a report headed by a truth-seeking executive director.

In their Preface to *The 9/11 Commission Report*, Kean and Hamilton said that the Commission sought "to provide the fullest possible account of the events surrounding 9/11."[29] In truth, what the Report provided was a fairly complete report of all the "events surrounding 9/11" that could be used to support the official account of the 9/11 attacks. The Report simply ignored all the "events surrounding 9/11" that have been cited as evidence for the alternative account of 9/11, according to which the attacks of 9/11 were able to succeed only because they were facilitated by the Bush administration and its agencies, especially the Pentagon.

I will now mention twelve facts that were omitted by the Zelikow Report:

1. The Alleged Hijackers

There is evidence that some of the alleged hijackers, including Waleed al-Shehri – said to have been on American Flight 11, which supposedly struck the WTC's North Tower – were still alive after 9/11. The Associated Press reported that al-Shehri spoke on September 22 to the U.S. embassy in Morocco, explaining that he lived in Casablanca, working as a pilot for Royal Air Maroc.[30] Defenders of the official account would later claim that this was a case of mistaken identity.[31] That it was *Der Spiegel*'s story that was absurd is shown in Jay Kolar's "Afterword" to "What We Now Know about the Alleged 9-11 Hijackers," which is in the paper-

ANOMALIES IN THE 9/11 COMMISSION REPORT

back edition of Paul Zarembka, ed., *The Hidden History of 9-11-2001* (New York: Seven Stories, 2008). As Kolar also shows, the BBC later adopted the same view as *Der Spiegel*. But a 2001 BBC article, entitled "Hijack 'Suspect' Alive in Morocco," made clear that the man of that name identified by the FBI as one of the hijackers was still alive:

> His photograph was released by the FBI, and has been shown in newspapers and on television around the world. That same Mr. Al-Shehri has turned up in Morocco, proving clearly that he was not a member of the suicide attack. He told Saudi journalists in Casablanca that ... he has now been interviewed by the American authorities, who apologized for the misunderstanding.[32]

Nevertheless, the 9/11 Commission, writing as if none of this discussion occurred, endorsed the FBI's inclusion of al-Shehri, with his photograph, on the list of hijackers. The Commission even said that al-Shehri was probably responsible for stabbing one of the flight attendants on American 11.[33]

2. The Atta-to-Portland Story

The first page of *The 9/11 Commission Report* says: "Among the [air] travelers [on September 11] were Mohamed Atta and Abdul Aziz al Omari, who arrived at the airport in Portland, Maine.... Atta and Omari boarded a 6:00 AM flight from Portland to Boston's Logan International Airport."[34]

This story raises puzzling questions. Why was Atta in Portland (Maine) the morning of the attacks? He was not only purportedly the "ringleader" of the hijackers but also the one who was supposed to pilot American 11 after it was taken over. If the commuter flight had been delayed for an hour, he would have been too late to make the connection to American 11. Why would he have taken such a risk? Both the 9/11 Commission and the FBI admitted that they had no answer to this question.[35]

According to the official story, in any case, Atta was already in Boston on September 10, but then took a rental car – a Nissan Altima – to South Portland, stayed overnight at the Comfort Inn, and then got to the Jetport in time to catch the 6:00 AM flight to Boston.[36] However, although Atta successfully made the transfer to American 11, his luggage did not. And after the attack on the North Tower, his luggage at the Boston airport was opened, and it contained much evidence, including Atta's will, that seemed to prove that the attacks had been carried out by al-Qaeda – at least if one did not ask why Atta would have taken his will on a plane that he had planned to crash into the World Trade Center.

The 9/11 Commission, in any case, reported this Atta-to-Portland story as if it had been told about Atta from the beginning. Actually, however, the original story was that two other alleged hijackers, Adnan Bukhari and Ameer Bukhari, drove the rented Nissan to Portland, stayed overnight, and then flew back to Boston the next morning in time to board American 11.[37] This second story is no longer present on the CNN website. Mohamed Atta, like a sensible fellow, stayed in Boston, and left a rented Mitsubishi at Boston's Logan airport. According to this original story, the authorities had found the materials that incriminated Atta and hence al-Qaeda in this Mitsubishi, not inside Logan Airport.[38]

But on September 13, CNN reported that neither of the Bukharis could have died on 9/11: Ameer Bukhari had died the previous year, and Adnan Bukhari was still alive.[39] As a result, authorities, with the help of the press, started changing the story. The full transition to what is now told as the official story did not emerge until September 16.[40] But *The 9/11 Commission Report* did not contain any hint that the story about Atta flying from Portland to Boston, which is on the first page, was a story that had undergone major alterations during the week after September 11.

3. What Mohamed Atta Was Like

Stories in the mainstream press, including *Newsweek* and the *San Francisco Chronicle*, had reported that Mohamed Atta had engaged in behavior that undermined the portrayal of him as a devout Muslim – behavior such as gambling, drinking alcohol, and enjoying lap dances.[41] These reports were even pointed out in a *Wall Street Journal* editorial entitled "Terrorist Stag Parties," which said: "[S]everal of the hijackers – including reputed ringleader Mohamed Atta – spent $200 to $300 each on lap dances in the Pink Pony strip club."[42] Moreover, investigative reporter Daniel Hopsicker reported that while Atta was in Florida, he used cocaine and lived with a stripper.[43] *The 9/11 Commission Report*, however, does not mention any of these reports. It instead portrays Atta as not only religious but even "fanatically so."[44]

According to Professor Dittmar Machule of Hamburg, who had been Atta's thesis supervisor in the 1990s, Atta's full name – like his father's – was Mohamed Al-Emir Atta, and this young man was actually very religious, so much so that he prayed regularly, never touched alcohol, and would not even shake hands with a woman upon being introduced. Professor Machule, said: "I would put my hand in the fire that this Mohamed El-Amir I know will never taste or touch alcohol."[45] The Mohamed El-Amir Atta that the professor knew was also described by him as "very small," being "one meter sixty-two" in height[46]– which means slightly under 5'4" – whereas the American Atta has been described as 5'8" and even 5'10" tall.[47] The 9/11 Commission never raised the possibility that the alcohol-drinking, cocaine-taking, lap-dancer-paying man going as "Mohamed Atta" was a different man than the devout Muslim student in Hamburg.

4. *World Trade Center 7*

With regard to the official account of the Twin Towers, the Commission ignored all of the problems, such as how fire could have caused steel-framed buildings to have collapsed, especially straight down, totally, and in virtual free fall, and also how ordinary building fires, even if ignited by jet fuel, could have caused steel to melt. But the most anomalous omission about the World Trade Center was the fact that the Commission did not even mention the fact that World Trade Center 7, which was not hit by a plane, also collapsed, completely destroying itself. Amazingly – at least for anyone who assumed that Kean and Hamilton, rather than Zelikow, was responsible for The 9/11 Commission Report – Hamilton evidently did not even know that "his" report did not mention WTC 7. This fact was revealed in an interview of Hamilton by Evan Solomon of the Canadian Broadcasting Corporation, which went like this:

Solomon: [W]hy didn't the Commission deal with the collapse of Building 7, which some call the smoking gun? …

Hamilton: Well, of course, we did deal with it.…

Solomon: [after the conversation had shifted to other topics]: I just want to clarify something that you said earlier. You said

ANOMALIES IN THE 9/11 COMMISSION REPORT

that the Commission Report did mention World Trade Center Building 7 in it .... It did mention it or it didn't?

Hamilton: The Commission reviewed the question of the Building 7 collapse. I don't know specifically if it's in the Report, I can't recall that it is, but it, uh....

Solomon: I don't think it was in the report.

Hamilton: OK, then I'll accept your word for that.

Solomon: There was a decision not to put it in the report?

Hamilton: I do not recall that was a specific discussion in the Commission and we rejected the idea of putting Building 7 in, I don't recall that. So I presume that the report was written without reference to Building 7 at all, because all of the attention ... was on the Trade tower buildings.[48]

5. Mineta's Testimony and Cheney's Descent to the Bunker

Solomon, asking when "Vice President Dick Cheney ... went down to the protective bunker," said: "[T]here was some suggestion that the Secretary of Transport[ation], [Norman] Mineta, testified in front of the Commission that he in fact talked to Dick Cheney at 9:20 a.m.... That was eventually omitted from the final report. Can you tell us a bit about what Secretary of Transport[ation] Mineta told the Commission about where Dick Cheney was prior to 10 a.m.?" Hamilton replied: "I do not recall." When Solomon started to ask a follow-up question, Hamilton said: "Well, we think that Vice President Cheney entered the bunker shortly before 10 o'clock." In saying this, Hamilton was, of course, endorsing what *The 9/11 Commission Report* had said.[49]

Later in the interview, Hamilton said, "I do not know at this point of any factual error in our report." Yet he had here been confronted with what is one of the most obvious and important falsehoods in *The 9/11 Commission Report*: The claim that Cheney, having not entered the bunker until almost 10:00, did not have the conversation with the young man reported by Mineta. In my book-length critique of this report, I filled four pages with evidence, highlighted by Mineta's testimony, that the Commission's claim that Cheney did not reach the bunker until shortly before 10 a.m. was a lie. And yet Hamilton could "not recall" Mineta's testimony – even though Hamilton had been the one questioning Mineta and had begun his questioning by saying to Mineta: "You were there [in the bunker] for a good part of the day. I think you were there with the Vice President."[50] But Hamilton did not want to deal with that question. He wanted simply to repeat the official account, in which there is no room for Mineta's memory about Cheney's presence from about 9:20 on.

6. The Importance of the Omission of Mineta's Testimony

The omission of Norman Mineta's testimony about Cheney and the young man is important because it revealed that Cheney and others in the underground shelter – known as the Presidential Emergency Operations Center – were aware by 9:26 that an aircraft was approaching the Pentagon.[51]

7. The Conflict between Cheney and Clarke on the Shoot-Down Authorization

Richard Clarke states that he received authority for fighters to shoot down any unknown non-military planes by 9:50,[52] whereas

The 9/11 Commission Report claims that Vice President Cheney did not give the shoot-down authorization until after 10:10 (several minutes after Flight 93 had crashed).[53]

8. Omitting PNAC on the Helpfulness of "a new Pearl Harbor"

The 9/11 Commission also omitted the fact that The Project for the New American Century (PNAC), many members of which had become key figures in the Bush administration, published a document in late 2000 saying that "a new Pearl Harbor" would aid PNAC's goal of obtaining funding for a rapid technological transformation of the US military.[54]

9. Omitting Bases for Attacking the Taliban

The Commission also omitted the fact that Unocal had declared that the Taliban could not provide adequate security for it to go ahead with its oil-and-gas pipeline from the Caspian region through Afghanistan and Pakistan.[55] It also omitted a report that at a meeting in July 2001, US representatives said that because the Taliban refused to agree to a US proposal that would allow the pipeline project to go forward, a war against them would begin by October.[56]

10. Omitting Rumsfeld's Intentions to Attack Iraq

The report headed by Zelikow, who had written *NSS 2002* providing justification for attacking Iraq, omitted the fact that some key members of the Bush administration, including Donald Rumsfeld and his deputy Paul Wolfowitz, had been agitating for a war with Iraq for many years.[57] It also omitted the notes of

Rumsfeld's conversations on 9/11 showing that he was determined to use the attacks as a pretext for a war with Iraq.[58]

11. The Conflict between Clarke and Rumsfeld about Rumsfeld's Location

The Commission endorsed the claim of Donald Rumsfeld, the Secretary of Defense, that he was in his office talking with a CIA briefer during the 9/11 attacks until the Pentagon was hit,[59] but the Commission failed to point out the contradictory account of counter-terrorism coordinator Richard Clarke, who said that Rumsfeld was in the Pentagon's videoconferencing center, participating in Clarke's videoconference.[60]

12. The Conflict between Clarke and Myers about Myers' Location

The Commission also endorsed the claim of General Richard Myers, the acting chairman of the Joint Chiefs of Staff, that he was on Capitol Hill during the attacks.[61] But it failed to point out the contradictory account by counter-terrorism coordinator Richard Clarke, according to whom Myers was in the Pentagon participating in Clarke's videoconference.[62]

Conclusion

The points in the first part of this paper provide reasons to suspect The 9/11 Commission Report to be untrustworthy. The points in the second part provide illustrations of the fact that this Zelikow Report is indeed untrustworthy.

CHAPTER THREE

Why the NIST World Trade Center Reports are False

BY KEVIN R. RYAN

Introduction

THIS PAPER WILL DISCUSS THE EVIDENCE RELATED TO THE official investigations conducted by the National Institute of Standards and Technology (or NIST), whose reports comprise the final official explanation for what happened at the World Trade Center on September 11, 2001.

Before I discuss the NIST reports, however, it is important to consider the low probability that the only three instances of a skyscraper suffering complete, global collapse due to fire all occurred on the same day and in the same place. There have been many raging building fires, much worse than existed in any of the WTC buildings, but no global collapse has ever resulted from those fires. Yet, the US government has told us that it *was* primarily fire that destroyed all three buildings at the WTC.

Photos and videos of the buildings show that the towers appeared to have exploded, starting at the top and then going all the way down. Also, high velocity bursts of debris shot out from ten to thirty floors below the collapse front.

At the top of each tower, the debris appeared to shoot upward and outward, as much of the solid structure turned to dust. This is counterintuitive to the idea that the building was being crushed downward. Large steel column assemblies were shot outward hundreds of feet, and some of them became embedded in surrounding buildings.

Many have asked: Is this what it looks like when a building is softened or weakened from fire? Independent investigators have done much work over the years to try and answer this question. In that time, peer-reviewed scientific articles have been published on various subjects related to the destruction of these buildings. One of those papers is called "Fourteen Points of Agreement with Official Government Reports on the WTC Destruction".[63] The points of agreement discussed therein lead to many problems that have yet to be explained.

One of the points of agreement is that all three buildings fell at near free-fall acceleration. A question NIST tried to answer was, "How could the WTC towers collapse in only 11 seconds (WTC 1) and 9 seconds (WTC 2), speeds that approximate that of a ball dropped from similar height in a vacuum (with no air resistance)?"

That is, one problem with the official story in this regard is that, if there were impact between an upper and lower section during the collapse, this would cause energy to be transferred and lost through deformations and structural breakage, which would slow the fall. But there was no deceleration, or slowing. The upper section, which appeared to be nothing but steel and dust, fell freely in each case.

WHY THE NIST WORLD TRADE CENTER REPORTS ARE FALSE

We also agree that the fires in the buildings, whether driven by jet fuel or office furnishings, could not have melted the steel structure. NIST made the point that – "In no instance did NIST report that steel in the WTC towers melted due to the fires. The melting point of steel is about 1,500 degrees Celsius (2,800 degrees Fahrenheit). Normal building fires and hydrocarbon (e.g., jet fuel) fires generate temperatures up to about 1,100 degrees Celsius (2,000 degrees Fahrenheit). NIST reported maximum upper layer air temperatures of about 1,000 degrees Celsius (1,800 degrees Fahrenheit) in the WTC towers."[64]

In other words, diffuse hydrocarbon fires such as these cannot produce temperatures high enough to melt steel. Unfortunately, many prominent media and political figures have suggested that very thing, and continue to do so.

It is also important to realize that the towers were designed for airliner impacts. John Skilling, the structural engineer in charge said that in the event of airliner impact, "the building structure would still be there."[65] We agree, so why did total collapse occur?

Each tower had 236 super-strength steel box columns making up the perimeter wall, and this was built around a core of 47 massive steel columns. The floor decking ran in a staggered arrangement between the core and the perimeter. To reduce the effects of fire, all of this steel structure was coated with a spray-applied fireproofing material before the buildings were occupied, and, in the aircraft impact zones, this fireproofing was upgraded in just the few years before 9/11.

Another point of agreement among all parties is that the theory that was claimed to be the most probable root cause for many years, called the pancake theory, is no longer supported by NIST.

The fire resistance of tall buildings like those at the WTC is ensured through testing of samples prior to construction. My former employer, Underwriters Laboratories (or UL), tested and certified the fireproofing used in the WTC towers, as seen in this quote from the company that manufactured the fireproofing.

"There is no reason for that product in a typical commercial environment to deteriorate," because "[the] product had been thoroughly tested and approved by Underwriters Laboratories."[66]

UL also tested the steel components used in the towers. This was well known because UL's fire protection manager, Tom Chapin, said so in a letter he sent to the New York Times in 2002. Tom wrote: "The World Trade Center stood for almost an hour after withstanding conditions well beyond those experienced in any typical fire. In that time, thousands of people escaped with their lives. ASTM E-119 and UL's testing procedures helped make that possible."[67]

UL tested the steel components used in the WTC towers to meet the 1968 New York City fire code. The column assemblies had to withstand 3 hours of intense fire, and the floor assemblies had to withstand 2 hours of intense fire, in a test furnace. Loring Knoblauch, the CEO of UL when I worked there, confirmed that UL tested the WTC steel. He later wrote to me and a few others, saying:

- "We tested the steel with all the required fireproofing on, and it did beautifully."
- "As we do not do follow-up service on this kind of product, we can give an opinion only on the test sample which was indeed properly coated."
- "We test to the code requirements, and the steel clearly met those requirements and exceeded them."[68]

WHY THE NIST WORLD TRADE CENTER REPORTS ARE FALSE

UL later participated in the NIST WTC investigation, which was a clear conflict of interest.

The NIST WTC Report for the Twin Towers

The NIST WTC report is over 10,000 pages. It was originally published only for the Twin Towers. And like previous reports on the subject, it was focused only on the fire-induced collapse hypothesis. NIST made no real effort to examine the explosive demolition hypothesis.

The structure of the NIST report for the towers includes one summary report (NCSTAR 1) and eight sub-reports. This does not include the two sub-reports issued three years later for WTC building 7, which will be discussed in the second half of this paper.

NIST said its goals were to explain "why and how WTC buildings 1 and 2 collapsed after the initial impact of the aircraft" and "why and how WTC 7 collapsed." The physical tests that NIST performed to reach its conclusions included tests to determine gas (i.e. air) temperatures and steel temperatures, and to investigate the possibility of floor failure and fireproofing loss.

Unfortunately for NIST, none of the tests it performed supported its conclusions. NIST therefore based its entire explanation on computer models. A summary of NIST's collapse explanation is as follows:

1. The aircraft severed columns
2. Loads were redistributed
3. Fireproofing was widely dislodged
4. High temperatures weakened columns and floors
5. Floors began to sag

6. Sagging floors pulled exterior columns inward causing them to buckle
7. Instability spread around entire building

Finally, "global collapse ensued."

The first step in NIST's sequence was that the aircraft severed a number of columns. Again, it is agreed that the core columns were massive and over-designed and the perimeter columns were made of super-strong steel.

According to NIST, only a small percentage of columns were severed (14% in WTC1 and 15% in WTC2). However, the towers were originally designed such that one "could cut away all the first story columns on one side of the building, and partway from the corners of the perpendicular sides, and the building could still withstand design live loads and a 100 mph wind from any direction" (i.e. a tower could lose more than 25% of its columns without a problem).[69]

The second step in NIST's sequence was that the gravitational load was redistributed among the remaining columns. NIST says loads on some columns were decreased (as much as 20%) and other loads were increased (up to 25%). But again, original design claims were that, "live loads on these [perimeter] columns can be increased more than 2,000% before failure occurs."[70]

The third, very critical step in NIST's sequence was that fireproofing was "widely dislodged." NIST acknowledged that removal of fireproofing was critical to their collapse scenario:

> "The towers would not have collapsed under the combined effects of aircraft impact and the subsequent multi-floor fires if the insulation had not been widely dislodged or had been only minimally dislodged by aircraft impact."

WHY THE NIST WORLD TRADE CENTER
REPORTS ARE FALSE

Again, the steel structure was covered with a spray-applied fireproofing material. There were requirements for the fireproofing with regard to bond strength and those requirements were met.

The test that NIST performed to establish the critical fireproofing loss involved shooting 15 rounds from a shotgun at steel plates and bars coated with fireproofing. NIST's final report included a 12 page appendix describing the shotgun test performed.[71] NIST WTC report NCSTAR 1-6A, Appendix C. It was not convincing. In fact, NIST did not explain how a Boeing 757 airliner could be converted into many thousands of shotgun blasts, which would need to be pointed in all directions in order to reach all of the steel surfaces.

Moreover, based on how much energy each shotgun blast would require, the energy requirements for this are too high. Previous calculations by engineers at MIT had shown that all the kinetic energy from the aircraft was consumed in breaking columns, crushing the floors and destroying the aircraft itself.[72]

NIST's tests indicate that 1 MJ of energy was needed per square meter of surface area to shoot the fireproofing off. For the areas in question (more than 6,000 square meters of column, floor deck and floor joist surface) the extra energy needed would be several times greater than the entire amount of kinetic energy that NIST says was available to begin with (2,500 MJ).

The fourth step in NIST's collapse initiation sequence requires large masses of steel columns and floors to be heated to temperatures that would make the steel soften. These temperatures do not support the NIST conclusions, but the physical tests that NIST performed resulted in even less agreement. The NIST report says that the gas (not steel) temperatures in the WTC towers were as high as

1000 °C. The highest steel temperatures referenced in the NIST report are 760 °C, which were produced by a computer model.

The physical tests NIST performed indicated that the steel saved for this purpose reached very low temperatures. NIST's stated goal for this test was to "estimate the maximum temperature reached by available steel."[73] NIST accomplished this by selecting steel samples from an "enormous amount" of steel, and by emphasizing "regions of impact and fire damage" in the selection process.[74]

The tests performed by NIST to determine steel temperatures were:

- A paint deformation test – The result showed that only 3 out of 170 WTC samples had reached a temperature of 250 °C.
- A test of steel microstructure – This test demonstrated that none of the WTC steel samples had reached a temperature of 600 °C.

These results did not support NIST's hoped-for conclusions – that the steel in the WTC towers had been softened or weakened from the fires.

Another point of agreement between NIST and independent scientists is that the fires in any given area were of short duration. NIST made it clear, as other scientists had observed, that "the initial jet fuel fires themselves lasted at most a few minutes," and "at any given location, the duration of [air, not steel] temperatures near 1,000 °C was about 15 min to 20 min. The rest of the time, the calculated temperatures were near 500 °C or below."[75]

NIST also claimed that the fires migrated around the core of each building over a period of time. For the north tower, this migration time lasted one full hour, according to NIST, before the fire reached the south wall where the collapse initiation occurred. This left less than 45 minutes of fire time at the south wall, where the fires would have migrated toward each other.

NIST claimed that the south wall bowed inward from the fires there, but the east and west walls, which had seen as much fire time, apparently showed no signs of bowing. Perhaps something else was happening at the south wall.

The fifth step in NIST's sequence was that floors began to sag. My former company, UL, participated in the NIST investigation by conducting tests on models of WTC floor assemblies to examine the floor response to fire. The result was that only very slight sagging occurred in the tests, and no collapse occurred. After 45 minutes in a high temperature furnace, all four test models sagged only about 3 inches in the middle, and the major joist portions did not sag at all.

NIST deceptively transferred this data into its computer models, which somehow suggested dramatic 42-inch sagging, with joists bending downward severely.

To reiterate, UL and NIST built and tested exact replicas of WTC floor assemblies. A photo of one of those floor assemblies after the test can be found in the NIST report.[76] This floor assembly was tested for fire resistance according to the standard method ASTM E-119. During this test, it was held in a furnace at a temperature of over 1000 °C for a period of two hours. The effects of the fire can be seen clearly – the mid-sections of the assembly sagged a few inches but the frame was not damaged, and the floor held its load without failure. The weight loaded onto the floor models tested was double what was known to have existed at the WTC. These experiments were performed by NIST and UL on 4 separate floor models, all of which had less fireproofing than the WTC floors were known to have on September 11.

NIST next contends that the sagging floors caused pull-in forces on exterior columns, causing them to fail. The first obvious problem with this is that sagging floors do not weigh more than non-sagging floors.

Moreover, to defeat the original design claims mentioned earlier, over 30 perimeter columns would have to be pulled in to cause a problem with structural stability. The floor assemblies formed an intense, staggered grid with the columns, however, and the force required to pull a perimeter column inward, and overcome that grid, was far greater than what a sagging floor assembly could provide.

The fact is that, even within NIST's computer models, the sagging and pulling effects that NIST's explanation depends on were not seen – not even for the most severe cases examined. Several quotes from the NIST report make that fact clear:

- *sagging of floors in such a wide range over fire floors was not predicted by the full floor model analyses*
- *locations and magnitudes of pull-in forces were not accurately simulated*
- *pull-in forces were applied in some locations where the full floor analyses did not predict the development of such behavior*[77]

NIST was simply not able to demonstrate this critical pull-in effect. Physical tests were not done, although that would have been decisive. The computer models did not indicate the forces were present either.

As a result, NIST made some fraudulent changes to the model. All the fireproofing was stripped off a large section of the com-

WHY THE NIST WORLD TRADE CENTER REPORTS ARE FALSE

puter modeled building, and exaggerated temperatures were applied for twice as long as NIST had said occurred in the failure zones. That is, NIST applied the exaggerated temperatures for 90 minutes instead of 45 minutes.

But even then the pull-in forces were not created in the computer, so NIST did something completely paradoxical. It disconnected the floors from the exterior columns, and then applied an imaginary pull-in force.[78]

This is the opposite of science.

The final step of NIST's sequence was that the instability, caused by perimeter columns pulling inward, spread around the entire perimeter of the building. That claim was necessary to explain the perfectly uniform fall.

No tests of any kind were performed to confirm this instability spread. And for several reasons, it does not appear to be realistic as structural engineers have stated in the past that: "A steel structure, generally speaking, does not collapse suddenly when attacked by fire. There are unmistakable warning signs, namely, large deformations."[79]

Table 3-1 below reviews some of the key tests that NIST did perform, and how the results were used.

THE 9/11 TORONTO REPORT

TABLE 3-1: NIST TEST RESULTS VS. NIST COMPUTER

Questions	Physical Tests	NIST Computer
What were WTC steel temperatures?	Up to 250 C	Up to 760 C
Fireproofing widely dislodged?	Unrealistic shotgun test	Fireproofing entirely removed
Pull-in forces created?	3 inches after 2 hours of fire	42 inches after < 1 hour of fire
What were the actual "collapse" dynamics?	No tests done	No comment

NIST has refused to share its computer models with the public. Therefore, the results cannot be independently verified.

NIST did not complete its objective because it did not tell us how the WTC towers collapsed. NIST simply proposed a collapse initiation sequence that is not supported by the evidence or the test results generated within the investigation.

But what evidence did NIST ignore when it ignored the actual collapse dynamics? The following questions are among those that remain unanswered.

What about resistance of structure below? If each floor each caused hesitation of only half a second, an extra 40 seconds would be needed. What about the observed "squibs"? What about the molten metal observed pouring from the building and the pools of molten metal in the rubble of both Towers and WTC 7? What about the intergranular melting and sulfidation found on the steel by the earlier FEMA investigation?

WHY THE NIST WORLD TRADE CENTER
REPORTS ARE FALSE

Ultimately, the NIST report for the WTC towers is false because NIST did not explain why and how the buildings collapsed, and the investigation was deceptive and unscientific. Additionally, NIST reported findings that were in direct contradiction to the physical testing performed and NIST omitted or distorted many important facts.

The NIST Report for WTC Building 7

NIST also issued a report on WTC 7, the third building that completely collapsed on 9/11. Although we should look closely at the final NIST explanation for this collapse, it is also informative to recognize that the previous government investigation, reported by FEMA in 2002, provided a best hypothesis that all agreed had only "a low probability of occurrence."

WTC building 7 was 47 stories tall, was not hit by a plane and yet, at 5:20 in the afternoon on 9/11, it fell vertically and symmetrically to the ground, in 6.5 seconds.

After seven years of waiting, NIST finally put out its official report on building 7 in 2008. No one could have predicted the sequence of events that NIST says led to this building falling.

It says that normal office fires caused fully fireproofed steel beams to fail in one area of the building, and this failure led to the entire structure falling as it did, into a neat rubble pile. To reiterate, the official story of the "collapse" of WTC 7 is that a typical office fire caused this 47-story building to completely destroy itself in a matter of seconds. If we were to accept the NIST WTC7 report, we would have to conclude that no tall buildings are safe from the possibility of total unexpected collapse due to office fires.

All parties have agreed from the start that the collapse of WTC 7 was very problematic. Here are some quotes from the NIST and FEMA reports that make this clear.

> *"The performance of WTC 7 is of significant interest because it appears the collapse was due primarily to fire, rather than any impact damage from the collapsing towers."*
> – **FEMA BPAT report on WTC 7**

> *"This was the first known instance of the total collapse of a tall building primarily due to fires."*
> – **NIST NCSTAR 1A, Executive Summary**

The low probability hypothesis that FEMA described was that diesel fuel fires, driven by diesel fuel tanks located within the building, created intense fires that caused the collapse. For years, NIST promoted the diesel fuel fires hypothesis, but NIST abandoned that hypothesis in its final report.

> *"Diesel fuel fires did not play a role in the collapse of WTC 7."*
> – **NIST final report on WTC 7**

NIST also suggested for years that the damage caused by falling debris from the north tower was a root cause of the collapse of building 7. Ultimately, NIST gave up on that hypothesis as well.

> *"Other than initiating the fires in WTC 7, the damage from the debris from WTC 1 had little effect on initiating the collapse of WTC 7."*
> – **NIST final report on WTC 7**

And contrary to some media reports, the building design was not an issue either.

WHY THE NIST WORLD TRADE CENTER REPORTS ARE FALSE

"Neither did the Con-Edison substation play a significant role in the collapse of WTC7."
– **NIST final report on WTC 7**

One serious problem that impaired the investigation was that most of the steel evidence was destroyed. The US House Committee on Science reported, in March 2002:

"In the month that lapsed between the terrorist attacks and the deployment of the [FEMA] BPAT team, a significant amount of steel debris…was removed from the rubble pile, cut into smaller sections, and either melted at the recycling plant or shipped out of the U.S. Some of the critical pieces of steel…were gone before the first BPAT team member ever reached the site."

Of course, this destruction of evidence was a violation of the U.S national standard for fire and explosive investigations (NFPA 921), which says "it is essential to prevent the destruction or removal of evidence."

Another serious problem was that NIST was clearly stumped for the first four or five years of the investigation, but then suddenly concluded that the answers were obvious. In 2006, NIST's lead investigator, Shyam Sunder, said "But truthfully, I don't really know. We've had trouble getting a handle on building No. 7."[80] Yet in 2008, when the final NIST report for WTC 7 was being issued, Sunder claimed that "the reason for the collapse of World Trade Center 7 is no longer a mystery" and "The public should really recognize the science is really behind what we have said… The obvious stares you in the face."[81]

THE 9/11 TORONTO REPORT

It is first important to note that NIST's allegedly obvious explanation is entirely computer-based. NIST did no physical testing at all to support its building 7 report.

A summary of the NIST explanation for what happened to WTC 7 can be found in the NIST WTC 7 report. In this summary statement, NIST claims that:

> "Fire induced expansion of the floor system surrounding column 79 led to the collapse of floor 13, which triggered a cascade of failures. In this case, the floor beams on the east side of the building expanded enough that they pushed the girder spanning between columns 79 and 44 to the west on floor 13. This movement was enough for the girder to walk off its support at column 79."[82]

NIST says fires on the northeast corner of floor 12 heated the ceiling that included the floor beams for floor 13, causing thermal expansion of the beams which pushed the girder at column 79 off its seat. NIST says that column 79 buckled due to the loss of support from that girder, and then the whole building collapsed in a matter of seconds.

One fact that contradicts this scenario is the presence of shear studs on the floor beams and the girder in question. The NIST interim report from 2004 said that most of the beams and girders were made composite with the floor slabs using shear studs. In a deceptive turnabout, NIST did a reversal in its final report, saying that no shear studs were installed on any of the girders.

Unfortunately for NIST, it was not just its own 2004 interim report that contradicted this vital aspect of the final theory. The presence of shear studs on all the girders was also described by John Salvarinas, the project manager for building 7 from the com-

WHY THE NIST WORLD TRADE CENTER REPORTS ARE FALSE

pany that supplied the steel components. A diagram from an academic paper that Salvarinas wrote in 1986 shows that there were 30 shear studs on that critical girder.[83]

NIST claims that thermal expansion caused the breakage of over one hundred high strength bolts. There were 28 shear studs on each of the affected floor beams, 30 shear studs on the critical girder, and 4 bolts at the column seat.

The mechanism that NIST claims caused all this damage is called differential thermal expansion, which happens when the expansion of the beam is much greater than the expansion of the concrete floor slab above it.

Thermal expansion is not a new phenomenon as NIST suggests, but has been a consideration throughout the history of structural design. That point was made by two building professionals from Australia who wrote a response to NIST on its building 7 report.[84] These building professionals reported that they had actually done physical tests to see what thermal expansion would do to floor assemblies. These were just the kinds of tests that NIST should have done.

Because they had actually done the tests, the Australians were able to state that the shear studs would not fail because in a building fire, the floor slab would be heated as well and the entire composite assembly would expand together. So NIST's final theory is at odds with actual experimental evidence from the testing of real floor assemblies.

Another problem with NIST's theory is the distance that girder would have had to be pushed for it to walk off its seat, as NIST suggests. NIST reported that the girder seat at column 79 was 11 inches wide. Therefore the girder had to be pushed at least 5.5

inches, or half of that distance, to walk off the seat. That fact was made clear in statements made within the NIST report.

To repeat, NIST's initial failure mechanism for WTC 7 was that the critical girder was pushed 5.5 inches by the floor beams. The 5.5 inches was needed in order for the vertical web of the girder, and therefore the center of mass of the girder, to move off of the seat.

Because thermal expansion is a function of temperature, we need to know what temperature NIST says the beams reached, so that we can estimate how much they expanded. This was a tricky question for NIST because at temperatures as high as 600 degrees Celsius the steel will lose strength and stiffness and therefore not be able to extend into the girder. At the same time, if the temperature is not high enough, there will not be enough expansion of the beams. What NIST settled on was the idea that the beam temperatures reached 400 degrees Celsius on the northeast corner of floor 12.

Related to this is another glaring problem in that NIST's computer model had all the steel heating to extreme temperatures and all the bolts and other connections breaking within a matter of about 2 seconds. This is an example of how NIST's computer modeling was not realistic.[85]

Once the temperature distribution needed for its theory was settled, NIST found a way to suggest that the differential thermal expansion could be possible, at least in the computer: NIST simply didn't heat the floor slab in the computer model.[86] Of course, differential thermal expansion cannot be measured if one of the materials you are trying to differentiate is not heated. One doesn't have to be a scientist to understand that, but the approach is what most scientists would call fraud.

WHY THE NIST WORLD TRADE CENTER REPORTS ARE FALSE

NIST's theory has more problems than that. Given NIST's temperature scenario, the amount of expansion by the beams would not satisfy the amount of expansion that NIST said was required, or 5.5 inches. NIST provided an example of the equation that scientists use to calculate thermal expansion.[87] When we put the correct values into the equation, using 53-foot long floor beams and the temperature of 400 °C (to retain rigidity), we see that the maximum expansion would be only 3.3 inches.

As we already know from NIST, 3.3 inches would not be enough to cause the girder to walk off its seat. The girder would have had to be pushed at least 5.5 inches for NIST's very improbable scenario to even begin. Therefore the basic premise of NIST's explanation of failure for WTC 7 is not realistic.

NIST also said that there were seven-hour fires in building 7, which gave the impression that the fires were very long and very hot. NIST reported that "WTC 7 endured fires for almost seven hours," and "Fires were ignited on at least 10 floors; however, only the fires on Floors 7 through 9 and 11 through 13 grew and lasted until the time of the building collapse."

However, early photographs did not show fires on floors 11 through 13, where NIST says the first failures occurred, until after 2 pm. And the building fell less than 3.5 hours later. So there could not have been seven hour fires in the areas NIST reported as failing first.

Underwriters Laboratories provided the fire resistance information for WTC 7. This fact was stated clearly in the NIST report for building 7.[88] NIST also reported that inspection of the fireproofing prior to 9/11 found that the fireproofing applied met the fire resistance requirements.[89] The requirements were that these steel components had to withstand 2 to 3 hours of intense fire in standard tests.

An additional contradiction that NIST avoided was that its investigators knew that the fire load in the building would only support about 20 minutes of fire in a given area.[90] When the NIST report talks about several hours of fire, it is deceptively referring to the time a fire lasts anywhere on a floor, not in one specific location on that floor. Underneath a specific floor beam, for example, the fire time is only about 20 minutes.

Another problem NIST did not explain is that the fires on floor 12 were completely burned out at least 30 minutes before the building fell.[91] And it is well know that steel cools quickly after a source of heat is removed. We should be able to verify how long the fires lasted in a given location because there are photographs available from various times during the day. But it turns out that NIST did not use the photographs to verify its computer simulations.

A comparison of a photo in NIST's report, taken at about 4 pm, and the NIST simulation of fires on floor 12 at the same time, shows no correlation between NIST's simulation and what really happened. At approximately 4 o'clock, NIST's computer simulation shows raging fires across the north side windows of floor 12. The photo from about the same time shows no fires in that area at all.[92] NIST admits that "the observed fire activity gleaned from photos and videos was not a model input."[93] Again, this is not science and this is another example of why the NIST report is false.

There are significant problems with NIST's description of the collapse dynamics as well. One problem is that the computer model output does not match what is seen in WTC7 collapse videos. Videos of the collapse show the building falling straight down with little deformation of exterior walls, whereas NIST's computer model suggests the building crumpled from the sides before falling.[94]

Another problem is that NIST has admitted that building 7 fell at free-fall acceleration for a period of time, and that simply cannot occur without the structure below being removed by some unexplained forces.

Overall, with regard to WTC building 7, we can say with absolute certainty that the NIST report is unscientific and false for the following reasons.

- No physical tests were done by NIST to confirm its explanation
  - Physical tests performed by other experts disprove the NIST hypothesis
- The fire hypothesis is contradicted by the known fire resistance plan
  - The fires in WTC 7 lasted only 20 minutes in each area while the steel components were rated for hours of fire resistance
- NIST's final theory was based entirely on computer simulations that are not based on evidence
  - NIST's fire modeling contradicts the photographic evidence
  - The fires in the critical areas (northeast corner of floor 12) were out long before collapse
  - NIST did not heat the floor slabs in its model of differential thermal expansion

- NIST ignored known facts about shear studs on the critical girder
- The maximum thermal expansion possible could not have caused the girder to "walk off" its seat
- The NIST computer result does not accurately model the collapse

Conclusion

Regardless of the fact that the NIST WTC 7 report is false in many ways, the scientific research community would like to see how NIST reached its conclusions. But as stated previously, NIST has refused to release its computer models to the public.

Structural engineer Ron Brookman made a Freedom of Information Act (FOIA) request to NIST in 2009 asking for the calculations and analysis behind the NIST claim of girder walk-off failures. NIST's official response was that release of that information might jeopardize public safety.

Has NIST's work on this subject been taken seriously with respect to building design and construction? The new, taller WTC 7 building was completed in 2006, at the time that NIST's lead investigator said, "I don't really know. We've had trouble getting a handle on building No. 7."

Therefore the people who owned and constructed the new building 7 did not take NIST seriously, nor could they have done so due to the lengthy delays in production of NIST's reports. Additionally, the NIST recommendations that have been adopted by the International Building Code council do not relate to the causes of destruction that NIST cited for the WTC towers and Building 7.

WHY THE NIST WORLD TRADE CENTER REPORTS ARE FALSE

In conclusion, this essay has demonstrated the need for a new investigation into what happened at the WTC on 9/11. Official reports produced have not explained why and how the buildings collapsed, and the investigations were deceptive and unscientific. NIST reported findings that were in direct contradiction to the physical testing performed, and omitted or distorted many important facts. NIST claims that it cannot share the details of the computer models that support its findings with the public and therefore these cannot be independently verified as required in science. Finally, NIST's explanations have not been taken seriously by the building construction community.

CHAPTER FOUR

Seeing 9/11 from Above: A Comparative Analysis of State Crimes Against Democracy

BY LANCE deHAVEN-SMITH, PhD

THE OFFICIAL ACCOUNT OF 9/11 IS THAT IT WAS A TERRORist attack with no U.S. foreknowledge. This version of events has been challenged by a wide range of evidence, much of which is covered at these hearings. Perhaps most important is eyewitness, chemical, and visual evidence indicating the Twin Towers and Building 7 at the World Trade Center were brought down by controlled demolition. The visual evidence is something everyone can see by watching videos of the Twin Towers explode into dust from the top down, and Building 7 collapse symmetrically and initially at free-fall acceleration into its own footprint. The appearance of controlled demolition not only casts doubt on the official account of how the buildings fell, it raises obvious questions about possible official foreknowledge and complicity. These doubts and questions are compounded by the government's failure to investigate the debris at the World Trade Center and the Pentagon for signs of explosives and incendiaries. This failure amounts to nonfeasance indicative of guilty knowledge. Official complicity is further suggested by the actions of U.S. governing authorities in the aftermath of 9/11: immediately invading Afghanistan, adopting an official policy of preemptive war, and manipulating intelligence to justify the invasion and occupation of Iraq. These actions are prima facie evidence of a preexisting agenda to contrive a pretext for waging wars of aggression in the Middle East to gain control of diminishing energy supplies. The case for suspecting 9/11 was an inside job driven by imperial ambitions is compelling and certainly sufficient to warrant national and international legal investigations.

Nevertheless, the official account of 9/11 continues to be defended by U.S. elites and accepted uncritically by large segments of the America public. No doubt, this lack of suspicion is reinforced by self-interest, nationalism, and resistance to cognitive dissonance, but it is also based to a considerable extent on what seems to be common sense. People doubt that U.S. public officials would have allowed, much less have planned and organized an attack that killed thousands of U.S. citizens and threatened the nation's centers of finance and government. Many Americans believe that the vast majority of public servants would refuse to go along with such a treasonous plot and that, in any event, elements of the government could not organize and execute such a complex operation without being detected or without someone talking.

This paper aims to dispel this seemingly straightforward perspective by analyzing 9/11 scientifically as a State Crime Against Democracy (SCAD). The analysis is scientific in the sense that it

SEEING 9/11 FROM ABOVE: A COMPARATIVE ANALYSIS OF STATE CRIMES AGAINST DEMOCRACY

employs theory-based empirical observation to uncover patterns of variation in a general phenomenon. Science has historically overcome popular prejudices by re-conceptualizing everyday experience and pointing out unnoticed facts that are more or less in plain sight. Before scientific discoveries in astronomy and physics in the 16th and 17th centuries, people believed the earth was the center of the universe and the sun, the planets, and the stars revolved around it. Common sense said the earth could not be spinning and flying through space, just as common sense today says 9/11 could not have been an inside job. Galileo opened people's eyes with the concept of gravity along with some surprising but irrefutable observations. This paper will do this, in a small way, with the SCAD concept and some novel observations about elite political criminality in the United States.

In a 2006 peer-reviewed journal article, I introduced the concept of State Crime Against Democracy to displace the term "conspiracy theory." The word displace is used rather than replace because SCAD is not another name for conspiracy theory; it is a name for the type of wrongdoing about which the conspiracy theory label discourages us from speaking. Later, this paper will discuss how the label, as it is used today, was formulated and popularized in the 1960s by the CIA. For now, it is enough to acknowledge that the term conspiracy theory is applied pejoratively to allegations of official wrongdoing, which have not been substantiated by public officials themselves.

In contrast, SCADs are not allegations; they are a type of crime. SCADs are defined as concerted actions or inactions by government insiders intended to manipulate democratic processes and undermine popular sovereignty (deHaven-Smith, 2006). By definition, SCADs differ from bribery, kickbacks, bid-rigging, and other, more mundane forms of political criminality in their potential to subvert political institutions and entire governments or branches of government. They are high crimes that attack democracy itself. When, as with 9/11, they involve making war against the United States, they are also acts of treason under the U.S. Constitution.

SCADs can be and are committed at all levels of government, but this paper centers on SCADs in high office because of their grave consequences. Examples of such SCADs that have been officially proven include the Watergate break-ins and cover up (Bernstein & Woodward, 1974; Gray, 2008; Kutler, 1990; Summers, 2000); the illegal arms sales and covert operations in Iran-Contra (Kornbluh & Byrne, 1993; Martin, 2001; Parry, 1999); and the effort to discredit Joseph Wilson by revealing his wife's status as an intelligence agent (Isikoff & Corn, 2007; Rich, 2006, 2007; Wilson, 2004).

Many other political crimes in which involvement by high officials is suspected have gone uninvestigated or have been investigated only superficially. Among these are the events referred to as 9/11. Additional examples include the fabricated attacks on U.S. ships in the Gulf of Tonkin in 1964 (Ellsberg, 2002, pp. 7-20); the "October Surprises" in the presidential elections of 1968 (Summers, 2000, pp. 298-308) and 1980 (Parry, 1993; Sick, 1991); the assassinations of John Kennedy and Robert Kennedy (Fetzer, 2000; Garrison, 1988; Groden, 1993; Lane, 1966; Pease, 2003; Scott, 1993; White, 1998); the election breakdowns in 2000 and 2004 (deHaven-Smith, 2005; Miller, 2005); the October 2001 anthrax letter attacks; and the misrepresentation of intelligence

SEEING 9/11 FROM ABOVE: A COMPARATIVE ANALYSIS OF STATE CRIMES AGAINST DEMOCRACY

to justify the invasion and occupation of Iraq (Isikoff & Corn, 2007; Rich, 2006).

This paper is divided into four parts. First, it will discuss how science and scientific concepts have been able, historically, to overturn mistaken beliefs that were widely accepted and strongly held. Second, it will explicate some dubious assumptions about elite political criminality that are embedded in our everyday perceptions of political crimes. It will also show that these assumptions create a blind spot which the SCAD concept can expose and overcome. Third, it will describe several patterns in SCADs and suspected SCADs and briefly point out what they suggest about the nature and institutional locus of state criminality in American politics. Finally, it will conclude by pointing out a few aspects of 9/11 that SCAD research suggests warrant more attention than they have thus far received.

Scientific Conceptualization

Although science is based on observation, scientific observation is more than merely looking and seeing. Modern science says the earth is spinning on its axis and revolving around the sun, and yet, clearly, the earth does not feel to us like it is moving. If the earth is spinning, why do we not fly off? What holds us to the ground? "Gravity," you say. But can you show me this gravity? What does it look like? Where can I find it? "It is invisible," you reply. But surely you jest. You ask me to believe in a mysterious force that I cannot see it, and the only reason you have for claiming the force exists is that (you say) the earth is spinning, when it obviously is not.

The concept of gravity is essential to the sun-centered model of the planetary system. It explains what holds people to the spinning earth as well as what holds the planets in their orbits around the sun. However, gravity is not something we can observe directly; it is a postulated force.

Galileo convinced people that gravity exists by showing them something remarkable they could see with their own eyes but had never noticed. The concept of gravity implied that, when dropped, physical objects would fall at the same rate of acceleration regardless of their size or weight because they are all pulled down by the same uniform force – the uniform force of the earth's "gravity," not the varying force of the objects' "weight." Galileo is said to have proved this by dropping objects from the leaning Tower of Pisa. The fact that objects of different weights fell at the same speed was an astounding discovery; people had seen objects fall countless times, but they had always assumed heavier objects fell faster than lighter objects. Thus, the concept of gravity pointed to an observable phenomenon that people's conventional beliefs had prevented them from seeing.

This is also how the theory of evolution overturned the accepted idea that all the plants and animals on earth had been created in the form and diversity they display today. Contradicting the Biblical account of creation, Darwin said plants and animals evolved from simple life forms to more complex, differentiated forms (or "species") through a process of "natural selection." However, most people initially considered it ludicrous, not to say insulting, to suggest that humankind had descended from apes. Moreover, speciation itself cannot be observed; it is something that has already happened. We came to accept evolutionary theory not because we actually saw evolution, but because the theory led to a number of novel discoveries that had been more or less in plain sight all along. One was the fact that the characteristics of animals vary with their environments. Rabbits in snowy regions are white while in sandy regions they are tan. Another discovery was the fossil record of dinosaurs and of intermediary species between apes and human beings.

The theory of evolution also allowed us to see things about ourselves that we had never considered. Darwin himself would point out to audiences that the origin of human beings from animals is evident in our bodies. Apes and dogs have a crease in their ears where their ears bend and they can raise and lower the tips. If you feel the back of your own ear, you will find an atavistic remnant of this same crease. It is a small indentation along the back of your ear about a third of the way down.

These examples show that it is often the surprising discovery or novel observation that causes people to accept scientific theories and abandon their taken-for-granted, commonsense beliefs about how the world works. Uncovered by concept-driven and theory-driven observation, these discoveries take two forms. Some are macro-discoveries in the sense that they zoom out and point to missing pieces that fill in a larger theoretical picture. Examples of macro-discoveries include, in biology, the intermediary species between apes and human beings, or in astronomy, Keplar's discovery that the planets move in elliptical orbits. Other discoveries are micro-discoveries in the sense that they zoom in, bringing obscure phenomena into focus. Examples of micro-discoveries include the crease in the human ear and the uniform acceleration of falling objects. In both cases, macro- and micro-, the world is seen in a new way because new concepts highlight overlooked facts and cause old perceptions to be re-interpreted. Where previously we had seen the earth as stationary and the sun as rising and setting, we now realize the sun is stationary and the earth is spinning.

Incident-Specific Myopia in Everyday Perceptions of Political Crime

The SCAD concept and SCAD research operate similarly in re-conceptualizing accepted perceptions of American politics and government. The everyday, common sense understanding of assassinations, defense failures, election breakdowns, and other unexpected political events is that they are isolated occurrences, each with its own special and distinct circumstances. This way of thinking, this tendency to see such events as unique and isolated, is common regardless of one's views about conspiracy theories. Allegations as well as denials of elite political criminality tend to be focused on only one event at a time. There are separate combinations of official accounts and conspiracy theories for the assassination of President Kennedy, the attempted assassination of President Reagan, the October Surprise of 1980, the disputed 2000 presidential election, and so on. The Toronto Hearings were a part of this pattern, but focused on 9/11.

Even when obvious factors connect events, each incident is examined individually and in isolation. For example, John Kennedy and Robert Kennedy were brothers, both were shot in the head (unlike other victims of assassination), both were rivals of Richard Nixon, and both were killed while campaigning. Nevertheless, their assassinations are generally thought of as separate and unrelated. It is seldom considered that the Kennedy assassi-

SEEING 9/11 FROM ABOVE: A COMPARATIVE ANALYSIS OF STATE CRIMES AGAINST DEMOCRACY

nations might have been serial murders. In fact, we rarely use the plural, Kennedy assassinations. In the lexicon, there is the Kennedy assassination, which refers to the murder of President Kennedy, and there is the assassination of Robert Kennedy.

This same "incident-specific myopia" is evident in perceptions of the disputed 2000 and 2004 presidential elections. Although both elections were plagued by very similar problems, and although in both cases the problems benefitted George W. Bush, the election breakdowns are not suspected of being repeat offenses by the same criminal network employing the same tactics and resources. This is not failing to connect the dots; this is seeing one dot and then another dot and never placing the dots on the same page.

Contemporary perceptions of 9/11 are no different. 9/11 and the anthrax letter attacks are viewed as separate and unrelated even though they occurred closely together in time and both were acts of terrorism.

It should be noted that this way of thinking about elite political crimes – this tendency to view parallel crimes separately and to see them as unrelated – is exactly opposite the way crimes committed by regular people are treated. If a man marries a wealthy woman and she is killed in a freak accident, and if this same man then marries another wealthy woman who also dies in an accident, foul play is naturally suspected, and the husband is the leading suspect. It is routine police protocol to look for patterns in burglaries, bank robberies, car thefts, and other crimes, and to use any patterns that are discovered as clues to the identity of perpetrators. This is Criminology 101. It is shown repeatedly in crime shows on TV. There is no excuse for our failure to apply this method to assassinations, election fiascos, and other crimes and suspicious events that shape national political priorities.

Normative Suppression of Suspicion

Americans fail to notice connections between crimes involving political elites in part because powerful norms discourage them from looking. The U.S. political class condemns, ridicules, and ostracizes anyone who speculates publicly about political criminality in its ranks. A clear example of these norms in action is the term "conspiracy theory" and its use as a pejorative to stigmatize suspicions of official complicity in troubling events. In today's public discourse, no epithet is more effective at silencing allegations of official wrongdoing. To call an idea a conspiracy theory is to imply that anyone who endorses it is paranoid and possibly psychologically troubled.

Although the conspiracy-theory label and its pejorative connotations are taken for granted by most Americans, they actually make no sense. First, as a label for irrational political suspicions, the concept is obviously defective because political conspiracies in high office do, in fact, happen. Given that some conspiracy theories are true, it is absurd to dismiss all unsubstantiated conspiracy theories as false by definition.

Second, ridiculing suspicions about political elites is blatantly inconsistent with American political traditions. In fact, the Declaration of Independence itself espouses a conspiracy theory. It claims that "a history of repeated injuries and usurpations" by King George proved the king was plotting to establish "an absolute tyranny over these states." The bulk of the document is devoted to detailing the abuses evincing the king's tyrannical designs.

SEEING 9/11 FROM A... OF STATE CRI...

Third, in disparaging s[...] nality, the conspiracy-theor[...] the post-WWII era, official [...] sinations, election fiascos, d[...] events to such unpredictable, [...] antiquated voting equipment, [...] cent mistakes, all of which sus[...] qui bono questions. In effect, [...] spiracy theories with coinciden[...]

If there is any logical reason for skepticism about conspiracy theories, it is the idea that conspiracy theories could not be true because secrets in the United States cannot be kept – someone would talk. This strikes many Americans as common sense. However, it is simply untrue, and Americans, of all people, should know it. The Manhattan Project took several years and involved tens of thousands of people, but it did not become known to outsiders, either in the public or inside the government, until the first atomic bombs were dropped. Even President Truman did not learn of the project until he had been president for a week (McCullough, 1992, pp. 376-379). Similarly, secrecy was maintained throughout World War II about America's success in breaking German and Japanese encryption systems. Clearly, when the U.S. government wants to keep secrets, it can do so even when the secrets must be harbored by many people and multiple agencies.

If the conspiracy-theory label is nonsensical, un-American, based implicitly on a "coincidence theory," and contradicted by obvious examples of well kept secrets, why did people start using it in the first place? The truth is the conspiracy-theory label and its pejorative connotations did not originate and spread sponta-

...tural communicative processes of civil society. ...y evidence shows the term was actively deployed by ...s a dismissive catchall for criticisms of the Warren Commission's conclusion that President Kennedy was assassinated by a lone gunman. The CIA issued instructions for its agents to urge "propaganda assets" and "friendly elite contacts (especially politicians and editors)" to rebut the Warren Commission's critics with a series of talking points. The CIA mobilized a coordinated media campaign labeling the Warren Commission's critics as "conspiracy theorists," questioning their motives, and alleging that "parts of the conspiracy talk appear to be deliberately generated by Communist propagandists."

Today, this tactic of covertly manipulating public discourse is being referred to as "cognitive infiltration." Cass Sunstein and Adrian Vermeule coined this term in a 2009 journal article on the "causes and cures" of conspiracy theories. Sunstein is a Harvard law professor appointed by President Obama to head the Office of Information and Regulatory Affairs. Especially alarmed about conspiracy theories of 9/11, Sunstein and Vermeule advocate a government program of "cognitive infiltration" to covertly "disrupt" online discussions by conspiracy-theory groups and networks (Sunstein and Vermeule 2009, 218-219, 224-226). The cynicism and hypocrisy of this proposal are breathtaking. Sunstein and Vermeule call for the government to conspire against citizens who discuss with one another suspicions of government conspiracies, which is to say they are urging the U.S. government to do precisely what they want citizens to stop saying the government does.

Given the insight-disabling effects of the conspiracy-theory meme, we should be wary of the term "cognitive infiltration," especially since it was put forward in a plan for manipulating public discourse. In the CIA's operation to stigmatize conspiracy theorizing, the agency injected a destructive meme into the communicative organs of civil society for the purpose of influencing public-opinion formation. When cognitive infiltration involves planting memes, it would be more accurately described as "linguistic thought control" or "subliminal indoctrination."

The SCAD Concept

The victim's "standpoint." The SCAD concept is intended to function like a corrective lens to shift the standpoint and widen the angle of political crime observation. In effect, everyday (case-by-case) perceptions of assassinations, defense failures, election fiascos, and similar events view these events from the perspective of a victim, a perspective that magnifies the threat and/or the vulnerability of the target. This is understandable; in the aftermath of shocking events, threats loom large in our thoughts because we may be frightened and are struggling to make sense of the incident and its implications.

The victim perspective is frequently evident in the photographic images that become iconographic: President and Mrs. Kennedy in their limo with the Texas School Book Depository rising above them in the background; a close-up, full-body picture taken from below eye level of Lee Harvey Oswald holding a rifle; Robert Kennedy prostrate on the floor, dying, surrounded by standing onlookers.

To this day, when we are reminded of 9/11, the images that come to mind "see" the destruction "from below." If they are images of the Twin Towers, their perspective is from street level looking up. For days or weeks after the events, the Twin Towers appeared in our mind's eye whenever we saw commercial airplanes flying overhead. Even now, it takes a willful act of imagination to visualize the hijacked planes from a different perspective. You can experience this for yourself: Try to visualize the scene from a standpoint above the buildings and the approaching plane. For many people, the image is vague, blurry, and unstable.

Of course, in the case of 9/11, the natural tendency to magnify the threat and see it "from below" was enhanced by the fact that the threat came from the sky, but it was also abetted by a decision of the U.S. government to sequester photos that looked down on the carnage. Before, during, and after the Twin Towers imploded, thousands of photos were taken of the World Trade Center from a police helicopter flying overhead. These are the only images in existence that show the destruction from above, and yet the photos were withheld from the public for over 8 years. They came out only because ABC News filed a request under the Freedom of Information Act with the National Institute of Standards and Technology (NIST), the agency responsible for investigating the WTC destruction.

Significantly, no official explanation for sequestering these photos has been offered despite a New York Times editorial criticizing the action after the photographs were released in February 2010. The editorial focused on how these photos would have changed popular perceptions of 9/11 had they been released sooner. The editorial was titled, "9/11 From Above." It is a troubled and troubling missive that flirts with dark suspicions but ultimately leaves them unspoken. The editorial says it is "surprising to see these photographs now in part because we should have seen them

SEEING 9/11 FROM ABOVE: A COMPARATIVE ANALYSIS OF STATE CRIMES AGAINST DEMOCRACY

sooner." Pointing out that "9/11 has resolved itself into a collection of core images," the authors imply that these images have left Americans with a picture of events that is blurry and too close up. Implicitly contrasting this collection of images with the new photos, the editorial says, because the photos from the helicopter were "shot from on high, they capture with startling clarity both the voluminousness of the pale cloud that swallowed Lower Manhattan and the sharpness of its edges." The authors do not explain what this reveals about 9/11, but they clearly believe it is significant, for they conclude by saying the photos "remind us of how important it is to keep enlarging our sense of what happened on 9/11, to keep opening it to history."

The SCAD standpoint. The SCAD construct shifts our perspective conceptually. It raises the standpoint of observation and inquiry above isolated incidents by directing attention to the general phenomenon of elite political criminality. Similar to research on white collar crime, domestic violence, serial murder, and other crime categories, SCAD research seeks to identify patterns and commonalities in SCAD victims, tactics, timing, those who benefit, and other SCAD characteristics. These patterns and common traits are macro-discoveries that offer clues about the motives, institutional location, skills, and resources of SCAD perpetrators. They also provide a basis for understanding and mitigating the criminogenic circumstances in which SCADs arise. In turn, as patterns and commonalities across multiple state political crimes are identified, they point to micro-discoveries by suggesting characteristics to look for when investigating individual incidents.

A variety of SCADs and suspected SCADs have occurred in the United States since World War II. Table 1 contains a list of 19 known SCADs and other counter-democratic crimes, tragedies, and suspicious incidents for which evidence of U.S. government involvement has been uncovered. The table identifies tactics, suspects, policy consequences or aims, and includes a summary assessment of the degree to which official complicity has been confirmed. For research purposes, the universe of SCADs must include not only those that have been officially investigated and confirmed, but also suspected SCADs corroborated by evidence that is credible but unofficial. Although including the latter brings some risk of error, excluding them would mean accepting the judgment of individuals and institutions whose rectitude and culpability are at issue.

Before discussing some telling patterns in Table 1, a general observation is appropriate: American democracy in the post-WWII era has been riddled with elite political crimes. This is evident from a simple review of elections. Presidential elections were impacted by assassinations, election tampering, and/or intrigues with foreign powers in 1964, 1968, 1972, 1980, 2000, and 2004. This amounts to over a third of all presidential elections since 1948 and fully half of all elections since 1964. Moreover, two-thirds of these tainted elections were marred by multiple crimes:

- 1964 included the assassinations of JFK and Oswald, plus the Gulf of Tonkin incident;
- 1968 included the assassination of RFK plus the 1968 October Surprise;
- 1972 included the stalking of Ellsberg, the crimes of Watergate, and the attempted assassination of Wallace; and
- 2004 included bogus terror alerts plus election tampering.

SEEING 9/11 FROM ABOVE: A COMPARATIVE ANALYSIS OF STATE CRIMES AGAINST DEMOCRACY

TABLE 4-1: CRIMES AGAINST AMERICAN DEMOCRACY COMMITTED OR ALLEGEDLY COMMITTED BY ELEMENTS OF THE U.S. GOVERNMENT

Crime or Suspicious Event, Time Frame, and *Modus Operandi*	Perpetrator Motive or Policy Implication	Suspected or Confirmed Perpetrator	Degree of Confirmation of Gov't Role
McCarthyism (fabricating evidence of Soviet infiltration). 1950-1955. MANIPULATION OF DEFENSE INFO/POLICY	Large scale purge of leftists from government and business. POLITICAL OPPORTUNISM	Joseph McCarthy, with others. Although his tactics were not investigated, they were discredited in Senate hearings, and a Democratic Senate censured the Republican Senator.	HIGH (Fried, 1990; Johnson, 2005)
Assassination of President Kennedy. 1963. ASSASSINATION	Lyndon Johnson's Presidency; Escalation of the Vietnam War. CONTROL WAR POLICY	Probably right-wing elements in CIA, FBI, and Secret Service. Possible involvement of Johnson and/or Nixon.	MEDIUM (Fetzer, 2000; Groden, 1993; Garrison, 1988; Lane, 1966; Scott, 1993; White, 1998)
Assassination of Lee Harvey Oswald. 1963. ASSASSINATION	Oswald's ties to the CIA remain hidden. A trial of Oswald is avoided. CONCEAL CRIME	Jack Ruby, who had ties to the CIA and organized crime. Part of overall JFK assassination plot.	MEDIUM (Scott, 1993)

Fabricated Gulf of Tonkin incident. 1964. PLANNED INTERNATIONAL EVENT	Large expansion of military resources committed to the Vietnam conflict. CONTROL WAR POLICY	President Johnson and Secretary of Defense McNamara falsely claimed that North Vietnam attacked a U.S. military ship in neutral waters.	HIGH (Ellsberg, 2002, pp. 7-20)
Assassination of Senator Robert Kennedy. 1968. ASSASSINATION	Weak Democratic nominee (Humphrey); election of Nixon; no further investigation of JFK assassination; continued escalation of Vietnam conflict. CONTROL WAR POLICY	Rightwing elements in the CIA and FBI, with likely involvement of Nixon. Suspicions of government involvement are based largely on number of bullets shot and failure to fully investigate.	LOW (Pease, 2003b)
October Surprise of 1968. 1968. MANIPULATION OF DEFENSE INFO/POLICY	Secure election of Richard Nixon as President by convincing South Vietnam to withdraw from Johnson's peace negations for ending the Vietnam War POLITICAL OPPORTUNISM	Nixon and intermediaries with South Vietnam leadership.	HIGH (Summers, 2000, pp. 298-308; also supported by tapes of Johnson and Nixon)

SEEING 9/11 FROM ABOVE: A COMPARATIVE ANALYSIS OF STATE CRIMES AGAINST DEMOCRACY

Burglary of the office of Daniel Ellsberg's psychiatrist's office. 1971. **BURGLARY**	Discredit Ellsberg. Exposure of the break-in prevented use of the stolen information. **CONTROL WAR POLICY**	President Nixon, White House staff, and CIA operatives or former operatives. The crime was discovered during Ellsberg's trial, not in an investigation of the break-in.	**HIGH** (Ellsberg, 2002)
Attempted assassination of George Wallace. 1972. **ASSASSINATION**	Wallace taken out of 1972 election and Nixon reelected. Wallace was likely to win 7 southern states, forcing the election to be decided by a Democratically controlled Congress. **POLITICAL OPPORTUNISM**	Arthur Bremer. Some circumstantial evidence points to the involvement of Nixon via the Watergate plumbers. Evidence includes comments of Nixon.	**MEDIUM** (Bernstein & Woodward, 1974, 324-330; Carter, 2000)
Watergate Break In. 1972. **BURGLARY/ WIRETAPPING**	Weak Democratic nominee (McGovern) and reelection of Nixon. **POLITICAL OPPORTUNISM**	President Nixon, White House staff, and CIA operatives or former operatives.	**HIGH** (Bernstein & Woodward, 1974)

Attempted assassination of Ronald Reagan. 1981. ASSASSINATION	V.P. Bush's role in the Administration is strengthened, especially in relation to covert operations in the Mid-East and Latin America. CONTROL WAR POLICY	John Hinkley. Evidence shows connections between Hinkley's family and the family of V.P. Bush.	LOW (Bowen, 1991; Wiese & Downing, 1981)
October Surprise of 1980. 1980. MANIPULATION OF DEFENSE INFO/POLICY	Secure election of Ronald Reagan as President by making deal with Iranians to sell them U.S. arms if hostages not released until after election POLITICAL OPPORTUNISM	Reportedly arranged in a meeting in Paris attended by George H.W. Bush, William Casey, and Robert Gates. Confirmed later by Iranian officials. Iran-Contra arms dealing appears to have been an extension of this earlier effort.	HIGH (Parry, 1993; Sick, 1991) Iran-Contra. 1984-1986.
Iran-Contra. 1984-1986. MANIPULATION OF DEFENSE INFO/POLICY	Release of hostages; civil war in Nicaragua. CONTROL WAR POLICY	President Reagan, Vice President Bush, CIA, military.	HIGH (Kornbluh & Byrne, 1993; Martin, 2001; Parry, 1999)

SEEING 9/11 FROM ABOVE: A COMPARATIVE ANALYSIS OF STATE CRIMES AGAINST DEMOCRACY

Florida's disputed 2000 presidential election. 2000. **ELECTION TAMPERING**	Legally mandated recount is blocked; G.W. Bush becomes president through U.S. Supreme Court decision. **POLITICAL OPPORTUNISM**	Jeb Bush and Katherine Harris developed flawed felon disenfranchisement program. Jeb Bush, Harris, and Tom Feeney colluded to block recount. Harris facilitated counting of fraudulent overseas military ballots.	**HIGH** (Barstow & Van Natta, 2001; deHaven-Smith, 2005)
Events of 9/11. 2001. **PLANNED INTERNATIONAL EVENT**	Bush popularity rises; defense spending increases; Republicans gain in off-year elections; military invasion of Afghanistan; pretext for invasion of Iraq. **CONTROL WAR POLICY**	Evidence of controlled demolition of buildings at WTC indicates official foreknowledge and complicity, probably at the highest levels.	**MEDIUM** (Griffin, 2004, 2005; Hufschmid, 2002; Paul & Hoffman, 2004; Tarpley, 2005)

Anthrax letter attacks. 2001. PLANNED INTERNATIONAL EVENT	Bush popularity rises; defense spending increases; Republicans gain in off-year elections; military invasion of Afghanistan; pretext for invasion of Iraq. CONTROL WAR POLICY	Officially blamed on Bruce Ivins but more likely part of the overall 9/11 operation. The anthrax has been traced to a strain developed by the U.S. Army. Circumstantial evidence of cover-up.	HIGH for involvement of U.S. bio-weapons expert(s)
Assassination of Senator Paul Wellstone. 2002. ASSASSINATION	Republicans regain control of the Senate after Wellstone's replacement. CONTROL WAR POLICY	Intelligence operatives.	LOW
Iraq-gate. 2003. MANIPULATION OF DEFENSE INFO/POLICY	U.S. gains control of Iraq oil production; Iran surrounded by U.S. armies; other Mid-East nations intimidated. CONTROL WAR POLICY	President Bush, Vice President Cheney, CIA Director fix intelligence to justify war. Bush misrepresents intelligence to Congress in State of Union address. CIA officer Valerie Plame is outed in an attempt to discredit Joseph Wilson.	HIGH (Clark, 2004; Dean, 2004; Wilson, 2004; Woodward, 2004)

SEEING 9/11 FROM ABOVE: A COMPARATIVE ANALYSIS OF STATE CRIMES AGAINST DEMOCRACY

Bogus terror alerts in advance of 2004 election. 2004. MANIPULATION OF DEFENSE INFO/POLICY	Bush wins reelection and support is maintained for the war on terror. POLITICAL OPPORTUNISM	Terror alerts to rally support for the President going into the 2004 presidential election.	HIGH (Hall, 2005)
Ohio's disputed 2004 presidential election. 2004. ELECTION TAMPERING	Bush wins electoral college vote with a 118,000 vote margin in Ohio. POLITICAL OPPORTUNISM	Republican election officials impede voting in Democratic precincts.	HIGH (Miller, 2005; Tarpley, 2005)

When we stop looking at SCADs one-by-one, and we telescope out and look at them collectively or, so to speak, "from above," we see a nation repeatedly abused. This abuse is another reason for the citizenry's incident-specific myopia; trauma fragments memory because traumatic events loom too large to be kept in perspective. Just as victims of child abuse and spouse abuse tend to have fragmented recollections of the abuse, America's collective memory of assassinations, defense failures, and other shocking events – the people's shared narrative and sense of history – is shattered into emotionally charged but disconnected bits and pieces.

SCAD patterns. For the purpose of illustrating the SCAD construct, I will focus on the patterns in Table 4-1 that are readily apparent.

1. Many SCADs are associated with foreign policy and international conflict. Such SCADs include the Gulf of Tonkin

incident; the burglary of Daniel Ellsberg's psychiatrist's office; the 1968 October Surprise; Iran-Contra; 9/11; the anthrax letter attacks; fake intelligence leading to the war in Iraq; the bogus terror alerts in 2004; and the assassinations of John Kennedy and Robert Kennedy. All of these SCADs contributed to the initiation or continuation of military conflicts.

2. SCADs are fairly limited in their modus operandi (MO). SCAD-MOs listed by order of frequency are assassinations (6), mass deceptions manipulating defense information or policy (6), planned international-conflict events (3), election tampering (2), and burglaries (2). With the possible exception of election tampering, all of these MOs are indicative of groups with expertise in the skills of espionage and covert, paramilitary operations.

3. Many SCADs in the post-WWII era indicate direct and nested connections to two presidents: Richard Nixon and George W. Bush. Nixon was not only responsible for Watergate and the illegal surveillance of Daniel Ellsberg, he alone benefitted from all three of the suspicious attacks on political candidates in the 1960s and 1970s: the assassinations of John Kennedy and Bobby Kennedy, and the attempted assassination of George Wallace. If JFK and RFK had not been killed, Nixon would not have been elected president in 1968, and if Wallace had not been shot, Nixon might not have been reelected in 1972. The SCADs that benefitted Bush include the election-administration problems in Florida in 2000 and in Ohio in 2004; the events of 9/11; the anthrax letter attacks on top Senate Democrats in October 2001; Iraq-gate; and

SEEING 9/11 FROM ABOVE: A COMPARATIVE ANALYSIS OF STATE CRIMES AGAINST DEMOCRACY

the series of specious terror alerts that rallied support for Bush before the 2004 presidential election.

4. The range of officials targeted for assassination in the post-WWII era is limited to those most directly associated with foreign policy: presidents (and presidential candidates) and senators. Most other high-ranking officials in the federal government have seldom been murdered even though many have attracted widespread hostility and opposition. No Vice Presidents have been assassinated, nor have any justices of the U.S. Supreme Court. The only member of the U.S. House of Representatives who has been targeted is Gabrielle Giffords in January 2011. If lone gunmen have been roaming the country in search of political victims, it is difficult to understand why they have not struck more widely, especially given that most officials receive no Secret Service protection. Why did no assassins go after Joe McCarthy when he became notorious for his accusations about communists, or Earle Warren after the Supreme Court's decisions requiring school desegregation, or Spiro Agnew after he attacked the motives of antiwar protestors, or Janet Reno after she authorized the FBI's raid on the Branch Dividians in Waco? If one assassination of a top public official were committed each year, and if targets were randomly selected, the odds of a president being killed in any given year would be 1 in 546. (There are 100 senators, 435 representatives, 9 Supreme Court justices, 1 vice president, and 1 president.) The odds of two presidents (Kennedy and Reagan) being shot by chance since 1948 are roughly 1 in 274,000. If Robert Kennedy is included (as a

THE 9/11 TORONTO REPORT

president-to-be), the odds of three presidents being targeted by chance since 1948 are approximately 1 in 149 million.

5. The same is also true of senators. Three senators have been confirmed to have been targeted for assassination since 1948: Robert Kennedy, Patrick Leahy, and Tom Daschle. If one assassination of a top public official were committed each year, and if targets were randomly selected, the odds of a senator being targeted in any given year would be 1 in 5.46 (or 100/546). However, the odds of three senators being targeted by chance over this time period are approximately 1 in 5 million. But of course senators are not being selected at random. Senators have been assassinated only when either running for president (Robert Kennedy) or when the Senate was closely divided and the death of a single senator from the majority party could significantly impact policy. Aside from RFK, the only well confirmed senatorial assassinations or attempted assassinations in the post-WWII era occurred in 2001 when Democrats controlled the Senate by virtue of a one-vote advantage over Republicans. In May of 2001, just four months after George W. Bush gained the presidency in a SCAD-ridden disputed election, Republican Jim Jeffords left the party to become an independent, and the Senate shifted to Democratic control for the first time since 1994. Five months later, on 9 October 2001, letters laced with anthrax were used in an unsuccessful attempt to assassinate two leading Senate Democrats, Majority Leader Tom Daschle and Judiciary Committee Chairman Patrick Leahy. The anthrax in the letters came from what is known as the "Ames strain," which was developed and distributed to bio-

medical research laboratories by the U.S. Army (Tarpley, 2005, pp. 311-318).

6. Ominously, the frequency of SCADs recently increased sharply, and the scope of government complicity has been growing wider. Figure 1 (below) is a bar graph of the frequency of SCADs by decade. SCAD frequency surged in the 1960s, declined in the 1970s and 1980s, dropped to zero when the Cold War ended in the 1990s, but then jumped dramatically in the 2000s. To some extent, the SCAD sprees of the 1960s and the 2000s reflected the criminality associated with Presidents Nixon and George W. Bush. However, the widening scope of government complicity across the decades suggests creeping corruption may be amplifying the untoward implications of criminally inclined presidential administrations.

The expanding scope of government complicity in elite political criminality can be observed in the trajectory from Watergate through Iran-Contra to Iraq-gate (cf., Bernstein, 1976). The crimes of the Nixon Administration were driven by the President's personal fears and animosities, and involved only a handful of top officials, most of whom participated only in cover-ups and, even then, reluctantly. Furthermore, Republican and Democratic members of Congress joined together to investigate and condemn the President's actions. In contrast, the Iran-Contra episode was systemic, organized, and carefully planned, and its investigation was impeded by partisan opposition even though (or perhaps because) it obviously appeared connected to the alleged 1980 October Surprise. Motivated by ideology, Iran-Contra emanated from the White House and garnered enthusiastic participation by high-ranking officials and career professionals within the State Department, the CIA, and the military. Even wider in scope and more deeply woven into governing institutions were the crimes apparently committed by the Bush-Cheney Administration (Conyers, 2007; Fisher, 2004; Goldsmith, 2007; Goodman, 2007; Greenwald, 2007; Loo and Philips, 2006; Wolf, 2007). Attacking the organs of deliberation, policymaking, oversight and legal review, they appear to have involved officials throughout the executive branch and perhaps leaders in Congress as well.

FIGURE 4-1: SCAD FREQUENCY AND SCOPE
OF GOVERNMENT COMPLICITY

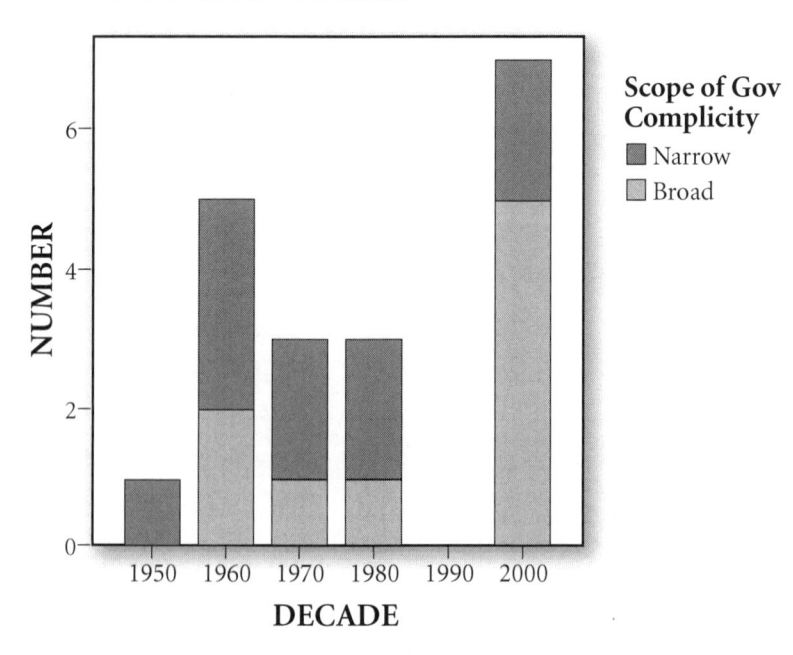

SEEING 9/11 FROM ABOVE: A COMPARATIVE ANALYSIS
OF STATE CRIMES AGAINST DEMOCRACY

Observations about 9/11

Presented below are some suggestions for future research and investigation. These suggestions are speculative in nature and, ultimately, may fail to bear empirical fruit. They are offered in the spirit of scientific curiosity and exploration, recognizing that science advances by making novel discoveries, not by veering clear of untraveled ground.

The SCAD heuristic

A potential heuristic for 9/11 research is to think in terms of what SCADs in general imply about the likely characteristics of 9/11 tactics, perpetrators, concealment, and so on. In a sense, this involves using SCAD patterns as a scope or template for searching through 9/11 evidence.

So what is seen when 9/11 is observed through a "SCAD scope"? First, of course, we see that 9/11 possesses many characteristics that have been observed in other SCADs and suspected SCADs in the post-World War II era. Table 2 lists SCAD characteristics, gives examples of SCADs that have those characteristics, and indicates how each factor is reflected in 9/11. In addition to 9/11, two or more SCADs or suspected SCADs in the table have the following traits: involved overlapping considerations of presidential politics and foreign policy; fomented militarism or cleared the way for wars or the continuation of wars; employed the skills and tactics of covert operations and psychological warfare; had crime scenes that were investigated superficially and cleaned up quickly; had incriminating photographic or documentary evidence that was either sequestered or ignored; garnered tendentious analyses by officials to explain away anomalous forensic evidence; plagued by "coincidences" that contributed to their success and concealment; occurred in pairs or clusters close in time; and have been associated with cognitive infiltration or other efforts by officials to deflect popular suspicions.

TABLE 4-2: 9/11 SCAD CHARACTERISTICS

SCAD Characteristic	Examples	9/11 Parallels
SCADs often appear where presidential politics and foreign policy intersect	Gulf of Tonkin incident and Congressional Resolution; The crimes of Watergate; the October Surprises of 1968 and 1980	9/11 put to rest questions about the disputed 2000 presidential election and rallied popular support around the President George W. Bush.
SCADs frequently foment or clear the way for wars or the continuation of wars	The Gulf of Tonkin incident, the assassinations of John and Robert Kennedy and Martin Luther King; the 1968 October Surprise;	9/11 and the anthrax letter attacks were the pretext for wars in Afghanistan and Iraq and for a policy of preemptive war. The anthrax letter attacks supported fears of Iraqi WMD
SCADs often employ the skills and tactics of covert operations and psychological warfare	Watergate wiretapping, Iran-Contra "cutouts," and forged documents on Iraqi acquisition of uranium	9/11 used airplanes as weapons and involved controlled demolition;

SEEING 9/11 FROM ABOVE: A COMPARATIVE ANALYSIS OF STATE CRIMES AGAINST DEMOCRACY

SCAD crime scenes are investigated superficially and are cleaned up quickly	President Kennedy's limousine was washed at Parkland Hospital; a doorframe riddled with bullets when Robert Kennedy was assassinated was "lost" by the Los Angeles Police Department	Debris from the WTC was cleaned up quickly and steel was shipped to China. NIST conducted no tests for signs of explosives and incendiaries
Incriminating photographic or documentary evidence is either sequestered or ignored	The Zapruder film was immediately purchased by *Look Magazine*; Iran-Contra documents were shredded by Oliver North; Howard Hunt's safe in the White House was cleaned out; the hard drives on Katherine Harris' computers were erased.	Videos from security cameras around the Pentagon were confiscated and withheld; videos of WTC collapses were not considered by NIST; photographs taken from a helicopter flying above WTC were sequestered until Feb. 2010.
Tendentious technical analyses are developed to explain away anomalous forensic evidence or frame favored suspect	In JFK assassination investigation, magic bullet theory developed to explain how JFK was wounded twice and John Connolly was wounded by two shots. After 2000 election, Florida appointed a commission that blamed the election fiasco on "voter error" and punch-card ballots, overlooking evidence of crimes and partisan intrigue.	NIST theory of the pancake collapse of the Twin Towers and the key-beam collapse of WTC7 (all based on computer simulation ignoring visual evidence). Silicon in mailed anthrax attributed to water used in growing (but unable to replicate when challenged by Congress). Anthrax traced by DNA to batch under control of Bruce Ivins (later rejected by NSF review).

LINES OF INQUIRY SUGGESTED BY SCAD PATTERNS		
SCAD Characteristic	**Examples**	**9/11 Parallels**
SCADs are plagued by suspicious "coincidences" – consequences benefitting certain officials, inexplicable breaches of procedure, administrative failures, investigative gaps, witness deaths, lost or destroyed evidence, etc.	JFK assassination: Nixon in Dallas that morning; limo route changed to include sharp turn at Texas School Book Depository; JFK limo washed at hospital; Oswald killed. 2000, 2004 elections: Results differ inexplicably from exit polls and in Bush's favor; insufficient staff & equipment at precincts where Democrats are concentrated; ballot design flaws favoring Bush.	All hijackers slip through airport screening; Confusion caused by war games; President sits in Florida classroom after second plane hits WTC towers; Three steel skyscrapers collapse at near free-fall acceleration into their own footprints; Larry Silverstein says he decided to "pull" WTC Building 7; Anthrax from US domestic lab mailed one week after 9/11. See Table 3 for more items.
SCADs usually occur in clusters and clustered SCADs have similarities or connections that point to likely suspects	The assassination of John Kennedy was followed by the murder of Lee Harvey Oswald while in police custody by a police-connected mobster; the attacks on Daniel Ellsberg were followed by Watergate and a multitude of "dirty tricks" to influence the Democratic primaries.	The 9/11 hijackings were followed by the anthrax letter attacks. Guilty knowledge indicated by White House being administered Cipro while Congressional leaders and the public were not warned Plame-gate/Iraq-gate

SEEING 9/11 FROM ABOVE: A COMPARATIVE ANALYSIS OF STATE CRIMES AGAINST DEMOCRACY

Cognitive infiltration is employed by public officials to subliminally deflect public suspicions and otherwise shape public perceptions of the SCAD	The term "conspiracy theory" was planted to stigmatize criticism of the Warren Commission report. Two days after the arrest at the Watergate, Nixon Press Secretary Ron Ziegler famously dismissed the crime as a "third-rate burglary attempt" (quoted in Ripley 1973). Whereas the crime was actually political espionage, election tampering, and wiretapping, to this day it is referred to as the Watergate burglary.	The term 9/11 exaggerates the threat of terrorism, limits the scope of investigation, and subliminally excites fear and foments social panic; also, withholding photographs taken from a helicopter flying above WTC impeded conceptualization of the destruction "from above."

Research on 9/11 has documented in detail all of the SCAD characteristics listed in Table 4-2 with the exception of those in the bottom three rows. The SCAD scope or template highlights these neglected factors and points to potentially promising lines of inquiry and analysis. Investigators should consider: (1) Estimating the statistical probability of 9/11's many "coincidences"; (2) Examining the actions of Bush, Cheney, and other Administration officials for signs of complicity not just in 9/11 but also in other crimes and suspicious events closely related to 9/11 in time, tactics, or consequences; and (3) Studying the communicative implications, origins, and diffusion of 9/11 terminology for signs of cognitive infiltration and "meme seeding."

THE 9/11 TORONTO REPORT

The improbability of 9/11.

9/11 stands out from other SCADs and suspected SCADs in the range of "coincidences" surrounding it that indicate official complicity. Table 4-3 expands on the examples listed in Table 4-2 (third row from the bottom). Those who accept the official account of 9/11 must attribute virtually all of these coincidental occurrences to chance. Doing so amounts to embracing a "coincidence theory" of 9/11 that defies scientific reasoning.

TABLE 4-3: THE "COINCIDENCE THEORY" OF 9/11
(in which all of the following factors are dismissed as unrelated, unintentional, or random occurrences)

Before the Attacks	During the Attacks	Immediate Effects and Aftermath	Related to the Investigation
Project for a New American Century says military buildup needed but not possible without a "new Pearl Harbor" — DOD project Able Danger identifies 4 of the future hijackers as part of an al Qaeda cell a year before 9/11. The Able Danger data are destroyed by order of DOD before 9/11.	All hijackers slip through airport screening — Air traffic controllers think hijackings may be part of war games — President sits in Florida classroom after being informed of second plane hitting WTC towers — Hijacked plane en route to DC is tracked for ~ 20 minutes but is not intercepted	Three steel skyscrapers collapse at near free-fall acceleration into their own footprints — Videos show what appears to be molten steel — Pools of molten steel reported during cleanup — Larry Silverstein says he decided to "pull" WTC Building 7	Terrorists identified within 24 hours — Next day, Bush tells Richard Clarke to look for connections between 9/11 and Iraq — Bin Laden denies involvement in 9/11 — US rejects offer by Taliban to turn over bin Laden if there is evidence he sponsored 9/11

SEEING 9/11 FROM ABOVE: A COMPARATIVE ANALYSIS OF STATE CRIMES AGAINST DEMOCRACY

US envoys meet with Taliban in summer 2001 and threaten war if a pipeline is not allowed to be built across Afghanistan — FBI field offices warn of Arabs seeking flight training but not training for take-offs or landings — FBI informant lives with one of the hijackers in California — Cheney appointed to head an Energy Taskforce which examines oil reserves and contracts in the Middle East — Cheney put in charge of war games — In July 2001, a top CIA official meets with bin Laden in Dubai where the latter is being treated for kidney disease	Cheney appears to give order not to intercept plane headed to DC — White House receives call using codename for Air Force One and saying it is next target — Pentagon workers report huge explosion minutes before aircraft hits — Firefighters report explosions in basement of towers — Firefighters and others report explosions in Building 7 in the morning — Cell phone calls said to be made from hijacked aircraft (later denied by FBI) — Plane targeting Pentagon executes complex air maneuver that exceeds plane's design capacity and most pilots' skills	Cleanup workers assured WTC is safe despite dust and fumes — Anthrax from US domestic lab mailed one week after 9/11 — Anthrax sent to leading Democrats in the Senate — White House pressures FBI to link anthrax mailing to Al Qaeda — Hole in Pentagon appears too small for commercial jet — Seismic record for collapses at WTC show seismic "spikes" at the beginning of the North Tower collapse, well before debris hits earth — Tapes made by air traffic controllers during debriefing immediately after the attacks are destroyed	WTC not tested for evidence of explosives or incendiaries — Steel at the site cut up quickly and shipped to China — Editor of Fire Engineers magazine condemns investigation of WTC destruction a farce — CCT video tapes around Pentagon confiscated within an hour of the strike — Bush and Cheney block an investigation for almost a year — Bush, Cheney, Rice say an no one could have imagined hijacked airplanes being used as weapons — Kissinger initially appointed Director of 9/11 Commission

THE 9/11 TORONTO REPORT

In July, Attorney General Ashcroft stops flying on commercial airlines	Aircraft hits Pentagon on side under construction where deaths least likely	BBC newscaster says Building 7 has collapsed *before* it actually collapses	Kissinger initially appointed Director of 9/11 Commission
—	—	—	—
War games are scheduled for 9/11/01, at least one of which involved hijacked aircraft	Sec. of Defense Rumsfeld, 2nd in military chain of command after the President, wanders around outside the Pentagon after the aircraft hits	Iowa State University destroys its comprehensive anthrax archives shortly after mailed anthrax is discovered, either at behest of or with approval of FBI	Zelikow appointed Director of 9/11 Commission despite conflicts of interest
—			—
In August, Presidential Daily Brief warns that bin Laden plans to strike in US, hijacked aircraft may be involved, mentions WTC			9/11 Commission not told terrorists' "confessions" extracted with torture
—		—	—
Signs of insider trading on American and United Airlines stock shortly before 9/11		Photographs taken from a helicopter flying above WTC on 9/11 were sequestered until Feb. 2010 and were released only pursuant to a Freedom of Information Act request.	9/11 Commission not allowed to see videotapes of interrogations
—			—
On Sept. 10, Pentagon officials cancel commercial air flights scheduled for 9/11			CIA videotapes of waterboarding destroyed
			—
			Building 7 not mentioned in 9/11 Commission Report
			—
			Zelikow is informed of findings of Able Danger but does not include this in the 9/11 Commission Report

SEEING 9/11 FROM ABOVE: A COMPARATIVE ANALYSIS OF STATE CRIMES AGAINST DEMOCRACY

The science for estimating the likelihood of events occurring by chance is called statistics. In probability theory, events are assumed to have a finite range of variation. A flipped coin can land on only heads or tails. The probability of any given outcome occurring by chance is the proportion that outcome comprises of the total number of outcomes in the range of possible outcomes. The flipped coin landing on heads is one variant out of two; the other variant is tails. So the probability of a flipped coin landing on heads is one out of two, or 0.5.

Common sense tells us that the odds of a multiple events occurring together by chance are low, but the science of statistics can help us estimate how low. As the number of coincidences increases, the odds of them occurring by chance rapidly becomes infinitesimal, which is to say, almost impossible. The odds of one variant occurring twice are equal to the odds of it occurring once squared. The odds of getting two heads in two flips are one-in-four (.5 x .5 = .25). The odds of something occurring three times are the odds of it occurring once cubed. The odds of getting three heads in three flips are 1 in 8 (.5 x .5 x .5= .125). Ten heads out of ten flips would be expected to occur one time in 1,024 tries.

The number of "coincidences" in Table 4-3 exceeds 50. The odds of getting 50 heads in 50 flips are less than one in a quadrillion. This mathematical exercise does not apply directly to 9/11, but it does suggest that the odds of all the coincidences in Table 3 occurring together are astronomically small.

The anthrax letter attacks

SCAD research suggests SCADs are committed in pairs or clusters. Examples include the assassination of John Kennedy which was followed two days later by the assassination of Lee Harvey

Oswald while in police custody; the stalking of Daniel Ellsberg which was followed by the crimes of Watergate and the attempted assassination of George Wallace; and the 1980 October Surprise which was followed by Iran-Contra. In the case of Watergate and Ellsberg, we know that the crimes in question had been committed by the same group, and that this group committed other crimes as well.

If this pattern holds for 9/11, then other crimes closely related in time or employing similar tactics were probably planned and organized by the same people. An obvious place to start looking for connections to 9/11 is with the anthrax letter attacks, but consideration should also be given to investigating other events and venues, including: who decided to withhold the photos taken of the WTC on 9/11 from a helicopter flying overhead; who forged the documents indicating (falsely) that Iraq had purchased yellowcake uranium from Niger; after the U.S invasion of Iraq, who authorized payments to a former Iraqi official for forging a letter suggesting (falsely) the Iraqis possessed WMD but had moved them to another country; who authorized the expedited flights out of the U.S. for the relatives of Osama bin Laden; who initiated and arranged the meeting between envoys of the Bush-Cheney Administration and Taliban officials where war was threatened if the U.S. was not allowed to build a pipeline for transporting natural gas across Afghanistan. All of these questions remain unanswered.

Officially, the anthrax letter attacks have been attributed to Bruce Ivins, a bio-weapons expert who allegedly had psychological problems. However, the case against Ivins contains several gaps. The anthrax in the letters has not been conclusively connected to the anthrax in Ivins' control; the high amount of silicon

SEEING 9/11 FROM ABOVE: A COMPARATIVE ANALYSIS OF STATE CRIMES AGAINST DEMOCRACY

in the mailed anthrax, which enhanced its lethality, may have required equipment and skills Ivins lacked; and Ivins did not have direct control of the equipment allegedly used to dry the anthrax.

Like 9/11, the anthrax letter attacks played into the Bush-Cheney agenda for invading Iraq. In fact, the Administration immediately suggested that the anthrax came from Iraq. The effort to implicate the regime of Saddam Hussein was thwarted only because the FBI investigation concluded the anthrax came from a strain developed by the U.S. military at the Army Medical Research Institute of Infectious Diseases at Fort Detrick, Maryland (Broad et al. 2001).

There is already circumstantial evidence in the public domain indicating the Bush-Cheney Administration had foreknowledge of the anthrax letter attacks. In the evening on 9/11, weeks before the anthrax mailings were discovered, medical officers at the White House distributed a powerful antibiotic (Cipro) to the president and other officials (Sobieraj 2001). Officials might claim that Cipro was administered simply as a precaution, but this innocent explanation is belied by the failure of anyone in the White House to tell Congress and the public that an anthrax attack was feared. Investigators should determine what kind of anthrax attack was feared; who issued the warning; who suggested that Cipro should be administered; to whom Cipro was given and for how long; and why other officials and the public were not warned. Those officials who were responsible for these decisions, especially those earliest in the decision chain, should be considered suspect of complicity in both 9/11 and the anthrax letter attacks, and their whereabouts and contacts on and immediately before and after 9/11, should be carefully tracked.

THE 9/11 TORONTO REPORT

Linguistic thought control

The possibility of linguistic thought control in relation to 9/11, the anthrax letter attacks, and other associated crimes, should be investigated. If any destructive memes were surreptitiously injected into public discourse, they may have characteristics similar to those of the conspiracy-theory label, which is normatively powerful but conceptually flawed and alien to America's civic culture.

A number of memes have been introduced by the military as part of the war on terror, but they do not qualify as linguistic thought control because they were not released into the public sphere surreptitiously. Examples include: war on terror; extraordinary rendition; enhanced interrogation; detainee; collateral damage; evil doers; Islamofascism; and Operation Iraqi Freedom. These memes skew and hamper communication, but they are recognized as artificial constructs, and hence their ability to distort public discourse is mitigated.

In contrast, memes warranting inspection as possible plants for linguistic thought control are those that are taken for granted as natural products of sense-making in civil society. The most important example discussed here for purposes of illustration is the term "9/11." If it was inserted into the organs of opinion formation during or immediately after the day of the hijackings, prior planning would probably have been necessary, which would be evidence of official complicity in the events of 9/11. Other examples of memes that warrant study include: ground zero, let's roll, al Qaeda, lone wolf terrorist, and homegrown terrorist.

Today, the term "9/11" is accepted as simply a straightforward name for the events on September 11, 2001. However as a label for "terrorist attacks upon the United States" (the phrase used in

SEEING 9/11 FROM ABOVE: A COMPARATIVE ANALYSIS OF STATE CRIMES AGAINST DEMOCRACY

the official title of the 9/11 Commission) 9/11 has characteristics of a conceptual Trojan horse similar to those of the conspiracy-theory meme. On the surface, the term 9/11 says almost nothing; it is not even a complete date. And yet it carries hidden associations and implications that reverberate in the national psyche.

First, the term 9/11 contains emotionally charged symbolism. The numbers 9-1-1 correspond to the phone number used to contact first responders when emergencies occur in the United States. This means references to 9/11 subliminally provoke thoughts among Americans about picking up the phone and calling for an ambulance or for help from police or firefighters. The 9/11 label would not have been possible if the events had not occurred on September 11; this itself suggests prior planning for a date with emotional connections. Nevertheless, state intervention into the discursive processes of civil society would have been necessary both to suggest the date as the label for the events and to drop the year from "9-11-01."

As a matter of fact, the connection between the abbreviated date (9/11) and the emergency phone number (9-1-1) was highlighted in what had to be one of the very first times the term 9/11 was used in the media. The 9/11 label was included in the headline of a story in the New York Times on September 12, 2001. The headline was "America's Emergency Line: 9/11." The first sentence of the article referred to "America's aptly dated wake-up call." Since then, the connection between the date and the emergency number has been mentioned in the New York Times only one other time – in an article published in February 2002. The author of the first article was Bill Keller, a senior writer who had served previously as chief of the Moscow Bureau during the years when the Soviet Union was collapsing. Keller was appointed Executive Editor of the New York Times in 2003 and was in that position when the Times withheld the story about the Bush-Cheney Administration's warrantless wiretapping until after the 2004 presidential election. Keller should be considered a "person of interest" in any legal investigation of the events of 9/11.

A second characteristic of the 9/11 label indicative of cognitive infiltration is that it deviates from America's naming conventions for the type of event it designates. With the possible exception of Independence Day, which is often referred to as July fourth, the 9/11 label marks the first time Americans have called a historic event by an abbreviated form of the date on which the event occurred. 9/11 is a first-of-its-kind "numeric acronym." Americans do not call Pearl Harbor, "12/7," even though President Roosevelt declared December 7, 1941, to be "a date that will live in infamy." Americans do not refer to the JFK assassination as "11/22." Historically, as these examples suggest, Americans have referred to crimes, tragedies, and disasters by their targets, locations, methods, or effects – not their dates. Americans remember the Alamo and the sinking of the Maine. They speak of Three Mile Island, Hurricane Katrina, the Oklahoma City bombing, and Watergate.

If Americans had followed this pattern for 9/11, the events would have been called something else. The hijackings. The attack on America. The airplane terror attack. Americans would tell themselves to remember the World Trade Center and the Pentagon.

Even when Americans want to refer to a specific day because of its historical significance, they seldom use the date. They speak of Independence Day, D-Day, VE Day, Election Day, etc. If they

SEEING 9/11 FROM ABOVE: A COMPARATIVE ANALYSIS OF STATE CRIMES AGAINST DEMOCRACY

had done this for September 11, it would have been called the Day of Terror or something like that.

Third, the term 9/11 should be suspected of being an artifact of linguistic thought control because the term shapes perceptions in ways that play into elite agendas for global military aggression. In drawing attention to a date as opposed to the method or location of the destruction, the term 9/11 suggests there has been a shift in the flow of history. 9/11 is an historical marker. There is the world before 9/11, and the world after 9/11. As Vice President Cheney and other officials said, "9/11 changed everything." Clearly, this framing suggests the need for a dramatic U.S. response and a determined, hardened attitude. Think how less convincing and urgent it would be to say the hijackings changed everything, or the collapse of the Twin Towers and Building 7 changed everything. When you refer to hijackings and buildings, you cannot avoid the realization that the threat of terrorism is in no way comparable to the threat the allies faced in World War II or to the dangers in the standoff between the United States and the Soviet Union in the Cold War. Using the term "9/11" to refer to the destruction at the World Trade Center and the Pentagon has the effect of exaggerating the threat posed by people who hijack airplanes and use them as weapons.

Fourth, by stressing the date, the term 9/11 draws our attention away from the victims, the destruction, and the military response. Imagine if we referred to the events in question as the Airplane Mass Murders, or the Multiple Skyscraper Collapse, or the National Air-Defense Failure. Each of these names points to a different investigative focus. 9/11, as a name, causes us to think in terms of chronology and historic change instead of failures and culpability.

THE 9/11 TORONTO REPORT

We should not be surprised that intelligence elites might develop and plant concepts in public discourse. It is very unlikely the conspiracy-theory label was a unique instance of CIA concept-creation and deployment. Recall the language used to sell the Iraq War. Could Bush, Cheney or Rice come up with the line, "We don't want the smoking gun to be a mushroom cloud"? Would they have known to reach back to World War II for their nomenclature, or to think of words and phrases like "Homeland Security," "Axis of Evil," "ground zero," and the like? Such wordcraft requires teams of people, historical research, linguistic analysis, advertising specialists, experts in propaganda, and more.

Recognize, too, that if officials were complicit in the events of 9/11, which ample evidence suggests, they would have been intensely concerned with how the 9/11 events were interpreted and perceived. Hence they would have been especially interested in what the events would eventually be called. The RAND Corporation, a CIA-connected think tank, began studying this phenomenon in the 1950s. Roberta Wohlstetter, wife of RAND game-theorist and nuclear-war strategist Albert Wohlstetter, examined the communicative context of Pearl Harbor, including how the attack came to be understood and referenced in popular culture, and how its meaning evolved. The parts of her study that were not classified were published as Pearl Harbor: Warning and Decision. Paul Wolfowitz, a student of Roberta's, cited this book when he appeared before Congress shortly after 9/11. Also, the topic of how historic events are popularly understood and conceptualized is reputed to be an area of expertise of Phillip Zelikow, the director of the 9/11 Commission and primary author of the Bush-Cheney Administration's first policy statement on preemptive war. Thus officials had both the motive and the capability to frame the events of September 11, 2001, as "9/11," and their extensive network of media assets gave them the means.

Fortunately, if the 9/11 meme is indeed an artifact of linguistic thought control, it should be possible to track the meme back to its source. The media record is still largely intact in the archives of the nation's major newspapers and television networks. Moreover, the length of time that would need to be covered is fairly short: a few weeks at most. Once the originating sources and conveyors are identified, they could be interviewed to determine their role in propagating the label.

Conclusion

The main theme emerging from the foregoing analysis is that SCADs appear to be surface indications of a deeper, invisible level of politics in which officials at the highest levels of government use deception, conspiracy, and violence to shape national policies and priorities. This manipulation of domestic politics is an extension of America's duplicity in foreign affairs and draws on the nation's well-developed skills in covert operations. Through their experience with covert actions, national security agencies have developed a wide range of skills and tactics for subverting and overthrowing regimes, manipulating international tensions, and disrupting ideological movements. Apparently, these skills are being used domestically as well as overseas.

On rare occasions when policymakers have been called to justify domestic covert operations and other deceptions, they have done so by asserting that public opinion, both domestic and international, is a critical battlefront in conflicts between democratic capitalism and its ideological and military opponents. Although the implications of this policy for popular control of government are seldom examined, the policy itself was and is no secret. As an assistant secretary of defense said in response to claims that public opinion had been manipulated during the Cuban missile crisis, "News generated by actions of the government as to content and timing are part of the arsenal of weaponry that a President has in application of military force and related forces to the solution of political problems, or to the application of international political pressure" (Wise and Ross, 1964, pp. 297-298). Richard Nixon put it more bluntly. In claiming that the president has the power to break the law when protecting national security, he said: "Well, when the president does it, that means that it is not illegal"(Frost, 1977).

CHAPTER FIVE

9/11 as a Deep Event: How CIA Personnel Helped Allow It to Happen

BY PETER DALE SCOTT

I WANT TO BEGIN BY THANKING THOSE RESPONSIBLE FOR these important Hearings in Toronto, and commending them for their sensible guidelines, even though these were inevitably going to disappoint some people. After ten years it is indeed worthwhile to reassess what we know and do and do not know about 9/11.

Today, we can confidently say:

- the most important truths still remain unknown, in large part because many of the most important documents are either unreleased or heavily redacted;
- the efforts at cover-up continue, if anything more aggressively than before;
- thanks to the collaborative efforts of many different people, we now understand 9/11 far better than

before, along with relevant earlier events, and above all the post 9/11 cover-up;
- In addition to the cover-up, there has been what 9/11 Commission Senior Counsel John Farmer has called either "unprecedented administrative incompetence or organized mendacity" on the part of key figures in Washington.[95]

Kevin Fenton's New Book on Systematic Withholding of Information from the FBI

Farmer's first alternative, that of "unprecedented administrative incompetence," is in effect the explanation offered by the 9/11 Commission Report, to deal with a) striking anomalies both on 9/11 itself, and b) the preceding twenty months during which important information was withheld from the FBI by key personnel in the CIA's Bin Laden Unit (the so-called Alec Station). But thanks to the groundbreaking new book by Kevin Fenton, *Disconnecting the Dots,* we can no longer attribute the anomalous CIA behavior to "systemic problems," or what Tony Summers rashly calls "bureaucratic confusion."[97]

Building on earlier important books by James Bamford, Lawrence Wright, Peter Lance, and Philip Shenon, Fenton demonstrates beyond a shadow of a doubt that there was a systematic CIA pattern of withholding important information from the FBI, even when the FBI would normally be entitled to it. Even more brilliantly, he shows that the withholding pattern has been systematically sustained through four successive post-9/11 investigations: those of the Congressional Inquiry chaired by Senators Bob Graham and Richard Shelby (still partly withheld), the

9/11 AS A DEEP EVENT: HOW CIA PERSONNEL HELPED ALLOW IT TO HAPPEN

9/11 Commission, the Department of Justice inspector general, and the CIA inspector general.

Most importantly of all, he shows that the numerous withholdings, both pre- and post 9/11, were the work of relatively few people. The withholding of information from the FBI was principally the work of what he calls the "Alec Station group" – a group within but not identical with the Alec Station Unit, consisting largely of CIA personnel, though there were a few FBI as well. Key figures in this group were CIA officer Tom Wilshire (discussed in the 9/11 Commission Report as "John"), and his immediate superior at Alec Station, Richard Blee.

The post-9/11 cover-up of Wilshire's behavior was principally the work of one person, Barbara Grewe, who worked first on the Justice Department Inspector General's investigation of Wilshire's behavior, then was transferred to two successive position with the 9/11 Commission's staff, where she was able to transfer the focus of attention from the performance of the CIA to that of the FBI.[98] Grewe subsequently left government to work at the Mitre Corp., a private firm doing CIA contract work with the CIA and another private firm, Ptech. Questions about Ptech and Mitre Corp's work on FAA-NORAD interoperability systems were raised in 9/11 testimony presented some years ago by Indira Singh; see Scott, *Road to 9/11*, 175. Whether or not Grewe conducted the relevant interviews of Wilshire and other relevant personnel, Grewe "certainly drew on them when drafting her sections of the Commission's and Justice Department inspector general's reports."[99] Kirsten Wilhelm of the National Archives told Fenton (p. 78) that "It appears Barbara Grewe conducted the interviews with 'John' [Wilshire] and Jane [Corsi]," another key figure. Wilhelm could find no "memorandum for the record" (MFR) for the Wilshire interview, which Fenton understandably calls "about the most important interview the Commission conducted" (p. 79). Summers, also citing correspondence with Kirsten Wilhelm, disagrees, saying that the report of Wilshire's interview exists, but "is redacted in its entirety" (Summers, 381, cf. 552). This is an important point to be focused on in future investigations.

Grewe's repositioning from post to post is a sign of an intended cover-up at a higher level. So, as we shall see, is Wilshire's transfer in May 2001 from CIA's Alec Station to the FBI, where he began a new phase of interferences with the normal flow of intelligence, obstructing the FBI from within it.[100]

The pattern begins with intelligence obtained from surveillance of an important al Qaeda summit meeting of January 2000 in Malaysia, perhaps the only such summit before 9/11. The meeting drew instant and high-level US attention because of indirect links to a support element (a key telephone in Yemen used by al Qaeda) suspected of a role in the 1998 bombings of US Embassies. As Fenton notes, "The CIA realized that the summit was so important that information about it was briefed to CIA and FBI leaders [Louis Freeh and Dale Watson], National Security Adviser Sandy Berger and other top officials."[101]

Yet inside Alec Station Tom Wilshire and his CIA subordinate (known only as "Michelle") blocked the effort of an FBI agent detailed there (Doug Miller) to notify the FBI that one of the participants (Khalid Al-Mihdhar) had a US visa in his passport.[102] Worse, Michelle then sent a CIA cable falsely stating that Al-Mihdhar's "travel documents, including a multiple entry US visa, had been copied and passed 'to the FBI for further investigation.'"[103] Alec Station also failed to watchlist the participants in the meeting, as was called for by CIA guidelines.[104]

This was just the beginning of a systematic, sometimes lying pattern, where NSA and CIA information about Al-Mihdhar and his traveling companion, Nawaf al-Hazmi, was systematically withheld from the FBI, lied about, or manipulated or distorted in such a way as to inhibit an FBI investigation of the two Saudis and their associates. This pattern is a major component of the 9/11 story, because the behavior of these two eventual hijackers was so unprofessional that, without this CIA protection from the "Alec Station Group," they would almost certainly have been detected and detained or deported, long before they boarded Flight 77 in Washington.

Fenton concludes with a list of thirty-five different occasions where the hijackers were protected in this fashion, from January 2000 to about September 5, 2001, less than a week before the hijackings.[105] In his analysis, the incidents fall into two main groups. The motive he attributes to the earlier ones, such as the blocking of Doug Miller's cable, was "to cover a CIA operation that was already in progress."[106] Lawrence Wright, "The Agent," *New Yorker,* July 10 and 17, 2006, 68; quoted approvingly in Peter Dale Scott, *American War Machine,* 199. However after "the system was blinking red" in the summer of 2001, and the CIA expected an imminent attack, Fenton can see no other explanation than that "the purpose of withholding the information had become to allow the attacks to go forward."[107]

Wilshire's pattern of interference changed markedly after his move to the Bureau. When in CIA, he had moved to block transmittal of intelligence to the FBI. Now, in contrast, he initiated FBI reviews of the same material, but in such a way that the reviews were conducted in too leisurely a fashion to bear fruit before 9/11. Fenton suspects that Wilshire, assisted by his FBI colleague Dino Corsi, anticipated a future review of his files; and was laying a false trail of documentation to neutralize his embarrassing earlier performance.[108] Fenton notes that Corsi worked at FBI HQ, which coordinated "liaisons with foreign services" (Fenton, 313).

I believe we must now accept Fenton's finding of fact: "It is clear that this information was not withheld through a series of bizarre accidents, but intentionally."[109] However I see a different explanation as to what those intentions originally were, one which is paradoxically much simpler, more benign and also more explicative of other parts, apparently unrelated, of the 9/11 mystery.

The Liaison Agreements with Other Intelligence Agencies

Initially, I believe, Al-Mihdhar and Al-Hazmi were protected because they had been sent to America by the Saudi GID intelligence service, admitted under the terms of the liaison agreement between the GID and the CIA.[110] Prince Turki al-Faisal, former head of the GID, has said that he shared his al Qaeda information with the CIA, and that in 1997 the Saudis "established a joint intelligence committee with the United States to share information on terrorism in general and on...al Qaeda in particular."[111] The 9/11 Commission Report adds that after a post-millennium review, the Counterterrorism Center (i.e. Alec Station) intended to proceed with its plan of half a year earlier, "building up the capabilities of foreign security services that provided intelligence via liaison."[112]

9/11 AS A DEEP EVENT: HOW CIA PERSONNEL HELPED ALLOW IT TO HAPPEN

This was a Blee specialty. Steve Coll reports that Richard Blee and his superior Cofer Black, excited about the opportunities presented by liaison arrangements, flew together into Tashkent in 1999, and negotiated a new liaison agreement with Uzbekistan.[113] According to Steve Coll and the *Washington Post*, this arrangement soon led, via Tashkent, to a CIA liaison inside Afghanistan with the Northern Alliance as well.[114]

Speaking as a former junior diplomat, let me observe that a liaison arrangement would probably have required special clearances for those facilitating the arrangement and sharing the liaison information.[115] This would explain the exclusion of the FBI agents who were not cleared for this information, as well as the behavior of other non-cleared CIA agents who proceeded to collect and disseminate information about the two hijackers. Alec Station needed both to protect the double identity of the two Saudis, and also to make sure that they were not embarrassingly detained by the FBI.

Almost certainly the CIA had relevant liaison arrangements, not just with the Saudi GID and Uzbekistan, but also with the Inter-Services Intelligence (ISI) of Pakistan, as well as the intelligence services of Egypt, and probably Yemen and Morocco. In particular there is reason to think that Ali Mohamed, the double agent who was protected by the FBI from being detained in Canada, thus allowing him to help organize the al Qaeda embassy bombings of 1998, was permitted under such arrangements to enter the US as an agent of foreign intelligence, probably Egyptian. According to Mohamed's FBI handler, Jack Cloonan, "all that information came from Ali," while the PDB itself attributes its key finding to what "an Egyptian Islamic Jihad (EIJ) operative told an [---] service."[116] (Ali Mohamed was definitely EIJ, and this service was probably Egyptian.)

But when Mohamed, like Al-Mihdhar and Al-Hazmi, was inappropriately admitted to the US, it was reportedly not by the CIA, but possibly by "some other Federal agency."[117] This was possibly a Pentagon agency, because from 1987 to 1989, Ali Mohamed "was assigned to the U.S. Special Operations Command [SOCOM] in Fort Bragg, the home of the Green Berets and the Delta Force, the elite counterterrorism squad."[118] SOCOM, which includes JSOC (the Joint Special Operations Command), has its own intelligence division;[119] and SOCOM is the command that first mounted the Able Danger program to track al Qaeda operatives, and then, inexplicably, shut it down.[120]

For this and other reasons, I would suggest reconceptualizing what Fenton calls the anomalous "Alec Station group" as an interagency liaison team (or teams) with special clearances, perhaps centered principally in Alec Station, but involving collaborating personnel in the FBI (such as FBI agent Dino Corsi, about whom Fenton has much to report), and possibly SOCOM. Corsi worked at FBI HQ, which as Fenton notes coordinated "liaisons with foreign services."[121]

Background: the Safari Club and William Casey

These arrangements, in one form or another, dated back at least to the 1970s. Then senior CIA officers and ex-officers (notably Richard Helms), who were dissatisfied with the CIA cutbacks instituted under Jimmy Carter's CIA director, Stansfield Turner, organized an alternative network, the so-called Safari Club. Subordinated to intelligence chiefs from France, Egypt, Saudi Arabia,

9/11 AS A DEEP EVENT: HOW CIA PERSONNEL HELPED ALLOW IT TO HAPPEN

Morocco and (under the Shah) Iran, the Safari Club provided a home to CIA officers like Theodore Shackley and Thomas Clines, who had been marginalized or fired by CIA Director Turner. As Prince Turki later explained, the purpose of the Safari Club was not just to exchange information, but to conduct covert operations that the CIA could no longer carry out in the wake of the Watergate scandal and subsequent reforms.[122]

In the Afghan covert war of the 1980s, CIA Director William Casey made key decisions in the conduct of that war, not with his own CIA bureaucracy, but together with the Saudi intelligence chiefs, first Kamal Adham and then Prince Turki. Among these decisions was the creation of a foreign legion to assist the Afghan mujahedeen in their war – in other words, the creation of that support network which since the end of that war we have known as Al Qaeda.[123] Casey worked out the details with the two Saudi intelligence chiefs, and also with the head of the Bank of Credit and Commerce International (BCCI), the Saudi-Pakistani bank in which Adham and Turki were both shareholders.

In so doing, Casey was in effect running a second CIA, building up the future al Qaeda in Pakistan with the Saudis, even though the official CIA hierarchy in Langley rightly "thought this unwise."[124] In *American War Machine*, I situated the Safari Club and BCCI in a succession of "second CIA" or "alternative CIA" arrangements dating back to the creation of the Office of Policy Coordination (OPC) in 1948. Fenton himself invokes the example of the Safari Club in proposing the possible explanation that Blee and Wilshire used a "parallel network" to track Al-Mihdhar and Al-Hazmi inside the United States. In his words, "Withholding the information about Almihdhar and Alhazmi only makes sense if the CIA was monitoring the two men in the US itself, either officially or off the books."[125] But a third option would be that the GID was monitoring their movements, a situation quite compatible with Saudi Prince Bandar's claim that Saudi security had been "actively following the movements of most of the terrorists with precision."[126]

Joseph and Susan Trento heard from a former CIA officer, once based in Saudi Arabia, that "Both Hazmi and Mihdhar were Saudi agents."[127] If so, they were clearly double agents, acting (or posing) as terrorists at the same time they were acting (or posing) as informants. In espionage, double agents are prized and often valuable; but to rely on them (as the example of Ali Mohamed illustrates) can also be dangerous.

This was particularly the case for the CIA with respect to Saudi Arabia, whose GID supported Al Qaeda energetically in countries like Bosnia, in exchange for a pledge (negotiated by Saudi Interior Minister Naif bin Abdul Aziz with Osama bin Laden) that Al Qaeda "would not interfere with the politics of Saudi Arabia or any Arab country."[128] Pakistan's ISI was even more actively engaged with al Qaeda, and some elements of ISI were probably closer to the ideological goals of al Qaeda, than to Pakistan's nominally secular government.

But in all cases the handling of illegal informants is not just dangerous and unpredictable, but corrupting. To act their parts, the informants must break the law; and their handlers, knowing this, must first fail to report them, and then, all too often, intercede to prevent their arrest by others. In this way, the handler becomes complicit in the crimes of their informants.

9/11 AS A DEEP EVENT: HOW CIA PERSONNEL HELPED ALLOW IT TO HAPPEN

Such corruption is very widespread, perhaps inevitable. In the notorious cases of Gregory Scarpa and Whitey Bulger, agents in the New York and Boston offices of the FBI were accused of giving their mob informants information that led to the murder of their opponents. Agents in the New York office of the old Federal Bureau of Narcotics became so implicated in the trafficking of their informants that the FBN had to be shut down and reorganized.

Even in the best of circumstances, decisions have to be made whether to allow an informant's crime to go forward, or to thwart it and risk terminating the usefulness of the informant. In such moments, agencies are all too likely to make the choice that is not in the public interest.

A very relevant example is the first World Trade Center bombing of 1993 – relevant because Khalid Sheikh Mohammed, the alleged mastermind of 9/11, was one of the 1993 plotters as well. The FBI had an informant, Emad Salem, among the plotters; and Salem later claimed, with supporting evidence from tapes of his FBI debriefings, that the FBI deliberately chose not to shut down the plot. Here is Ralph Blumenthal's careful account in the *New York Times* of this precursor to the mystery of 9/11:

> Law-enforcement officials [i.e. the FBI] were told that terrorists were building a bomb that was eventually used to blow up the World Trade Center, and they planned to thwart the plotters by secretly substituting harmless powder for the explosives, an informer said after the blast.
>
> The informer was to have helped the plotters build the bomb and supply the fake powder, but the plan was called off by an *F.B.I. supervisor who had other ideas about how the informer, Emad A. Salem, should be used*, the informer said.

The account, which is given in the transcript of hundreds of hours of tape recordings Mr. Salem secretly made of his talks with law-enforcement agents, portrays the authorities as in a far better position than previously known to foil the Feb. 26 bombing of New York City's tallest towers. The explosion left six people dead, more than 1,000 injured and damages in excess of half a billion dollars. Four men are now on trial in Manhattan Federal Court in that attack.[129]

The next day, the *Times* published a modest correction: "Transcripts of tapes made secretly by an informant, Emad A. Salem, quote him as saying he warned the Government that a bomb was being built. But the transcripts do not make clear the extent to which the Federal authorities knew that the target was the World Trade Center."

What makes the 1993 even more relevant is that Salem, according to many sources, was an agent of the Egyptian intelligence service, sent to America to spy on the actions of the Egyptian "Blind Sheikh" Omar Abdel Rahman.[130] This raises the possibility that the F.B.I. supervisor who had "other ideas" about how to use Emad Salem, was a member of a liaison team, with special knowledge he could not share with other FBI agents. It may have been, for example, that the Egyptian intelligence service declined to let Salem's cover be blown. This hypothesis is both speculative and problematic, but it has the advantage of offering a relatively innocent explanation for otherwise baffling behavior.

This explanation does not at all rule out the possibility that some officials had more sinister motives for allowing the bombing to take place and covering it up afterwards. Sheikh Omar Abdel Rahman was at this very time a key figure in a sensitive Saudi pro-

9/11 AS A DEEP EVENT: HOW CIA PERSONNEL HELPED ALLOW IT TO HAPPEN

gram, signed on to by U.S. officials as well, of supplying mujahedeen warriors in Bosnia against Serbia.[131] It is clear from both investigative and prosecutorial behavior that a number of different US agencies did not want to disturb Rahman's activities. Even after Rahman himself was finally indicted in the 1995 conspiracy case to blow up New York landmarks, the US Government continued to protect Ali Mohamed, a key figure in the conspiracy.

Worse, the performance of the FBI in allowing the bombing to proceed was only one of a series of interrelated such performances, climaxing with 9/11. The first was in connection with the murder in New York of the Jewish extremist Meir Kahane. The FBI and NY police actually detained two of the murderers in that case and then released them, allowing them to take part in the WTC bombing of 1993. A key trainer of the two men was Ali Mohamed, whose name was systematically protected from disclosure by the prosecuting attorney, Patrick Fitzgerald. Then in 1994, when Ali Mohamed was detained in Vancouver by the Canadian RCMP, the FBI intervened to arrange for Ali Mohamed's release. This freed Mohamed to proceed to Kenya, where he became the lead organizer of the 1998 Embassy bombing in Nairobi.

Following this atrocity, Ali Mohamed was finally detained by the Americans, but still not indicted. He was apparently still a free man when he readily confessed to his FBI handler, Jack Cloonan, that he knew at least three of the 9/11 hijackers, and had helped instruct them in how to hijack airplanes.[132]

We have to conclude that there is something profoundly dysfunctional going on here, and has been going on since before 9/11, indeed under both political parties. The conditions of secrecy created by special clearances have not just masked this dysfunctionality; they have, I would argue, helped create it. The history of espionage tells us that secret power, when operating in the sphere of illegal activities, becomes, time after time, antithetical to public democratic power.

Add to these conditions of unwholesome secrecy the fundamentally unhealthy, indeed corrupt, relationship of U.S. intelligence agencies to those of Saudi Arabia and Pakistan. This has been profoundly anti-democratic both at home and in Asia. The US dependency on Saudi oil has in effect subsidized a wealth-generated spread of Islamic fundamentalism throughout the world, while what ordinary Americans pay for oil and gas generates huge sums, which Saudis then recycle into the financial institutions at the pinnacles of Wall Street.

In like manner, America's unhealthy relationship to the ISI of Pakistan has resulted in a bonanza in Afghanistan for the international heroin traffic. In short the bureaucratic dysfunction we are talking about in 9/11 is a symptom of a larger dysfunction in America's relationship to the rest of the world.

Liaison Agreements and the Protection of Al-Mihdhar and Al-Hazmi

Even without the suggestive precedent of the 1993 WTC bombing, it is legitimate to posit that liaison agreements may have inhibited the round-up of Khalid Al-Mihdhar and Nawaf Al-Hazmi. Let us consider first Fenton's finding of fact: "It is clear that this information [about the two men] was not withheld through a series of bizarre accidents, but intentionally."[133] This finding I consider rock hard. But we can question his explanation:

9/11 AS A DEEP EVENT: HOW CIA PERSONNEL HELPED ALLOW IT TO HAPPEN

that "the purpose of withholding the information had become to allow the attacks to go forward."[134]

I believe that in fact there are a number of possibilities about the intention, ranging from the relatively innocent (the inhibitions deriving from a liaison agreement) to the nefarious. Before considering these, let us deconstruct the notion of "letting the attacks go forward." Clearly, if the hijackers were not detained at the airport gates, people would have been killed – but how many? Recall that in the Operation Northwoods documents, the Joint Chiefs wrote, "We could develop a Communist Cuban terror campaign" in which "We could sink a boatload of Cubans."[135] Would the loss of four planeloads of passengers have been a qualitatively different tragedy?

Of course 9/11 became a much greater tragedy when three of the planes successively hit the two Towers and the Pentagon. But I suspect that the liaison minders of the two Saudis did not imagine, any more than we can imagine, that their targets were capable of such a feat. Recall that their flying lessons, even in a Cessna, were such a fiasco that the lessons were quickly terminated. Their instructor told them "that flying was simply not for them."[136]

Let me suggest that there are three separable ingredients to the 9/11 attacks: the hijackings, the strikes on the buildings, and the unexpected collapse of the three WTC buildings. It is at least possible that the Alec Station liaison team, as a group, never contemplated more than the first. The video of the South Tower attack, in which Flight 175 does not even begin to slow down, persuades me that this flying feat was achieved by robotics. The robotics engineers need not be American; they could be from any group or country – though I very much doubt that Al Qaeda had a Robotics Command in the caves of Tora Bora.

A minimal, least maligning initial explanation for the withholding of information about two of the hijackers would be the hypothesis I proposed in the case of Emad Salem – the constraints established by a liaison agreement. But just as in 1993, the secret power created behind the wall of restrictive clearances may have been exploited for ulterior purposes. The dangerous situation thus created – of potential would-be-hijackers being protected from detention at a time of expected attack – may have inspired some to exploit it as a pretext for war.

One clue to this more sinister intention is that the pattern of withholdings detailed by Fenton is not restricted exclusively to the two Saudis and their CIA station handlers. There are a few concatenating withholdings – above all the Able Danger info at SOCOM and an important intercept, apparently by NSA, of a call between hijack organizers KSM and Ramzi bin Al-Shibh, apparently about the hijackers and Moussaoui.[137]

If the NSA was withholding information from relevant audiences, it would recall the role of the NSA at the time of the second Tonkin Gulf Incident in August 1964. Then the NSA, at a crucial moment, forwarded 15 pieces of SIGINT (signals intelligence), which indicated – falsely – that there had been a North Vietnamese attack on two US destroyers. At the same time NSA withheld 107 pieces of SIGINT, which indicated, correctly that no North Vietnamese attack had occurred.[138] NSA's behavior at that time was mirrored at the CIA: both agencies were aware of a powerful consensus inside the Johnson administration that had already agreed on provoking North Vietnam, in hopes of creating an opportunity for military response.[139]

We know from many accounts of the Bush administration that there was also a powerful pro-war consensus within it, centered on Cheney, Rumsfeld, and the so-called cabal of PNAC (the Project for the New American Century) that before Bush's election had been lobbying vigorously for military action against Iraq. We know also that Rumsfeld's immediate response to 9/11 was to propose an attack on Iraq, and that planning for such an attack was indeed instituted on September 17.[140] It is worth considering whether some of those protecting the hijackers from detention did not share in these warlike ambitions.

Did Richard Blee Have an Ulterior Motive for Withholding Information?

As Fenton speculates, one of those seeking a pretext for an escalated war against Al Qaeda may have been Richard Blee. We saw that Blee, with Cofer Black, negotiated an intelligence-sharing liaison agreement with Uzbekistan. By 2000 SOCOM had become involved, and "U.S. Special Forces began to work more overtly with the Uzbek military on training missions."[141] In the course of time the Uzbek liaison agreement, as we saw, expanded into a subordinate liaison agreement with the Northern Alliance. Blee, meeting with Massoud, agreed to lobby in Washington for more active support for the Northern Alliance.[142]

After the Cole bombing in 2000, Blee was pushing to expand the mission still further, into a joint attack force in conjunction with the Northern Alliance forces of Massoud. There was considerable objection to this while Clinton was still president, largely on the grounds that Massoud was known to be supporting his forces by heroin trafficking.[143] But in the spring of 2001 a meeting of department deputies in the new Bush administration revived the plans of Blee, Black, and Richard Clarke for large-scale covert aid to Massoud.[144] On September 4, one week before 9/11, the Bush Cabinet authorized the drafting of a new presidential directive, NSPD-9, authorizing a new covert action program along these lines in conjunction with Massoud.[145]

Blee was no longer a minority voice, and six weeks after 9/11 he would be named the new CIA station chief in Kabul.[146] Fenton reports that in this capacity Blee became involved in the rendition of al Qaeda detainees, and suggests that the motive may have been to obtain, by torture, a false confession (by Ibn Shaikh al-Libi) to Iraqi involvement with al Qaeda. This false confession "then formed a key part of Secretary of State Colin Powell's embarrassing presentation to the UN before the invasion of Iraq."[147]

Did SOCOM Have an Ulterior Motive for Closing Down Able Danger?

What ensued after 9/11 went far beyond Blee's program for paramilitary CIA involvement with the Northern Alliance. The CIA component in Afghanistan was soon dwarfed by the forces of SOCOM: George Tenet reported that by late 2001 the US force in Afghanistan consisted of about 500 fighters, including "110 CIA officers, 316 Special Forces personnel, and scores of Joint Special Operations Command raiders creating havoc behind enemy lines."[148]

In the Bush administration, Stephen Cambone, who earlier had collaborated with Rumsfeld and Cheney in signing the PNAC's statement, *Rebuilding America's Defenses,* became one

9/11 AS A DEEP EVENT: HOW CIA PERSONNEL HELPED ALLOW IT TO HAPPEN

of the active promoters of using SOCOM special forces to operate covertly against al Qaeda, not just in Afghanistan, but "anywhere in the world."[149]

It is possible that anything Blee may have done in Alec Station to prepare the way for 9/11 was only one part of a larger interagency picture, in which an equivalent role was played by SOCOM's shutting down of the Able Danger project. This might help explain a handwritten notation around 10 PM on 9/11 by Stephen Cambone, then a Deputy Secretary under Rumsfeld in the Pentagon, after a phone call with George Tenet:

AA 77 – 3 indiv[iduals] have been followed since Millennium & Cole

1 guy is assoc[iate] of Cole bomber

2 entered US in early July

(2 of 3 pulled aside & interrogated?)[150]

The "guy" here is probably Al-Mihdhar, and the "Cole bomber" probably Khallad [or Tawfiq] bin Attash, a major al Qaeda figure connected not just to the Cole bombing but also to the 1998 embassy attacks. One wants to know why Tenet was sharing with a hawk in the Pentagon information that has apparently never been shared by anyone outside the CIA since. And is it a coincidence that Cambone, like Blee, oversaw a program – in this case staffed by SOCOM special operations personnel – using torture to interrogate detainees in Afghanistan?[151]

Just as Blee was reportedly a special prot g of George Tenet at CIA, so Cambone was notorious for his fierce loyalty to first Dick Cheney and later Donald Rumsfeld in the Pentagon. It is not known whether he was associated with the Continuity of Government (COG) planning project where Rumsfeld and Cheney, among others, prepared for the warrantless surveillance and detention measures that were (as I have argued elsewhere) implemented beginning on the morning of 9/11.[152] Nor is it known if he was associated in any way with Cheney's Counterterrorism Task Force in the Spring of 2001, which has been alleged to have been a source for the war games, including rogue plane attacks, which added to the disarray of the US response, on 9/11, to the four hijacked planes.

I want to conclude with a little historical perspective on the dysfunction we have been looking at. In a sense, 9/11 was unprecedented – the greatest mass murder ever committed in one day on U.S. soil. In another sense it represented a kind of event with which we have become only too familiar since the Kennedy assassination. I have called these events deep events – events with a predictable accompanying pattern of official cover-ups backed up by amazing media malfunction and dishonest best-selling books. Some of these deep events, like the Kennedy assassination and 9/11, should be considered structural deep events, because of their permanent impact on history.

It is striking that these two structural events – the JFK assassination and 9/11 – should both have been swiftly followed by America's engagement in ill-considered wars. The reverse is also true: all of America's significant wars since Korea – Vietnam, Afghanistan (twice, once covertly and now overtly), and Iraq – have all been preceded by structural deep events.

In two recent books I have been reluctantly compelled, against my own initial incredulity, to list more than a dozen significant parallels between the Kennedy assassination and 9/11. Thanks to

9/11 AS A DEEP EVENT: HOW CIA PERSONNEL HELPED ALLOW IT TO HAPPEN

Kevin Fenton's brilliant research, I can list a further analogy. The CIA files on Lee Harvey Oswald, more or less dormant for two years, suddenly became hyperactive in the six weeks before the Kennedy assassination. Fenton has demonstrated a similar burst of activity in FBI files on the two Saudis in the weeks before 9/11 – a burst initiated by Tom Wilshire, at a time suspiciously close when the hijackers settled on a final date for their attack.

America, I argue in my latest book, has become dominated by a war machine in Washington, a war machine that has been building incrementally since Eisenhower warned us about it in 1961. We should see the actions of Wilshire and Blee in the context of this war machine, and the secret consensus in 2001 – just as earlier in 1964 – that had already become settled on the need for further war.

CHAPTER SIX

Evidence of Insider Trading before September 11th Re-examined

BY PAUL ZAREMBKA

THIS CHAPTER ADDRESSES EVIDENCE OF INSIDER TRADING before September 11th, which is sometimes referred to by the broader phrase, informed trading. Insider trading refers to using private knowledge of an anticipated event in order to profit financially by engaging in financial market transactions. In the first weeks after September 11, 2001, a number of financial publications called attention to substantial insider trading in put options occurring before the attacks. Some of these early examples were surveyed by the present author,[153] which also commented on certain exaggerations, for example, an incorrect doubling of the put-option volumes. Quickly, scholarly commentary died out.

One financial transaction that can allow an individual to bet that the price of a stock will fall, and profit from it, is the purchase of a put option. Purchasing a put option entitles the owner to sell a stock at a contractually stated price, called the "strike price," at any time until the contract expires. If the market price of the stock drops below the strike price, the owner of the put option can buy the stock (if not already owned) and simultaneously sell the same stock at that strike price, making a profit if the cost of the option itself does not exceed the net revenue.

This chapter deals with *evidence* of insider trading only. It does not deal with speculation, nor does it deal with certain open questions about financial issues surrounding September 11th that otherwise deserve investigations, such as the following:

Large increases in the M1 money supply in the United States have been reported for July and August 2001 and explanations have been sought.

- Huge financial transactions have been reported to have taken place at computers at the World Trade Center minutes before the attacks.
- Selling short (borrowing a stock and selling it, then returning it later through purchasing).
- Activity in markets outside the United States.
- Disappearances of gold and securities from the World Trade Center.
- The specific financial firms directly hit by planes, and the financial investigations sabotaged by the WTC or Pentagon attacks.
- Insurance payoffs, particularly to the owner of destroyed buildings, particularly to Larry Silverstein.

EVIDENCE OF INSIDER TRADING BEFORE SEPTEMBER 11TH RE-EXAMINED

This is not a complete list of issues deserving investigation. However, some of the above seem to have only one testimonial behind them. This paper will instead focus on the issue of insider trading. This issue was addressed, however imperfectly, by the 9/11 Commission. The 9/11 Commission's treatment of insider trading will be examined first, followed by the evidence that has emerged since.

The 9/11 Commission and Insider Trading

In 2004, the *9/11 Commission Report* stated in a footnote that the government's investigations had produced no evidence of insider trading before the attacks.[154] Yet, it offered little of its evidence to the public. When a FOIA request was filed with the Securities and Exchange Commission, which was the government entity primarily responsible for investigating insider trading prior to 9/11, asking for the documentary evidence behind that Commission footnote, the SEC replied on December 23, 2009 that "the potentially responsive records have been destroyed."[155] Such a response is curious, given that certain documents discussed below were made public on January 14, 2009. These documents would have provided at least a partial response to the FOIA request.

On January 14, 2009, two memos from the SEC's investigation were made public.[156] The simpler one, prepared on May 11, 2004 for the 9/11 Commission, stated that the volume of put-option trades for United on September 6, 2001 (for a $30 strike price with expiration on October 20, 2001) had been erroneously reported in the SEC data: the correct value should have been 1500 – i.e., for 150,000 shares – not 2000. The memo explained that the SEC had missed the actual cancellation of an intended 500 put sale (included, but not a purchase). The Option Clearing House had the correct number.[157] Still, judging by the reported change in the next day in open interest, a 500 purchase did indeed occur on September 7. Open interest is the amount of the put contract remaining unexercised. In other words, a volume of 2000 occurred over two days, not one day (1500, then 500). This would not seem to affect Poteshman's work, discussed below, since he used the *change in open interest* for his measure rather than volume data, but it does raise a general concern about the SEC data. A volume level of 2000 for the first day does appear both in Zarembka (p. 66) and in Chesney, et al. (2010, p. 35, Table 2) and is implicitly retained in the Commission's own report despite that 2004 memo it had received (Zarembka, p. 68).

The second SEC memo that was released was prepared on September 17-18, 2003. It stated that, on September 9, 2001, the *Options Hotline* newsletter and its editor Steve Sarnoff faxed to its approximately 2,000 subscribers a recommendation to buy put options on American Airlines stock.[158] The memo further stated that the SEC interviewed 28 people who purchased these options and 26 had said that they had done so because of the newsletter. This memo reported 27 additional subscribers, not interviewed, as additional purchasers of that put option.

The same memo went on to report that an unnamed large institutional investor in hedge funds had purchased the 2000 United Airlines put-options – i.e., for 200,000 shares – but this was explained away by the fact that the same investor had also *purchased* 115,000 shares of American stock on September 10. This information does appear in the Commission's report at page 499, footnote 130.

EVIDENCE OF INSIDER TRADING
BEFORE SEPTEMBER 11TH RE-EXAMINED

A third memo for the 9/11 Commission, this one dated April 24, 2004, reported an interview with Ken Breen, Deputy Chief, Business and Securities Fraud Section, Department of Justice. It reports that Breen "was not sure about potential trading in index futures (because the volume is so great that analysis proved impossible)."[159] In other words, the exhaustive governmental investigation was not so exhaustive after all, by its own admission.

Discerning Evidence of Insider Trading before September 11th

Having first considered the government's investigation into insider trading associated with 9/11, this paper will next describe three econometric studies undertaken by academic econometricians. The first two have been peer-reviewed and published in well-established journals; the third has been a lengthy work in progress and is planned for submission shortly.

Each of the papers cited here has reference to data as quantiles. Quantiles are defined by the accumulation of the probabilities of occurrences of a random variable. A quantile at 50% means that one half of the occurrences of random variable had already occurred over the frequency distribution and one half have yet to occur. A quantile at 95% means that 19 out of 20 occurrences of the random variable had already occurred with 1 in 20 yet to occur; a quantile at 99% means 99 out of 100 had already taken place. Thus, an event at a quantile of 95% would be rare, and at 99% would be quite rare.

THE 9/11 TORONTO REPORT

Analysis: The Econometric Evidence in Poteshman

The first study is a scholarly article by Poteshman (2006) in the *Journal of Business*.[160] Using econometric modeling, Poteshman claimed high probability of insider trading for American Airlines and United Airlines put-option purchasing shortly before September 11th. Were they random, the American purchases had only a 1% probability of occurrence. The United Airlines put-option purchasing was less improbable, but on September 6 had only a 4% probability of occurrence. Poteshman obtained both measures by comparing of the airline values reported on p. 1720, Table 4, to the benchmark values reported on p. 1713, Table 1 in his article.

Since the government had provided so little evidence of its position, some sharp criticism and reference to Poteshman's results ensued.[161]

The article by Poteshman in the *Journal of Business* well describes the problem at hand, and is applicable to all three works. Hinting at the end about a useful two-pronged approach, Poteshman writes that, in general, option market activity:

> is motivated by a number of factors such as uninformed speculation (i.e., noise trading), hedging, trading on public information, and trading on private information. Consequently, when a statistic obtains a value that is extreme relative to its historical distribution, one can infer that there was an unusual amount of activity related to one or more of the option trading motivations. Although the statistics do not distinguish between trading motivations, if an extreme value is observed just before an important piece of news

EVIDENCE OF INSIDER TRADING
BEFORE SEPTEMBER 11TH RE-EXAMINED

becomes public, then it is reasonable to infer that there was option market trading based on private information rather than a shock to the trading from one of the other motivations. Indeed, the fact that the statistic has obtained an extreme value indicates that a shock to trading from another motivation would have to be unusually large to account for the observed option market trading. Of course, it is possible that the typical option trading from the other motivations varies systematically with changes in the state of the option or underlying security market. This is the reason that conditional as well as unconditional distributions for the statistics will be computed in the next section.[162]

Poteshman's work examines several measures for the probabilities of insider trading occurring, while addressing market options for American Airlines, United Airlines, the index for airline stocks, and the S&P 500. The easiest one of three to understand and the one he seems most comfortable exploring is discussed here, which is the evidence regarding volumes of put-option contracts. The volume of a put-option contract is measured by the change in a contract's open interest from one day to the next day (purchases less sales less exercises of options) compared to the average of such change measured by a 126 trading day period, going backwards in time from 22 trading days before the date in question. This is also normalized for the standard deviations of those 126 trading days. The statistical results for the four trading days before September 11th are reported in Table 6-1.

TABLE 6-1: PUT-OPTION MARKET VOLUME STATISTICS[163]
BEFORE SEPTEMBER 11TH

Volume Statistics	Sept. 5	Sept. 6	Sept. 7	Sept. 10
AMR	-.02	.08	.65	3.83
UAL	-.12	1.45	1.23	.15
Airline Index	-.13	.63	.66	.85
S&P 500	-.07	.25	.54	.85

Poteshman compares these AMR and UAL statistics to his benchmark data for the 1,000 largest market capitalization firms from January 2, 1990 through September 4, 2001. Compared to the historical record of the large companies, the AMR datum for September 10th in the table has only a 1% probability of occurrence and the UAL datum of September 6 has a 4% probability of occurrence. The airline index datum for September 6th has a 6% probability of occurrence and the S&P datum for September 7th, a 5% probability.

Poteshman also considers a four-trading day interval in addition to the daily values reported in Table 1. For those who consider this measure to be more appropriate, probabilities are somewhat less unlikely. In any case, the above results are not conditional upon any underlying factors. Poteshman also introduces four conditioning factors, "total option volume, the return on the underlying asset, the abnormal trading volume of the underlying asset, and the return on the overall stock market."[164] He under-

EVIDENCE OF INSIDER TRADING
BEFORE SEPTEMBER 11TH RE-EXAMINED

takes quantile regressions for these four factors and obtains very similar results.

Analysis: The Econometric Evidence in Wong, et al.

The article by Wong et al. (Wong) has the most detailed discussion of option trading executions.[165] It then undertakes a complex statistical investigation of S&P 500 option trading before September 11th, centering first on whether they were purchased in-the-money (above the market, and thus costing a higher price), at-the-money (at the market level), or out-of-the-money (below the market). They also consider the type of strategy used, including the use of call options. Calls are the contractual right to purchase stocks for a determined "strike price" before an expiration date. They are a less obvious strategy for anticipating a decline in an asset price.

Wong first contrast the 2001 period for contracts expiring on September 22, 2001 with the same September expiration in 2000. Both time periods were in declining market environments. For the period between January 1 and June 30, 2000, the S&P 500 declined 15 points, while for the period January 1 to June 30, 2001, the S&P 500 declined 96 points. They consider these as "control periods" (pp. 15-16). They find that "the trading volume for the SPX index put options during the control periods is not significantly different between 2001 and 2000 ... the years 2000 and 2001 being similar in regard to option activity in a time period before intense trading began in September index put options" (p. 37).

Continuing the comparison of 2001 to 2000, they examine a short sub-period after the S&P 500 closed at 1134 on August 31 to September 10, 2001 when it closed at 1093, a decline of 39 points in five trading days. A year earlier, the S&P 500 had closed at 1518 on August 31, 2000, while on September 8 (September 10 was a Sunday) it had closed at 1495, a decline of 23 points, also in five trading days. Wong find that "the mean and the standard deviation of the trading volumes for September 2001 contracts were more than double those for September 2000 contracts during sub-period [September 1 to September 10] for both call and put, but not so much during the other sub-periods" (p. 20). They also find many more extreme volumes in the 2001 period.

Wong then investigate the various types of puts and calls available in the market, and also consider alternative strategies. Studying statistical results, they conclude that there was:

> a significant abnormal increase in the trading volume in the option market just before 9-11 attacks in contrast with the absence of abnormal trading volume far before the attacks. This only constitutes circumstantial evidence that there were insiders who tried to profit from the options market in anticipation of the 9-11 attacks. More conclusive evidence is needed to prove definitively that insiders were indeed active in the market. Although we have discredited the possibility of abnormal volume due to declining market, such investigative work would still be a very involved exercise in view of the multitude of other confounding factors e.g. coincidence, confusing trading strategies intentionally employed by the insiders, noises from the activities of non-insiders.[166]

Wong do not claim definitive results, but rather significant statistical evidence of insider trading. Their procedure attempts to discount the importance of a declining overall market, which some have attempted to use as a basis for a counter-argument

EVIDENCE OF INSIDER TRADING
BEFORE SEPTEMBER 11TH RE-EXAMINED

against the evidence of insider trading. A counter-argument could begin by observing that August was an up-market in 2000 and down-market in 2001. However, there are no empirical studies published that have compared options market behaviors in up markets as compared to down market, so no presumptions about the importance of market direction in options activity level should be made without evidence.

Wong do not attempt to compare their results with Poteshman's regarding the S&P 500. Poteshman noted the fact that "the option volume on SPX options was more than 100 times greater than that on either AMR or UAL options. Consequently, it would be much more difficult to detect an option market bet."[167] Wong do observe that "any 9-11 insider would not trade directly the airline options in large volume to avoid drawing attention after the 9-11 attacks."

Analysis: The Econometric Evidence in Chesney, et al.

Chesney, et al., (Chesney) offer the most detailed evidence that points to insider trading in advance of 9/11.[168] To understand what they are offering, first consider American Airlines stock (AMR) for the authors' time period of January 1996 to April 2006. It is representative of their general methodology and they provide details for this particular example, which has been of so much concern within the 9/11 movement. Technical details are placed in footnotes following the Table 2 presentation of their results below.

Chesney start with 137,000 AMR put-option contracts. These represent, on average, about 54 possibilities per trading day over the ten-plus years of data they analyze (about 250 trading days per year). They first identify for each day that put-option contract across strike prices and expiration dates with largest increment in open interest.[169] These 2560 data points are highly unusual. After accounting for intraday speculation[170], they record the prior two years of data for each time *t*, beginning in January 1998 and ending in April 2006. This leads to a measure q_t, that denotes, for date *t*, the frequency such a value occurred based upon the prior historical record. They are referred to as probabilities. For the AMR option on September 10, as one example, q_t is reported as 1.2%. This reflects 6 occurrences in the two years of 500 data points on and before that day. Generally for their study, q_t must refer to data that had occurred no more than 5% of the time, i.e., no more than 25 times for the prior two years.[171]

A second, additional criterion attempts to account for hedging transactions – buying a put option to guard against a fall in an existing stock position, or buying stock to guard against a fall in a put-option's value as the stock rises. They offer a rather complicated procedure, not elaborated here. The two criteria, as they report, reduce the considered spikes for AMR put options down to 141 instances, which is still a fairly considerable number.

Instead of stopping here, as a third criterion, Chesney focus upon the most profitable, using *ex post* information on the behavior of the stock price. Let r_t be the option's return at time t. The maximum return over the available contracts after time t is then represented by r_t^{max}. AMR on September 10th had a put-option contract price of $2.15 for a $30 strike price and October 20, 2001 expiry. The maximum gain for that contract therefore turned out to be one exercised on September 17 as the stock price fell to an $18 close[172] and the option price rose to $12, about a $10 gain per

EVIDENCE OF INSIDER TRADING
BEFORE SEPTEMBER 11TH RE-EXAMINED

contract on $2.15 invested, or 453%. That particular r_t^{max} is reported in Chesney with a typo of 458%.

Now, this third criterion is formulated as a pair of conditions that are presented here in a footnote.[173] The introduction of this third criterion leads to *only 5 incidents* for AMR: May 10 and May 11, 2000, August 31 and September 10, 2001, and August 24, 2005, rather than 141 without the third criterion.

For the entire set of fourteen companies studied, only 37 incidents are identified: 13 spikes identifiable before September 11th as reported in Table 2, 14 associated with earnings announcements (10 beforehand, 2 on same day, 2 after), 6 associated with mergers and acquisitions (4 beforehand, 2 same day), and 4 not identified. In other words, spikes are being shown to *relate to real events, most frequently anticipating them.*

The gains from exercising put options, reported below in Table 6-2 for the 13 identified cases of informed trading before September 11th, do not depend upon the econometric procedure, but rather are factually based, close to the maximum possible. As can be seen, the American purchases on September 10th are by no means the most profitable. The Merrill Lynch put-option purchase generated almost four times the subsequent gains as that for American. The extensive put purchases for Boeing were even more profitable.

These trades could have been background for Sarnoff's September 9th recommendation to his subscribers regarding American. That is, an option advisor's knowledge of prior airline put-option purchases by others may have factored into his or her own recommendations. If the advisor turns out to be wrong, there is a good excuse available: "I was not alone." In other words, the evidence on American Airlines that Poteshman and Chesney, et al. present may not be direct evidence of insider trading at all, but instead may have been informed by previous trading activity in other related stocks. If correct, those other put options trades require particularly careful investigations. Indeed, if a person actually had prior information about what was to happen on September 11th, why would he or she engage in put-option purchasing for the most obvious of choices, American and United, and subject himself or herself to easy detection?

TABLE 6-2: EVIDENCE OF INFORMED PUT-OPTION PURCHASES[174]

Put Option	2001 Date	Change in open interest	Gain from exercising the put options	Proxy for probability as an informed trade
Boeing	29 Aug.	2828	$1,972,534	0.998
Boeing	5 Sept.	1499	1,805,929	0.998
Boeing	6 Sept.	7105	2,704,701	0.998
Merrill Lynch	10 Sept.	5615	4,407,171	0.998
J.P. Morgan	30 Aug.	3145	1,318,638	0.998
J.P. Morgan	6 Sept.	4778	1,415,825	0.998
Citigroup	30 Aug.	4373	2,045,940	0.998
United	6 Sept.	1494	1,980,387	0.998
American	31 Aug.	473	662,200	0.984
American	10 Sept.	1312	1,179,171	0.998

EVIDENCE OF INSIDER TRADING
BEFORE SEPTEMBER 11TH RE-EXAMINED

Bank of America	7 Sept.	3380	$1,774,525	0.994
Delta	29 Aug.	202	328,200	0.998
KLM	5 Sept.	100	53,976	0.998

What the prior paragraph is suggesting is that spikes in put-option purchases are not independent events, but, in actuality, can be interrelated. Therefore, one cannot conclude on the basis of this evidence that the joint probability of their occurrences is "astronomically low." The joint probability would still be very low, but not "astronomically low." In this case, Boeing put-option purchasing moves to the center of attention, not just for the magnitude of profits reported in Table 2, but as possible background leading options specialists to notice the unusual activity and purchase put-options on American Airlines a few days later.

As to the United put-option purchasing, the SEC reports that it was related to a large stock purchase of American Airlines stock by the same investor. Poteshman did not find the option purchase to be highly improbable on a random basis. Chesney, et al.'s procedure for delimiting hedging transactions would not capture such an example of purchasing American Airlines stock while also purchasing put-options on United.

In sum, it is reasonable to accept the SEC's reporting about American and United Airlines and not consider them to represent direct evidence of insider trading. However, these are the only pieces of evidence on the issue of insider trading put forward publicly from SEC investigations. Specifically, Boeing as well as Merrill Lynch, J.P. Morgan, Citigroup, and Bank of America deserve careful attention as a result of Chesney, et al.'s work. Nevertheless, the government has demonstrated that it can withhold evidence for years and later release it to the public. Jumping too quickly to conclusions and making accusations can backfire.

The total gains without United and American Airlines reported in Table 2, and then also including other individual stocks not yet analyzed by Chesney, should fall short of $30 million in total. This level is reported in order to keep in mind the *maximum* potential of insider put-option trading benefits before September 11th. This is not necessarily the total number of dollars made by the traders in these options. Insider trading could have occurred in individual stocks as Chesney, et al., find, and also served as unsuspecting background to investors and their advisors for United and American Airlines put-option purchases.

Boeing, Merrill Lynch, J.P. Morgan, Citigroup, and Bank of America

For Boeing, Merrill Lynch, J.P. Morgan, Citigroup, and Bank of America, there does not appear to be any public news that would motivate large put-option purchases for them before the dates found in Chesney, et al.'s research. Note that the cited downgrade of Boeing[175] came after the dates the option purchases were made.

In any case, research work by Chesney, et al., fails to suggest spikes in put-option trading occurring merely due to rating changes by analysts of corporations. Indeed, 33 of theirs are associated with September 11th, or earnings announcements, or mergers and acquisitions; only 4 remain unidentified.

EVIDENCE OF INSIDER TRADING
BEFORE SEPTEMBER 11TH RE-EXAMINED

The SEC Evidence regarding One Named Financial Advisor

Returning to the insider trading evidence addressed by the 9/11 Commission, the tip that Steve Sarnoff, editor of *Options Hotline*, offered subscribers on September 9 for placing put options on American Airlines is reported by Mike Williams.[176] Nothing appears unusual with the recommendation itself. If the SEC memo is believed, somewhat more than 50 of 2000 subscribers seem to have acted upon the recommendation – i.e., about two and one-half percent. Nothing appears unusual with this outcome. The 1312 change in open interest on September 10th represents an average of a bit less than 26 put-options purchases per subscriber who purchased, representing 2600 shares each. Yet, consider the implications of taking this at face value.

Joe Duarte, another financial advisor, lists ten newsletters dealing with option trading (*www.joe-duarte.com/free/directory/options-newsletters.asp*). *Options Hotline* does not happen to be one of them, perhaps suggesting that Sarnoff has no dominance. Search the web and get many more. Recommendations are being made by newsletters daily, weekly, monthly. If two to three percent of subscribers are following recommendations to buy put options on stocks, we should see many, many examples similar to what occurred for American on September 10, 2001. Therefore, what happened that day for American would be a rather common event, not a very unlikely one, and that volume on American put options would *not* have shown up as unlikely, as a statistical matter.

Absent informed trading, newsletters should be nothing more than *instruments*, rather than causes, of these market behaviors being analyzed.

It is not only American Airlines, but, as discussed in detail below, *nine* other put options showing statistically anomalous spikes before September 11th. Chesney find *only 37 examples* in a decade of some 1.5 million pieces of put-option data on fourteen companies, *13 of such examples were related to September 11th*. These spikes should have been innocent of *ex post* shock events because spikes are always expected in random statistical outcomes. Instead, most are centered on prior to shock events.

Two Caveats

Let me put one consideration to rest. Some critics of the 9/11 truth movement, such as Kay [177], claim that the entire movement is filled with people who go down a rabbit hole, never willing to leave it. In this case, the suggested claim could be that Sarnoff himself should be added to a conspiracy about 9/11, added in January 2009, as soon as the government released its evidence as to *who made what recommendation and with what effect* regarding American on September 10. Such an approach would address the contradiction we have identified, but it would be at the expense of having no evidence for such an assertion.

We wish to stay with *evidence*, evidence from the econometricians, the government, and anywhere else obtainable. In other words, we wish to fully examine the contradiction.

Regarding evidence, we have to be careful. For Boeing, Mike Williams, seeking to expose myths among skeptics of the official story of September 11th, cites a Dutch article of September 11, 2006 placed on the site physics911.net.[178] This article made only a tangential mention of Boeing, thus representing no more than the proverbial "straw man" – a data source is not even provided.

EVIDENCE OF INSIDER TRADING
BEFORE SEPTEMBER 11TH RE-EXAMINED

Williams then provides a news report referring to one analyst's public downgrading of Boeing on September 7th, apparently being unaware that put-options purchases cited by Poteshman were on United and occurred on September 6th. Chesney also reported on this, as discussed previously.[179]

A Contradiction and Its Deepening

Through the above, we have arrived at a contradiction: an econometric result of high probability of insider trading in American Airlines stock and somewhat less for United contradicts against the US government's September 2003 memo (released in 2009). This contradiction might be resolved by simply asserting that Poteshman himself never claimed certainty and that an event of low probability had been all that had occurred. However, two other econometric studies have been added to the scientific literature since the Poteshman paper.

The first study by Wong examined put options on the S&P 500 index and found additional econometric evidence of insider trading before September 11th. Recall, this is the index that Ken Breen of the U.S. Department of Justice had, in April 2004, alleged was impossible to analyze because the volume was so great. Furthermore, the result is significant because some have speculated that option trading was heightened in the period before September 11th because of a falling market. As explained in detail above, Wong obtained their results even after trying to account for a falling market.

The second study by Chesney examined about 1.5 million put-option trades for 14 companies: 5 airline companies including American and United, 5 bank stocks, and 4 others, for the period of January 1996 to April 2006. They report, with high probability, informed trading before September 11th in each of the put options for Boeing, Merrill Lynch, J.P. Morgan, Citigroup, United, American, Bank of America, Delta, and KLM (ordered here from the highest calculated gains downward).

In sum, ten financial instruments, including the S&P 500 put option, each exhibited, with high statistical probability, evidence of insider trading before September 11th, sometimes more than once. American and United Airlines are identified by separate methodologies, seven additional companies are identified by Chesney, and the S&P 500 is identified by Wong. The joint probability of all of these being nothing more than random outliers seems astronomically low.

The government, however, deepened its position. In that September 17-18, 2003 memo, the SEC refers to investigations of "103 companies and 38 index products and broad-based funds." It finds no evidence of any insider trading. It dismissed dramatic comments shortly after September 11th, even by a person as well positioned as the German Central Bank President Ernest Welteke. The report definitively concludes with the SEC's lead investigator Joseph J. Cella, III, Chief of Market Surveillance, Division of Enforcement, SEC, saying that "he has no questions about any trade and is confident there was no illicit trading pre 9/11 in the United States."

The sharp contradiction between the scientific results and the government's position is too great to ignore. Can it be resolved? On the one hand, are three distinct econometric methodologies implemented with option trading data each erroneous in some manner? Is the competence of the econometricians, including authors of two articles that were screened through peer review evaluations, in serious doubt? On the other hand, if the SEC is accurately reporting the motivating factors about American and United put-option purchases, could the SEC be wrong about many or all of the other financial instruments, for which no evidence has been made public? Having repeatedly said that the attacks were a complete surprise, has the government been influenced to avoid acknowledging any insider trading before September 11th? Worse, is it aware of insider trading and is it lying?

Concluding Recommendations

- United and American options activity should not be recognized as direct evidence of insider trading. Nevertheless, by themselves, they convey little of the larger question.

- Ken Breen, Department of Justice, reported to the Commission in an interview released in 2009 that, for put-options on indexes, "the volume is so great that analysis proved impossible". Therefore, Wong's result regarding the S&P 500 is not contested in the background reports to the 9/11 Commission, despite what the Commission asserted. Wong's results demand further investigation.

- To the best of the present author's knowledge, none of the three econometric methodologies and results has been contested in the professional literature. Typically, controversial results generate opposition. The three separate methodologies presented here should be considered convincing in that that they are solid scientific works. Therefore, the econometric research results presented above must be considered meritorious until proven otherwise.

- Demand that the SEC publicly report the details of its findings on Boeing, Merrill Lynch, J.P. Morgan, Citigroup, Bank of America, Delta, and S&P 500 index put-option trading before September 11th. This reporting should be at least as detailed as that already released for American and United Airlines.
- Add to that demand of the SEC any additional corporations exhibiting evidence of insider trading before September 11th, e.g., in the expanded material in Chesney, et al.

In addition:

- Promote an independent investigation into the events of September 11th, inclusive of subpoena powers, that includes investigations of put-option purchasing.
- Incorporate into that independent investigation the financial issues cited in the introduction, but not examined in detail in this paper, most of them having billions of dollars at stake.

CHAPTER SEVEN

Anomalies in the Official Accounts of American 77 and United 93

BY DAVID RAY GIFFIN

THIS CHAPTER COVERS THE ANOMALIES IN THE OFFICIAL accounts of American Flight 77 and United Flight 93. These "anomalies" are features in the official accounts of these flights that *would not be expected on the assumption that these accounts are true.*

Part I: American Flight 77

I. Is the 9/11 Commission's New Story about American 77 Believable?

One of the things that would not be expected, on the assumption that the official account of American Flight 77 is true, is that three years after 9/11, the original official story about this flight would be replaced with a radically different story. According to the original story, told in a press release of September 18, 2001 called "NORAD's

Response Times," NORAD was notified about American 77 at 9:24 AM, roughly 14 minutes before the Pentagon was hit.[180]

This report raised a difficult question for the military. Why were the F-16s from Langley Air Force Base, about 130 miles away, not able to get to the Pentagon in time to prevent the attack? This question leaves aside the perhaps more important question of why the Pentagon, surely the most well-protected building on the planet, had to rely on fighters from an Air Force base 130 miles away, when there were always fighters at nearby Andrews Air Force Base on alert to protect Washington D.C. and the Pentagon. Even if we accept the [absurd] idea that the Pentagon needed to rely on fighters from Langley, those fighters could have easily reached the Pentagon in 14 minutes. In their 2006 book, the co-chairs of the 9/11 Commission, Thomas Kean and Lee Hamilton, in fact wrote: "[I]f the military had had the amount of time they said they had … , it was hard to figure how they had failed to shoot down [the plane]."[181]

The 9/11 Commission would avoid this conclusion by providing a new story, according to which the FAA had not told the military about American 77 at 9:24. In fact, the 9/11 Commission claimed, the FAA never did notify the military, until after the Pentagon was struck.

There was, however, an FAA memo that went in the opposite direction: Whereas the Commission claimed that the 9:24 notification time was too early, this memo stated that the FAA had notified the military much earlier than 9:24. This memo, written on May 22, 2003, was created in response to a request that day by the 9/11 Commission, during a public hearing, to clarify the

ANOMALIES IN THE OFFICIAL ACCOUNTS OF AMERICAN 77 AND UNITED 73

FAA's notification of the military about the flights, especially American 77. This memo said:

> Within minutes after the first aircraft hit the World Trade Center, the FAA immediately established several phone bridges that included ... DOD [the Department of Defense] .... The U.S. Air Force liaison to the FAA ... established contact with NORAD on a separate line. The FAA shared real-time information ... including information about ... all the flights of interest, including Flight 77 ... NORAD logs indicate that the FAA made formal notification about American Flight 77 at 9:24 a.m., but information about the flight was conveyed continuously during the phone bridges before the formal notification.[182]

According to this memo, therefore, the military had been told about Flight 77 long before 9:24.[183]

During the 9/11 hearing the next day, Commissioner Richard Ben-Veniste read this memo into the record and said: "So now we have in question whether there was an informal real-time communication of the situation, including Flight 77's situation, to personnel at NORAD."[184] A military general, Craig McKinley confirmed this point, saying that the FAA was indeed in contact with the military.

Given the way this conversation was going, the 9/11 Commission would be expected to say that the FAA told the military about Flight 77's troubles even before 9:24, so the military definitely should have been able to intercept the flight and prevent any attack on the Pentagon. But this is not how it went.

Rather than saying that the FAA had told the military about this flight before 9:24, the Commission declared: "NEADS

[NORAD's Northeast Air Defense Sector] never received notice that American 77 was hijacked."[185] By making this assertion, the 9/11 Commission had to state that military officers had given false testimony. The Commission said:

> In public testimony before this Commission in May 2003, ... NORAD officials stated that at 9:24, NEADS received notification of the hijacking of American 77. This statement was incorrect.[186]

The 9/11 Commission complained that NORAD's original story, which had been repeated by generals during the 9/11 Commission Hearings of 2003, had

> made it appear that the military was notified in time to respond, raising questions about the adequacy of the response. Those accounts ... overstated the FAA's ability to provide the military with timely and useful information that morning... Thus the military did not have 14 minutes to respond to American 77, as testimony to the Commission in May 2003 suggested.[187]

This new official story by the 9/11 Commission got the military off the hook for not preventing the attack on the Pentagon. But this new story is not believable for two reasons. The first reason is that the 9/11 Commission accuses the military leaders of telling an irrational lie. If the Commission's new story, according to which the military was completely guiltless, were the truth, why would military leaders have invented the original story, which implied that the military was guilty – guilty of standing down or at least incompetence? This would have been a completely irrational lie. The second reason why the Commission's new story is

ANOMALIES IN THE OFFICIAL ACCOUNTS OF AMERICAN 77 AND UNITED 73

unbelievable is that it contradicts many previously established facts. Below are four examples.

A. **The FAA Memo:** The earlier-quoted FAA Memo of May 22, 2003, stated that the 9:24 notification time was wrong by being too late, not too early. The Commission dealt with this point by simply ignoring it – even though 9/11 Commissioner Richard Ben-Veniste had read this memo into the Commission's records.[188]

B. **Wald's NYT Story:** Four days after 9/11, Matthew Wald of the *New York Times* published a story entitled "Pentagon Tracked Deadly Jet but Found No Way to Stop It." This story said: "During the hour or so that American Airlines Flight 77 was under the control of hijackers, up to the moment it struck the west side of the Pentagon, military officials in a command center on the east side of the building were urgently talking to law enforcement and air traffic control officials about what to do. But … the fighter planes that scrambled into protective orbits around Washington did not arrive until 15 minutes after Flight 77 hit the Pentagon."[189] The 9/11 Commission dealt with this story by simply ignoring it.

C. **Indianapolis Ignorance:** The FAA's air traffic control center in Indianapolis was handling the flight when it started showing signs of being in trouble. The 9/11 Commission claims that the Indianapolis Center did not notify the military even when, at 8:56, it lost this flight's transponder signal, its radar track, and its radio. Why? Because the Indianapolis controller concluded, the 9/11 Commission claimed, that "American 77 had experienced serious electrical or mechanical failure," after which it had crashed.[190] Why would the controller have made this conclusion at this time, when it was known that two planes had already been hijacked, one of which had crashed into the World Trade Center? Because, the Commission claimed, no one at Indianapolis Center "had any knowledge of the situation in New York" until 9:20. But this claim strains credulity. Television networks had started broadcasting images of the World Trade Center at 8:48. These images included, at 9:03, the crash of the second airliner into the South Tower. Millions of people knew about these events. How can we believe that no one at Indianapolis Center "had any knowledge of the situation in New York" until 9:20? General Mike Canavan, director of civil aviation security, told the 9/11 Commission: "[A]s soon as you know you had a hijacked aircraft, you notify everyone.... [The notification] gets broadcast out to all the regions."[191]

D. **Military Liaisons:** The Commission's account, according to which the military did not know about Flight 77, is contradicted by the presence of military liaisons at the FAA's headquarters in Washington and its Command Center in Herndon, Virginia. The Commission claimed that, although the fact that Flight 77 was lost was known at Herndon by 9:20 and at FAA headquarters by 9:25, this knowledge did not get passed to the military. However, Ben Sliney, the operations manager at the Command Center, said:

> [A]t the Command Center ... is the military cell, which was our liaison with the military services. They were present at all of the events that occurred on 9/11.... If you tell the military you've told the military. They have their own communication web.... [E]veryone who

needed to be notified about the events transpiring was notified, including the military.[192]

Conclusion

The 9/11 Commission's new story about Flight 77 is impossible to believe. This story rests entirely on the assumption that the "NORAD tapes," which the Pentagon gave to the 9/11 Commission in response to a subpoena, had not been doctored. But Philip Zelikow was a good friend of Steven Cambone, the undersecretary of defense for intelligence,[193] generally considered Rumsfeld's "right-hand man." There was also plenty of time for the tapes to be doctored, as they were not delivered until about a month after they had been subpoenaed.[194] The suggestion that the tapes had been doctored is speculative, of course, but so is any suggestion that they had *not* been doctored. It should not simply be presupposed that the tapes, as delivered to the 9/11 commission, provide "the authentic military history of 9/11."[195] The authenticity of the tapes must be evaluated in light of the total evidence.

II. Was the Pentagon Attacked by Al-Qaeda?

It has been widely thought that the 9/11 Truth Movement is hopelessly divided about how the Pentagon was damaged: Some believe that the Pentagon was struck by a Boeing 757, perhaps American Flight 77, while others believe that there was no 757. Some of those in the latter camp even suggest that those who believe that the Pentagon was struck by a 757, perhaps American 77, have endorsed the official theory about the Pentagon.

However, to focus on this contrast is to focus on a secondary issue. The primary issue is the following: who was responsible for the Pentagon attack? People who regard the Pentagon as struck by a 757 and perhaps even American 77 have endorsed the official theory only if they hold that the Pentagon was attacked by Flight 77 *under the control of al-Qaeda*. The crucial point in the official account is that the attack on the Pentagon was planned and carried out by al-Qaeda, not by our own military.

Given this perspective, there is consensus in the 9/11 Truth Movement regarding the central issue about the Pentagon attack, because all members of the 9/11 Truth Movement hold that *the Pentagon was not struck by American 77 under the control of al-Qaeda*.

This point can be illustrated with reference to a paper by Frank Legge and another paper by David Chandler and Jon Cole. Legge leans toward the 757 view, saying that "it cannot be conclusively proved that no 757 hit the Pentagon."[196] Chandler and Cole incline to the American 77 view, saying that "the physical evidence does not rule out the possibility that it was American Airlines Flight 77 that actually crashed into the Pentagon."[197] There are six points that demonstrate the consensus about the Pentagon within the 9/11 Truth Movement because they show that Legge and Chandler-Cole reject the official view of the Pentagon as fully as those who believe that the Pentagon was not struck by a Boeing 757.

1. The Pentagon Should Not Have Been Struck

The Pentagon was probably the best protected building in the world. Without some kind of stand-down order, it simply could not have been attacked, especially by amateur hijackers. Legge has articulated this point, saying: "[The Pentagon] should have been well defended.... There was ample time to send up fighters to intercept, as is the normal procedure."[198] Chandler and Cole asked, rhetorically: "How could the Pentagon, the hub of the US military, have been so poorly defended that it could be hit .... after

ANOMALIES IN THE OFFICIAL ACCOUNTS OF AMERICAN 77 AND UNITED 73

the buildings in New York City had already been hit and other hijacked planes were known to still be in the air?"[199]

2. Cheney's Confirmation of a Stand-Down Order

According to the *9/11 Commission Report*, Dick Cheney entered the bunker under the White House – technically the PEOC (the Presidential Emergency Operations Center) – "shortly before 10:00, perhaps at 9:58."[200] However, according to virtually all reports, including statements by Richard Clarke[201] and David Bohrer (Cheney's photographer),[202] Cheney had entered the PEOC closer to 9:15 AM. The most important of these reports came from Norman Mineta, who was the Secretary of Transportation. In testimony to the 9/11 Commission, Mineta said that he "arrived at the PEOC at about 9:20 AM," shortly after which he overheard an ongoing conversation involving Cheney, which occurred "[d]uring the time that the airplane was coming in to the Pentagon." Mineta said:

> "[T]here was a young man who would come in and say to the Vice President, 'The plane is 50 miles out.' 'The plane is 30 miles out.' And when it got down to 'the plane is 10 miles out,' the young man also said to the Vice President, 'Do the orders still stand?' And the Vice President turned and whipped his neck around and said, 'Of course the orders still stand. Have you heard anything to the contrary?'"

What were "the orders"? Mineta assumed, he said, that they were orders to have the aircraft shot down. But no aircraft approaching Washington was shot down. Mineta's interpretation also made the young man's question unintelligible. Given the fact that the airspace over the Pentagon is categorized as "forbidden," meaning that commercial aircraft are never permitted in it, plus the fact that two hijacked planes had already crashed into the Twin Towers, the expected orders, if an unidentified plane were approaching that airspace, would have been to shoot it down. Had Cheney given those orders, there would have been no reason for the young man to ask if the orders still stood. His question made sense only if the orders were to do something unexpected: *not* to shoot it down. The most natural interpretation of Mineta's story, accordingly, was that he had inadvertently reported that he had heard Cheney confirm stand-down orders.

This interpretation would also make sense of what the 9/11 Commission did in response to Mineta's story: Its Report did not mention Mineta's story, and by claiming that Cheney entered the PEOC "shortly before 10:00," the Commission claimed, implicitly, that there was no time for the exchange with the young man described by Mineta. This portion of Mineta's testimony was also removed from the Commission's video archive.[203]

Mineta's testimony, combined with the 9/11 Commission's reaction to it, provides strong evidence, convincing to at least most members of the Truth Movement, that Washington insiders, including Cheney, were behind the Pentagon attack. Chandler and Cole asked: "Why was Norman Mineta's testimony about Cheney's response to the approach of the aircraft discounted in the 9/11 Commission report?"[204] Legge, calling Mineta's testimony "crucial," wrote: "There is little doubt that Cheney had it in his hand to block this attack [on the Pentagon]."[205]

ANOMALIES IN THE OFFICIAL ACCOUNTS
OF AMERICAN 77 AND UNITED 73

3. Hani Hanjour's Incompetence

The official story is rendered especially dubious by its claim that the Pentagon was struck by a Boeing 757 flown by al-Qaeda's Hani Hanjour. As the title of a *New York Times* story revealed in 2002, Hanjour, who had been taking lessons in a single-engine plane, was known as "a trainee noted for incompetence," about whom an instructor said: "He could not fly at all."[206]

And yet on September 11, 2001, before Hanjour had been declared by authorities to have been the pilot of the plane that hit the Pentagon, a *Washington Post* story said: "[J]ust as the plane seemed to be on a suicide mission into the White House, the unidentified pilot executed a pivot so tight that it reminded observers of a fighter jet maneuver.... Aviation sources said the plane was flown with extraordinary skill."[207] A *Post* story the following year stated: "[A]viation experts concluded that the final maneuver of American Airlines Flight 77 ... was the work of 'a great talent.'"[208] This was clearly impossible: A man who could not safely fly a single-engine plane could not possibly have flown a giant airliner with "extraordinary skill," like "a great talent."

Legge agrees that Hanjour's "poor flying skills" rule out the possibility that he flew a 757 into the Pentagon.[209] Chandler and Cole ask, rhetorically: "How could an untrained pilot have performed the difficult maneuvers?"[210]

4. Wedge 1 Required an Extraordinary Maneuver

Moreover, the extraordinary maneuver would have been so difficult in a 757 that the official story could not be saved by simply choosing a less incompetent al-Qaeda trainee. Ralph Kolstad, who was a top US Navy pilot before becoming a commercial airline pilot, has said: "I have 6,000 hours of flight time in Boeing 757's and 767's and I could not have flown it the way the flight path was described."[211] If the maneuver could not have been executed in a 757 by one of America's top pilots, it could not have been executed by any of the alleged hijackers.

It might be thought that this point would rule out the 757 view, but Legge is able to affirm this view with "the possibility that the plane was hijacked by an on-board device, pre-programmed to take over the autopilot,"[212] and Chandler and Cole agree.[213]

5. Al-Qaeda Would Have Crashed into the Roof

If al-Qaeda masterminds had wanted only to strike the Pentagon, they would not have targeted Wedge 1, thereby requiring an amateur pilot to fly a trajectory that even an expert professional probably could not have executed. The masterminds would have had the pilot simply crash into the roof, thereby having a 29-acre target. Chandler and Cole say that the plane was not flown by al-Qaeda, because if it had been, it most likely would "have simply dived into the building."[214]

6. Al-Qaeda Would Not Have Targeted Wedge 1: Still More Reasons

The targeting of Wedge 1 provides still more reasons to conclude that al-Qaeda was not in charge. First, al-Qaeda operatives would have wanted to kill the secretary of defense and top military officers. But their offices were as far from Wedge 1 as possible. Second, Wedge 1 was the only part of the Pentagon that had been renovated, making it less vulnerable to attacks, so an attack on Wedge 1 caused less damage than would have an attack on any other section of the Pentagon. Third, the renovation was not quite

ANOMALIES IN THE OFFICIAL ACCOUNTS OF AMERICAN 77 AND UNITED 73

completed, so Wedge 1 was only sparsely occupied. Accordingly, whereas the attack on Wedge 1 killed 125 Pentagon employees, a strike on any other part of the Pentagon would have caused many more deaths.

Summary

Points 4 through 6 show that the al-Qaeda "mastermind" behind the attack on the Pentagon would have been the stupidest mastermind conceivable. A rational assessment of the evidence shows that the Pentagon attack was not engineered by al-Qaeda. Members of the 9/11 Truth Movement have differing beliefs about what damaged the Pentagon, but they can and do have consensus on the fact that the Pentagon was not struck by American 77 under the control of al-Qaeda.

III. A Final Question: Did Barbara Olson Make Calls from American 77?

One of the best-known features of the official story of 9/11 is that Barbara Olson – a commentator on CNN and the wife of US Solicitor General Theodore "Ted" Olson – made two calls to her husband from American 77 shortly before it struck the Pentagon. Ted Olson reported that the first call lasted "about one minute"[215] and the second one "two or three or four minutes."[216]

The success of Ted Olson's reports is shown by the fact that virtually everyone, it seems, "knew" that the hijackers had box-cutters, even though the reported Olson calls were the only "phone calls from the planes" in which box-cutters, called "cardboard cutters," were mentioned.

In the first five years after 9/11, there were many reasons given as to why these reported calls from Barbara Olson were improbable, perhaps impossible – whether from cell phones or seat-back phones. Then in 2006, the FBI, providing evidence for the trial of Zacarias Moussaoui,[217] indicated that the calls could not have been made in either way. On the one hand, the FBI ruled out the possibility that Barbara Olson could have used a cell phone, saying: "All of the calls from Flight 77 were made via the onboard airphone system."[218] On the other hand, the FBI report indicated that, although Barbara Olson did attempt a call from a seat-back phone, it was "unconnected" and (therefore) lasted "0 seconds."[219]

This anomaly in the official account of Flight 77 has thus far not been mentioned by the mainstream press, with only (to my knowledge) one exception.[220]

Part II: United Flight 93

I. The Reported Calls to Deena Burnett

The anomaly about the reported Olson calls provides a bridge to United Flight 93, because one of its distinctive features is that there were more reported phone calls from this flight than from the rest of the flights combined. These reported calls are of great importance, because it was the "phone calls from the 9/11 planes" that first convinced the public that America had been attacked by al-Qaeda hijackers. Evidence that these calls had been faked would, therefore, be of utmost importance. From the evidence in the previous point, it would appear that the Olson calls were somehow faked.

Strong evidence for fakery is also provided by the reported calls of Tom Burnett from United 93. His wife, Deena Burnett, reported that she had received "three to five cellular phone calls" from him.[221] She knew he was using his cell phone, because, the

ANOMALIES IN THE OFFICIAL ACCOUNTS OF AMERICAN 77 AND UNITED 73

FBI report from that same day said, "Burnett was able to determine that her husband was using his own cellular telephone because the caller identification showed his number."[222]

This gives us another major anomaly. On the one hand, it seems impossible to dismiss Deena Burnett's testimony as based on either dishonesty or confusion, so we have no reason to doubt that her caller ID indicated that she was called from her husband's cell phone. On the other hand, cell phone calls from United 93's altitude at that time of over 40,000 feet were, given the technology available in 2001, so unlikely that they can be called impossible. Even Deena Burnett herself, having been a flight attendant, wrote: "I didn't understand how [Tom] could be calling me on his cell phone from the air."[223]

Indeed, even the FBI – in spite of having recorded on 9/11 that Deena Burnett had reported that her caller ID indicated that her husband had called her from his cell phone – stated, in its report provided for the Moussaoui trial, that Tom Burnett's calls were made from a passenger-seat phone.[224]

There would seem to be no escape from the conclusion that the calls to Deena Burnett, having not come from her husband flying at roughly 40,000 feet on United 93, had in some way been faked. And if one call was faked, this raises the likelihood that all of the reported calls were faked – because if United 93 and the other 9/11 planes had really been taken over in surprise hijackings, no one would have been prepared to fake a single call.[225]

II. When Did the Military Know that United 93 Was in Trouble?

Another question about United 93 is when it showed signs of being in trouble. There were contradictory reports. In 2003,

THE 9/11 TORONTO REPORT

NORAD officials told the 9/11 Commission that the FAA reported "a possible hijack of United Flight 93" at 9:16[226] and that the Langley fighters had been scrambled at 9:14 to intercept United 93. But the 9/11 Commission in 2004 called both of these claims "incorrect," saying instead: "By 10:03, when United 93 crashed in Pennsylvania, there had been no mention [to the military] of its hijacking."[227]

The FAA controller in Cleveland had detected signs of hijacking at 9:28 – even hearing "We have a bomb on board" – and yet the Cleveland FAA reportedly did not contact the military. The 9/11 Commission, trying to explain why not, gave an unbelievable account of incompetence and even stupidity in the FAA.[228] Besides being unbelievable, the 9/11 Commission's claim was contradicted by at least four prior reports.

First, in his 2004 book, Richard Clarke said that during his White House videoconference, FAA Administrator Jane Garvey reported, at about 9:35, a number of "potential hijacks," which included "United 93 over Pennsylvania,"[229] while both Donald Rumsfeld and General Richard Myers were listening. The 9/11 Commission was able to claim that the military did not learn of Garvey's report by denying that Rumsfeld and Myers were involved in the video conference.

Second, an ABC program on the first anniversary of 9/11 had Karl Rove, David Bohrer (Cheney's photographer), and Cheney himself discussing the hijacked United 93 and considering it "the biggest threat."[230] Brigadier General Montague Winfield, who had taken a leadership position in the Pentagon's National Military Command Center, recalled: "We received the report from the FAA

ANOMALIES IN THE OFFICIAL ACCOUNTS
OF AMERICAN 77 AND UNITED 73

that Flight 93 had turned off its transponder, had turned, and was now heading towards Washington, DC."[231]

Third, General Larry Arnold, the commander of NORAD's US continental region, indicated in a January 2002 interview that the military learned about UA 93's troubles between the crash into the second tower and the attack on the Pentagon: "By this time," he said, "we were watching United Flight 93 wander around Ohio."[232] He also said that at 9:24: "Our focus was on United 93, which was being pointed out to us very aggressively I might say by the FAA."[233] This report by Arnold, who was involved in the events, differed radically from the 9/11 Commission's claim, according to which the FAA never contacted the military about United 93.

Fourth, the 9/11 Commission's claim was also, of course, incompatible with the testimonies, quoted above, about the military liaisons at the FAA Command Center. It seems impossible for us to say what was really going on with UA 93. But we can confidently say that the 9/11 Commission's account was false.

III. Did the Military Shoot United 93 Down?

Rumors that the military had shot down Flight 93 existed from the start. Major Daniel Nash, one of the pilots from Otis Air Force Base sent to fly over New York City, reported that when he returned to base, he was told that a military F-16 had shot down an airliner in Pennsylvania.[234] This rumor became sufficiently widespread that it came up during General Richard Myers' confirmation interview with the Senate Armed Services Committee on September 13. Chairman Carl Levin, saying that "there have been statements that the aircraft that crashed in Pennsylvania was shot down," added: "Those stories continue to exist."[235]

Myers replied: "Mr. Chairman, the armed forces did not shoot down any aircraft."[236] That same day, NORAD said: "Contrary to media reports that speculate that United Airlines Flight 93 was 'downed' by a U.S. fighter aircraft, NORAD-allocated forces have not engaged with weapons any aircraft, including Flight 93." NORAD said that this should put an end to the rumors.[237]

But the rumors continued. In 2002, for example, Susan Mcelwain, who lived near the crash site, reported that within hours of the crash, she had received a call from a friend who said that her husband, who was in the Air Force, had called and said: "I can't talk, but we've just shot a plane down."[238]

Although the 9/11 Commission did not directly acknowledge this controversy, it made a three-fold argument to rule out the possibility that UA 93 could have been shot down. The first argument was that the military did not know about the hijacking of United 93 until after it had crashed. As we have seen, there is much evidence against this claim.

The second argument was that Cheney, having not arrived in the PEOC until almost 10:00, did not give the shootdown authorization until some time after 10:10, and that Richard Clarke, who had asked for this authorization, did not receive it until 10:25.[239] This claim is also refuted by strong evidence. These claims were meant to rule out the possibility that UA 93 was shot down, because it, the Commission said, came down at 10:03 (or 10:06), But Clarke himself indicated that he, after asking for the authorization shortly after 9:30 and then being "amazed at the speed of the decisions coming from Cheney," received the authorization between 9:45 and 9:50.[240] Also, a *Newsday* story published two weeks after 9/11 said that the authorization was given "after Flight 77 crashed into the Pentagon,"

ANOMALIES IN THE OFFICIAL ACCOUNTS OF AMERICAN 77 AND UNITED 73

meaning about 9:38.[241] In 2003, *U.S. News and World Report* wrote: "Pentagon sources say Bush communicated the order [to shoot down any hijacked civilian airplane] to Cheney almost immediately after Flight 77 hit the Pentagon."[242] Colonel Robert Marr, the head of NEADS, said that he had "passed that [order] on to the pilots," so that "United Airlines Flight 93 [would] not be allowed to reach Washington, DC."[243] So there was plenty of time for the plane to have been shot down.

The Pentagon's third argument was that the military was not in position to shoot UA 93 down. But a reporter in Nashua – which is where the Boston Air Traffic Control Center is – wrote: "FAA air traffic controllers in Nashua have learned through discussions with other controllers that an F-16 fighter stayed in hot pursuit of another hijacked commercial airliner until it crashed in Pennsylvania."[244] Deputy Secretary of Defense Paul Wolfowitz said: "We responded awfully quickly, … and, in fact, we were already tracking in on that plane that crashed in Pennsylvania."[245] A CBS story then said: "U.S. officials were considering shooting down the hijacked airliner that crashed in western Pennsylvania, but it crashed first…. [A]dministration officials say that, had the jetliner continued toward Washington, the fighter jets would have shot it down."[246]

Still other stories reported that the military was in position to shoot United 93 down.[247] So the claim by the military and the 9/11 Commission was very strongly contradicted by numerous reports.

The Alleged Crash Site

The falsity of the official story about Flight 93 is further suggested by descriptions of the alleged crash site. One television reporter said: "There was just a big hole in the ground. All I saw was a crater filled with small, charred plane parts. Nothing that would even tell you that it was the plane.... There were no suitcases, no recognizable plane parts, no body parts."[248] A newspaper photographer said: "I didn't think I was in the right place.... I was looking for anything that said tail, wing, plane, metal. There was nothing."[249]

Debris, instead, was found many miles away, and much of it was debris that could not have blown there. John Fleegle, an employee at Indian Lake Marina, reported that the debris that washed ashore included "pieces of seats, small chunks of melted plastic and checks."[250] Newspapers reported that debris was found in New Baltimore, which was beyond a mountain ridge more than eight miles from the alleged crash site.[251]

Also, although Flight 93 reportedly was carrying more than 37,000 gallons of fuel when it crashed, tests of the soil and groundwater at the official crash site found no evidence of contamination.[252]

Perhaps the strangest feature of the crash site was that there were evidently two of them. According to CNN reporter Brian Cabell, speaking from the official crash site, the FBI had "cordoned off a second area about six to eight miles away from the crater." He then asked: "Why would debris from the plane ... be located 6 miles away?"[253]

The Flight Path(s)

Parallel to this evidence of two crash sites was evidence for two flight paths. According to the Flight Data Recorder, the plane came in from the north, a path that was confirmed by some witnesses in the Shanksville area. But other residents reported that the plane came from the east, with people fishing at the Indian Lake Marina reporting that the plane flew right over the lake.[254]

Conclusion

This chapter has shown that there are many anomalous features in the official stories of Flights 77 and 93, which deserve the attention of future official investigations of the events on September 11, 2001.

CHAPTER EIGHT

Eyewitness Evidence of Explosions in the Twin Towers

BY DR. GRAEME MacQUEEN

MANY OF US ARE CONVINCED THAT THE TWIN TOWERS OF the World Trade Center were brought down on September 11, 2001 through controlled demolition. But the question at once arises: if this is what happened, would somebody not have noticed?

The answer is that many people did notice. There is a good deal of eyewitness evidence for the demolition of buildings 1 and 2. This paper will give a brief overview of this evidence.

Before we look at the evidence, we must first confront one of the most common objections in response to it. Eyewitness evidence, say the objectors, is "soft," untrustworthy, and unreliable. According to such critics, it does not matter how many eyewitnesses there are to an event or who these eyewitnesses are or how their accounts relate to each other; the best plan is just to dismiss everything they say. This is an odd view. There is no support for it either in social scientific studies of eyewitness testimony or in the scholarly literature on criminal investigation.[255]

Eyewitness evidence certainly has its vulnerabilities: we know that eyewitnesses can misperceive, misremember and deceive. However, as with other kinds of evidence, we have developed ways of checking to see if what the witnesses report is accurate. For example, we look for *corroborating evidence* – further eyewitness evidence as well as evidence of entirely different kinds.

Moreover, eyewitness evidence is highly relevant to the investigation of explosions. The National Fire Protection Association's manual on fire and explosion investigations states clearly that in an explosion investigation, "the investigator should take into consideration all the available information, including witness statements."[256]

The present paper offers not only an overview of eyewitness evidence of explosions but also a critique of the handling of this evidence by the 9/11 Commission and the National Institute of Standards and Technology. But both of these organizations make extensive use of eyewitness evidence and obviously consider it valid and important. Therefore, disagreements with NIST and the 9/11 Commission on the legitimacy of eyewitness testimony are not at the level of principle but at the level of application.

One especially important source of eyewitness testimony is the oral histories of the Fire Department of New York (technically, World Trade Center Task Force Interviews), released in 2005 by the City of New York.[257] The *New York Times* had taken the city to court to obtain the release of the documents, and when the material was released the newspaper hosted the oral histories in the form of a series of separate PDF files on its website.

EYEWITNESS EVIDENCE OF EXPLOSIONS IN THE TWIN TOWERS

The oral histories were collected by the World Trade Center Task Force of the FDNY after New York City fire commissioner Thomas Von Essen decided it would be important to have a record of what the members of the department experienced on that day. The Task Force interviews comprise 10-12,000 pages of statements by approximately 500 "FDNY firefighters, emergency medical technicians and paramedics collected from early October, 2001 to late January, 2002."[258]

Professor David Ray Griffin, with the help of able researchers, was the first scholar to ferret out fascinating descriptions of explosions from this material.[259] The author of the present paper published a subsequent article after reading the oral histories, "118 Witnesses: the Firefighters' Testimony to Explosions in the Twin Towers."[260]

The presentation and analysis below build on this earlier work. As the evidence is presented, three important points will emerge. First, the conviction that the Towers came down because of explosions was common on 9/11. Second, there is substantial eyewitness evidence supporting this conviction. Third, this evidence has been ignored or suppressed by both the 9/11 Commission and NIST.

The explosion hypothesis was common on 9/11

In discussions of the events of 9/11, it is often implied that the original, obvious, and natural hypothesis concerning the destruction of the Twin Towers is some variety of gravity-driven collapse. It was obvious to everyone on 9/11, we are led to believe, that the Towers came down because the buildings simply could not withstand the plane strikes and subsequent fires and therefore gave way. Those who say the buildings came down because of explosions – who hold to an "explosion hypothesis" in the broad sense – are, according to this view, late arrivals. They are folks, it is argued, who came along after 9/11 and over-thought an initially simple situation due to a conspiratorial mind-set.

In fact, it is easy to prove that this is a falsification of history. Proponents of the explosion hypothesis were extremely common on 9/11, especially at the scene of the crime. Many people made their judgment on the basis of what they directly perceived while close to the buildings, while others accepted as a matter of course that complete and energetic pulverization of these enormous buildings must have entailed explosions. Below are five of many examples supporting these views.

1. In a video clip preserved from 9/11, ABC television reporter N. J. Burkett is seen standing close to the Twin Towers. He draws our attention to the firefighters at the scene and to the burning buildings themselves. Suddenly, the South Tower begins to come apart behind him. As the pulverized debris shoots into the air, Burkett says: "A *huge* explosion now, raining debris on all of us. We better get out of the way!"

   Mr. Burkett's statement shows no evidence of over-thinking the situation or of a conspiratorial mindset. He certainly did not come along after 9/11: he expressed his judgment before the debris of the building had even reached the ground. Then he ran for his life. Half an hour later he would run for his life again as the North Tower came down.[261]

2. In CNN's same-day coverage of the events of 9/11, Mayor Giuliani was asked questions about explosions in the Twin

EYEWITNESS EVIDENCE OF EXPLOSIONS IN THE TWIN TOWERS

Towers on two separate occasions. The second occasion is a press conference at about 2:39 p.m. A female reporter (off screen) asks the Mayor: "Do you know anything about the cause of the explosions that brought the two buildings down? Was it caused by the planes or by something else?"[262]

Notice that she does not ask if there were explosions: she assumes there were. She does not ask if these explosions brought down the Towers: she assumes they did. She merely wants to know what caused the explosions – the planes or "something else."

3. In footage known as the "Matthew Shapoff video," acquired from NIST through a Freedom of Information Act request, there are several people (off screen) chatting while they watch the events at the World Trade Center unfold at a distance and film them with their video camera. Suddenly, through their camera we see the North Tower begin to throw pulverized debris in all directions in huge plumes as it disintegrates. After a horrified, "oh, my God!" we hear a male voice, presumably that of Shapoff, exclaim as follows: "That was a bomb that did that! That was a fuckin' bomb that did that! There's no goddamn way that could have happened!"[263] Again, this is a spontaneous reaction to what Shapoff was observing.

4. New York firefighter Christopher Fenyo, in a passage from the World Trade Center Task Force interviews, speaks of a debate that began among firefighters who were on the scene. The debate started after the destruction of the South Tower but before the destruction of the North Tower – in other words, between about 10:00 and 10:30 a.m.

"...At that point a debate began to rage because the perception was that the building looked like it had been taken out with charges."

As with Shapoff, the statement concerns not just explosions generally but the intentional destruction of the building with explosives. That is, people were already debating a sub-category of the explosion hypothesis, the controlled demolition hypothesis, before 10:30 on the morning of 9/11.

5. The FBI's name for its investigation of the 9/11 incidents is PENTTBOM, which stands for "Pentagon/Twin Towers Bombing Investigation." Is it possible that when this name was assigned someone in the FBI thought a bombing had taken place? (Recall that according to the current official narrative there was no bombing at any of the affected locations.) On the day of 9/11, *USA Today's* foreign correspondent Jack Kelley was seen telling his TV audience that the FBI's "working theory" at that time was that "at the same time two planes hit the building...there was a car or truck packed with explosives underneath the building, which exploded at the same time and brought both of them down."[264] Given that Kelley was later shown to have routinely fabricated stories for *USA Today*, his allegations about the FBI would have to be corroborated. However, the general hypothesis ascribed here to the FBI – the buildings were brought down through the use of explosives—was common on 9/11. For example, Albert Turi, FDNY Chief of Safety, told NBC's Pat Dawson not long after the destruction of the Towers that, in Dawson's words, "according to his [Turi's] theory he thinks that there were actually devices that were planted in the building."[265]

EYEWITNESS EVIDENCE OF EXPLOSIONS IN THE TWIN TOWERS

These five examples have been offered in support of the contention that the explosion theory, even in its most robust form (deliberate destruction through explosives), was familiar to eyewitnesses on the day of 9/11. It was widely accepted as a reasonable theory. That many people held this theory does not mean it is correct, but it suggests that if this theory is to be rejected it must be rejected on the basis of evidence, not because it is regarded as late, unnatural, exotic or conspiratorial.

There is strong eyewitness evidence supporting the explosion hypothesis.

The eyewitness evidence is strong in terms of both *quality* and *quantity*. The quality of the evidence is found in the richly detailed, mutually corroborating accounts of what was witnessed. At the same time, the quantity of evidence is impressive in both the number and variety of eyewitnesses who discuss explosions in their statements.

Quality

A conversation between Dennis Tardio and Pat Zoda about the destruction of the North Tower was captured on film by the Naudet brothers on the day of 9/11.[266]

Tardio and Zoda repeatedly affirm each other's accounts, both with words and with hand gestures. The hand gestures are like a series of karate chops starting high and going quickly downward. The witnesses evidently want to suggest that there were many discrete, energetic events that they observed, and that these started high up and then moved rapidly down the building at regular intervals.

THE 9/11 TORONTO REPORT

Zoda says, as he moves his hand: "Floor by floor, it started poppin' out." Tardio concurs and uses the same hand gesture: "It was as if they had detonated, detonated (Zoda: "Yeah, detonated, yeah"), you know, as if they were planted to take down a building: boom, boom, boom, boom, boom, boom, boom." Zoda adds: "All the way down. I was watching and running."

These are firefighters and they are used to encountering the standard sorts of explosions that occur in building fires. But they do not talk about smoke explosions, or "boiling-liquid-expanding-vapor" (BLEVE) explosions, or any of the other expected forms of explosion. Instead, they are talking about, and acting out with dramatic gestures, something altogether different. They say that what they saw resembled a controlled demolition.

The next example is Paul Lemos, who, on 9/11, was in the vicinity of the World Trade Center to participate in the filming of a commercial. Lemos was interviewed on videotape on 9/11 near the World Trade Center, with WTC-7 still standing in the distance.[267] He was filmed by a different film maker at a different location than the firefighters just described. This footage appears to be *entirely independent of the Tardio/Zoda footage just discussed*. However,

EYEWITNESS EVIDENCE OF EXPLOSIONS IN THE TWIN TOWERS

when Lemos begins describing the demise of the North Tower, he uses the same hand gestures as Tardio and Zoda: rapid chops that start high and move at regular intervals down the building.

Here is what he says as he performs his gestures:

"All of a sudden I looked up and about twenty stories below…the fire…I saw, from the corner, boom, boom, boom, boom, boom, boom, boom, boom, boom…just like twenty straight hits, just went down and then I just saw the whole building just went 'pshew'…and as the bombs were goin' people just started running and I sat there and watched a few of 'em explode and then I just turned around and I just started running for my life because at that point the World Trade Center was coming right down…"

Lemos is even bolder than Tardio and Zoda, in that he does not qualify his statement by saying "*as if* they had detonated." He refers openly to "bombs" and he says he watched them "explode."

In any case, the Tardio/Zoda footage and the Lemos footage are both rich in detail and mutually corroborating. The rich detail is apparent from the transcript, and the corroboration comes not just from the language used but also the hand gestures. These men clearly perceived the same event and came away with the same idea – that explosive devices in the buildings were used to bring them down.

Lemos also tells an interesting anecdote about a conversation with a person who was introduced to him as an architect, which is relevant to the tampering with and suppression of eyewitness evidence. Lemos states, "…now, they told me afterwards it wasn't explosions. I was talking to one of the architects that they pulled in." It is unclear who "they" is referring to in this statement, but a reasonable supposition can be made that "they" refers to the authorities on the scene. Therefore, it appears that the authorities had an architect there on 9/11 telling people like Paul Lemos what they had and had not perceived.

Regardless of whether or not this "architect" had a sinister purpose, we can be sure of the following facts about the architect: (1) unlike Lemos, he was not himself an eyewitness (he had been "pulled in" to the scene); (2) he would not have had time to carry out a thorough canvassing of eyewitnesses; (3) he certainly did not have time to do a comprehensive review of photographs and videos of the collapse; and (4) there is little possibility he could have studied the remains of the building in any detail – either the steel or the dust. Despite all of this, he feels he can tell an eyewitness what that eyewitness did *not* perceive. Not only is the architect making an unwarranted judgment, his behavior is extremely irregular insofar as it makes conducting an unbiased

EYEWITNESS EVIDENCE OF EXPLOSIONS IN THE TWIN TOWERS

investigation much more difficult. Homicide investigations, fire investigations, and explosion investigations have strict principles, and in each case it would be unheard of to walk onto a crime scene and taint the evidence by interfering with an eyewitness.

This discussion of the architect is also important because of its wider significance. In the months following 9/11, many eyewitnesses muted, qualified and even rejected their own initial judgments after hearing that authorities had adopted a structural failure hypothesis that had no room for explosions. The structural failure hypothesis that was most common during that period, and that was widely advanced as correct, was the "pancake" hypothesis of sequentially failing floors. The pancake hypothesis has since that time been discredited and abandoned (it was specifically rejected by NIST) but in the early days it did a fine job of weakening the confidence of eyewitnesses who thought they had perceived explosions.

Examples of firefighters revising their judgment of what they had perceived on the basis of what authorities were saying at the time are common in the World Trade Center Task Force interviews.

Dominick DeRubbio says in his description of the destruction of the South Tower: "It was weird how it started to come down. It looked like it was a timed explosion, but I guess it was just the floors starting to pancake one on top of the other."

James Drury says in his statement about the North Tower:

"…we started to hear the second roar. That was the north tower now coming down. I should say that people in the street and myself included thought that the roar was so loud that…bombs were going off inside the building. Obviously we were later proved wrong…"

THE 9/11 TORONTO REPORT

John Coyle starts his important statement about the South Tower in a very tentative way:

"The tower was—it looked to me—I thought it was exploding, actually. That's what I thought for hours afterwards… Everybody I think at that point still thought these things were blown up."

All of these witnesses recall their initial impressions of what they saw and thought (and in the case of Drury and Coyle the initial impressions of their friends and colleagues who were also on the scene), and then try to back away from these impressions. Thus, we have clear evidence of both how common the explosive demolition theory was on 9/11, and how it was later marginalized – not by sound science but by speculative theories given a stamp of approval by authority figures.

Returning now to the issue of corroboration, there are additional evidentiary sources that corroborate the descriptions given by Zoda, Tardio and Lemos of regular, descending energetic events. First, here are three examples of corroborating eyewitness testimony.

Ross Milanytch, an employee at nearby Chase Manhattan Bank, says of the South Tower: "It started exploding…It was about the 70th floor. And each second another floor exploded out for about eight floors, before the cloud obscured it all."

John Bussey, a reporter for the *Wall Street Journal*, said this of the South Tower:

"Off the phone, and collecting my thoughts for the next report, I heard metallic crashes and looked up out of the office window to see what seemed like perfectly synchronized explosions coming from each floor, spewing glass and

EYEWITNESS EVIDENCE OF EXPLOSIONS IN THE TWIN TOWERS

metal outward. One after the other, from top to bottom, with a fraction of a second between, the floors blew to pieces."[268]

Kenneth Rogers of the New York Fire Department said this about his experience with the South Tower:

"…we were standing there with about five companies and we were just waiting for our assignment and then there was an explosion in the south tower… A lot of guys left at that point. I kept watching. Floor after floor after floor. One floor under another after another and when it hit about the fifth floor, I figured it was a bomb, because it looked like a synchronized deliberate kind of thing."

Corroboration can be even more impressive when it involves an entirely different form of evidence. Paul Lemos explicitly says that he was watching the North Tower, and, more specifically, a corner of the North Tower, when he saw the explosions. Evidence that corroborates his judgment that there were explosions occurring at a corner of the North Tower is found in high quality footage filmed during its destruction.[269] This footage clearly shows a rapid sequence of forceful and focused ejections, apparently explosive, moving down the building. The size and velocity of these ejections can be measured, which means their existence and basic characteristics are not open to question. Thus, there is a high degree of corroboration among the different eyewitness accounts, and between eyewitness evidence and other evidence.

Some who object to this compilation of eyewitness testimony say that what these witnesses experienced may not have been explosions at all. Falling bodies, crashing elevators, snapping columns and even sonic booms have all been proposed as alternative explanations. These assertions can be addressed by analyzing, quite closely, the statements of another eyewitness.

The witness is Sue Keane. She was, on 9/11, an officer in the Port Authority Police Department (PAPD) where she had been for eight years. Before this she had spent 13 years in the U.S. Army, where she received training on how to respond to explosions.

Listed below are six common characteristics of explosions as described by former FBI explosives expert James Thurman in his book, *Practical Bomb Scene Investigation*.[270] These characteristics are matched to selections from statements Sue Keane gave to the authors of the book, *Women at Ground Zero*.[271] These statements, given within a few months of the 9/11 events, are supported by her separate handwritten submission to the Port Authority Police Department.

1. Sound

Keane: "A couple of minutes later, it sounded like bombs going off. That's when the explosions happened."

2. Positive blast pressure phase

"The windows blew in…we all got thrown." "Each one of those explosions picked me up and threw me."

3. Partial vacuum during positive blast pressure phase

"There was this incredible rush of air, and it literally sucked the breath out of my lungs."

4. Negative blast pressure phase

"Everything went out of me with this massive wind… Stuff was just flying past. Then it stopped and got really quiet, and then everything came back at us. I could

EYEWITNESS EVIDENCE OF EXPLOSIONS IN THE TWIN TOWERS

breathe at this point, but now I was sucking all that stuff in, too. It was almost like a back draft. It sounded like a tornado."

5. Incendiary or thermal effect

"…he threw me under the hose, which in a way felt great, because I didn't realize until then that my skin was actually burning. I had burn marks, not like you'd have from a fire, but my face was all red, my chest was red."

6. Fragmentation and shrapnel

"…there was stuff coming out of my body like you wouldn't believe. It was like shrapnel. It's still coming out."

The handwritten PAPD report of this brave and obviously traumatized individual, which corroborates the above account in several crucial respects, is directly available in the PAPD documents released in 2003.[272] One page of that report is reproduced on the following page.

> **The Port Authority of New York and New Jersey**
> **HAND-WRITTEN MEMORANDUM**
>
> PA 2265 11-72   (3)
>
> To: _____
> From: _____
> Date: __/__/__
> Subject: _____
>
> Massive amounts of debrie, concrete dust and bodies or part were more frequent at this point. Then there was an eerie silence and it was like you knew something was going to happen, there just seemed to be one explosion after another. I was seperated from the guys from the bridge (GWB) by another explosion, masive again sucking the air out of your lungs and then just a wind more intense this time with larger pieces of debrie flying. When things cleared, there were still civilians in the area and myself, a NYPD cop and 2 firemen then attempted to get the rest of the people out. Since I only knew how to get back to Tower 5, that is how we got the rest of the group out across the plaza, by looking up and only letting them go 2 or 3 at a time.
> This is starting to get hard to write I'll try again in a few days.

On what reasonable grounds can we exclude Sue Keane's statements as we attempt to determine the causes of the destruction of the Twin Towers?

In summary, the eyewitness testimony of Tardio/Zoda, Lemos and Keane are examples of "quality," meaning evidence that is rich in detail. Below, the issue of "quantity" of eyewitness evidence is considered.

EYEWITNESS EVIDENCE OF EXPLOSIONS IN THE TWIN TOWERS

Quantity

It is difficult to formulate a complete account of eyewitnesses who describe, expressly or implicitly, explosions near the time of the destruction of the Twin Towers. Neither the FBI, nor the 9/11 Commission, nor the National Institute of Standards and Technology have published a count. I have compiled the most complete known list of witnesses to explosions at the Twin Towers. There are 156 such witness statements. The two graphs presented below summarize certain aspects of the list.

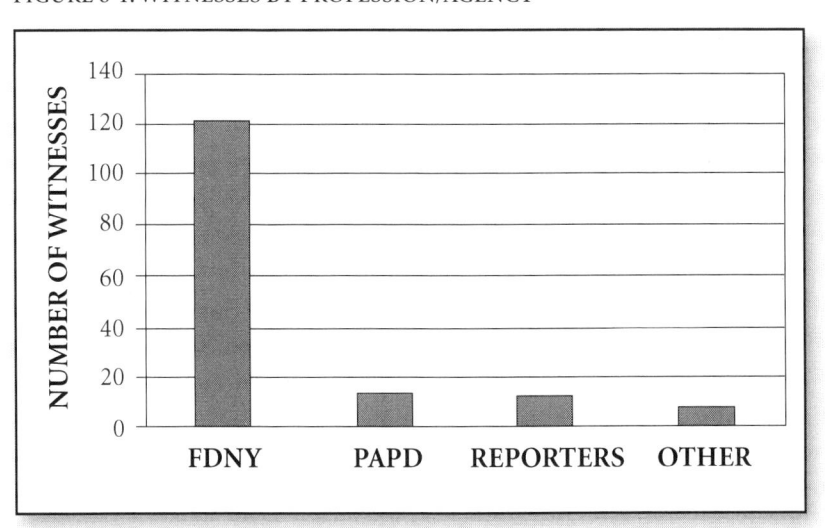

FIGURE 8-1: WITNESSES BY PROFESSION/AGENCY

Of the 156 eyewitnesses, 121 are from the Fire Department of New York. Another 14 witnesses are from the Port Authority Police Department. Thirteen are reporters, most working for major television networks. Eight are listed as "other," usually people who worked in the vicinity of the Towers.

Members of the FDNY and PAPD are typically referred to as "first responders." So 135 out of 156 witnesses, or 87% of the total, are first responders. This is significant because these people have much more experience with explosions than most people. Moreover, their statements were given to superior officers as part of their professional duties, and the circumstances in which the statements were collected make this eyewitness evidence very strong.

The reporters also occupy an important position in the list because their accounts in most cases are directly captured on videotape. Their voice inflections and often their body language can be examined in detail. The reporters' accounts are also important because they are in most cases given spontaneously, with little reflection, very soon—minutes or even seconds—after the event they witnessed. Spontaneous witness statements are widely viewed as credible because there is little time for internal or external filtering of what is stated. In fact, the U.S. Federal Rules of Evidence typically do not admit into court statements made by witnesses outside of court, which are referred to as hearsay. However, one exception to the rule against hearsay is the "excited utterance" exception. The excited utterance exception allows hearsay to be admitted when it is "a statement relating to a startling event or condition made while the declarant was under the stress of excitement caused by the event or condition." (Fed. Rules Evid. 803(2)) As expected, with respect to 9/11, the distorting tendencies in recollection have worked *against* the explosion hypothesis, for the simple reason that people progressively adjusted their stories as time went on to better accord with what they were being told by authority figures.[273]

Before discussing the next graph, it is appropriate to describe how the list of explosion witnesses was compiled. Eyewitnesses are included in the list if they use, in their statement, at least one

EYEWITNESS EVIDENCE OF EXPLOSIONS
IN THE TWIN TOWERS

of the following terms: "explosion" (or the corresponding permutations of "to explode"), "blast," "blow up" (or "blow out") "bomb" (or "secondary device"), or "implosion." There is also a category called "other CD," which includes cases that do not use one of these terms, but that are in some respects strongly suggestive of controlled demolition. The point of this method is not merely to be able to quantify explosion reports, but to reduce the list compiler's role in the interpretive process. Eyewitnesses are included in the list not because an outside observer interprets what they witnessed as explosions, but because the eyewitnesses themselves interpret what they witnessed as explosions.

Additionally, there are processes available to investigators that can help check the quality of the evidence. The witnesses can be closely scrutinized (names, occupations, reliability, experience); motives for deception can be looked at; quality of sources can be examined; chain of custody for all witness accounts can be verified; and, of course, corroboration through other evidence of both similar and dissimilar kinds can be confirmed. Corroboration is so massive in the present case that the other processes have received less attention.

The "explosion" category is by far the largest, with 112 eyewitnesses. However, the "bomb" category, with 32 eyewitnesses, is extremely important as well. Most of the people on this list speaking of bombs are firefighters, and it is clear from their use of the word "bomb" that they are not talking about the sort of explosion they expect to encounter in a high-rise fire.

Now, there are three common objections to the demolition argument as based on eyewitness evidence. Two have been addressed already: eyewitness evidence is "soft" and can be disregarded; and eyewitnesses may have mistakenly reported explosions

FIGURE 8-2: WITNESSES BY TERM USED

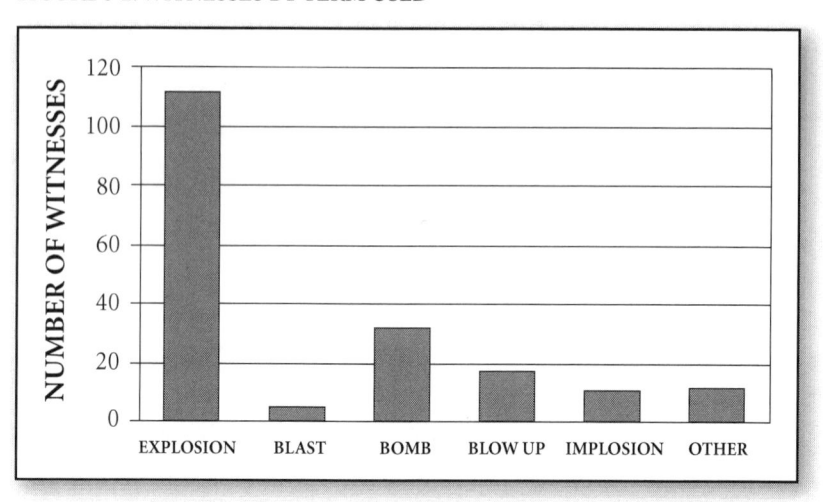

[Bar chart showing number of witnesses by term used: EXPLOSION ~110, BLAST ~3, BOMB ~32, BLOW UP ~17, IMPLOSION ~10, OTHER ~11]

when, in fact, non-explosive events (such as falling elevators) were at issue. The third objection is the only one that can be taken seriously. It is this: there are many natural forms of explosion that occur in large fires, and the mere fact that there were *explosions* does not mean that *explosives* were used. It is an unjustified leap, claim these objectors, to go from eyewitness statements about explosions to the controlled demolition hypothesis.

The types of explosions that typically accompany a fire are described in detail in various publications, probably most authoritatively in the National Fire Protection Association's *Guide for Fire and Explosion Investigations*. There the NFPA describes four types of explosion that would have been expected to accompany the fires in the Twin Towers.

1. BLEVE ("boiling-liquid-expanding-vapor-explosion," as with an exploding boiler)
2. Electrical explosion

EYEWITNESS EVIDENCE OF EXPLOSIONS IN THE TWIN TOWERS

3. Smoke explosion (i.e. backdraft)

4. Combustion explosion (e.g., natural gas, jet fuel vapor)

There are three characteristics of the eyewitness statements that rule out all four types of explosion. That is, these four sorts of explosions may well have occurred, but they do not account for the main explosions witnesses say they perceived. Here are the three characteristics that must be explained.

Identification

If the explosions encountered were the type typically encountered in fires, the firefighters would be expected to recognize them as such and name them. There are very few instances where they do so. On the contrary, they clearly feel these were different types of explosion than those they were used to encountering, as evidenced by, for example, the number of references to bombs.

Power

Many eyewitnesses clearly thought they were watching explosions destroy the Twin Towers ("I looked up, and the building exploded...The whole top came off like a volcano") But none of the common four types of fire-related explosions could accomplish this. Recall that according to NIST, the Twin Towers were essentially intact beneath the point where they were hit by the planes. While BLEVEs and combustion explosions sometimes destroy structures such as wood frame houses, there are no examples of these explosions causing the destruction of such robust steel structures as are at issue here. Also, there is no evidence that the right conditions for such explosions (for example, the necessary quantities of natural gas or jet fuel) existed in the Twin Towers at the time their dramatic destruction began.

Pattern

As described above, many eyewitnesses reported regular, rapid energetic events in sequence down the building, which cannot be explained by any of the four common types of explosion. If these patterned ejections are the result of explosions, they can only be explosions resulting from explosives.

Eyewitness evidence was ignored/suppressed by the 9/11 Commission and NIST

The discussion above gives a brief overview of the eyewitness testimony available to investigators. The last main point here is that this evidence has been ignored or suppressed by both the 9/11 Commission and NIST.

In its 585 pages, the 9/11 Commission Report contains one partial sentence referring to eyewitness reports of explosions at the time of collapse. The context is a discussion of firefighters who were on upper floors of the North Tower when the South Tower came down. The sentence fragment is as follows: "...those firefighters not standing near windows facing south had no way of knowing that the South Tower had collapsed; many surmised that a bomb had exploded..."[274] In other words, according to the 9/11 Commission, a subcategory of firefighters – those in upper floors of the North Tower with an impeded view—mistook the collapse of the South Tower for a bomb. The implication here is that the explosion witnesses, presumably few in number, made a mistake.

EYEWITNESS EVIDENCE OF EXPLOSIONS IN THE TWIN TOWERS

Of course, a careful examination of the available eyewitness testimony, as set forth above, would show that it is categorically false that all or most of the explosion witnesses were in the upper floors of the North Tower, and that only those with an impeded view thought a bomb had exploded. The truth is that witnesses were in a great variety of locations and many of them had an exceptionally clear view of the Towers.

The National Institute of Standards and Technology gave even worse treatment to the eyewitness testimony. One of NIST's stated objectives is to "determine why and how WTC 1 and WTC 2 collapsed following the initial impacts of the aircraft."[275] But in the 295 pages of this report, there is not a single reference to eyewitnesses who perceived explosions in the Twin Towers.

Some may argue that this is not surprising because NIST deals with hard evidence, not soft evidence. NIST is concerned with things like column size, temperatures reached, and the yield strength of steel; NIST does not deal with eyewitnesses. This is a misconception. The truth is that NIST openly discussed its attention to eyewitnesses.

Very early in its investigation of the Twin Towers, NIST adopted a sophisticated method of collecting eyewitness evidence, and the results can be seen in Chapter 7 ("Reconstruction of Human Activity") of the NIST final report. Telephone interviews, face-to-face interviews, and focus groups were all used.[276] Note, for example, the following statement: "225 face-to-face interviews, averaging 2 hours each, gathered detailed, first-hand accounts and observations of the activities and events inside the buildings on the morning of September 11."[277] Although Chapter 7 is not about the destruction of the Towers, elsewhere NIST explicitly recognizes the relevance of eyewitness evidence to the understanding of how the buildings came down.[278] [33] Yet NIST somehow fails to note even one eyewitness reference to explosions or bombs, not only among its interviewees but also in the literature. It misses, for example, all of the 156 eyewitnesses used as the basis of this paper, even though it had access to all of the sources used to compile the list.

The 9/11 Commission and the National Institute of Standards and Technology, apparently following the lead of the FBI, have violated standard principles of investigation. Whether this is evidence of incompetence or of deliberate cover-up is irrelevant to my present argument. Either way, it is obvious that the official investigations carried out to this point have been grossly inadequate and that a new and thorough investigation is essential.

CHAPTER NINE

WTC 7: A Refutation of NIST Analysis

BY DAVID CHANDLER

THE FIRST INDICATION THAT WORLD TRADE CENTER Building 7 was intentionally demolished comes from direct observation and common sense. If it is viewed coming down, there is really no question. All support has been removed and the building falls straight down. It has been seen many times, always and only as a result of demolition. Buildings do not fall through themselves naturally at the acceleration of gravity. The late Danny Jowenko, a building demolition expert in Holland, was shown Building 7 collapsing for the first time during a live interview. His response: "This is a controlled demolition. No question about it. They simply blew up columns and the rest caved in afterwards." He was then asked "You sure?" and replied "Absolutely. It's been imploded. This was a hired job, performed by a team of experts. ... It's without a doubt a professional job. They know exactly what they're doing."[279]

Only later did he learn that this building came down on 9/11. NIST asks its readers to discount their perceptions, and their common sense, and believe only NIST. However, we cannot overlook the fact that:

- The NIST report was produced by a government agency in an administration that was notorious for censoring scientific reports for political purposes.
- The claim that an event resembling controlled demolition was caused by office fires is patently absurd.
- NIST's analysis leading to this conclusion was based solely on computer modeling and ignored contradictory physical evidence.
- The data and assumptions that went into NIST's computer models have not been made public.
- The NIST report has not been peer reviewed.
- Before NIST even began its study, the crime scene had been systematically and intentionally destroyed.
- NIST refused to search for residue of explosives.

As our colleague Frank Legge has put it,

"The evidence for explosives in controlled demolition of all three buildings is both compelling and obvious, hence the failure of NIST to consider this possibility is prima facie evidence of corruption."

Common sense is not a perfect guide to truth, but neither is blind faith in authority figures. Our senses can be fooled, but authority figures can lie. When something doesn't pass the smell

WTC 7: A REFUTATION OF NIST ANALYSIS

test, we honor our good sense by validating it with critical observation, experimentation, and analysis – in other words, with science. As individuals, some of us may not have the talents or resources to validate our own perceptions about 9/11, but as a community, we do. The role of the many scientists who question the official story of 9/11 is to engage with the evidence, to engage with the public, and to witness to the Truth.

Description of World Trade Center 7 and Its Collapse

World Trade Center Building 7 (sometimes referred to as WTC 7, Building 7, or the Solomon Smith Barney Building) was a tall, trapezoidal building, situated a little more than 100 meters north of the North Tower, across Vesey Street. It was 47 stories (174 m; 571 ft.) tall. Its footprint was nearly the size of an American football field. It had 58 perimeter columns and 25 core columns. The tenants of the building in 2001 included Salomon Smith Barney, the IRS Regional Council, the US Secret Service, the DOD, the CIA, the NYC Office of Emergency Management, the Securities & Exchange Commission, and several banks and insurance companies. The 23rd floor housed a specially reinforced bunker for the NYC Office of Emergency Management.[280] Needless to say, it was an extremely security-minded place.

On the morning of 9/11, WTC 7 was hit by debris from the collapse of the North Tower. But whereas the Twin Towers were hit by jet liners flying at approximately 500 mi/hr[281], the few large projectiles that hit WTC 7 were more like small trucks. The measured speed of the fastest of them was 78 mi/hr, essentially highway speed.[282] The planes that hit the Twin Towers had about 1500 times the kinetic energy of the most energetic debris that hit WTC 7. Ultimately NIST discounted debris damage as a factor in the collapse of the building, but it is still cited and still plays a role in the public perception.

There were fires on a limited number of floors that moved around the building, staying in any one place no more than 20-30 minutes, exhausting the fuel and moving on. In its final report, NIST claims that in the northeast corner of the 12th floor, intense, prolonged fires caused thermal expansion in the overhead beams, pushing a girder off its seat connecting it to Column 79. This failure, they claim, cascaded down several floors leaving the column unsupported and causing it to buckle. The failure of this single column, they say, is what ultimately brought the building down.[283]

Chris Sarns, a researcher with Architects and Engineers for 9/11 Truth, has analyzed photographs showing the actual progression of the fires.[284] He found that the fires on the 12th floor had burned past the northeast corner earlier in the day and were essentially out, in that area, by 5:00 pm. NIST needed fires around column 79 for their theory to work, so it appears they adjusted their computer model, in contradiction with the visual evidence provided by photographs available of that same area, to show a fire around Column 79 when it was needed to support NIST's conclusion.

Throughout the day there were sounds of explosions and reports that WTC 7 was going to come down. Sometime after both towers had collapsed, Ashleigh Banfield reported for MSNBC, "We just heard one more explosion. That's about the fourth one we've heard." Several reporters, including Vince Dimitri, CBS, and Ashleigh Banfield, MSNBC, reported that fire officials expected Building 7 to collapse.

WTC 7: A REFUTATION OF NIST ANALYSIS

BBC news famously jumped the gun and reported the collapse of WTC 7 in detail about 20 minutes prior to its actual occurrence.[285] Other reporters, who apparently knew the NY skyline better, seemed to have had the same script but showed confusion when what they were reading didn't match what they saw. At 4:15 Aaron Brown reported for CNN, with Building 7 standing in the background behind him, "We are getting information now that one of the other buildings, Building 7 in the World Trade Center complex is on fire and has either collapsed or is collapsing, and I, I, you, to be honest can see these pictures a little bit more clearly than I." Someone on CNN even reported that a 50-story building went down at 10:45 am.[286] As crowds filled the streets to watch from behind police lines, WTC 7 fell at 5:20 pm.

The final demise of the building began with the collapse of the East Penthouse, preceded by a loud, sharp, percussive boom, recorded by a television camera on West St. near Harrison St.[287] After several seconds the West Penthouse started to fall into the building, but before it even disappeared, the rest of the building let go and fell along with it.

For well over 2 seconds, the downward acceleration was constant and equal to the acceleration of gravity within the margin of error of the measurements. In other words, for this building, even though it was falling straight down through its own supporting structure, freefall actually happened. Furthermore, there was a sharp onset of freefall.[288] The building was holding steady, then it simply let go. In approximately 2.5 seconds of freefall, it fell over 100 feet – the equivalent of 8 stories.

Some argue, erroneously, that the resistance in the case of WTC 7 was not significant because the falling weight was so great. It is true that the falling weight was great, but the strength of the supporting structure was even greater. The structure was built to support 3 to 5 times the actual load. The energy absorbed during destruction of the structure would therefore not be negligible and the resulting downward motion would not approximate freefall unless the strength of the structure was being removed by some other force. Furthermore, note that when the falling section of the building did eventually engage with the lower structure, deceleration resulted. If the structure had enough strength to decelerate the falling building after it achieved a considerable speed, it should have produced measurable resistance from the beginning. The conditions allowing freefall in the first 2.5 seconds are clearly very different from the conditions that existed during the rest of the descent of the building.

An alternative analysis could consider the energy associated with Building 7's descent. When an object falls, the potential energy is converted to kinetic energy. During freefall, *all* of the potential energy is converted into kinetic energy. But, if any of the energy is used for other purposes along the way, such as crushing concrete or deforming steel, or throwing things around, there will be less energy available to be transformed into kinetic energy. This would reduce the speed of the fall. For freefall to occur, none of the energy could have been diverted to other uses, so the energy that destroyed the structure had to have come from some other source. The *observed fact* of freefall is literally proof of demolition.

WTC 7: A REFUTATION OF NIST ANALYSIS

The NIST Report

The preface of the NIST report on WTC 7 states:

NIST is a nonregulatory agency of the U.S. Department of Commerce. The purpose of NIST investigations is to improve the safety and structural integrity of buildings in the United States, and the focus is on fact finding. ... NIST does not have the statutory authority to make findings of fault nor negligence by individuals or organizations. Further, no part of any report resulting from a NIST investigation into a building failure or from an investigation under the National Construction Safety Team Act may be used in any suit or action for damages arising out of any matter mentioned in such report.[289]

Choosing NIST to be the investigative body determined from the outset that this would be a limited, building safety investigation without the statutory authority to become a forensic criminal investigation. We have not had a real, fully empowered, forensic investigation at all. Therefore, we should not be asking for a *new* investigation. We should instead be asking for a *real* investigation.

The final draft of the NIST WTC 7 report was released for public comment in August 2008, and the final report was released on November 25, 2008. In both of these, NIST discusses the rate of fall of the building.

A standard way to understand the motion of the roofline would be to track it frame-by-frame using the many videos of the collapse that were made available to NIST. NIST did not initially do this; at least such analysis is not mentioned in their published report. In the final draft released for public comment, NIST claimed it measured the overall *time* it took for the roofline to move between two points, like starting and stopping a stopwatch. The ending point of NIST's collapse time was when the roofline reached the level of the 29th floor. Their starting point was 5.4 seconds earlier, which one would presume would coincide with the downward motion of the roofline. This they compared with the expected freefall time, which they calculated to be 3.9 seconds. They therefore proclaimed that the collapse time was 40% longer than freefall time.[290]

This was a stunningly invalid and meaningless measurement. The only way to validly compare the motion of the building to the acceleration of gravity is to actually measure the acceleration of the building throughout its collapse. The acceleration is found from the slope of the velocity versus time graph. In mathematical terms, acceleration is the derivative of velocity with respect to time. A valid measurement of acceleration cannot be obtained from two data points unless it is assumed, *a priori*, that the acceleration between those two points is uniform, and it is improper to assume uniform acceleration without a valid reason for doing so.

What NIST did is equivalent to connecting the first and last points on the actual velocity versus time graph, and ignoring everything that happened in between. This is not a valid way to measure what they say they are measuring, yet this was the basis of their initial denial that freefall occurred.

NIST apparently *wanted* to claim that freefall did not occur, because they knew that actual freefall would be a smoking gun for demolition. They also must have known that freefall *did* occur, because it is easily measurable by tracking the roofline, they had access to all the relevant videos, and the scientists at NIST are not incompetent. To cover up the inconvenient fact of freefall, they

WTC 7: A REFUTATION OF NIST ANALYSIS

focused on the deceptive, and completely meaningless notion of "freefall time" and said the collapse time of the building took longer than freefall time. Moreover, to support this deception, they had to falsify the collapse time measurement, as described below.

The ending point of NIST's collapse time measurement is when the roofline reaches the level of the 29th floor. The starting point, 5.4 seconds earlier, which they claimed was the start of downward motion, is during a period of quiescence after the collapse of the East Penthouse, about a second before the beginning of the collapse of the West Penthouse, and about a second and a half before the actual descent of roofline of the main building. It is just plainly dishonest to claim that the collapse time of the main part of the building is 5.4 seconds.

Jeremy Hammond has looked carefully at the question of how NIST measured their collapse time.[291] NIST's measurements are based on a video taken from a camera on West Street near Harrison Street, which they labeled Camera 3. This camera has an upward-looking view from near ground level toward WTC 7. That video shows a kink that develops in the roofline prior to the fall of the building. Other upward-looking views also show this kink. Jeremy did a frame-by-frame comparison of the pixels in the Camera 3 video, trying to reconstruct NIST's measurement. He found that there is actually movement of the roofline that coincides with NIST's start time, but what they were measuring was the development of this kink. He also determined, by comparison with other videos, that the kink was not a vertical dip in the roofline at all, but rather a horizontal fold towards the interior of the building. The simple proof of this is that the fold is visible only when viewed from below. For videos with a line of sight level with the roofline, the roofline stays flat even as it falls to the ground. Since Camera 3 has an upward-angled line of sight, a horizontal fold is indistinguishable from a vertical dip. Furthermore, by choosing a tracking point near the center of the roofline, NIST maximized the ambiguity. It appears that this was the basis of their claim that the downward motion of the roofline began 1.5 seconds before downward motion actually began. The scientists at NIST had access to many videos from different perspectives. They had to be aware that the collapse of the building was a three-dimensional event and that their chosen video had a line of sight that introduced ambiguity into the measurement.

On August 26, 2008 NIST held a technical briefing conference and I was able to ask the following question: "Any number of competent measurements using a variety of methods indicate the northwest corner of WTC 7 fell with an acceleration within a few percent of the acceleration of gravity. Yet your report contradicts this, claiming 40% slower than free fall, based on a single data point [I meant to say two data points]. How can such a publicly visible, easily measurable quantity be set aside?"[292]

Shyam Sunder, NIST's lead investigator, answered that freefall happens when there is no structural resistance. He said that freefall would have taken 3.9 seconds but their model showed it should come down in 5.4 seconds. He also said that the 5.4 seconds of their model was reasonable because there was structural resistance in this case, that there was a series of failures that had to take place, and they were not all simultaneous. However, the question I posed was how the video evidence that freefall actually occurred could be set aside. Sunder's answer is that their *computer model* showed that freefall could not have occurred. That is the substance of his answer. Sunder is elevating their model above the direct physical evidence. That is not science. Sunder's response typifies the entire investigation. NIST substituted computer models for actual physical evidence. Taking the evidence out of the picture insulated them from having to go where the evidence leads.

NIST's model is based on the assumption that WTC 7 came down as a natural collapse due to fire, gravity, and buckling columns. Since their model could not produce a freefall collapse, and since the video evidence shows that freefall actually occurred, their model is wrong, and the assumptions behind their model are wrong. NIST does not acknowledge this or try to account for the discrepancy in any way.

Shyam Sunder, in interviews, has touted the "robustness" of modern modeling software, describing how entire airplanes are designed start-to-finish based on computer models. This is an irrelevant distraction. NIST was not tasked with designing a plane or designing a building. NIST was tasked with an investigation of how a *particular* building *actually* came down. If explosives were used to destroy Building 7, NIST would never discover them in a computer model. Even if the computer model can be made to collapse, it does not mean that is the way the building actually collapsed.

Conclusions drawn from computer models are essentially restatements of the assumptions that were programmed in. NIST could have made their model work if, at a mouse click, eight floors of support, in the model, were suddenly removed, but that would require that the fall of WTC 7 be interpreted as a demolition.

In the August 2008 Final Draft for Public Comment, the strategy was to try to cover up the fact that during a significant portion of collapse, the building underwent freefall acceleration. That strategy didn't work, because the public comments that were submitted let NIST know that many people understood the deception they were attempting to perpetrate on their readers.

In the final report released in November 2008[293], NIST continued to assert that their earlier analysis was correct. The entire original timing analysis is still in the final report. But then they added what they described as a "more detailed" analysis. Using video frame tracking measurements, they computed a velocity versus time graph from which the acceleration was computed as a function of time. They said they were still using the Camera 3 video, so they still had the issue of the ambiguous lateral motion, which made it look as though the downward motion begins sooner and undergoes a more gradual transition into freefall acceleration. They then divided the graph into three stages. The fall of the main part of the building starts in Stage 2 and continues into Stage 3. However they tack on the erroneous early measurements as Stage 1, leading to an overall time for their three stages of 5.4 seconds.

They also did one more thing. They added a straight regression line through their Stage 2 data. They even gave the equation of the line, which shows that the slope is exactly equal to the acceleration of gravity. In other words, NIST admits in the final report that WTC 7 fell in absolute freefall for over 2 seconds.

WTC 7: A REFUTATION OF NIST ANALYSIS

FIGURE 9-1: VELOCITY V. TIME GRAPH FROM NIST FINAL REPORT ON WTC 7

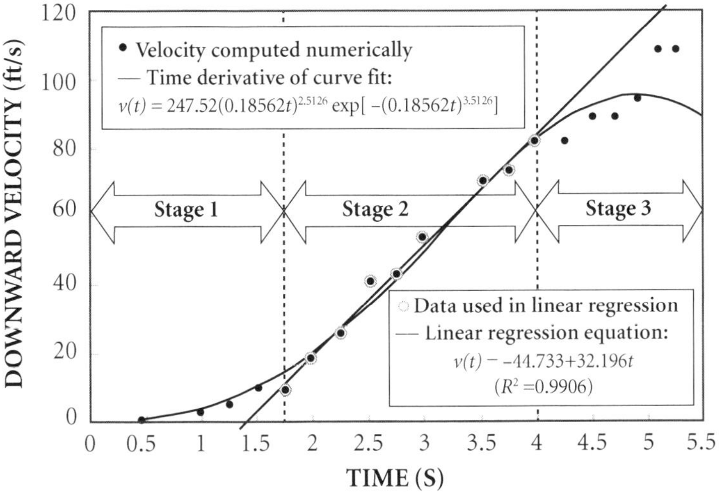

- Velocity computed numerically
- Time derivative of curve fit:
  $v(t) = 247.52(0.18562t)^{2.5126} \exp[-(0.18562t)^{3.5126}]$

Stage 1 | Stage 2 | Stage 3

○ Data used in linear regression
— Linear regression equation:
$v(t) = -44.733 + 32.196t$
($R^2 = 0.9906$)

DOWNWARD VELOCITY (ft/s) vs TIME (S)

Downward velocity of north face roofline as WTC 7 began to collapse

Whether or not the whole process took 5.4 seconds or any other amount of time is irrelevant. Knowing the exact start time of the fall is irrelevant. What really matters is the slope of the graph *during* the fall. The fact that NIST acknowledges 2.25 seconds of absolute freefall acceleration should be the end of the story. Freefall acceleration happened over a significant interval, and NIST has finally admitted it. The straight line on this graph means that NIST acknowledges that WTC 7 came down without resistance and without doing any work for over 100 feet. It means all support over that distance was suddenly removed by something *other than* the falling mass. It literally means the NIST final report confirms that WTC 7 had to have been a demolition. This is what should have been reported in newspaper headlines around the world.

NIST's three stages add up to 5.4 seconds, so in a weasel-worded conclusion they claim their original analysis is vindicated:

"As noted above, the collapse time was approximately 40 percent longer than that of free fall for the first 18 stories of descent. The detailed analysis shows that this increase in time is due primarily to Stage 1. The three stages of collapse progression described above are consistent with the results of the global collapse analyses discussed in Chapter 12 of NIST NCSTAR 1-9."[294]

Their concluding statement is not actually saying the admitted period of *freefall* acceleration is consistent with their collapse analysis. There is nothing in their analysis that justifies a period of freefall. They are saying the overall 5.4 seconds of the three stages taken together is consistent with their analysis.

So, we are back to NIST's two data points connected with a straight line. They simply ignore the very real period of freefall, point instead to their artificial 5.4 second construct, and then they walk away from it.

In interviews and other appearances, Shyam Sunder has attempted to minimize the significance of the freefall observation by discounting the visible collapse as seen in videos. He claims that the interior had already collapsed and what we are seeing is just the "facade" of the building. (Note, by the way, that what Sunder calls a facade is actually a load-bearing wall.)

Of course we are seeing only the surface, but what can be seen on the surface contains evidence about what lies behind. If there were an internal collapse ahead of time, the falling beams and girders would apply torques to the exterior walls, which would have created visible distortions. If the interior collapse could propagate the length of the building, why didn't it propagate to the much closer exterior walls of the building and therefore become visible?

The structure was rigid right up until a fraction of a second before global collapse. Then there was a clear transition point where the structure literally went limp. This occurred suddenly, just before it started to fall. The windows under the East Penthouse broke when the East Penthouse fell into the building, but no more window breakage occurred until after the building began to fall. Had the bulk of the interior collapsed ahead of time as NIST claims, we would have seen the same external signs we saw in the smaller, earlier collapse of the East Penthouse. Likewise, the West Penthouse was fully supported by interior columns right up to about a half second before global collapse. When the West Penthouse did collapse, it fell only about half its height before the rest of the building joined it in freefall. The West Penthouse remained partially visible throughout the freefall interval.

When the building fell there were roiling clouds of debris that raced down the street, which some have likened to volcanic pyroclastic flow. The release of these debris-laden clouds was simultaneous with the visible collapse. Had the bulk of the building collapsed earlier, with just a visible facade left to fall, the debris clouds would have occurred earlier.

Remember the context of this separation of interior and exterior collapse: Sunder is trying to justify the observation of freefall. He is claiming the "real" collapse occurred as their model predicted, slower than freefall, and that what we can see from the exterior was merely a thin shell, so supposedly its freefall is inconsequential. As suggested above, this entire construct is false.

However, even assuming the construct is not false, and that only a facade remained, the exterior columns would have retained their full strength, but without the load. They would be expected to remain, perhaps many seconds, swaying, tipping, then buckling one-by-one, much as happened to the straggler columns in the North Tower of the WTC following its collapse. The simultaneous, straight-down freefall of a postulated thin veneer wall would be even more mysterious than the freefall of the loaded structure.

All of this is a fantasy, of course. The entire building fell nearly simultaneously with the West Penthouse, with accompanying window breakage and simultaneous release of a massive debris cloud. NIST has no escape from freefall acceleration of the entire structure.

The NIST WTC 7 report has never been peer reviewed. There has been no transparent public forum for critiquing or correcting the final report. It does not constitute science. It is instead an authoritarian declaration by a government agency that has repeatedly demonstrated its unwillingness to consider the one hypothesis that could account for all of the observations – explosive demolition. The fact that NIST attempted to deny the obvious freefall acceleration, then attempted to hide their *acknowledgment* of freefall in a transparently false construct, together with the fact that they used an inappropriate camera angles and inappropriate analytical methodology, all point to NIST's role in furthering a criminal cover-up.

Conclusion

The most significant fact in all this is that we have measured and NIST has reluctantly confirmed that WTC 7 went through a significant period of freefall.

- Dynamically, this means all column support was suddenly and simultaneously eliminated.
- Practically, this means this was an intentional demolition, and that it had to have been planned and set up in advance of 9/11.
- Politically and sociologically, given the extreme security consciousness of the agencies that occupied in the building, the only way the building could be prepared for demolition would be through deep insider connections.
- Ultimately, this means that the insiders who were involved in planning and executing the demolition of WTC 7 on 9/11 had to be in coordination with the entire event of 9/11, including the demolitions of the Twin Towers, the airplane hijackings, and the subsequent cover-up.

CHAPTER TEN

Evidence for Extreme Temperatures at the World Trade Center

BY KEVIN R. RYAN

THERE IS SIGNIFICANT EVIDENCE THAT HAS BEEN UNCOVered over the last ten years related to the existence of unusually high temperatures at the World Trade Center, both during the destruction of the three buildings and afterward for several months.

Much of the evidence has been catalogued in two peer-reviewed scientific papers. One of these papers is called "Extremely High temperatures during the WTC destruction," and it was published online at the Journal of 9/11 Studies in January, 2008.[295]

The authors included four PhD physicists, one PhD chemist and several others including me. The second of the two papers is called "Environmental Anomalies at the WTC, evidence for energetic materials," and it was published both online and in print by a Springer journal called The Environmentalist in 2008.[296] The authors include myself and two of my colleagues.

The first paper discusses the maximum temperatures that were cited by the National Institute of Standards and Technology (or NIST) at the WTC. In its report on the WTC destruction, NIST reported gas temperatures as high as 1000 °C. It is important to note that these are gas temperatures, not the temperatures of solid materials.

Others who have publicly supported the fire-induced collapse hypotheses for the WTC buildings, such as Professor Thomas Eagar of MIT, have suggested the same maximum temperature while still others have proposed that a slightly higher gas temperature of 1100 °C might theoretically have existed.

One problem with the maximum temperatures cited by officials is that there are many eyewitnesses who claimed to see molten metal at the WTC. Approximately 1000 °C cannot melt the steel in the WTC buildings. Just a few of the eyewitness statements regarding molten metal can be found below. The first one is from a man who worked for John Skilling, the design engineer of the WTC towers.

> "There was a 'river of steel flowing' at the B1 level of the WTC debris pile."
> – Leslie Robertson[297]

> "Going below, it was smoky and really hot… The debris past the columns was red-hot, molten, running."
> – Richard Garlock, Structural Engineer / LERA

EVIDENCE FOR EXTREME TEMPERATURES AT THE WORLD TRADE CENTER

"I talked to many contractors and they said they actually saw molten metal trapped, beams had just totally been melted because of the heat."
– Herb Trimpe, Chaplain at Ground Zero

"[I was shown slides of] molten metal, which was still red hot weeks after the event."
– Dr. Keith Eaton of Institute of Structural Engineers

"In some pockets now being uncovered they are finding molten steel."
– Dr. Alison Geyh, Johns Hopkins School of Public Health

"[I] saw pools of literally molten steel"
– Peter Tully, president of Tully Construction

"Feeling the heat, seeing the molten steel, the layers upon layers of ash, like lava, it reminded me of Mt. St. Helens… Shards of steel lay upon shards of steel, shifting and unstable, uncovering red hot metal beams excavated from deep beneath layers of subfloors."
– Ron Burger, structural engineer

"A fire truck 10 feet below the ground that was still burning two weeks after the Tower collapsed, its metal so hot that it looked like a vat of molten steel."
– Vance Deisingnore, ASHA Officer at the WTC, reporting to Jim McKay, Post-Gazette Staff Writer, on Sept 11, 2002

"I saw melting of girders in World Trade Center"
– Abolhassan Astaneh-Asi, the first structural engineer given access to the WTC steel via a National Science Foundation Grant

"You get down below and you'd see molten steel – molten steel running down the channel rail, like you're in a foundry, like lava."
– FDNY Fire Department Captain

NIST ignored all of these witness statements about molten metal in reporting maximum temperatures of 1000 °C.

There are also photographs that show bright orange and yellow molten metal pouring from the south tower, and being pulled from the debris pile at ground zero. NIST said that they found no evidence of molten metal, but also said if molten metal had been present, it would have had to have been aluminum from the plane. The molten metal could not have been molten aluminum, as molten iron or steel is yellow/orange, and molten aluminum is silvery gray when poured in daylight. Experimental demonstrations have been done to show this, which can be found at The Journal of 9/11 Studies.

The temperature required to melt steel (1538 °C) is far above the maximum gas temperature cited in the official report (1000 °C). In a structural fire, steel temperatures lag behind gas temperatures for a number of reasons, including the thermal conductivity of steel, the effects of convection, and the fireproofing that is applied. Achieving a *steel temperature* of 1538 °C at the WTC would require *gas temperatures* that are well above 1538 °C and far above the maximum of 1000 °C cited in the NIST report.

EVIDENCE FOR EXTREME TEMPERATURES AT THE WORLD TRADE CENTER

When the temperatures cited in the NIST report are achieved, for example in a testing furnace when the air temperature is raised quickly and held at 1,000 °C and heat is not conducted away by a large building structure, it takes approximately two hours for protected steel to reach just 600°C, which is still below the melting temperature of most forms of aluminum.[298] And obviously the steel temperatures cannot exceed the gas temperatures in such an environment, to produce molten iron or steel. These facts demonstrate that the NIST reports do not address the evidence.

I have seen evidence of the previously molten metal at the WTC myself, in the form of metallic microspheres that I have found in all of the nearly dozen WTC dust samples I have examined. Photomicrographs of the first examples that I received, in 2007, are published online.[299]

I extracted the particles from a sample of WTC dust that had been given to me by someone who was at Ground Zero after the destruction of the buildings. Dr. Steven Jones of Brigham Young University had been examining WTC dust samples as well and I was interested in seeing for myself what he had seen.

After realizing that such findings could be used in a legal proceeding at some point in the future, my colleagues and I began asking that samples collected by these independent sources be accompanied by documentation that recorded the time, date and other necessary information including sample location. Each sample was provided with this information as well as the signature of the collector and sometimes a witness as well. The process evolved into the use of a standard chain of custody form similar to that which I have used for many years in my experience as a laboratory manager.

I have extracted the metallic microspheres and other paramagnetic particles from the dust in several ways. One way is to slide a magnet along the side of the bag containing the dust and capture what is attracted with a spatula. Another way is to place a stronger magnet into a plastic bag and insert that bag into the dust sample. Removing the bagged magnet and inverting the bag allows the particles to be captured.

It is interesting to note that the United States Environmental Protection Agency (or EPA) once considered using iron microspheres as a signature characteristic to identify WTC dust.[300] For an unknown reason, EPA decided to not designate the iron spheres as a signature characteristic of WTC dust, despite the fact that it was known to be an unusual identifying characteristic of that dust.

The first paper mentioned above begins with a discussion of such metallic microspheres, as well as the finding of semi-transparent, silicate-rich microspheres. Two independently collected samples were received for this study. Both samples were collected indoors and shortly after the 9/11/2001 event. One sample was collected on an indoor window sill on 9/14/2001, just three days after the disaster while the search for survivors in the rubble was ongoing, in a building four blocks from ground zero. The other sample was acquired inside a fourth-floor apartment, whose upper windows broke during the WTC collapse, a few days later.

An important point to recognize is that the presence of these metallic and silicate microspheres, as well as much more such evidence, had already been reported by other independent researchers apart from the US EPA. The RJ Lee Group was one of those independent groups. RJ Lee is a corporation specializing in industrial forensics. It was hired by lawyers for Deutsche Bank to

EVIDENCE FOR EXTREME TEMPERATURES AT THE WORLD TRADE CENTER

characterize the WTC dust as the Deutsche Bank building, located at Ground Zero, was being assessed after 9/11.[301]

RJ Lee produced a report that corroborates and expands upon the findings of our research group.

The second independent group to have corroborated our findings was the United States Geological Survey (USGS), which is a federal source for science about the Earth, its natural and living resources, natural hazards, and the environment. USGS coordinated an interdisciplinary environmental characterization of the entire area around the WTC after 9/11.

RJ Lee reported that the quantity of iron spheres in the WTC dust was 5.87%. This is an enormous amount relative to what is found in typical dust samples from office buildings. In fact, RJ Lee reported that it is 150 times as much.

The spherical shape of the particles indicates that they were at one time molten (liquid) metal. As with water falling or spraying through air, molten metal forms spheres due to surface tension. The cohesive forces between liquid molecules are responsible for this. When a liquid is falling or sprayed through the air, the molecules at the surface do not have other like molecules on all sides of them and consequently they cohere more strongly to those directly associated with them on the surface. This forces liquid surfaces to contract to the minimal area.

The WTC dust spheres indicate not only that the iron or silicate was molten at one point, but that, due to the small size of the spheres, a violent disturbance of some kind would have been necessary to shatter molten metal into the sizes seen. Various explosive or incendiary processes are likely explanations.

The RJ Lee report says that lead was melted and that such particles are absent in typical office dust.

"Various metals (most notably iron and lead) were melted during the WTC Event, producing spherical metallic particles. ... high heat exposure of the WTC Dust has also created ... spherical, vesicular siliceous [silicate particles] and [these]...are classic examples of high temperature or combustion by-products and are generally absent in typical office dust..."[302]

Surprisingly, these researchers also reported that alumino-silicates were evaporated at the WTC, as indicated by the Swiss cheese appearance of some of the particles examined in the dust.

RJ Lee also reported a "vesicular alumino-silicate particle" which exemplifies a "round open porous structure having a Swiss cheese appearance as a result of boiling and evaporation".[303]

The United States Geological Survey found the same iron and silicate spheres throughout the WTC dust and could not find an explanation.

Two members of our research team submitted a Freedom of Information Act request to the USGS for any other information that might not have been reported. To our surprise, the USGS responded with data showing that their group had found molybdenum microspheres in the WTC dust. The presence of these molybdenum spheres indicates that there was molten molybdenum at the WTC site. The temperature required to melt molybdenum is 2,623 °C.

Our research team, led by Dr. Steven Jones and Dr. Jeffrey Farrer at Brigham Young University, analyzed the metallic microspheres we found in the WTC dust by a technique called X-ray Energy Dispersive Spectroscopy, or XEDS. This is a technique

EVIDENCE FOR EXTREME TEMPERATURES AT THE WORLD TRADE CENTER

that provided the elemental composition of the spheres. In other words, it told us what elements the spheres were composed of. The result was that the spheres we found were very high in iron and low in other elements. This agreed with the findings of the RJ Lee group.

The discoveries related to these high temperatures continued. RJ Lee further reported that lead had not only melted, it had "volatilized." That is, lead had actually vaporized at the WTC, according to the RJ Lee research report, which said: "The presence of lead oxide on the surface of mineral wool indicates the existence of extremely high temperatures during the collapse which caused metallic lead to volatilize, oxidize, and finally condense on the surface of the mineral wool."

The RJ Lee report further stated – "Some particles show evidence of being exposed to a conflagration such as spherical metals and silicates, and vesicular particles." A vesicular formation is a round open porous structure having a Swiss cheese appearance as a result of boiling and evaporation. These kinds of vesicular formations are abundant in particles extracted from WTC dust samples.

The most important point of all this is that the official US government investigators into the WTC disaster reported gas temperatures that were far lower than what would be required to explain these findings from RJ Lee, the USGS, and our research team.

As shown in Table 10-1 on the following page, the temperatures required to melt iron, vaporize lead, melt molybdenum, and vaporize alumino-silicates give evidence for an environment at the WTC that was nearly two thousand degrees hotter than what official investigators have reported as maximum gas temperatures.

TABLE 10-1: TEMPERATURES REQUIRED BASED ON THE EVIDENCE

Process and material	°C	°F
To melt iron (spherule formation)	1,538	2,800
To vaporize lead	1,740	3,164
To melt molybdenum	2,623	4,753
To vaporize aluminosilicates	2,760	5,000

More corroboration for these findings is found in the official US government report that preceded the current one published by NIST. The first report was from the Federal Emergency Management Administration (FEMA). Appendix C of the FEMA WTC report provided strong evidence of extremely high temperatures at the WTC, in the form of highly corroded and eroded steel samples saved from the buildings that had been destroyed.[304]

FEMA described samples of steel that had been thinned to razor-sharpness. In some cases there were inexplicable holes in the steel. The fire engineering professors who found these samples could not come up with an explanation for it. They also could not explain the sulfidation of the steel. That is, steel had been chemically changed at the micro-structural level in ways that indicated a chemical eutectic mixture had been achieved between sulfur, iron and oxygen, causing the steel to melt.

The New York Times called these findings "the deepest mystery uncovered in the [WTC] investigation."[305] That mystery has never been officially solved and the related evidence was completely ignored by NIST.

EVIDENCE FOR EXTREME TEMPERATURES AT THE WORLD TRADE CENTER

Other evidence for extremely high temperatures at the WTC site includes the finding of fused metal and concrete artifacts like the "meteorite", and also thermal hot spots measured by a NASA remote sensing instrument that measures temperature via electromagnetic radiation emitted from the ground. Surface temperatures in the debris piles were found to be as high as 750 °C (or 1350 °F) a week after 9/11.

There is an explanation available for all this officially unexplained evidence. This explanation is that the thermite reaction was present and occurring at the WTC on 9/11 and afterward, in the pile at Ground Zero. The thermite reaction is an extremely exothermic chemical reaction between aluminum powder and a metal oxide. The metal oxide is typically iron oxide but copper oxide, molybdenum oxide and vanadium oxide are also used, among others.

The temperature at which thermite burns approaches 3,000 °C for some mixtures, which would explain the evidence for high temperatures described above. The reaction products of an aluminum/iron oxide thermite mixture are molten iron, and aluminum oxide, which quickly forms a white dust cloud as it cools. Additives like sulfur improve the burn properties of thermite. A sulfur-containing thermite, which is called thermate, would explain the evidence found by the FEMA investigators.

The color of the molten iron product from thermite reactions is yellow-orange, just like the photos of molten metal witnessed at the WTC. The photographs of molten metal at the WTC, pouring from the south tower and found in the debris pile, exhibit the yellow-orange color, unlike molten aluminum, which is silvery gray when poured in the daylight.

Even though a thermite reaction is a good explanation for the molten iron, some have suggested that it is an innocuous explanation because there was aluminum in the planes and rusty metal (or iron oxide) in the buildings. Such claims suggest that innocent components of the buildings and planes coming together might have caused the thermite reaction to occur.

Unlike NIST, however, we actually tested that hypothesis. A colleague of Dr. Steven Jones poured molten aluminum over a rusty steel rail and found that the thermite reaction will not occur in that scenario. This was expected because thermite mixtures are powders mixed in an exact ratio and require a high temperature ignition device to ignite.

Of course, the "natural thermite" hypothesis would also fail to explain the molten molybdenum found by USGS and the RJ Lee group.

The second of the two peer-reviewed scientific articles referred to above focuses on air emissions data produced by EPA and the University of California Davis. Before going into the environmental data, the paper reviews some important facts about the environment at ground zero in the days, weeks and months after 9/11. The fires at ground zero could not be put out, and continued to burn in one place or another throughout the pile for months, even into February 2002.

This was despite the fact that:

- Several inches of dust covered the entire area after the destruction of the WTC buildings.
- Millions of gallons of water were sprayed onto the debris pile.
- Several rainfall events occurred at the site, some heavy.

EVIDENCE FOR EXTREME TEMPERATURES AT THE WORLD TRADE CENTER

- A chemical fire suppressant called Pyrocool was pumped into the piles, but had no effect.[306]

Such characteristics are not typical of structure fires and cannot be explained by typical office fire phenomena.

The EPA data discussed in the paper was released to my local investigative group, which is called the 9/11 Working Group of Bloomington. This data shows certain patterns of extreme emissions occurring at the WTC site. Figure 10-1 shows an example of those unusual patterns. These five chemicals, all of the type called volatile organic compounds or VOCs, exhibited spikes in detection on the same dates.

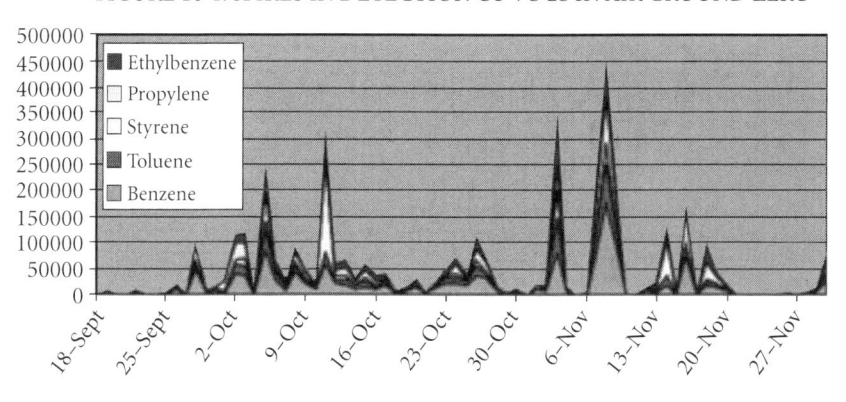

FIGURE 10-1: SPIKES IN DETECTION OF VOCS IN AIR GROUND ZERO

All of these compounds were emitted into the air at high levels on the dates given. These chemicals are the byproducts of the combustion of plastics, which often burn only partially in a fire.

The levels at which these VOCs were seen at the WTC site were unprecedented. As an example, consider that benzene has been seen at levels as high as 26 parts per billion (ppb) in structure fires. Benzene is also seen in high-traffic areas of urban settings, with mean levels of 4 ppb. At the WTC site, benzene was detected in bursts of 80,000 ppb and higher.

These VOC levels indicate that plastics and other organic materials were burning to completion and doing so very rapidly within the pile at ground zero.

Similar spikes in other chemical compounds were seen. Specifically, there were spikes in detection of iron, aluminum, and compounds of silicon and sulfur. There were also spikes in detection of rare metals, like vanadium, and an unusual synthetic organic chemical called 1,3-diphenylpropane (1,3-DPP).

The EPA noted that it had never before seen 1,3-DPP in any of its environmental testing. Erik Swartz, a research scientist at EPA, noted that 1,3-DPP was pervasive and was found at levels that "dwarfed all others."[307] One use of 1,3-DPP is to stabilize the structure of nanocomposite materials.[308]

The EPA findings were corroborated by aerosol data produced by a team from the University of California Davis near the WTC site in October 2001. The UC Davis data exhibited spikes in the detection of silicon compounds as well as aluminum and iron compounds.

When publishing their results, the UC Davis team noted several problems could not be explained. They reported as follows:

- We see very fine aerosols typical of combustion temperatures far higher than [expected in] the WTC collapse piles.
- We see some elements abundantly and others hardly at all, despite similar abundances in the collapse dust.
- We see organic species in the very fine mode that would not survive high temperatures.[309]

EVIDENCE FOR EXTREME TEMPERATURES AT THE WORLD TRADE CENTER

These data are compelling when one considers that there is a form of thermite that contains silicon compounds and organic materials. This material is sometimes referred to as nanothermite or superthermite. And although this essay does not go into the discovery of nanothermite at the WTC, which is discussed elsewhere in this volume, we should recognize two facts.

First, the compounds detected at the WTC site, in spikes and at extreme levels, indicate the presence of violent fires occurring on specific dates. These compounds also match well with sulfur-containing thermate and/or with nanothermite. Secondly, the official investigators are not willing to examine or even discuss these data.

I have made nanothermite myself, via formulations published by U.S. national research laboratories, and I have ignited that nanothermite. When we look at the ignition residues, they are strikingly similar in appearance to WTC dust particles that were extracted with a magnet. Both are the same colors, and show the same metallic microspheres. Both also exhibit the same kind of relative size and vesicular formations that suggest high temperature reactions or explosive effects.

There are two more important points of evidence relating to the high temperatures at the WTC site. The first is that the huge dust cloud that arose from the destruction of the buildings was similar to that of a volcano. In other words, it was pyroclastic-like and appeared to be driven by energy sources that exceeded the energy available from a simple gravitational collapse. Calculations by researcher Jim Hoffman, based on photographs of the size and distribution of the clouds, have confirmed that the energy is not accounted for by gravitational effects alone.[310]

Another striking fact is that the dust cloud was very hot and was burning people and setting objects on fire. In the public domain, there are photos of the many vehicles that were set on fire or burned in the area.

Paul Curran, a member of the New York City Fire Patrol, was asked what he thought was the cause of these vehicle fires. Curran responded:

> "I believe it must have been from the debris falling and the heat just started hitting the cars and starting cars on fire. There were an awful lot of cars burning, an awful lot. It had to be radiated heat or just stuff falling on cars and setting them on fire. There were numerous cars burning, numerous."

There were also many witnesses to the cloud being very hot and burning people as it passed by. The following are excerpts from some of their testimonies:

> "Then the dust cloud hits us. Then it got real hot. It felt like it was going to light up almost."
> **– Thomas Spinard, FDNY Engine 7**

> "A wave – a hot, solid, black wave of heat threw me down the block."
> **– David Handschuh, New York's Daily News**

> "…the hot billowing cloud of death chasing us through the narrow streets of lower Manhattan"
> **– Andred Fagan**

> "When I was running, some hot stuff went down my back, because I didn't have time to put my coat back on, and I had

EVIDENCE FOR EXTREME TEMPERATURES AT THE WORLD TRADE CENTER

some – well, I guess between first and second degree burns on my back."
– Marcel Claes, FDNY Firefighter

"I was running, and stuff was coming down. This time fire was coming down, because I could feel the heat. I grabbed a firefighter's turnout coat that just seemed to be in front of me. I grabbed it. I threw it over my shoulders. I didn't make it much further than that. …It was really hot, because this time there was fire. I know that because my neck burned."
– Louis Cook, FDNY Paramedic Division

"By the time it took me to break the back window of the SUV my safety coat was already on fire, my socks were on fire."
– Ronald Thomas Coyne, EMT Battalion 44

"Sal ran west somewhere and got blown off, got burnt on the back of his back."
– James Curran, FDNY

"…and then we're engulfed in the smoke, which was horrendous. One thing I remember, it was hot. The smoke was hot and that scared me"
– Paramedic, Manuel Delgado

"I remember making it into the tunnel and it was this incredible amount of wind, debris, heat…."
– Brian Fitzpatrick, FDNY Firefighter

"A huge, huge blast of hot wind gusting and smoke and dust and all kinds of debris hit me."
– Firefighter, Louis Giaconelli

"This super hot wind blew and it just got dark as night and you couldn't breathe."
– **Firefighter Todd Heaney**

"The whole block I think was on fire. All the parked cars were on fire. There were a couple of firemen hooked up right to a hydrant fighting the car fires."
– **Firefighter, Peter Giammarino**

As for the air emissions, many courageous people responded to the tragedy in New York by working to search for survivors, clean up the site, and get lower Manhattan back into working order. Thousands of these people have become sick and are dying from the exposure to that environment. The US government ignored them for many years but finally passed a bill last year providing limited medical support.

The unavoidable conclusion is that there is a great deal of evidence for the presence of unusually high temperatures at the WTC site on 9/11 and in the months afterward.

CHAPTER ELEVEN

The Official Collapse Narrative and the Experimental Method

BY JONATHAN H. COLE, P.E.

How did the Twin Towers fall down?

THE ANSWER TO THE QUESTION OF HOW THE TWIN TOWers fell down depends on when the question was asked. On the day of the event, recall what the news said live, as we watched those terrible events unfold:

" … huge explosion that we all heard … "
– LIVE FOX News Alert

" …and another explosion … "
– CNN

"We presume because of the initial explosion that there may have been secondary explosions as well that were detonated in the building by these terrorists."
– NBC4, Tom Brokaw

"The entire building has just collapsed as if a demolition team set off; when you see the old demolitions of the old buildings; it pulled it down on itself and it is not there anymore."
– ABC News

"Um … if you wish to bring … anybody who has ever watched a building being demolished on purpose knows that if you're going to do this you have to get at the …at the under infrastructure of a building and bring it down."
– ABC Live Coverage, Peter Jennings

" … an enormous explosion now in the remaining World Trade …"
– CNBC, Mark Haines

"It happened the same way, the explosion started high in the building and worked its way down. There, you see the building imploding. It… it…do you see what's happening? I think we're safe, I think I'm on safe ground Bill, I don't think… this was clearly…the…the way the structure is collapsing…this was the result of something that was planned. This is…it's not accidental, that the first tower just happened to collapse and then the second tower just happened to collapse in exactly the same way.
– CNBC, Mark Haines

Well over a hundred eyewitnesses heard explosions at the World Trade Center – not the explosions due to the impact of the planes, but additional, secondary explosions. So on the very day of the event, had you had asked "Why did those towers fall?" the answer was clear that day: the towers were brought down with explosives.

THE OFFICIAL COLLAPSE NARRATIVE
AND THE EXPERIMENTAL METHOD

The Floor by Floor "Pancake" Collapse

Several of our institutions and media experts later presented the "floor by floor" progressive "Pancake Collapse" Theory. PBS, with its popular NOVA program *Why the Towers Fell* explained:

The heat of the fire would have softened both the floor trusses and the outer columns they were attached to. When the steel became weak the trusses would have collapsed. And without the trusses to keep them rigidly in place, the columns would have bent outward and then failed. Once the trusses failed, the floors they were holding cascade down with a force too great to be withstood. The result is what's called a progressive collapse, as each floor pancakes down onto the one below.

NOVA did not show the actual video of the towers' destruction. Rather, they used an animation of the floors without the towers' perimeter columns so that it appeared as if the floors were floating in space around the central core columns. Yet even with their simulation, the central core columns remained standing after the floors pancaked. How those core columns ultimately fell remained unexplained by NOVA.

The phenomena we observed when the towers fell did not match the animations presented to the public by NOVA. For example, entire floor systems did not collapse straight down on the one below. Rather, we observed only portions of the floors being demolished, racing well ahead of the balance of the floors. In addition, we observed much of each tower's mass being blown outward and away from the lower floors, so much of upper mass could not possibly have impacted the underlying floors.

The strong inner core columns of the Twin Towers were cross-braced and could stand on their own. Videos show much of the core standing well after the majority of the floors were demolished, and then eventually they too fell straight down. This straight down fall of the "spire", or inner core columns, remained unexplained with the "Pancake Collapse" Theory.

And when we observe other building collapses that have indeed "pancaked," for example from earthquakes, we clearly see stacks of floors in the rubble.

New Zealand earthquake collapse clearly indicating pancaked floors

Yet, there were no stacks of floors observed at Ground Zero. This Pancake Theory still persists today even though the NIST, after years of study and millions of dollars, concluded: *"NIST findings do not support the 'Pancake' Theory of collapse which is premised on a progressive failure on the floor systems in the WTC Towers."*[311]

THE OFFICIAL COLLAPSE NARRATIVE
AND THE EXPERIMENTAL METHOD

The "Pile Driver" Collapse

Others besides NIST also disagreed with the Pancake Theory. Some claimed it was a "Pile Driver" collapse.

Professor Zdenek Bazant and others published a series of scientific papers replete with equations purporting to describe how the upper top "block" of floors crushed the lower, larger section down to the ground, and then, that upper block crushed itself back up.

SCENARIO OF PROGRESSIVE COLLAPSE AT THE WORLD TRADE CENTER TOWERS

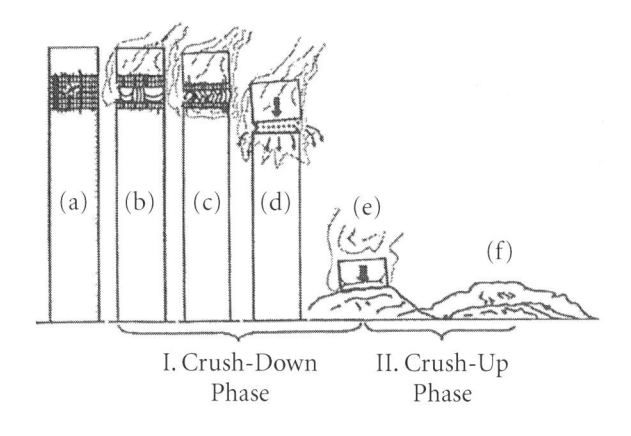

(a) (b) (c) (d) (e) (f)

I. Crush-Down Phase   II. Crush-Up Phase

Like the Pancake Theory, this Pile Driver Theory neglected to explain how that upper block fell through those inner core columns, or why the "spire" of core columns remained standing for a few seconds and then fell straight down.

In addition, no one observed or recorded this upper block crushing all the way to the ground or the remarkable crush-up phase. Again, much of the falling debris was blown well outside the underlying tower so that material could not have possibly impacted the lower undamaged structure.

The Pile Driver Theory's crush-down crush-up scenario ignores Newton's Third Law, which holds that *for every action there is an opposite and equal reaction*. How, then, can a smaller top block, acting by gravity alone, crush a larger stronger lower block without also destroying itself well before it could destroy the entire lower larger block?

NEWTON'S THIRD LAW

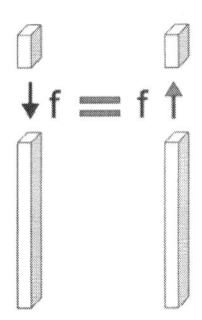

$$\downarrow f = f \uparrow$$

For every action there is an equal and opposite reaction

The core of the Scientific Method is to test the hypothesis by experiment for confirmation. The critical "experiment" step in the scientific method demonstrates what actually happens in the real world, because experimental results are governed only by the laws of physics. The best hypothesis is the hypothesis that addresses the most evidence, and can be confirmed by a repeatable experiment. Richard Feynman, the Nobel Prize winning physicist, understood that many beautiful theories regardless of their elegance or complexity are invalid if not proved by real world experiments.

THE OFFICIAL COLLAPSE NARRATIVE AND THE EXPERIMENTAL METHOD

To test this Pile Driver Theory, I conducted several rudimentary experiments that attempted to demonstrate the principal of this crush-down crush-up hypothesis. The experiments were not an attempt to recreate the towers' collapses. Instead, they were intended to test how similar materials would behave when they impact under the force of gravity alone.

The experiment was relatively simple. I would drop one concrete block onto a stack of several concrete blocks. Not one repetition of this experiment resulted in the block that was dropped destroying the entire stack of blocks. Instead, the falling block damaged the top block and damaged itself, directly in line with what one would expect from Newton's Third Law. Therefore, my experiment failed to support the Pile Driver Theory of falling objects. And so far, no other real world experiment, regardless of its sophistication, has been able to demonstrate this remarkable crush-down crush-up aspect of the Pile Driver Theory.

Since the Pile Driver hypothesis concept has yet to be verified by any real world experiment, and just the opposite has been demonstrated…it's wrong.

The Mysterious 'Eutectic Steel'

Jonathan Barnett, a fire professor from Worchester Polytechnic Institute was surprised to find some unique pieces of steel at Ground Zero that had intergranular melting. The New York Times said it was "…*perhaps the deepest mystery uncovered in the investigation.*" Since office and jet fuel fires cannot melt steel, what heat caused these pieces of steel to melt?

Other professors at WPI did an analysis on this steel and found that it had been attacked by a eutectic mixture that included sulfur. The FEMA Report, which included those professors' findings in its Appendix C, said: *"No clear explanation for the source of the sulfur has been identified."* So the critical question was: *Where did that sulfur come from?*

The voluminous official NIST study, taking years to complete, never answered that question. Institutional experts from other universities did attempt to answer it. Dr. Frank Greening published a research paper, which concluded

> *"that sulfur emissions...were relatively small compared to those involving diesel fuel...and CaSO4 in gypsum wallboard..."*

The BBC corporate media experts agreed saying:

> *"The sulfur came from masses of gypsum wallboard that was pulverized and burned in the fires."*

However, gypsum wallboard is commonly used to protect steel from fire, not attack it. Despite this incongruence, the gypsum explanation for the creation of sulfur stuck, even though no experiments were ever conducted to verify such bold conclusions.

Realizing that an experiment could be conducted relatively simply, I decided to undertake this task. Using a structural steel beam, I surrounded it with crushed concrete, gypsum wallboard, diesel fuel, plastics and aluminum to simulate the materials available in the WTC fires. I then placed it in a fire and fed that fire with ample fuel, driving the temperatures high enough to make the steel beam glow red and melt aluminum. The fire burned for over 24 hours, and later the steel was exposed. Despite the long duration of exposure to high temperatures, no intergranular melting was observed at all. Rather, the steel was still very sound and serviceable.

THE OFFICIAL COLLAPSE NARRATIVE AND THE EXPERIMENTAL METHOD

After I posted a video showing my experiments and its results, titled *"9/11 Experiments: The Mysterious Eutectic Steel"* to YouTube, Dr. Greening admitted:

> *"I am prepared to admit that my initial proposal of how the steel was sulfided during the 9/11 events needs to be modified. Certainly it looks like diesel fuel, gypsum, concrete and aluminum alone are not going to do it."*

Yet even after this experiment and admission by Dr. Greening, there are still some who ignore the scientific method and still claim today that only typical office materials burning caused the steel to melt. Dave Thomas, in the July/August 2011 issue of the *Skeptical Enquirer Magazine*, stated:

> *"This occurred because sulfur released from burned drywall corroded the steel as it stewed in the pile for weeks."*

To-date, no experiment with diesel fuel and wallboard can replicate this intergranular melting, and that awkward question for the official story still remains unanswered today: *Where did the sulfur come from?*

Can Thermitic Material Melt Steel?

In an effort to explain what was never explained by NIST or FEMA, namely the sulfur source which caused the intergranular melting, the flowing metal observed pouring from the South Tower minutes before its demise, and that high percentage of iron-rich microspheres found by the USGS in the dust, independent scientists have pointed out that all of this evidence could easily be explained as a result of a thermitic reaction.

Thermite is a specific mixture of iron oxide and powdered aluminum, and thermate includes just the right percentages of thermite, mixed with sulfur and other chemicals. It is the added sulfur that helps form a eutectic that lowers the melting point of steel. Thermite has been used for welding railroad tracks and destroying military arms for years. Moreover, the natural byproducts of a thermitic reaction include iron microspheres.

The suggestion of some type of thermitic material being used in part to destroy the twin towers did not fit well with the official explanation, so it was ignored in the NIST and FEMA/ASCE reports. To counter this suggestion, the scientific arm of the corporate media conglomerates attempted to discredit the thermite reasoning by conducting their own experiments, which were intended to downplay thermite's capability to melt or cut steel.

The National Geographic Channel, using New Mexico Tech University experts, provided experimental "proof" that thermitic material could not have been used to demolish the Twin Towers because large quantities of thermite cannot cut or even melt a steel column. National Geographic and its experts premised their experiment by stating

> "If thermite melts through [a] steel column, the theory of a thermite controlled demolition may have some validity."

They then posed a simple question to the viewer:

> "Can thermite of any type burn through steel beams?"

By inference, if the thermite won't melt the steel column in their experiment, the viewer can assume that the theory of thermite controlled demolition has no validity.

THE OFFICIAL COLLAPSE NARRATIVE
AND THE EXPERIMENTAL METHOD

Their experiment used 175 pounds of thermite powder surrounding a steel column, held in place by steel plates shaped like a funnel against the column. Although the thermite reacted with an eruption of smoke, intense bright light and tremendous heat, the column remained virtually undamaged after the experiment. Accordingly, an average viewer could now conclude that thermite must not have been used, since the National Geographic experiment, conducted by trusted experts, "proved" that thermite could not even damage the tiny steel column used in their experiment. It could then be assumed that thermite could not harm the massive box columns that supported the towers.

Although the experimental television show Mythbusters refuses to discuss the events of 9/11 on its website, they reinforced this notion that it would take massive amounts of thermite to do any real damage. They ignited 1000 pounds of thermite in an attempt to cut a car in half. But even with all that thermite, it barely managed to melt through the car's thin metal roof.

In addition, websites referenced by many supporting the official 9/11 story have said:

> "The thermite would have also needed to cut sideways. Not an easy feat for thermite. You see, it's a powder, which burns chaotically. Maybe with some device but no working device has been proven to me to work to cut a vertical column."

The results of the National Geographic and Mythbusters experiments, along with the official story-supporting websites, leave the public believing that:

- Thermite cannot melt steel.
- Thermite cannot cut a column, horizontally or vertically.

- It would take a large amount of thermitic material to do any real damage to a steel beam.

I decided to conduct my own experiments to see if the above conclusions were correct.

The Great Thermate Debate

In one of my experiments, I made small amounts of thermite, which were held loosely in place with clay tiles on each side of a welded steel connection. When I ignited the thermate, it yielded similar results to the National Geographic experiment; that is, there was virtually no damage to the steel.

Indeed, it appears powdered thermate/thermite placed loosely against steel, where the vast majority of the energy is dissipated away from the steel column, does little or no structural damage. But what if that energy was somehow more focused? I decided to fabricate a crude thermite torch that would direct the energy released by the thermite reaction in a specific direction.

Using short segments of steel box tube, I had a slot milled along one corner of the steel box. I then welded on a bottom plate and small angle clips on each side near the top of the box segment. I placed less than 2 pounds of powdered thermate in a plastic bag, and placed the bag inside the small box segment. Finally, I attached the top plate, held by angle clips.

This assembly was then clamped to a steel column and ignited with a magnesium strip. This time, it sliced right through the web of a wide flange. After examining the debris from the experiment, it appeared to me that the second half of the thermate inside the slotted steel tube was less constrained, and therefore did not cut as well as the first half. So, I built a variable container intended to

THE OFFICIAL COLLAPSE NARRATIVE AND THE EXPERIMENTAL METHOD

keep the volume constant during the reaction, using a sliding steel piston kept under relatively constant pressure. Bolting this mechanism to a vertical steel column also resulted in a damaged column, but this time cut horizontally.

I made several variations of thermate containers that, when ignited, could slice off large diameter bolts from either side. In addition, my thermitic "box cutters" were configured such that they could be placed inside replicas of the towers' perimeter box columns and cause significant damage. Moreover, igniting thermite held in simple iron pipes mounted adjacent to a wide flange resulted in the flange being melted away and thinned to razor sharpness, similar to that "eutectic steel" piece found by Jonathan Barnett.

Full details of my experiments can be seen on a YouTube video called *9/11 Experiments: The Great Thermate Debate*.[312] My experiments were not intended to suggest that crude containers holding ordinary thermite were somehow bolted to the tower walls. Rather, my point was to demonstrate that the corporate media's experiment intended to "prove" to the public that large amounts of thermite could not do any damage was wrong. As demonstrated, the results of my experiments proved that small amounts of thermate indeed can do serious damage to steel. Thus, the theory that thermitic materials could certainly have been used in the towers demolition has not been disproved by the experiments shown in National Geographic and Mythbusters.

In 2009, a peer-reviewed scientific study was published describing a very high-tech energetic material found in the WTC dust called nanothermite, further supporting the independent theory that the towers' demise was intentional and due, at least in part, to thermitic material. If ordinary experiments with "old fashioned" thermate could damage steel, modern high-technology and energetic nanothermate should produce far better destructive results.

Yet, any suggestion of thermitic material being used in the towers' demolition is still being dismissed with statements like those of Dave Thomas in Skeptical Enquirer Magazine:

> *"Thermite is simply not practical for carrying out a controlled demolition, and there is no documentation of it ever having been used for this purpose."*

First, the independent scientists suggesting that thermitic materials were used in the towers and WTC 7's demolition are not saying that *only* thermitic material was used. Rather, it may have been, and probably was, used in conjunction with other explosives. Secondly, prior use of a product, especially an innovative product, is not necessarily a prerequisite for proving that something cannot be done. Finally, even in the case of ordinary thermite, the statements are not true.

In 1935, a three million pound steel tower, which was taller than World Trade Center 7, was taken down with 1500 pounds of thermite placed on the outside of the steel support columns.[313]

THE OFFICIAL COLLAPSE NARRATIVE AND THE EXPERIMENTAL METHOD

POPULAR MECHANICS 657

Skyride Tower Felled by Melting Steel Legs

Intense heat was employed by wrecking engineers in toppling the 3,000,000-pound east tower of the "Skyride," a major attraction of Chicago's Century of Progress. Huge "overshoes" in the form of cupolas made of steel and lined with firebrick were constructed around two legs of the tower and filled with 1,500 pounds of thermite, a mixture of aluminum and iron oxide. When fired by electricity the thermite generated a temperature of more than 5,000 degrees about the two legs, melting the ten-foot sections almost instantly, causing the tower to tip and then to crash. A microphone attached to the tip of the tower broadcast the noise of the fall by radio, and the spectacle

East Tower of Skyride Crashing after Two Legs Had Been Melted by Thermite in Cupolas, Below

was viewed by a crowd estimated at more than 100,000. The west tower had been wrecked several weeks earlier with dynamite. The 628-foot twin towers, the cables which supported the cars passing between them and the elevators cost more than $1,750,000 to erect.

BRAKE TESTER MOUNTED IN CAR

Mounted on steering column or the dash, a brake tester for automobiles, trucks and buses keeps accurate check on the efficiency of brakes. It gives approximate stopping distance and test readings can be made at twenty, thirty or forty miles per hour. The device works on the decelerometer principle, its pointer moving across the face of the dial as the car is braked to a stop. The dial shows one section, "Not Safe," another, "Good," and a third "Excellent," the section in which the pointer stops indicating the approximate condition of the brakes. The instrument is easy to operate.

Why couldn't thermite also work to help destroy the World Trade Center buildings, perhaps if it was placed inside the steel box columns that supported them?

Over the years we have been given many conflicting and inaccurate theories by the media and institutional experts, including:

- The office fires melted the steel – The office fires didn't melt the steel.
- The truss connections broke first – The truss connections didn't break.
- The columns bowed outward – The columns bowed inward.
- It was a progressive pancake collapse – It wasn't a progressive pancake collapse.
- It was a pile driver collapse – although no experiment can support this claim.
- Collapse was inevitable – even though collapse is not inevitable.
- Sulfur came from the drywall – Sulfur did not come from the drywalls.
- The experts could not melt steel with thermite – but a novice could.

And remarkably, there is absolutely no official theory given by the government or any of their agencies for the total collapse of the Twin Towers. Today, we really only have the official "Collapse *Initiation* Theory" asserted by NIST. Those theories, regardless of how official they may be, were never confirmed by experimentation and therefore prove nothing.

THE OFFICIAL COLLAPSE NARRATIVE AND THE EXPERIMENTAL METHOD

Tell them to prove it!

No matter what theory you are told and regardless of who is talking, tell them to prove it by experiment using the scientific method. Regardless of how beautiful or logical it is, or how it fits with your perception of world events, if that theory doesn't agree with experiment…it's wrong.

Not one fire-only collapse theory put forth to-date can be supported by the experimental method. The crush-down crush-up pile driver theory is wrong because it defies Newton's third law, doesn't match observation and has not been supported by any known experiment. The "pancake" theory is wrong because it defies momentum laws, cannot explain the fall of the core, doesn't match observation, and cannot be replicated experimentally.

Here is some of the evidence that must be explained:

- The measured uniform downward acceleration of the tower roofline, with no "jolts" observed to amplify the downward force.
- The explosive ejections of building material seen well ahead and before any possible impact from the primary destructive wave front.
- The straight down collapse of the inner core columns, or "spire," well after the rest of the towers demise.
- The initial "antenna drop" observed on tower one.
- The lack of "pancaked" floors at Ground Zero.
- The acknowledged free-fall of WTC 7 for over 100 feet – a total impossibility with any type of progressive collapse not assisted by explosive demolition.

- The energy to create all the dust and powdered concrete.
- The cut up steel segments found at Ground Zero.
- The sulfur and resulting eutectic formations found in the steel.
- The iron microspheres.
- The molten iron or steel observed, and
- The nanothermite found in the dust.

The only theory that adequately addresses this evidence is the intentional "controlled demolition" hypothesis, using some combination of incendiaries and explosives. And the use of explosives is exactly what was clearly understood by those who were there on the very day of the event, before the experts had time to tell us what to think:

> "…the way the structure is collapsing…this was the result of something that was planned …it's not accidental, that the first tower just happened to collapse and then the second tower just happened to collapse in exactly the same way. How they accomplished this, we don't know but clearly this is what they wanted to accomplish."
> **– CNBC, Mark Haines**

Over the last ten years, there never really was a single "official collapse narrative" of how those towers came down on 9/11. Rather, there was a bewildering array of theories that contradicted each other and themselves, and did not address significant evidence. The main common element among all of the official accounts is that they deny that explosives were used – the only

THE OFFICIAL COLLAPSE NARRATIVE
AND THE EXPERIMENTAL METHOD

hypothesis that best addresses all the evidence and can be supported by experiment, using the scientific method.

The twin towers didn't just naturally "fall down" from airplane impact damage, fires and gravity alone. They were intentionally blown up.

CHAPTER TWELVE

Advanced Pyrotechnic or Explosive Material Discovered in WTC Dust

BY RICHARD GAGE, AIA;
GREGG ROBERTS AND ANDREA DREGER

STARTING IN 2007, A GROUP OF INDEPENDENT RESEARCHERS began examining the dust from the World Trade Center disaster to see if identifiable residues might help explain the highly energetic destruction that was observed in the videos. Naked-eye and microscopic examination revealed numerous tiny metallic and magnetically attracted spheres and red/gray chips, quite distinctive in the dust samples.

The existence of iron-rich microspheres in the WTC dust was documented in 2004[314] and 2005[315]. But nothing yet had been published about the red/gray chips in the dust until Steven Jones first described them in 2007. What might have been misinterpreted as the residue of common paint when seen with the naked eye proved to be a highly energetic advanced nano-composite material.

THE 9/11 TORONTO REPORT

In April 2009, a team of scientists that included physicist Steven Jones (formerly BYU), chemist Niels Harrit (University of Copenhagen, Denmark), physicist Jeffrey Farrer (Brigham Young University), and six other authors published their findings regarding the red/gray chips in the peer-reviewed paper "Active Thermitic Material Discovered in Dust from the 9/11 World Trade Center Catastrophe."[316]

Red/gray chips from four different WTC dust samples were examined using scanning electron microscopy, X-ray energy dispersive spectroscopy (XEDS), and differential scanning calorimetry. The main findings of the study are as follows:

The material in the red layer consists of intimately mixed particles of iron oxide and aluminum embedded in a carbon-rich matrix. The particles range in size from tens to hundreds of nanometers. Elemental aluminum was present in thin plate-like structures, while iron oxide was present as faceted grains, roughly 100 nm across – about a thousand times smaller than a human hair.

Iron oxide and aluminum are the ingredients of thermite, an incendiary that burns unusually hot at approximately 4500°F, producing aluminum oxide and molten iron. The carbon content of the matrix indicates the presence of an organic substance.

When the red/gray chips were heated to about 430°C (806°F), they ignited, releasing relatively large amounts of energy very fast. This behavior matches "fairly closely an independent observation on a known super-thermite sample," as reported in a paper published by researchers associated with Lawrence Livermore National Laboratories. The residue of the ignited red/gray chips included iron-rich spheres, "indicating that a very high temperature reaction had occurred, since the iron-rich product clearly

ADVANCED PYROTECHNIC OR EXPLOSIVE MATERIAL DISCOVERED IN WTC DUST

must have been molten to form these shapes." The chemical signature of the spheres and spheroids "strikingly matches the chemical signature of the spheroids produced by igniting commercial thermite, and also matches the signatures of many of the microspheres found in the WTC dust."

The scientists concluded, based on all their findings, that the red layer of the red/ gray chips "is active, unreacted thermitic material, incorporating nanotechnology," and that it "is a highly energetic pyrotechnic or explosive material." See the published study for the remainder of the findings.

Energetic nanothermitic compounds have been researched since the 1990s. One "advantage" of nanothermites stated in the literature is their ability to enhance the destructive effect of high explosives; the high rate of reaction in nanothermites allows the main explosive charge to release its energy even faster when nanothermite is used as an igniter.[317] Such igniters also do not leave behind lead-containing residues as lead azide igniters do. Nanothermitic composite materials have been extensively researched by US national labs. The energy release of these special materials can be tailored for various applications[318], they can be designed to be explosive by adding gas-releasing compounds[319] (such as what the matrix of the WTC chips' red layer might consist of) and they have potential for easy storage and safe handling.

As of 2002, the production process at the Naval Surface Warfare Center for ultra fine grain (UFG) aluminum, alone, required several pieces of high-tech equipment. The article states: "The current state of UFG aluminum production is that this is an area that still requires considerable effort."

Red/gray chips, with a red layer that comprises ultra fine grain aluminum platelets intimately mixed with faceted grains of nano-sized iron oxide, embedded in a carbon-rich matrix, cannot have been widely available in 2001. Niels Harrit, lead author of the study, stated "These new findings confirm and extend the earlier finding of previously molten, iron-rich microspheres in the World Trade Center dust. They provide strong forensic evidence that the official explanation of the WTC's destruction is wrong."

Given the explosive nature of the destruction of the WTC Twin Towers along with the finding of this high-tech nanocomposite pyrotechnic or explosive material in the WTC dust samples, there exists strong evidence to compel all who are aware to be active in supporting a real investigation into the destruction witnessed on 9/11.[320]

CHAPTER THIRTEEN

Evidence of Explosives at the Pentagon

BY BARBARA HONEGGER

Introduction

THIS CHAPTER PRESENTS COMPELLING EVIDENCE THAT the central fact of the Pentagon attack on September 11, 2001, is the same as at the World Trade Center: inside-the-building explosives, which no foreign terrorists could have had the access to plant, making the official narrative of what happened on 9/11 impossible. Physical evidence and eyewitness testimony converge to show that internal as well as external explosions went off just after 9:30 a.m., when the official narrative claims Flight 77 was still miles from Washington and did not approach the building until 9:37:46, and that these primary explosions went off at locations far removed from the official story "plane penetration path" in Wedge One. They occurred in Wedge Two and in the innermost rings well beyond the alleged C Ring "exit" hole.

The FBI knows that explosives are central to the actual 9/11 plot

The FBI's code names for terrorist investigations known to have been carried out by means of bombs or explosives end in BOM[B] – for example, the acronym for its Oklahoma City bombing investigation is OKBOM.[321]

It is therefore highly significant that the official FBI code name for the investigation of the September 11 attacks is PENTTBOM, which stands for **PEN**tagon **T**win **T**owers **BOM**bing. In this acronym, the abbreviation for Pentagon comes first, followed by that for the Twin Towers, with the notable absence of an abbreviation for Pennsylvania. Robert Mueller, who was FBI director on 9/11, confirmed this to *Time* magazine: "The [FBI's] SIOC [Strategic Intelligence Operations Center] filled to capacity on 9/11 and remained that way through PENTTBOM, the FBI's cryptonym for 'Pentagon,' 'Twin Towers' and 'Bombing'," reconfirming *Newsweek*'s report in the immediate wake of the attacks.[322] Despite the clear inference that the 9/11 investigation, the largest in the agency's history,[323] was focused on bombs or explosives, FBI briefers lied to the "Jersey Girls" when they asked why the investigation was called PENTTBOM. They were told it was because "all the FBI's investigations [code names] end in BOM."[324] This is provably false: even the acronym for the agency's investigation of the 9/11-related anthrax attacks is AMERITHRAX, not AMERIBOM. The truth is, the entire U.S. government knows why the investigation of the September 11 attacks was called PENTTBOM, has from the very beginning, and has made a conscious decision to keep the American people, including more than 6,000 victims' family members, not only in the dark but actively deceived

EVIDENCE OF EXPLOSIVES AT THE PENTAGON

about what really happened to cause the mass murder of nearly 3,000 of their fellow citizens.

Reports of primary explosions throughout the chain of command

As detailed by Professor Graeme MacQueen at the Toronto Hearings, more than 100 firefighters, first responders and other eye- and ear-witnesses heard and felt explosions inside the WTC Towers in New York City, including at least two dozen reporting massive basement-level explosions in WTC 1 before the first plane hit more than ninety floors above. Similarly, Pentagon eye- and ear-witnesses gave testimonies to Department of Defense historians and to the mainstream media that they experienced massive explosions at the Pentagon, some more than five minutes before Flight 77 is said by the official story to have come anywhere near the building.

Only minutes before the attack on his own building, Secretary of Defense Rumsfeld, who was in his office in a section of the Pentagon opposite the alleged impact point, "predicted" that there would be "another event" in addition to the two that had then already taken place in New York City,[325] and shortly after the attacks told Sam Donaldson of ABC News that his first thought in the wake of the attack was that a bomb had gone off. When Donaldson asked, "What did you think it was?" Rumsfeld replied, "A bomb?"

The 9/11 Commission staff report on its interview with Navy Capt. Charles Joseph "Joe" Leidig, acting deputy director of operations for the Pentagon's National Military Command Center on 9/11, notes, "He [Leidig] had no awareness of AA77 coming back to Washington. His first awareness was a call from the SECDEF's [Secretary of Defense Rumsfeld's] three-star aide who asked if he felt the explosion in the building, and asked Leidig to investigate whether it might be a terrorist attack."[326]

Many other military officers and enlisted personnel inside the building also experienced and reported explosions. Lt. Nancy McKeown, who was in the Naval Command Center on the first floor of the second-in D Ring, said, "It sounded like a series of explosions going off…It sounded like a series of bombs exploding, similar to like firecrackers when you light them and you just get a series going off." This is almost identical language to the firefighters' descriptions of preplaced explosives going off in the World Trade Center towers in New York City on 9/11. McKeown yelled "Bomb!" when she heard and felt a major explosion, after which tiles fell from the ceiling.[327] Lt. Col. Thurman, who was on the second floor of the same D Ring, said, "To me, it didn't seem like a plane. To me, it seemed like it was a bomb. Being in the military, I have been around grenade, artillery explosions. It was a two-part explosion to me. It seemed like there was a percussion blast that blew me kind of backwards in my cubicle to the side. And then it seemed as if a massive explosion went off at the same time." Army Lt. Col. Victor Correa, who was on the second floor in the Army Personnel area just above the alleged impact point, said, "We thought it was some kind of explosion, that somehow someone got in here and planted bombs because we saw these holes."[328] John Yates, a security manager for the Assistant Secretary of the Army for Manpower and Reserve Affairs who was in the same area as Correa just above the alleged impact point, said, "There was no noise. I mean, I did not hear a plane. Just suddenly

EVIDENCE OF EXPLOSIVES AT THE PENTAGON

the room just exploded, and I was blown through the air."[329] Even a local mayor who was at the Pentagon that morning had a similar experience, reported by the Frederick (Maryland) *News-Post*. Thurmont Mayor Marty Burns "was leaning against an office doorway when an explosion rocked the Pentagon…Pentagon employees assumed it was a bomb… 'Where's the next bomb?' Burns and his Pentagon colleagues wondered. Even outside the building, Burns saw no indication that a plane had caused the damage."[330] Lt. Col. Brian Birdwell, who had just come out of a restroom off Corridor 4 in the vicinity of the B Ring, said, "I heard the sound of a very loud explosion. In my number of years in the artillery community, I hadn't heard anything that loud. I thought it was a bomb."[331]

And standing outside the Navy Annex about three football fields' distance from the building, witness Terry Morin recalled, "I saw the flash and subsequent fireball rise approximately 200 feet above the Pentagon. There was a large explosion noise and the low frequency sound echo that comes with this type of sound. Associated with that was the increase in air pressure, momentarily, like a small gust of wind. For those formerly in the military, it sounded like a 2,000-pound bomb going off…"[332] Though this report is from a pilot who had just experienced a large plane fly overhead and to his right along the south side of the Annex, he nevertheless described what the official story alleges to have been an impact, which he could not see, with bomb-related references.

I conducted an interview with Ft. Monmouth Army financial auditor Michael Nielsen, who was on temporary duty assignment at the Pentagon before and on 9/11. He was in the Army financial management area, soon to be among the most destroyed by the attack, only minutes before the Pentagon explosion on the morning of 9/11. He had just returned to his temporary duty office on the ground floor near the building's cafeteria when he heard and felt a massive explosion. Immediately afterwards, he said, hundreds of Pentagon personnel ran by him down the corridor and out the exit, yelling "Bombs!" "A bomb went off!" and "It was a *bomb*!"

Even Chairman of the Joint Chiefs of Staff Gen. Hugh Shelton, the highest-ranking military officer in the U.S. chain of command, experienced what he thought was the residue of explosives. On page 434 of his biography *Without Hesitation*, Gen. Shelton noted that upon his arrival at the Pentagon he was struck by an overpowering smell of cordite, or gun smoke, a substance used in bombs that has a distinct and very different odor from burning jet fuel. "The smell of cordite was overwhelming," he said. Pentagon worker Don Perkal told MSNBC, "People shouted in the corridor outside that a bomb had gone off. Even before stepping outside, I could smell the cordite. Then I knew explosives had been set off somewhere."[333] Department of Defense attorney Gilah Goldsmith reported that immediately after hearing "an incredible whomp noise," she "saw a huge black cloud of smoke" that "smelled like cordite or gun smoke."[334]

Army witness April Gallop, who experienced a massive explosion as she pressed the 'on' button on her computer in Room 1E517 in Wedge Two off Corridor 5, more than 100 feet north of the official story alleged impact point, also smelled cordite and thought that it was a bomb. "Being in the Army with the training I had, I know what a bomb sounds and acts like, especially the aftermath," and it sounded and acted "like a bomb," Gallop told me in an under-oath videotaped interview.[335] She also restated

EVIDENCE OF EXPLOSIVES AT THE PENTAGON

this in her court filing and in a videotaped interview with former Minnesota Governor Jesse Ventura for a TruTV episode on the Pentagon attack aired December 17, 2010.[336] The force of the explosion or the impact of debris falling on her stopped her wrist watch at or just after 9:30,[337] almost 8 minutes before the official story says Flight 77 came anywhere near the building. Cordite produces a strong detonation shock wave but is cool burning, which would explain why Gallop could experience a major explosion and yet remain unburned (see Fig. 13-1).

FIG. 13-1

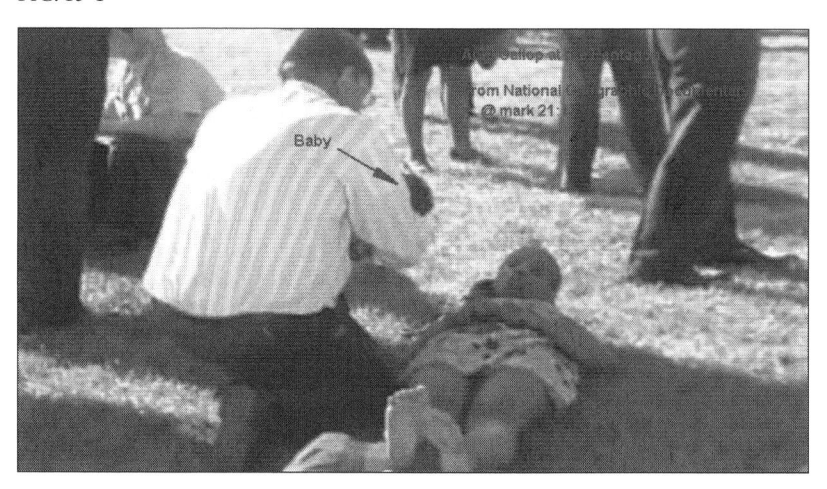

Army survivor April Gallop rests on the Pentagon lawn after having lost one of her shoes while escaping the destruction from an explosion that went off near her desk in Wedge 2 at just after 9:30. The official story claims that she exited through the entrance point of a plane and through a raging inferno consuming over 11,000 gallons of remaining jet fuel, yet Gallop was unburned, including on the bottoms of her feet. Her infant son is being held by the man kneeling at the left.

In sworn videotaped testimony I submitted as evidence in these Hearings, Gallop stated that there was no jet fuel and no fire on the floor as she walked out. "I had no jet fuel on me...I didn't smell any jet fuel...I didn't see any airplane seats. I didn't see any plane parts...I didn't see anything that would give me any idea that there was a plane [in the building]," she said under oath. As the explosion at or near her desk in Wedge Two was many minutes before and many dozens of feet from the alleged impact point in Wedge One, they wouldn't, however, have been expected. The only fires Gallop said she did see were "flames coming out of the computers" on desks around the perimeter of the large Army administrative area in the outer E Ring where she worked. In her original interview with an Army historian soon after the attack, Gallop said that her computer "blew." This was also experienced by other workers closer to the official alleged impact point further south in Wedge 1. As everything went black, witness Tracy Webb, whose office in 2E477 was on the second floor of the outer E ring off Corridor 4 effectively above the alleged impact point, also saw her "computer burst into flames."[338]

Pentagon wall clocks and April Gallop's wristwatch were stopped by primary explosions 5 to 8 minutes before the official story says Flight 77 approached the building

Multiple, independently set electric or battery-operated wall clocks in areas of the Pentagon that sustained major damage – including one outside in the heliport fire house off the west wall – were stopped by explosions shortly after 9:30, when the plane the official story claims was Flight 77 was still miles from the area. The Navy, whose Naval Command Center was destroyed by an explosion, immediately posted a photo of one of these wall clocks,

EVIDENCE OF EXPLOSIVES AT THE PENTAGON

stopped at 9:31:40 (right clock in Fig. 13-2) on an official Department of Defense website. The heliport firehouse clock, stopped at 9:32:30, is in the official 9/11 exhibit at the Smithsonian Institution National Museum of American History (left clock in Fig. 13-2).[339] The photo caption on its website states that "the blast" from the Pentagon attack "knocked the heliport clock from the wall, freezing it at 9:32."

FIG. 13-2

Some of the west section Pentagon wall clocks stopped shortly after 9:30 on Sept. 11, consistent with the early media reports.

Clearly, if a major violent event caused the destruction at the Pentagon shortly after 9:30, the official story that Flight 77 struck the building at 9:37:46 cannot be the whole or even the most important part of what really happened at the nation's military command center on 9/11.

THE 9/11 TORONTO REPORT

Early press and media reports of the Pentagon attack time were correct

Before the Bush-Cheney administration settled on the official story that the Pentagon was attacked at 9:37:46 – almost 9:38 – mainstream press reports on the time of the attack were accurate:

about 9:30 – *Reuters*, reported 3:57 p.m. on 9/11/01
about 9:30 – *USA Today*, reported 6:11 a.m. on 9/12/01
about 9:30 – *New York Times*, reported on 9/12/01
shortly after 9:30 – *U.S. News and World Report*, reported on 9/12/01

Preplaced explosives may have triggered the E Ring collapse

Because they contain no definitive evidence of a plane approach prior to the appearance of a fireball, the 'five frames' videotapes from the two security cameras outside the west wall are clear evidence only for an explosion either in or outside the wall, and there is evidence that the later collapse of a portion of the outside E Ring may also have been due to explosives. The contractor American Petrography Services was hired to do an "autopsy" on the concrete from the structural support columns in the alleged plane penetration path, including those supporting the outside wall. APS found temperatures so high and "concentrated for [such] a long period of time" in the portion of the building which later collapsed, that some of the concrete "turned to mush."[340] The samples "that came from columns near the crash site" also had "a reddish hue and tints of bright orange…that could be seen with the naked eye" due to the presence of iron. This section of the building experienced "the most extreme conditions" that the president of the company had ever seen, and though its analysis proposed that "the red and orange colors came from tiny amounts of iron in the rock that were oxidized in extreme heat," the iron could instead have been due to intense heat generated by superthermitic reactions on the columns, similar to those known to have occurred at the WTC, which produce molten iron at temperatures exceeding 4000 degrees F. This temperature is more than sufficient to cut through the steel reinforcement inside the columns that collapsed approximately 20 minutes after the attack, as well as to turn their concrete to "mush," whereas the far lower temperature of a quickly-burning jet-fuel-initiated office fire of approximately 500 degrees F[341] is not.

Shaped charge explosives created the alleged C Ring "exit" hole

After studying photos of the alleged "exit" hole in the inner wall of the C Ring, such as in Fig. 13-3 below, shaped charge explosives expert Michael Meyer concluded that the round, clean-edged hole not only could not have been made by a plane or plane parts, but has the exact signature of being created by shaped charge explosives. "It is physically impossible for the C Ring wall to have failed in a neat, clean circle like that [due to kinetic impact from a plane or plane parts]," Meyer emphatically stated.

FIG. 13-3

Earliest known photo, by a DoD photographer, of the near-perfectly-round 9- to 12-foot diameter alleged "exit" hole in the inner wall of the middle C Ring.

As for claims that any part of the debris seen in these photos was from a plane, Terry Mitchell of the Office of the Assistant Secretary of Defense for Public Affairs Audio/Visual Division, who was given early access to the A-E Drive between the C and B Rings into which the hole opens, showed a photo like the one in Figure 13-3 to the media at the Pentagon's September 15 news briefing and clearly explained: "This is a hole in [the C Ring] – there was a punch out. They suspect that this was where a part of the aircraft came through this hole, although I didn't see any evidence of the aircraft down there...This pile here is all Pentagon metal. None of that is aircraft whatsoever. As you can see, they've punched a

EVIDENCE OF EXPLOSIVES AT THE PENTAGON

hole in here. This was punched by the rescue workers to clean it out." Reporters asked, "We're trying to figure out how it came into the building" and how far it penetrated,[342] which Mitchell evaded answering. The circled and crossed "V" spray-painted on both sides of the hole after it was made is, in fact, the international triage marking symbol for "confirmed dead Victims removed."[343] The fact that a data file was downloaded from the Flight Data Recorder (FDR) four hours *before* the official story says the FDR was allegedly found just inside this C Ring hole[344] and that the only data fields that could have definitively identified the black box as having come from the plane that flew as Flight 77 on 9/11, or not, were intentionally "zeroed out"[345] suggests that this most important piece of "wreckage" was manipulated and then planted to make it appear that part of a plane had penetrated to the C Ring. This was almost certainly done by the agency in charge of all evidence at the Pentagon – the FBI – the same FBI whose September 11 investigation code name is PENTTBOM.

Some researchers have suggested that the C Ring "exit" hole could have been created by a quasi-liquid "slurry" of unburned jet fuel, wreckage and debris moving through the alleged "plane penetration path," but this is physically impossible. In addition to former NASA Dryden Research Division Director of Research Engineering Dwain Deets having shown that all possible paths between the alleged E Ring "impact" point and alleged C Ring "exit" hole had steel-reinforced columns still standing, such a "slurry" would had to have reconstituted and refocused itself after being progressively shredded and dispersed from impacting multiple intervening columns, finally forming itself into a perfectly-focused cone of energy capable of exploding a near-perfectly-round hole in the inner C Ring wall.

THE 9/11 TORONTO REPORT

The Pentagon *itself* initially said there were three "exit" holes, not one

The Pentagon originally claimed that there were *three*, not just one, "exit holes" on the inside of the C Ring. This is shown by Fig. 13-4, a graphic based on information from Pentagon sources published in the *Washington Post* shortly after the attacks.

FIG. 13-4

*Aerial photograph with overlays based on Pentagon sources showing **three** C Ring "exit" holes denoted by three dots labeled 1, 2 and 3 at the right of the picture. These are the precise locations of the **three** openings in the C Ring wall with black soot above them in in Fig. 14-5, the official Pentagon aerial photo of that same portion of the C Ring wall taken shortly after the attack.*

EVIDENCE OF EXPLOSIVES AT THE PENTAGON

FIG. 13-5

*Official Department of Defense aerial photo of the west section of the Pentagon following the collapse of a section of the outer E Ring (top center) showing **three** openings in the C Ring wall in the identical positions as the dots labeled 1, 2 and 3 representing **three** "exit holes" in the aerial photo with graphic overlays in Fig. 13-4. The "exit" hole furthest to the right/north, to which the official story later claimed the landing gear of Flight 77 penetrated at its furthest point into the building, has significantly less blackening from fire and smoke above it than the two further to the left/south.*

Although the left and middle openings in Figure 13-5 were not artificially created like the one on the right which the official story later claimed to be the sole "exit" hole – they are a roll-up door and a door – the point is not that just one of the three is a new and artificial wall breach, but that the Pentagon itself initially referred to all three as "exit holes," clearly putting them in the same category as personnel exit/entry locations, as was explicitly stated by DoD's own spokesman Terry Mitchell at the September 15 press briefing. And because it is unlikely for any single impactor – whether a plane, a drone or a missile – to be the cause of *three* exit holes, this is strong evidence that, at the time the Pentagon gave this information to the *Post*, the official story that a plane caused the northernmost "exit" hole had not yet been consolidated.

Fire and Destruction in the Innermost A and B Rings Far Beyond the C Ring "Exit" Hole

Compelling evidence against the official story that a plane caused all of the internal damage at the Pentagon is that there was fire and destruction in the innermost B and A Rings – one and two rings further in towards the center courtyard than the alleged C Ring "exit" hole that was allegedly the furthest penetration point of any part of a plane.

I interviewed the then Acting Assistant Secretary of Defense for Special Operations on 9/11, Robert Andrews, a former Green Beret and the top civilian official then in charge of special operations under Secretary of Defense Donald Rumsfeld. In this position, Andrews oversaw the Special Operations Command, one of whose operations was the Al Qaeda-tracking-and-data-mining "Able Danger" group which identified three of the four alleged 9/11 hijacker cells more than a year before the attacks and was ordered shut down shortly after Bush, Cheney and Rumsfeld took office. Andrews related the following: Immediately after the second WTC attack of 9:03, Secretary of Defense Rumsfeld left his office on the Potomac side of the Pentagon and went across the hall to his Executive Support Center (ESC)[346] which was set

EVIDENCE OF EXPLOSIVES AT THE PENTAGON

up for teleconferencing. The first Department of Defense statement released just before 10:00 a.m. EDT on 9/11 stated that Rumsfeld was "directing the response" from his "command center in the Pentagon,"[347] which was the ESC. From the ESC, Rumsfeld then joined the secure video teleconference of top government officials convened by National Security Council counter-terrorism 'czar' Richard Clarke out of the White House Situation Room media room. Clarke, in his book *Against All Enemies*, confirmed that Rumsfeld was among the first officials to come on to this teleconference.

Clarke's account and Robert Andrews' confirmation of it are thus completely at odds with the official story and the 9/11 Commission Report, which claim that no one could "locate" Rumsfeld until approximately 10:30 a.m. when he suddenly appeared in the National Military Command Center. Also, the fact that Rumsfeld, the military's top civilian official, was on the White House teleconference with the top official of the Federal Aviation Administration, FAA Director Jane Garvey, also calls into question the claim that NORAD fighters weren't scrambled in time to intercept the second/WTC2, third/Pentagon and fourth/Pennsylvania planes because the military and FAA had difficulty communicating: the top-most officials of the Pentagon and the FAA were talking to each another almost continuously for hours while Rumsfeld was in the ESC as well as being videotaped on Clarke's teleconference, a record which the Bush-Cheney administration refused to make public and which was withheld even from the 9/11 Commission. This videotape is thus "The Butterfield Tape" of September 11 and must be declassified and released to a new independent investigation. (During the Watergate scandal, a secretly-recorded tape of President Nixon's Oval Office conversations revealed by Alexander Butterfield became the "smoking gun" which forced Nixon to resign rather than face impeachment in the House and trial by the Senate.)

According to Andrews, immediately after the second WTC tower was struck at 9:03, he and an aide left his office and ran down to Rumsfeld's west section Counterterrorism Center (CTC). While they were in the CTC, a sudden violent event caused the ceiling tiles to fall and smoke to pour into the room. Andrews immediately looked at his watch, which read c. 9:35 but which was set fast to ensure timely arrival at meetings, so the actual time was closer to 9:32. He and the aide then immediately left the CTC to join Secretary Rumsfeld in his Executive Support Center across the hall from his main office. En route to the ESC, Andrews said that when he and his aide entered the corridor on the innermost A ring of the west section, "we had to walk over dead bodies" to get to the central courtyard. This is in the A Ring, two rings further in towards the center from the alleged "exit" hole in the C Ring which the official story says was the furthest any part of the plane or damage from it penetrated.

Once in the Pentagon's inner courtyard, Andrews and his aide ran to Rumsfeld's Executive Support Center, where he joined the Secretary as his special operations/counterterrorism adviser during Clarke's White House video teleconference. When they arrived, he was already on the teleconference,[348] and while there, Andrews said Rumsfeld spoke with President Bush. Whether this was via Clarke's teleconference or by phone or other means was not stated. The fact that Rumsfeld personally spoke with Bush while he was in his Pentagon ESC was published on an official DoD website, of the Naval Postgraduate School.

EVIDENCE OF EXPLOSIVES AT THE PENTAGON

In addition to the deaths, and by inference violent events that caused them, that occurred on the inside of the innermost A Ring, there also was massive damage and fire on the inside of the B Ring. This, again, is one ring further in towards the center court-yard from the official story alleged plane "exit" hole on the inside of the C Ring. The day after 9/11, the *Washington Post* reported "the attack destroyed at least four of the five 'rings' that spiral around the massive office building…A 38-year-old Marine major…said he and dozens of his colleagues rushed to the area in the Pentagon that appeared most heavily damaged – the B Ring between the 4th and 5th corridors." The major said that the B Ring area "was decimated" and "that heat and fire, it could eat you alive in three seconds." In his interview with the Army's Center of Military History, Lt. Col. Victor Correa, who was in Room 2C450 in the middle C Ring at the time of the attack, said he saw "the windows in the B Ring go out and come in – like the pressure, the blast made the windows go out,"[349] consistent with a massive internal explosion inside the B Ring. Also, members of the Pentagon Rescue Team told the *Washington Post* that "When we got into the building, we started to feel the heat right away, and as we walked deeper down the hallways, it got hotter and hotter. It was just fire everywhere. Not so much smoke, but just fire all around us. You couldn't see the plane, just debris everywhere you looked."[350]

It is physically impossible for any impactor that allegedly penetrated only to the middle C Ring as the official story holds, to cause massive damage, fire and deaths in the two rings further in. And no foreign terrorist – Al Qaeda or otherwise – could have had the access to plant explosives anywhere inside the Pentagon, regardless of the ring.

THE 9/11 TORONTO REPORT

Evidence that some of the inside explosives were targeted

Once it is realized that the real story at the Pentagon – as at WTC 1, 2 and 7 in New York City – is inside explosives, the possibility that specific offices or functions were targeted not only becomes possible, it becomes likely. No foreign terrorist would have chosen the hardest-to-hit place on the Pentagon – just above the ground on the only wedge that had just been hardened, that was the least populated and presented the greatest obstacle course including a hill, highway signs, light poles, a tall antenna, a chain-link fence and six-foot-high spools – as a target. Outside terrorists would have chosen the surest, simplest, fastest dive straight into the roof over the "highest value" targets – the offices of the Secretary of Defense and top ranking military brass on the opposite side of the building. It therefore had to have been, rather, the perceived necessity by insiders of taking out one or more functions located on the first floor of the Pentagon's west side that was the real reason for both the explosives placed in those areas and the requirement to create the appearance of a plane impact on such a "mission impossible" target to account for the damage.

The two Pentagon areas with by far the most physical destruction and fatalities were the Army administrative area on the first floor of the outer E Ring, and the Naval Command Center on the first floor of the second-in D Ring and third-in C Ring, and there is evidence that both areas were, indeed, targeted by inside explosives. Pentagon sources even said so to the *Washington Post* immediately after the attacks.

EVIDENCE OF EXPLOSIVES AT THE PENTAGON

The Naval Command Center

Shortly after the attacks, the *Washington Post* published the graphic in Figure 13-6 entitled "The Targeted Ones" sourced to the "U.S. Navy, Navy personnel and Department of Defense" showing the Naval Command Center (NCC) as an internal target of the Pentagon attack,[351] all of whose offices were beyond the point in the E Ring beyond which the *Pentagon Building Performance Report* said the plane's fuselage did not penetrate. The Center's functional divisions are detailed in the office layout blow-up at the top, in which the "intel cell" – the Naval Intelligence cell – in the right corner is designated by '8' in the legend:

FIG. 13-6

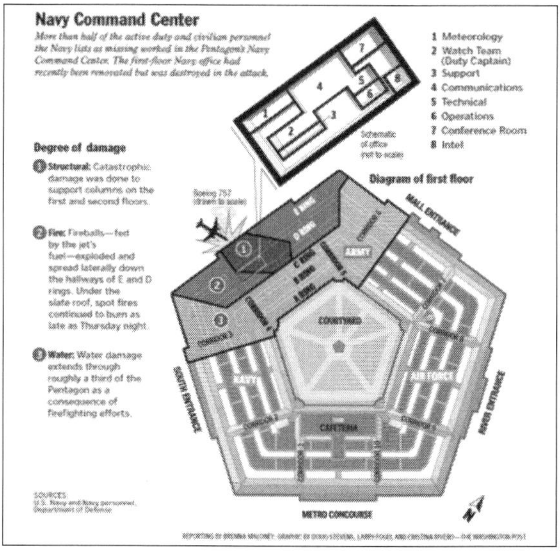

Graphic of "The Targeted Ones" in the Pentagon's Naval Command Center, based on information obtained from Navy and Defense Dept. sources and published in the Washington Post.

The Naval Command Center was the second-most-destroyed area of the Pentagon on 9/11, after the Army personnel and administrative area, which is addressed below. Center personnel had recently moved to their new offices on the first floor of the D and C Rings. The NCC was the only military-service command center in the targeted west wedge; the other service command centers, for the Air Force and Army, as well as the National Military Command Center and offices of the Secretary of Defense and Joint Chiefs of Staff, were all in untargeted wedges.

Significantly, in the report on its investigation of the damage to the building – the *Pentagon Building Performance Report* – the American Society of Civil Engineers states that the sole upward-thrust section of the second-floor floor slab in the alleged "plane penetration path" was likely due to an "independent" explosion, not impact and fire, as the official story claims an impactor penetrated essentially level and fire would have at the most collapsed the floor downwards: "The explosion, suggested by the raised [second-] floor section, might represent an independent explosion." This second-floor concrete slab that was thrust upwards by a major force is, not surprisingly, above the first-floor Naval Command Center that experienced a massive and reportedly targeted explosion.

The official story codified in the *9/11 Commission Report* and repeated by most of the main-stream media holds that all but one of the military personnel present in the Naval Command Center on the morning of September 11 died in the attack and that the alleged sole survivor was Lt. Kevin Shaeffer.[352] One possibility as to why it was targeted is what Shaeffer told the quarterly magazine *CHIPS*: "The Navy Command [Center] would have been able to prove what hit the World Trade Center if we had not been hit" by

EVIDENCE OF EXPLOSIVES AT THE PENTAGON

the explosion.[353] Notably, had it not been targeted, the NCC also could have ordered Navy fighters to intercept any errant planes that it determined NORAD was not responding to in a timely manner, which on 9/11 was all of them.

That something extremely important and apparently highly threatening to Bush-Cheney administration higher-ups was being pursued by the Naval Command Center's intel cell is underscored by yet another cover-up – of the real number of NCC personnel killed there in the attacks. The official story holds that 42 of 43 military personnel who were in the Pentagon's Naval Command Center on September 11 died,[354] with Lt. Kevin Shaeffer being the sole survivor. But I was told something quite different by the military officer in command of the Navy Anti-Terrorism Division in the NCC on 9/11, Coast Guard Reserve Rear Adm. Jeffrey Hathaway.[355] After the USS Cole was attacked in Aden Harbor, Yemen, on Oct. 12, 2000, Hathaway was put in charge of Navy counterterrorism force protection, for which he had been assigned to the NCC before September 11. Admiral Hathaway said that Shaeffer was not the only survivor, but that "the majority of the 18- to 19-person *intelligence cell* who were in a hardened room inside the Naval Command Center also survived" [emphasis added] the explosion. Whether the minority of the "18 to 19" who did not survive included the seven members of the super-secret Chief of Naval Operations-Intelligence Plot (CNO-IP) is unclear. In any case, what is clear is that there was a decision by the highest levels of the Bush-Cheney-Rumsfeld administration to hide the fact that there were more survivors of the attack on the Naval Command Center than just Kevin Shaeffer, who they were, what they knew and what they were doing that caused them to be targeted.

The Army Financial Audit Area

The Army's administrative, personnel and financial management/audit offices were the most heavily damaged areas with the greatest number of casualties. Nearly three dozen of the 125 Pentagon victims were auditors, accountants and budget analysts, all or almost all of whom worked in the Army area. The day before 9/11, Secretary of Defense Rumsfeld had publicly announced that the Pentagon was "missing" $2.3 Trillion dollars.[35] Some reports gave the amount as $2.6 Trillion. To put this number in perspective, after more than a decade, the total cost of both the Iraq and Afghanistan wars is, according to some reports, approximately this same amount. The question naturally arises, were the auditors in the Army area who were trying to "follow the money" – and the computers that were helping them do it – intentionally targeted by the inside explosives at the Pentagon on September 11? I was the first to suggest this possible nexus, in *The Pentagon Attack Papers* published in *The Terror Conspiracy* by Jim Marrs.[356] Recall also that the only fires seen by April Gallop, who told a conference audience that her office was not far from the Army auditors, were those coming out of computers. Michael Nielsen, the Army financial auditor I interviewed, said that the auditors' computers could indeed have been targeted and that their records were, in any case, destroyed.

Similar to the heavily damaged Army financial management/audit area, there is also reported reason to suspect that the Naval Command Center's intelligence cell was targeted because it was looking into what could have become grounds for a financial scandal with potential major geopolitical implications. A recent analysis claims that the NCC intel cell was investigating $240 Billion in secret securities that had been illegally used to sabotage the Soviet Union's economy during the Cold War, that these securities were to become redeemable the day after the attacks, and that some of the financial entities involved in the covert securities had their offices and related records in the World Trade Center Towers.[357] Given this context, it may prove important that Phillip Zelikow – a former member of President George H.W. Bush's National Security Council, a close colleague of and co-author with President George W. Bush's NSC Director Condolezza Rice, an expert in the creation and maintenance of "Myths of State" and the Executive Director of the 9/11 Commission which codified the "New Pearl Harbor" State Myth – headed the Harvard study that used the CIA's own documents to "exonerate" the agency of charges that the Bush Sr./Team B faction politicized and fixed "intelligence" on the Soviet Union around covert Cold War policy decisions. As one of the most secret policy decisions, if this nexus were true, would have been the use of billions to sabotage the Soviet Union, Zelikow and George Bush Sr. would have shared a special interest in seeing that documents on this most sensitive of covert operations reportedly investigated by the Naval Command Center be destroyed. Zelikow also defended the "Myth of State" that the original Pearl Harbor was a surprise attack in an Amazon.com review of Robert Stinnett's ground-breaking book *Day of Deceit*, in which Stinnett exposed President Roosevelt's provocation of Japan and setting up of Navy ships at Pearl Harbor as "sitting ducks" to ensure a "successful" attack.

In addition to the potential strategic and financial motives, there is yet another reason that the Naval Command Center's intelligence cell and adjacent damaged Defense Intelligence

Agency (DIA) offices may have been internally targeted: their likely participation in Able Danger, the pre-9/11 Special Operations Command data mining and analysis team that had identified two of the three "Al Qaeda" cells and four of the lead hijackers allegedly responsible for the 9/11 attacks, including 'ringleader' Mohammed Atta, and which Secretary of Defense Rumsfeld shut down in late January 2001 immediately after taking command of the Pentagon, perhaps not wanting the future hijackers to be tracked.

Naval Command Center survivor Kevin Shaeffer's testimony is also strong evidence that the NCC explosion was a primary event, unrelated to any possible plane impact. He insisted that the massive orange fireball that destroyed the Center, which Lt. Cmdr. Tarantino described as "a bombed out office space,"[358] happened "at precisely 9:43." As the official story claims that a plane impacted at 9:37:46, over five minutes before, and that whatever allegedly penetrated through to the C Ring did so in less than one second, or by 9:37:47, even if the official story were true Flight 77 could not have been the source of the Naval Command Center explosion and destruction at 9:43. The time difference between the first explosion, which we now know to have been at 9:32:30, stopping the heliport clock, and the NCC explosion at 9:43 makes it likely that the "second huge explosion" heard and felt by renovation team member Terry Cohen, which she said was "about 15 minutes later" than the first,[359] was the one which almost killed Shaeffer and was also the second explosion reported by Gallop. Still another primary explosion, which occurred at about 10:10, was reported live by local television.[360]

EVIDENCE OF EXPLOSIVES AT THE PENTAGON

The Pentagon attack is central to the 9/11 plot

Though the attacks on the World Trade Center towers in New York City were more spectacular, it is the attack on the Pentagon, the nation's most iconic military facility, that most fully turned the 9/11 attacks into the "New Pearl Harbor" called for by the Project for the New American Century one year earlier. It was the Pentagon attack that ensured that the Bush-Cheney administration could use the combined attacks as a pretext for being "at war"; for establishing the first-ever U.S. mainland combatant command, NORTHCOM; for rolling out its entire global domination agenda; and for creating and consolidating the domestic surveillance state. Alone, the attacks on the World Trade Center could have been credibly argued to be "a bigger World Trade Center '93" or "a bigger Oklahoma City," both of which had been addressed by the civilian courts. The Pentagon attack is thus the core of the real 9/11 plot, without which George W. Bush could not have become the "war president" he wanted to be before gaining office; without which the pretext for "preemptive" wars in Afghanistan, Iraq and beyond would not have existed; without which Vice President Cheney could not have realized his long-sought goal of concentrating power in a "unitary executive" with near-absolute authority over defense and foreign policy;[361] and without which Bush could not have credibly invoked his Article II commander-in-chief military powers to justify every violation of the Constitution and U.S. and international law in the wake of the attacks.

Because the "New Pearl Harbor" – the Pentagon – *had* to be successfully attacked, such a critical pretext for endless war could not be left to foreign terrorists. It had to be planned and, most importantly, controlled and executed by the very insider cabal who then used it to roll out their entire global domination and domestic surveillance agenda. Foreign terrorists could never have come up with a plot so perfectly resonant with the original Pearl Harbor deep within the American psyche: an expertly scripted kamikaze attack by suicide pilots using planes as weapons, only this time to attack buildings instead of ships. Khalid Shaikh Mohammed, Ramzi Binalshibh and the other "9/11 Five" awaiting "trial" in Guantanamo at most planned a 9/11-like attack, but they are not the real terrorists. The real terrorists are insiders who are still at large and must be brought to justice through a new, truly independent 9/11 investigation.

CHAPTER FOURTEEN

In Denial of Democracy: Social Psychological Implications for Public Discourse on State Crimes Against Democracy Post-9/11

BY LAURIE A. MANWELL

Dr. Martin Luther King had this to say more than forty years ago about his responsibility to challenge his own government regarding its war on Vietnam:

"A time comes when silence is betrayal; that time has come for us. Even when pressed by the demands of inner truth, men do not easily assume the task of opposing their government's policy, especially in time of war. And I knew that I could never again raise my voice against the violence of the oppressed in the ghettos without having first spoken clearly to the greatest purveyor of violence in the world today, my own government."

This essay will cover the betrayal of truth that continues today and break the silence about events that present a profound challenge to our most closely guarded beliefs about government and democracy. The public's attention must be brought to bear upon the state crimes against democracy related to the events of September 11, 2001, and the perpetrators and profiteers must be prosecuted for their crimes against humanity – crimes that have affected people worldwide, a decade past and continuing onward with no foreseeable end.

State Crimes Against Democracy

These events are collectively referred to as "State Crimes Against Democracy" or (SCADs), following Professor Lance deHaven-Smith. SCADs are actions which are undertaken in direct violation of sworn oaths of office by officials in order to circumvent, exploit, undermine or subvert laws, the constitutional order, or the public awareness essential to popular control of government. SCADs are dangerous to democracy because they are not isolated events, but a pattern of actions – or in some cases, inactions – which facilitate a progression towards closing down an open and free society.

American Behavioral Scientist Paper

The work discussed here is based on an international collaboration with five other academics – Drs. Lance De-Haven-Smith, Matthew Witt, and Christopher Hinson in the United States, and Dr. Kym Thorne and the late Dr. Alexander Kouzmin in Australia. A research paper of mine, along with six others, was published in the February 2010 special issue of American Behavioral Scientist on State Crimes Against Democracy. It focuses on scientific studies of attitudes, biases, and faulty beliefs that can prevent people from processing information that challenges pre-existing assumptions about government, reasoned dissent, and public discourse in a democratic society.

All of the information I present is based on widely accepted scientific research. Some of the concepts and explanations are quite complex and replete with technical jargon, so I will attempt to simplify things where appropriate, but there will be times when important distinctions between concepts require more technical terminology.

Although there are many theories as to why some people refuse to look at evidence that the official account of 9/11 is false, they are not all equally valid. It is neither valid nor accurate to claim that just because a person will not examine evidence that the official account is false, that person is simply in denial. The human brain is the most complex organ in the body – and thus, the mechanisms by which the mind processes, interprets and responds to information are equally complex. For example, the human brain is composed of hundreds of billions of neurons, each with thousands of synapses, creating a vastly complex and intricate neural network consisting of a hundred trillion to up to a quadrillion connections. At any one time, this organ is processing an infinite amount of information from its internal and external environment, most of which we are unconscious of. However, it is often that information – of which we are largely unaware – that has the most significant influence over our thoughts, feelings and behaviors – even those thoughts, feelings and behaviors that we adamantly believe to be consciously determined.

Evidence from neuroscience tells us that the way in which we perceive the world around us is not necessarily as it is. For example, we assume that when we are looking at something, we are consciously analyzing it based upon the visual information that is entering the brain from the eyes. But this is not entirely accurate. In fact, visual stimuli transduced by the rods and cones in the eyes, and sent by electrochemical signals to the central nervous system via the optic nerves, does not go directly to the occipital cortex which is the primary region responsible for processing visual information. Instead, it first goes to the lateral geniculate nucleus of the thalamus, another region of the brain that is part of the limbic system and important in emotional arousal. To put this in simpler terms, this means that you can experience an emotional reaction to something you see before you are consciously aware that you have even seen it – this, in turn, affects how you see it.

Perhaps one of the most elegant examples is the discovery of what are commonly known by neuroscientists as "mirror neurons." A mirror neuron is a neuron that is activated in the brain both when an organism performs an action itself – such as reaching or grasping for an object – and when that organism observes that same action performed by another organism. Research by psychologists in this area also suggests that this may be one mechanism by which people come to internalize not only the behaviors of others, but their emotions and ideas as well. Since this is a relatively new area of research, I will instead focus on some of the more established social-psychological mechanisms that may later be shown to have a biologically-based origin.

Overview

Here is a brief overview of five main areas that will be covered. First, I will present a framework for discussing psychological resistance that emphasizes the difference between a direct and indirect approach to discussing evidence of SCADs, which also recognizes the important role that the information environment and motivated reasoning play in such discussions. Second, I will review one of the most important psychological foundations of democracy, which is political tolerance, and its corollary, political aggression. Third, I will give some examples of psychological constructs that can interfere with people's examination of evidence of State Crimes Against Democracy, such as cognitive dissonance, threatened self-esteem and perceived threats to oneself or one's worldviews. Fourth, I will talk about the problems inherent in challenging people's assumptions about government, dissent, and public discourse, specifically in discussing evidence of SCADs such as 9/11. Here I will explain how people's defensiveness interferes with the public debate that is crucial for the survival of democracy. Finally, I will discuss the implications of research in psychology for social truth and justice movements and reform initiatives using the events of 9/11 as the primary example.

Framework: Direct and Indirect Approaches

Explanations of political assassinations, terrorist attacks, and other national tragedies that differ from official state accounts are sometimes dismissed by the general public because they evoke strong cognitive dissonance, a psychological phenomenon which occurs when new ideas or information conflict with previously formed ideologies and accepted beliefs.

One approach to dealing with cognitive dissonance arising from conflicting beliefs is to directly challenge the false belief itself, for example, by presenting evidence that the belief is factually incorrect. This is what most of the presentations at the Toronto Hearings did, and rightly and appropriately so. What I want to focus on – and even demonstrate – is the other method, the indirect approach.

The indirect approach, rather than challenging false beliefs directly, first points out the potential for the creation and persistence of false beliefs in general. This entails first demonstrating mechanisms by which beliefs can be manipulated, and then subsequently exploring what specific beliefs may have been generated falsely. Thus, before I challenge any false beliefs that may be held about the events of 9/11, I will first explain, in detail, how people can come to hold false beliefs. I expect that after I demonstrate this, the reader will better understand why the direct approach often not only fails to change a false belief, but sometimes serves to strengthen it.

In psychology, a false belief generally refers to one that has been manipulated, often purposely and outside of the person's awareness, and sometimes in a very specific direction or misdirection. An elegant and robust example comes from the work of Solomon Asch in the 1940's and Harold Kelley in the 1950's, and later replicated by others, including Neil Widmeyer and John Loy in the late 1980's; this experimental manipulation of beliefs is referred to as the "warm-cold effect."

Consequences of the "Warm-Cold" Effect

In a classroom setting, students in Widmeyer and Loy's experiment were given different introductions to a visiting professor and later asked to describe the professor and his lecturing abilities. Before the professor appeared, half of the students were informed that he was a "rather cold person" and the other half informed that he was a "rather warm person." In addition, students in both groups were also told that he was either a professor of physical education or a professor of social psychology. All students experienced the same lecture, which was delivered in a very neutral manner. The results showed that students who were led to believe that the lecturer was a warm person not only reported that he was much more likable than students led to believe that he was a cold person, they also reported that he was a more competent teacher. This is an example of a false belief because the liking or disliking, and perceptions of competency and incompetency, arose from the warm or cold introduction, not from the professor's actual mannerisms or methods of teaching, which were identical for all students. Most importantly, the information regarding the professor's area of expertise, as either a professor of "physical education" or "social psychology," had no effect on students' perceptions.

This experimental example has real world consequences for a functioning democracy. People can be manipulated, for example by the media, into falsely believing that they like or dislike a presidential candidate because of his or her public policy when, in fact, their perception arises solely from the media's framing of the candidate merely as either likable or dislikable. The issue of competency to hold the highest positions of public office does not even need to come into the equation.

Indeed, the creation and persistence of false beliefs can have very serious consequences. A case was presented by Steve Hoffman and colleagues in their paper entitled "There Must Be a Reason: Osama, Saddam, and Inferred Justification," which attempted to explain the strong – but false – belief held by many Americans that Saddam Hussein was involved in the terrorist attacks of September 11. It also demonstrates why the direct approach often serves only to strengthen the false belief. Here is a quote from their introduction:

Ronald Reagan once remarked that "the trouble with our liberal friends is not that they are ignorant, but that they know so much that isn't so" (Reagan, 1964). His comment goes to the heart of one of the most contentious issues in democratic theory: how should democracies handle false beliefs? False beliefs present a potentially serious challenge to democratic theory and practice, as citizens with incorrect information cannot form appropriate preferences or evaluate the preferences of others. Kuklinski and colleagues (2002) have demonstrated that incorrect beliefs – as distinct from mere lack of information, a more thoroughly studied phenomenon (e.g., Delli Carpini and Keeter 1997) – are widespread and underlie substantial differences in policy preferences." (p. 142)"

One explanation that Hoffman and colleagues discuss is referred to as the "information environment" explanation, which suggests that the false belief about Saddam Hussein and 9/11 arose primarily from the Bush administration's campaign, which was riddled with false information and innuendo that explicitly and implicitly linked Saddam with Al Qaeda.

However, Hoffman and colleagues were able to show, experimentally, that there is another "social psychological" explanation – that of inferred justification – which contributed to the creation and persistence of this false belief. They gave participants "challenge interviews" wherein reliable information was given to counter their false belief: primarily two newspaper articles reporting that the 9/11 Commission had not discovered any evidence linking Saddam to 9/11 and a quote from President Bush himself denying any claims of a link between Saddam and Al Qaeda. The responses were varied, and very interesting. Here are some examples of the strategies that people used to resist information that contradicted their beliefs.

First, several respondents, who had earlier claimed to believe that Saddam was linked to Al Qaeda, simply denied making this claim, even though it was recorded on the initial survey. In one case, a participant begins by saying that he did believe that Iraq was involved in the 9/11 attacks but then corrects his statement claiming that he knew it was Afghanistan all along. In fact, when the interviewer actually shows him his prior written response he continues to deny believing what he answered even though it is clearly laid out before his eyes.

Some of the other strategies that participants used to resist persuasion included the following, which are well known to psychologists:

Counter-Arguing

Directly rebutting the information. For example, some respondents could not provide any evidence to support their belief so they fabricated a reason. These people claimed that Saddam had to have been involved because of his hostility towards the US and support for terrorism: To quote one respondent: "I believe he was definitely involved with it because he was definitely pumping money into the terrorist organizations every way he could. And he would even send $25,000 to somebody who committed suicide to kill another person, to their family."

Attitude Bolstering

Bringing forth facts that support one's position without directly refuting the contradictory information. This was the most commonly used strategy. People would often change the topic or start talking about other good reasons why the U.S. was justified in going to war with Iraq. For example, some people responded that President Bush should not be judged so harshly for having acted on faulty information. One responded stated: "Well, I think he used the information that he had at the time; if that information was faulty I can't see that it could be his fault."

Selective Exposure

Ignoring the information without rebutting it or supporting it with other positions. In fact, many people simply refused to continue to engage in the discussion with contradictory information; one participant even said "I'm gonna pass on this one, for now."

Disputing Rationality

Arguing that opinions do not need to be grounded in facts or reasoning. The researchers' example of how this strategy was used by one person is telling:

> "**Interviewer:** …the September 11 Commission found no link between Saddam and 9/11, and this is what President

Bush said. (pause) This is what the Commission said. Do you have any comments on either of these?

Respondent: Well, I bet they say that the Commission didn't have proof of it but I guess we still can have our opinions and feel that way even though they say that."

Inferred Justification

A strategy that infers evidence supporting the respondent's beliefs. Basically, respondents retrospectively invented the causal links necessary to justify a favored politician's action. Inferred justification operates as a backward chain of reasoning that justifies the favored opinion by assuming the causal evidence that would support it.

God Have Mercy on Them – We Will Not

Lest you think that these kinds of reactions are merely responses in a laboratory setting, I have a personal story that I hope will trouble you as much as it did me. It occurred during a very friendly and casual conversation with a gentleman I had just met who was a life-long resident of Florida. We talked about the weather first, then our careers, then about our families and our concern for their futures, and then finally, politics and the future of America. "Well, I'll tell you what I think really needs to happen to set this country straight," he said. Since this gentleman had, so far, given wonderful advice on how to stay married for over forty years while raising a family, how to build a successful career, and how to be an upstanding member of one's community, and even how he had fought in the Vietnam war – I listened carefully. This is what he said: "What this country needs is for some of those al-

Qaeda terrorists that attacked us on 9/11 to walk into an American household, put a gun to the head of the father of the house, line up that man's wife and children against a wall, and make him watch, while they shoot everyone in his family. THEN," he said, raising his voice just a little, "the people in this country will understand what we are fighting to protect over there in Iraq."

After struggling to maintain my composure, I turned to ask him if he would volunteer his family for this, in order to save his county. But I did not. Instead, I gently asked him if a family in the Middle East might view some American soldiers as he views al-Qaeda terrorists. (I had in my mind a famous photograph taken mere moments after Samar Hassan, a five-year old Iraqi girl, covered in the blood of her family, had just witnessed her mother and father being shot and killed by American soldiers who opened fire on her family's car as they were on their way to take her sick brother to the hospital.) He appeared to be honestly surprised by such a scenario, one in which the tables had been turned and the Americans were viewed as the terrorists.

Now, I really did understand the point he was trying to make: unless it happens to them, in their own backyards and perhaps even within their own homes, many people won't take action against what they believe is wrong with their country. Yet the point he did not realize he was making is more revealing: unless whatever is happening is happening to an American, it just isn't important.

This widespread, deeply entrenched and false belief in "American exceptionalism" is a great threat to true democracy, by which I mean democracy for all. The type of democracy that is packaged and sold to us by the government and news and entertainment media is what I will refer to throughout this paper as "democracy for the few." It is meant for some, but not for all.

The point of this story is to emphasize how honest, decent, hard-working, and upstanding people can come to believe that democracy and freedom from wars of aggression belong only to them and not to all citizens of the world, whether they live in Afghanistan, Iraq, Pakistan, or Libya. This is the type of biased belief system that permits SCADs to continue.

"Democracy for the Few"

Indeed, the use of repression and terror, including threats of censorship, suppression of information, imprisonment, and torture, by leaders to silence political opponents and dissidents is not exclusive to authoritarian states. Such tactics can also be employed by leaders of democratic states – a fact that can be difficult for people to acknowledge, especially if it is not consistent with their belief system.

A recent Human Rights Watch World Report repudiated many leaders and governments worldwide as "despots masquerading as democrats." The report described how leaders use rhetoric, fear mongering, and suppression of a free press to undermine the rule of law. These charges are relevant to the current state of democracy in North America (Roth, 2008). I'll quote the report here:

> "Few governments want to be seen as undemocratic…. Determined not to let mere facts stand in the way, these rulers have mastered the art of democratic rhetoric that bears little relationship to their practice of governing…. The challenge they face is to appear to embrace democratic principles while avoiding any risk of succumbing to popular

preferences. Electoral fraud, political violence, press censorship, repression of civil society, even military rule have all been used to curtail the prospect that the proclaimed process of democratization might actually lead to a popular say in government.... Because of other interests – energy, commerce, counterterrorism – the world's more established democracies too often find it convenient to appear credulous of these sham democrats. Foremost has been the United States under President George W. Bush. In a troubling parallel to abusive governments around the world, the US government has embraced democracy promotion as a softer and fuzzier alternative to defending human rights.... Talk of human rights leads to Guantanamo, secret CIA prisons, waterboarding, rendition, military commissions, and the suspension of habeas corpus.... To make matters worse, the Bush administration's efforts to rationalize the invasion of Iraq in terms of democracy promotion has made it easier for autocrats to equate pressure on them to democratize with an imperial, militarist agenda. (pp. 1-4)"

We must be ever vigilant of the motives of leaders who would persuade us to surrender our property, liberty, and humanity, one priceless piece at a time. How can we do this? First and foremost by educating ourselves and our fellow citizens on the how "We the People" can be manipulated by our government and its compliant news media into forfeiting our civil liberties and duties. We need to challenge the long-standing and often erroneous assumptions about the role of government, public discourse and dissent in democratic societies. We can start by identifying some of the social psychological factors that can prevent people from examining evidence of crimes committed by the state.

Psychological Foundations of Democracy

One of the most important social psychological foundations of democracy is political tolerance. Democracy requires tolerance of different political views. Democracy specifically requires tolerance of alternative political views, especially those that may be unpopular, such as public discourse on threats posed by the state toward its citizens. A person's level of political tolerance largely determines his or her support for civil liberties and his or her degree of participation in civic duties, such as voting, showing support for free speech, or protesting government restrictions on freedom.

Research on political tolerance shows it is strongly influenced by an individual's level of commitment to democratic values, individual and collective personalities, and the degree of threat perception of others towards oneself. Although people with more political knowledge and experience tend to be more tolerant of dissimilar views, perceptions of threat can greatly decrease political tolerance in general. Failure to internalize important principles of democracy, such as political tolerance, majority rule, protection of minority rights, free speech, and equal voting, leads to apathy and double standards, or "democracy for the few."

In addition, the information environment, such as media and culture, can greatly influence political tolerance. For example, if the mainstream media portrays a group as violating social norms, public tolerance for that group will decrease. However, if a group is portrayed as behaving properly and in an orderly fashion, then far more people – often a majority – will tolerate the group and its activities, even if the group is generally unpopular or has an extremist image.

In two experiments, Falomir-Pichastor and colleagues tested the theory that when an aggressive act is committed, it is the perception of the perpetrator's political association as either democratic or authoritarian that determines whether the act is perceived as legitimate or not.

The results were telling: When people who commit aggressive acts were viewed as democratic, and their victims were viewed as authoritarian, the aggression was perceived as legitimate. However, any aggression committed against a democratic group was always perceived as highly illegitimate, regardless of whether the aggressor was seen as authoritarian or democratic. Hence, the less socially valued the group, the more legitimate any transgression against it was viewed, even when aggressive acts consisted of deadly force. Falomir-Pichastor's summary stresses the importance of such research in the post-9/11 world:

"In recent years, democratic nations have initiated a number of armed conflicts and wars, albeit not against other democratic nations, but against nondemocratic states...How can these aggressive state behaviors be justified without giving up the democratic principles of peace and rationality?

"We suspect that political leaders take advantage of democracy's good reputation...The results of the present studies provide potentially important insights for understanding how real intergroup and international conflicts are framed by elites to maximize their legitimacy and attract the necessary popular support (Nelson and Kinder, 1996). Many past and recent military interventions have been justified by portraying them as an opposition between 'good,' democratic forces and 'evil,' nondemocratic forces. Unfortunately, such a claim has a high price because it implies that democratic lives count more than nondemocratic lives. We hope that the present research can contribute to a better understanding of the dynamics underlying not only public support for, but also widespread opposition to, Western-democratic aggressions against nondemocratic targets." (p. 1683-1684, 1693)

Psychological Barriers to SCADs Inquiry

Although people may harbor some cynicism about bureaucrats and politicians, most do not want to believe that public officials in general, and especially those at the highest levels, would participate in election tampering, assassinations, mass murder, or other high crimes – especially in democratic societies. For example, although public cynicism toward government was high in the months prior to 9/11 (e.g., fewer than 30% of U.S. citizens indicated that they trusted their government to "do what is right"), trust in U.S. officials in Washington rose significantly (more than doubled to 64%) in the weeks following the attacks, suggesting that heightened focus on national security breeds support for incumbent foreign policy makers.

Claims that state intelligence and other officials within democratic states could conspire with criminal elements to kill innocent civilians are difficult for citizens of those states to comprehend, even when backed by substantial evidence. Evidence that U.S. officials have used the attacks of 9/11 as a means to manipulate the mass public into accepting two major wars of aggression has been dangerously ignored by mainstream media and academia until recently, as discussed by social psychologists McDermott and Zimbardo (2007, p. 365):

"An alternate hypothesis for the current system that bears examination suggests that leaders strive to manipulate public opinion through the strategic use of fear and anger in order to gain political power and advantage.... If leaders want or need backing for a particular campaign that is likely to be unpopular or expensive in lives and material, such as war, or restrictions on civil liberties, then the effective use of anger, threat, and fear can work to enhance public support. In this way, a terrorism alarm can simultaneously serve as both a political and a strategic tool."

To expose and prosecute officials responsible for orchestrating SCADs, people first must be presented with information of such crimes within the public sphere and, second, must be able to objectively consider evidence supporting those allegations, even facts that challenge their preexisting beliefs about democratic governance and citizen trust in leaders. As one of America's most prominent criminal prosecutors explains in his recent book, The Prosecution of George W. Bush for Murder:

"You have to disabuse yourself of any preconceived notion you may have that just because George Bush is the president of the United States he is simply incapable of engaging in conduct that smacks of great criminality. Because if you take that position, a position that has no foundation in logic, you're not going to be receptive to the evidence"

Thus, protecting democracy demands that citizens be made aware of how they can be manipulated by government and media into forfeiting their civic liberties and duties. Citizens need information vital to protecting them from crimes against democracy that, as history has repeatedly demonstrated, are particularly common in times of disaster, collective shock, and national threat.

Social Motivations and Goals

People's behaviors are largely regulated by social motivations and goals. Motivations are the processes that initiate an individual's behavior directed towards a particular goal, and motives and goals are focused either on desired or rewarding end states (approach) or on undesired or punishing end states (avoidance). For example, one's beliefs that another person is harmless may lead one to feel safe in approaching and interacting with that person in a positive way – a response based on approach-oriented motives or goals. Alternatively, one's beliefs that another person is threatening may elicit fear, leading one to avoid any interaction with that person or interact in ways that provoke confrontation – a response based on avoidance-oriented motives or goals.

These cognitive-behavioral mechanisms also underlie self-fulfilling prophecy, wherein one's motives, goals, or stereotypes directly influence interpersonal behavior in ways that tend to confirm, rather than disconfirm, preexisting beliefs. Conversely, interactions that disconfirm one's beliefs may lead to cognitive dissonance, which can be a powerful motivator for changing both public behavior and private beliefs.

For example, if a person works for a government institution because he believes strongly in democracy and government by the people, but he has recently discovered that colleagues are using the rule of law for personal gain, he would likely experience inner conflict and tension between these cognitions. To resolve cognitive dissonance, he could publicly voice his concerns, becoming a "whistleblower," even at the expense of his employment. Alternatively, he could change his opinion on the matter in two ways: Either he was wrong about his strong belief in democracy, or he was wrong in the belief that his colleagues had done something to violate the rule of law.

The attitude that is the weakest is the one that is also the most vulnerable to change; hence, in this situation, the person in question would most likely change his mind regarding the most recently formed belief about his colleagues – the path of least resistance – as opposed to his longstanding belief about government.

Research indicates that many people experiencing cognitive dissonance change their beliefs to make them consistent with otherwise dissonance-causing information; but occasionally some do not, as exemplified by the case of researcher Dr. Jeffery Wigand and the tobacco industry. After discovering that his employer, Brown and Williamson Tobacco Corporation, was intentionally manipulating the effect of nicotine in cigarettes, Wigand exposed the company's practice of "impact boosting" in the mainstream media. He was fired, testified in court, was constantly harassed, and was subjected to death threats because of his actions.

With respect to alleged SCADs, there have been many whistleblowers who, rather than change their beliefs, chose to publicly expose the problems they encountered in their respective fields of expertise. In response to the U.S. government's official account of the attacks of September 11, 2001, hundreds of officials, academics, and professionals have publicly expressed their objections – including the courageous Kevin Ryan who testified at the

Toronto Hearings, and who has co-authored several academic papers on 9/11.

Unfortunately, when people are confronted with evidence contradicting the U.S. official account of 9/11, it is unlikely that immediate, prolonged discussion and debate regarding evidence supporting alternative accounts will change their minds. However, the more the general public is presented with dissenting opinions and the more accessible to conscious processing that information becomes, the more this familiarity can lead to increased support for those dissenting opinions. By implication, social truth and justice movements and reform initiatives need to include strategies for resolving the cognitive dissonance and worldview defense reactions that their claims and proposals regarding SCADs inevitably provoke.

TMT: Mass Manipulation of Behavior via Mortality Salience

Basically, Terror Management Theory (TMT) proposes that, because people feel threatened by the fact that eventually they will die, they create a belief system that brings meaning and purpose, and thus a feeling of security, to their lives. This helps us understand why some people will vigorously defend any threats to their belief system.

Threatening the validity of a person's worldview, and hence the "security-providing function of that worldview," can result in vigorous cognitive-behavioral defenses, reactions collectively referred to as worldview defenses (Greenberg, Solomon, & Pyszczynski, 1997), ranging from contempt to physical aggression directed toward the source of the dissonant information. According to TMT, people create and defend cultural belief systems to deal with the existential dilemma of an "inevitable fate of nonexistence" after death:

> "The two most illuminating implications of TMT for understanding social behavior concern self-esteem and prejudice. By explicating how self-esteem comes to serve an anxiety-buffering function, the theory can explain the groping for self-esteem that seems to play such a prevalent role in human behavior – including the facts that those with high self-esteem fare much better in life than those lacking in self-regard, and that threats to self-esteem engender anxiety, anger, and all sorts of defensive reactions (from self-serving attributions to murder). The theory also offers an explanation for what is humankind's most tragic and well documented flaw: the inability to get along peacefully with those different from ourselves. If culturally derived worldviews serve a deep security-providing psychological need and are yet fragile constructions, it makes perfect sense that we respond to those espousing alternative worldviews with a combination of disdain, efforts to convert those others to our views, and aggression."

TMT is supported by research repeatedly showing that when people are exposed to information that increases death-related thoughts, known as mortality salience, they display more worldview defenses, such as showing greater bias toward their country or religion (known as compensatory conviction) and increased support for charismatic leaders, especially in times of national threat.

TMT dual-defense model proposes that mortality salience first activates proximal defenses, serving to immediately remove from conscious awareness thoughts related to death (e.g., via suppression, minimization, and denial), followed by distal defenses, acting to preserve one's self-esteem and worldview (e.g., via out-group stereotyping and in-group favoritism). Research indicates that increases in mortality salience can trigger displays of psychological dissociation and related behaviors; that is, threatening thoughts and emotions that are associated with an event are mediated independently of conscious awareness, rather than integrated, putatively to protect one from re-experiencing trauma.

Following the attacks of September 11, 2001, heightened mass anxiety and fear have likely been fostered by classical conditioning of emotionally laden thoughts and behaviors. For example, repeated media presentations of highly emotional images, such as images of the WTC Twin Towers being destroyed, paired with the horrific screams of witnesses, have produced enduring fear and aversion associated with these events. Because subliminal exposure to 9/11-related cues can bring death-related thoughts closer to consciousness, the phrase "9/11" – which is eerily similar to the "911" emergency response in North America – has become implicitly associated with traumatic death, destruction, and terrorism. The effect for many Americans and Canadians has been a corresponding increase in defensive and aggressive behavior when exposed to reminders of 9/11.

For example, in one study, when Americans were exposed to reminders of their mortality and 9/11, their support for U.S. President Bush and his counterterrorism policies increased. In another study, New York residents who continued to report greater distress (e.g., being angry, suspicious, or frightened and avoiding certain cities and events) a year after the attacks also displayed a greater willingness to surrender some of their civil liberties (e.g., favoring the use of citizen identification cards at all times to show police immediately upon request and allowing the U.S. government to monitor e-mails, telephone calls, and credit card purchases). Clearly, prompting people with reminders of 9/11 may arouse strong emotions that can be used by both government officials and mainstream media to manipulate citizens' behaviors.

The majority of research on TMT indicates that people's motivations to reduce the anxiety that arises from reminders of death and 9/11 can result in strong religious and patriotic displays and intolerance for people holding different cultural and political beliefs. Similarly, justification of the current social system can serve to reduce anxiety arising from uncertainty when the system's faults are exposed. These findings do not bode well for progressive social change in the face of injustice and crimes perpetrated by the state against its citizens.

System Justification Theory

According to System Justification Theory (SJT), there are many "social psychological mechanisms by which people defend and justify the existing social, economic, and political arrangements, often to their own detriment." As with reducing the negative effects of mortality salience proposed by TMT, justification of the system maintains "consistency, coherence, and certainty." SJT is supported by research showing that people can be strongly motivated to shorten their evaluations of information in order to reduce uncertainty, confusion, or ambiguity, also known as the "need for closure." The persistence of faulty beliefs, then, at both individual and societal levels, may perform an important psychological function, for example, by promoting feelings of safety and justice rather than permitting acknowledgment of potential vulnerability and exploitation.

Hence, system justification motives may interfere with SCADs inquiry because people are highly motivated to defend the institutions with which they are most familiar (e.g., religious, political and economic institutions, as well as military insititutions), behavior that is supported largely by selective attention and interpretation of information (Jost et al., 2008):

Research by DeSensi and Petty (2007) on authoritarianism and political conservatism indicates that system justification is a mechanism for some people to resist change and to rationalize inequalities in the status quo, even to their own detriment. In addition, social change is largely impeded by the low occurrence of collective action and protest against the system unless it is brutally unjust, and by the fact that criticism of the system can paradoxically increase justification and rationalization of the status quo, particularly when alternatives appear unlikely. This is especially true for alternatives proposed by a minority of dissenters, as research shows that information appearing to represent the majority opinion tends to induce "immediate persuasion," in comparison to minority opinions, which often induce "immediate resistance."

Contributing to people's failure to think critically about the validity of their worldviews is another psychological phenomenon known as "naive realism" – the tendency to believe that one always sees and responds to the world as it objectively is. Thus when others do not agree it is because their cognitions and behaviors are not based on reality.

Threats to Self and Worldviews Posed by SCADs

Naive realism, cognitive dissonance, TMT, and SJT all indicate that uncertainty reduction and threat management generally support the persistence of preexisting worldviews in the face of evidence that challenges those worldviews.

It is not surprising, therefore, that when confronted with the inconsistencies of the events of September 11, 2001 – for example, conflicts between information widely reported by the mainstream media, government, and the 9/11 Commission on the one hand, and dissimilar information presented by less-well-known alternative media, dissenting experts, scholars, and whistleblowers on the other – many people initially react by aggressively defending the official story, even to the point of fabricating arguments to support their beliefs.

The specific role of defensive denial in supporting flawed ideological belief systems was recently highlighted in two case studies analyzing the psychodynamics of attitude change. Bengston and Marshik's (2007) identification of several mechanisms of attitude resistance (e.g., dissociation, narcissistic withdrawal, and hyper-rationalization) underscored the fact that merely arousing cognitive dissonance is not a sufficient catalyst for changing behavior. Bengston and Marshik also identified several mechanisms of attitude change (e.g., moral culpability, realism, and experiential enlightenment) and discussed both findings in regard to public education on matters of democratic responsibility:

"For [democratic governance] to work as a viable alternative to rule by sheer power, citizens have to be not only knowledgeable but also educable – able to learn from civil experience and debates about policy to take a more perspicuous view of what constitutes their interests than they might have started with. But defensiveness has its appeal. If it did not, if ideologues and neurotics would not be amply gratified by their illusions and delusions, they would have no reason to resist moving forward. And so it is a measure of teaching effectiveness, on par with successful psychoanalysis, that it can cultivate open-mindedness in persons who would otherwise be happily closed-minded."

However, according to SJT, when changes to the collective worldview become inexorable, people's defense of the status quo begins to weaken in response to a growing support for the emergent worldview. According to Jost et al. (2008):

"The implication of a system justification analysis for social change is that it will either come not at all or all at once, the way that catastrophic change occurs in dynamic systems and in tipping point phenomena."

Democracies are not immune to government officials using fear and propaganda to gain popular support for policies of external aggression and internal repression. As North Americans struggle with repercussions of the attacks of September 11, 2001 – the deaths of nearly 3,000 people from 90 countries on that day, the U.S. declaration of a global war on terrorism, the erosion of civil liberties by the passing of PATRIOT Acts I and II, and the hundreds of thousands of deaths caused by the 9/11 wars in

Afghanistan and Iraq – American and Canadian citizens continue to be manipulated by their governments and media into forfeiting their freedoms and duties in exchange for security. These are grave matters that continue to be ignored by the mainstream media, the putative "watchdog" of democracy. As a political culture grows increasingly intolerant, public dissent is often demonized. Thus we find a persistent, broad refusal to challenge current political posturing despite overwhelming evidence that the Bush administration misled or outright lied about the events of 9/11 and its ensuing wars.

The integrity of a free press, where dissenting opinions and public discourse are presented – a matter integral to democracy – is already disappearing in Canada, according to a report on the news media from the Senate of Canada (2006). One of the greatest threats to democracy is mainstream news media's collusion with government in censoring information, especially in times of war (Williams, 1992):

> "Wars prosecuted by democratic societies are done so in the name of the people. If the public supports a war then it has a responsibility for the consequences. Citizens have rights and responsibilities, and surely one of the responsibilities in wartime is to see – or at least be provided with the opportunity to see – the price being paid to prosecute the war, whether this is the body of your neighbor's son or innocent civilians killed in the crossfire. Even if people do not want to accept their responsibilities it is difficult to argue that they have a right to be protected from seeing what happens on the battlefield. This would appear to deny a necessary democratic impulse."

IN DENIAL OF DEMOCRACY

According to alternative news media, this "necessary democratic impulse" is being weakened to the detriment of both "democratic" and "nondemocratic" lives, albeit unequally, as reported by Escobar (2008):

"Roughly two minutes of coverage, per network, per week. This is what the 3 major U.S. networks [ABC, CBS, NBC] now think that the drama in Iraq is worth...the networks are not telling Americans that more than one million Iraqis have been killed due to the 2003 U.S. invasion, according to sources as diverse as the medical paper The Lancet, [the website] Iraq Body Count, the British polling firm Opinion Research Business, and the website Just Foreign Policy. The networks are not even discussing the different numbers of violent Iraqi deaths, which may range from 600,000 to 1.2 million. The networks are not talking about the Pentagon underreporting or not reporting Iraqi civilian deaths. As Donald Rumsfeld used to say, the Pentagon "don't do body counts." The networks are not talking about the millions of Iraqi widows of war. The networks are not talking about almost 5 million displaced Iraqis – 2.4 million inside Iraq and 2.3 million in Jordan and in Syria. And the networks are not talking about – and especially not showing – U.S. soldiers coming home in body bags. Iraq is a human disaster worse than 9/11."

The effect of government and media manipulation on political tolerance is summarized by Snow and Taylor (2006):

"The dominance of censorship and propaganda is a triumph of authoritarian over democratic values. During times of international crisis like the Cold War or now in the so-called 'Global War on Terror,' authoritarian values of secrecy, information control and silencing dissent would appear to take precedence over democracy, the First Amendment and a free press. The general trend since 9/11, especially in the U.S., has been away from openness and toward increasing government secrecy coupled with what can seem a rise in contempt among inner circle policy-makers for a public's right to know that may override national and homeland security concerns."

Post-9/11 Political Tolerance

Essentially what we have is a system that creates threats which result in fear of terrorism that then needs to be managed by justifying the very system that created it in the first place. Two examples are denial of deep state politics and defense of disaster capitalism.

Perhaps the most serious threat to political tolerance, and thus democracy, is the one-percent doctrine – a policy, emanating from the Bush administration, of preemptive aggression against any state or non-state actor posing even a "1% chance" of threat, which must be treated as a 100% certainty. For example, as the November 2008 U.S. presidential election neared, neoconservatives continued to invoke the threat of "radical Islamic extremism" as the "absolute gravest threat" to the existence of America, even conceding that another 9/11-like terrorist attack would be "a big advantage to [Republican Presidential candidate John McCain]."

IN DENIAL OF DEMOCRACY

Incredibly, the Bush administration and mainstream media were still following in the same steps that led up to the wars on Afghanistan and Iraq, this time preparing to support a possible Israeli-led war on Iran before President Bush left office in January 2009. In fact, Pentagon officials have acknowledged that covert operations against Iran including plans to use "surrogates and false flags – basic counterintelligence and counter-insurgency tactics" similar to those used in Afghanistan, have been underway since 2007 with congressional approval and no major public debate. In fact, war propagandists are now predicting that Israeli and U.S. strikes on Iranian nuclear facilities will be welcomed by the Arab world, stating that their reaction will be "positive privately ... [with] public denunciations but no action," words sounding alarmingly familiar to Vice President Dick Cheney's erroneous prediction that Iraqi's would greet Americans "as liberators." Furthermore, the rhetoric of fear in attempting to link 9/11 terrorism to Iran cuts across both conservative and liberal party lines. In a speech as the Democratic presidential candidate, Barack Obama made repeated references to the terrorist threat facing the United States as "a powerful and ideological enemy intent on world domination" with the "power to destroy life on a catastrophic scale" if terrorists were permitted nuclear bombing capabilities:

> "The future of our security – and our planet – is held hostage to our dependence on foreign oil and gas. From the cave-spotted mountains of northwest Pakistan, to the centrifuges spinning beneath Iranian soil, we know that the American people cannot be protected by oceans or the sheer might of our military alone. The attacks of September 11 brought this new reality into a terrible and ominous focus."

Within the first 6 months of taking office, President Obama expanded the war in Afghanistan and Pakistan, using fear-provoking rhetoric similar to that of the Bush administration.

This continued shift toward ever-increasing authoritarianism and imperialism, precipitated by the mass fear and propaganda of 9/11, brings in its wake an ever more closed security state (Wolf, 2007; see Figure 1). According to Wolf (2007), all of the 10 historical steps prospective despots employ to close down open societies are well underway in North America: (a) invoking national external and internal threats, (b) establishing secret prisons, (c) recruiting paramilitary forces, (d) surveiling ordinary citizens, (e) infiltrating citizens' groups, (f) arbitrarily detaining and releasing citizens, (g) targeting dissenting individuals, (h) restricting the free press, (i) reframing criticism as "espionage" and dissent as "treason," and (j) subverting the rule of law.

In an increasingly fearful and intolerant political culture, this authoritarian mindset, escalated primarily by the events of 9/11, is also a disastrously dissociative one: it exemplifies "democracy for the few." This belief system places a premium on democratic rather than nondemocratic lives and compartmentalizes this fear of terrorism, separating it from a patriotic fervor to spread democracy and capitalism through war and occupation to anti-American states in the Middle East. These disparate beliefs are fueled by the imperialist agenda of American leaders committed to both military and economic conquest of regions in the Middle East.

The Bush administration implemented numerous policies that promote disaster capitalism – economic profiteering in the aftermath of collective shocks, such as terrorist attacks, natural disasters, and war – both in America and abroad in regions where it maintains military control. Huge profits can be acquired in the aftermath of wars through "post-conflict reconstruction" loans provided by the International Monetary Fund (IMF) and World Bank, organizations "often consulted prior to the onslaught of a major war" and that have been pivotal in channeling "foreign aid" to both Iraq and Afghanistan.

These policies have permitted collusion between war profiteers and elite opinion makers in Washington on one hand and the news media on the other to support a growing disaster capitalism complex, one in which corporately controlled media fail to investigate allegations of a "global war [being] fought on every level by private companies whose involvement is paid for with the public money" while simultaneously promoting "the unending mandate of protecting the United States homeland in perpetuity while eliminating all 'evil' abroad." (Klein)

U.S. officials have also used justification of free-market economic systems to minimize focus on the human disaster in Iraq and to rationalize and defend the exportation of American capitalism as a means to support democracy in the Middle East. Recently, the major U.S. entertainment conglomerate Disney announced its plans to increase profits by building an amusement park on expropriated Iraqi national park land in the middle of one of the most violent war zones in the Middle East, even though it clearly will not service the immediate needs of the Iraqi people.

To preserve what is left of North American democracy, and our responsibility for tolerance and restraint toward citizens of non-democratic states, the culture of fear and political intolerance and a governing dissociative mindset of "democracy for the few" must be subjected to immediate serious public scrutiny and debate.

This must begin with the thorough and scientific vetting of evidence that contradicts the U.S. government's official account of 9/11, on which two wars of aggression have been predicated, with the possibility of a third looming in the near future.

Reform Initiatives for SCADs Inquiry

The importance of continued public education and debate about SCADs in the post-9/11 world cannot be overemphasized, especially with governments and media attempting to silence dissenting voices, often with ad hominem attacks. Many scholars have already subjected labels such as "conspiracy theorist" to critical scrutiny.

In a recent sociological analysis, Husting and Orr (2007) discussed the inherent dangers of applying "conspiracy" labels to public exchanges of ideas and scholarly dialogues in a democracy:

"In a culture of fear, we should expect the rise of new mechanisms of social control to deflect distrust, anxiety, and threat.... Our findings suggest that authors use the conspiracy theorist label as (1) a routine strategy of exclusion; (2) a reframing mechanism that deflects questions or concerns about power, corruption, and motive; and (3) an attack upon the personhood and competence of the questioner.... The mechanism allows those who use it to sidestep sound scholarly and journalistic practice, avoiding the examination of evidence, often in favor of one of the most important errors in logic and rhetoric – the ad hominem attack."

Accordingly, social truth and justice movements and reform initiatives must address the social and psychological defense mechanisms that their inquiries into SCADs can provoke in the mass public. This approach needs to address both short-term and long-term solutions. First, immediate strategies to increase public awareness of SCADs should focus on framing information in neutral, nonthreatening language that gradually introduces people to the most serious of charges. Alternative accounts should be repeatedly presented within the public sphere with specific requests for citizens to themselves scrutinize the information presented to them and pass their findings along to others.

This suggestion is supported by research showing that (a) when controlling language is used to influence a message, it can arouse psychological reactance in people that results in rejection of that message; (b) civic participation is greatly increased when people are recruited to become involved during discussions of social responsibility; and (c) message repetition increases familiarity, which can translate into message tolerance and/or acceptance.

Regarding alleged 9/11 SCADs, public messages should encourage people to compare information presented by the 9/11 Commission Report (2004) with facts reported by nongovernmental sources and to contact their political representatives to follow up on any questions that they have not had answered.

Additional long-term solutions should include future public policy changes focused on increasing public education on media literacy and the social and psychological manipulation of citizens by the state. This proposal is supported by research showing that knowledgeable citizens possessing "firm, well-grounded political opinions are less susceptible to priming than audience members who know little about issues that dominate the news" and that "majority decisions tend to be made without engaging the systemic thought and critical thinking skills of the individuals in the group" but that dissident minority influence has been most effective when it "persisted in affirming a consistent position, appeared confident, avoided seeming rigid and dogmatic, and was skilled in social influence." (Zimbardo, 2008, p. 267) Moreover, when people are educated about and highly motivated to reduce their interpersonal biases, they "exhibit less prejudice" and develop more "shared social beliefs." Regarding SCADs, secondary- and postsecondary-level education should include courses on political psychology that deal with the social psychological foundations of democracy and citizens' rights and responsibilities to protect themselves from manipulation by the state and media.

Conclusion

I briefly reviewed, first, the social psychological foundations of democracy, secondly, research suggesting how preexisting beliefs can interfere with SCADs inquiry, especially in relation to the events of September 11, 2001, and, thirdly, strategies to educate the public as to how it can be manipulated by government and media into forfeiting civil liberties and duties. In the same year that William Golding, in *Lord of the Flies*, proffered his warning about the importance of dissent in a climate of fear, another great spokesman, Edward R. Murrow, also reminded us of the necessity of dissent to fulfill our responsibility of defending democracy from rampant fear:

> "We must not confuse dissent with disloyalty. We must remember always that accusation is not proof, and that conviction depends upon evidence and due process of law. We will not walk in fear, one of another. We will not be driven

by fear into an age of unreason, if we dig deep in our history and our doctrine, and remember that we are not descended from fearful men – not from men who feared to write, to speak, to associate and to defend causes that were, for the moment, unpopular."

We can and must take seriously the citizen's call to action and not allow fear to override the demand for interpersonal tolerance of different political views. We can and must create dissonance in the public psyche to encourage social responsibility and education on matters of national interest. We can and must investigate the current state of affairs for ourselves and not delegate accountability to elected officials who may harbor alternative agendas. We can and must remember that trading freedom for security destroys present and future collective power to participate in democratic governance. We can and must believe that change is possible when we choose to be a part of it. We can and must dissent in the face of everyday denials of democracy.

CHAPTER FIFTEEN

Reflections on the Toronto Hearings

BY DAVID A. JOHNSON, PH.D., FAICP

Preface

TEN YEARS AGO, ON SEPTEMBER 11, 2001, I WAS AT MY COMputer working on a paper. It was a gorgeous day in North Carolina and indeed on the entire east coast. I flipped over to the news and discovered that a plane had hit one of the World Trade towers in New York. Then I watched in horror as a second plane hit the South Tower, indicating that this was not an accident but something else. An hour later the South Tower collapsed, followed by the North Tower. I had been in those buildings on a number of occasions. Now, unbelievably, they were gone and nearly 3,000 people had perished. Like most people, I was grateful for the quick identification of the evil men who had committed this most horrendous of crimes on American soil. For several years following the attacks, like most people, I accepted the official explanations, wondering, though, whether this terrible event could have been prevented by our powerful military and intelligence agencies in Washington and around the world.

New York is my native city and I have written two books about its development and redevelopment. When the World Trade Center was first proposed I was working in New York as a city planner. We planners hotly debated whether the World Trade Center made good development sense. I supported the project because it appeared to solve several problems. The motivation for building the World Trade Center was to keep the financial district of lower Manhattan tightly clustered around the downtown – the area historically best served by public transportation. So I knew those buildings and had examined the architects' plans. I never liked the design very much. The spaces in the buildings were dark and gloomy. But the engineering was unique. A powerful central spine contained the structural elements that held the buildings up. This was supplemented at the perimeter by a web of Vierendeel trusses welded together to form a powerful box supporting the buildings. When a year or so after the attacks, I re-examined the videos of the collapses of the Twin Towers, something began to look very wrong to me. I had been trained in structural engineering in architecture school and had worked under the direction of professional engineers, verifying the structural design adequacy of scores of buildings. The videos of the September 11 collapses just didn't look right to me. Where were the robust spines in the centers of the two structures after collapse? My doubts persisted for several years, even after the release of Joint Congressional Hearings, the 9/11 Commission Report, and the two studies of the dynamics of collapse issued by the National Institute of Standards and Technology.

The Toronto Hearings

In September of 2011, on the Tenth Anniversary of 9/11, I was asked to serve with three panelists – two highly respected Canadian academics and the honorary chief judge of the Supreme Court of Italy – to hear testimony about that terrible day and alternatives to the official scenarios that had sought to explain the sequence of events that changed the course of history. I accepted the assignment reluctantly, but with the hope that I might have my doubts about the official story dispelled. September 11th is a difficult topic to internalize emotionally and weigh objectively. For four intense days we sat through the testimony of eighteen witnesses who had devoted much of their recent lives trying to sort out the facts of 9/11 and separate them from the inevitable speculations and theories that have swirled around the attacks, how they unfolded and the physical and human damage inflicted. The presentations ranged from rigorous and persuasive to tentative and open-ended, and occasionally controversial.

The Hearings began with a moment of silence to remember the victims and their families. This was followed by a video presentation by several 9/11 family members. It continues to be extremely painful to hear the relatives of victims express their frustration at the failure of the official investigations to bring answers to their questions and closure to their grief. This is especially poignant considering the extraordinary lengths the families went through to force a reluctant federal establishment even to hold an investigation, an investigation that turned out to be deeply flawed.[362]

There is no need to repeat here the details of the evidence and unanswered questions presented by the expert witnesses at the Toronto Hearings. The aggregate weight of the facts and deductions offered should give any thoughtful person reason to question the validity of the official version of events offered by the 9/11 Commission and the National Institutes of Standards and Technology (NIST). Several elements of the testimony stand out to this observer. The analyses of David Chandler showing free-fall movements in the collapses of the twin towers and WTC 7 are strong evidence of controlled demolition. Professor Paul Zarembka's rigorous analysis of the unusual number of call options made on the stocks of the two airlines involved is also important. These were not random investments but statistically unexplainable except by the possibility of prior knowledge of the plan to attack the World Trade Center and Pentagon. The 9/11 Commission did not look deeply into who might have been behind these lucrative deals. The experiments of Jon Cole showing how thermite easily cuts through steel and the identification of unignited nanothermite residues in the dust by Niels Harrit provide sufficient grounds to demand an independent review of the conclusion that explosives were used to bring down the three WTC buildings. Particularly dramatic was Professor Harrit's simple visual experiment of drawing a powerful magnet under a bag of dust from the area around Ground Zero. As he passed the magnet under the plastic envelope, clusters of iron spheroids were attracted from the dust. Iron spheroids are by-products of a thermitic reaction.

REFLECTIONS ON THE TORONTO HEARINGS

Richard Gage's analysis of the building destruction noted numerous phenomena that appeared to be incompatible with the official version of how the buildings failed. These include the following observations:

- Total disintegration of the tower buildings above the crash zone, immediately after the onset of collapse.
- Pulverization of concrete floors, forming enormous dust clouds. Energy levels needed to cause such pulverization appear far in excess of the potential gravity-based energy stored in the structure during construction.
- Cascades of extruded clouds of material in all directions from a level just above the crash zones, bearing a striking resemblance to high-energy explosive photographs available on the Web.
- Clouds of dust moving vertically, high in the sky above the twin towers, suggesting rising hot air particle suspensions. A structure simply collapsing from beam and column failure would be unlikely to emit such high level clouds of dust.
- Flashes of red fire around the entire perimeter of the floor just below the crash zone just at the onset of collapse. A collapse due entirely to structural failure would not exhibit such conflagration. Explosives might. (Flashes on lower floors would not have been visible after the initiation of collapse due to the pervasive smoke and dust surrounding the lower portions of the buildings.)
- Photographs of key core columns cut at 45 degrees at the base of the building have been shown as evidence.

A 45-degree burn would be the way a supporting column would be destroyed by a thermitic charge, permitting the structure to slide off its foundation support and bring down the central core above it. (Verification is needed to ensure that these were not made in the cleanup aftermath.)

- It is highly improbable that WTC 7 could collapse uniformly and instantaneously from the failure of a single column (Column 79) as suggested by NIST. All columns would have to fail at the same level and at the same moment as 79 for the building to collapse in the way it did – in free fall for 100 feet. Columns simply do not keel over in empathy with a single nearby failed column. Serial column failure is possible but only in a delayed sequential fashion, yielding an asymmetrical failure. This, however, is not how this building came down.

- NIST declined to address what ensued immediately upon so-called initiation of collapse for the Twin Towers, assuming what followed was "inevitable," without describing or explaining the mechanism of serial collapse or the pulverization of 108 floors of concrete in each tower. References to "pancaking" are misleading as the residual debris showed no evidence of slabs dropping serially as the collapse proceeded.

- First responders and other on-site witnesses reported multiple explosions prior to and during the collapses of the three buildings.

REFLECTIONS ON THE TORONTO HEARINGS

That more than 1,600 professional engineers and architects agree with Mr. Gage and have signed a petition demanding an independent investigation is notable, (though it has gone totally unnoticed by the mainstream media). The architect and engineer petition signers believe that only controlled demolitions can explain these phenomena. This proposition needs to be further examined. (The NIST engineers, when asked whether they had looked for explosives, said they had not, even while arguing that no explosives had been used in the building collapses at the World Trade Center.)

Other speakers at the Toronto hearings presented a lengthy list of unanswered questions, inconsistencies, and anomalies in the narratives of the official reports. Professors David Ray Griffin, Graeme MacQueen and chemist Kevin Ryan provided detailed and persuasive challenges to the official story. Their dogged research, ignored by the mainstream media, cries out for a wider audience and a rigorous but fair review by independent authorities. Jay Kolar's talk on the identities of the alleged 19 hijackers also raises disturbing questions about the individuals so quickly named as the perpetrators of the crimes of September 11. Barbara Honegger's view that the official story of the Pentagon attack is false also deserves further verification or refutation. There are simply too many unanswered questions remaining about the events of that day to close the books and simply move on as our Washington politicians would like us to do. Even the chairs of the 9/11 Commission have admitted that they were set up to fail. It is not too late to demand a real investigation. Indeed, it will never be too late until the true facts are revealed and justice is done.

THE 9/11 TORONTO REPORT

Professor Lance deHaven-Smith in his presentation on 9/11 and State Crimes Against Democracy, SCADS for short, showed how unaccountable units of government can and have through history undermined democratic states and institutions. Of course, there have been State Crimes Against Humanity perpetrated from earliest times. But State Crimes Against Democracy are a relatively new phenomenon, if you discount such events as the transformation of the Roman Republic into the Roman Empire. Democracies are not necessarily fragile entities but they are vulnerable to efforts to undermine them, as we saw in Weimar Republic in Germany in the 1930s. The question of interest here is whether the 9/11 attacks were part of a SCAD, an unthinkable notion, of course, but one that would require a new investigation to put to rest.

Professor Peter Dale Scott's incisive presentation reinforced the need to "connect the dots" concerning the events of 9/11. Scott's conception of "deep state politics" is a disturbing complement to the idea of SCADS as a driving force of a centralized state dominated by long-term secretive planning for control of strategic resources and global hegemony. Again, the verdict is not in as to the degree to which "deep politics" dominates US and global decision-making, but the possibility clearly needs to be considered.

Other speakers at the Toronto Hearings showed how salient facts were ignored or misrepresented in the official reports. They also noted unexplained anomalies, and the numerous unanswered questions that remain. I will not repeat their findings here in detail. The reader is invited to look carefully at their testimony in this report. At the conclusion of the Hearings, the only reasonable conclusion one could come to is that the official reports have failed to provide a satisfactory explication of the events of 9/11/01. The American people and the international community deserve and are owed a real investigation. It is not too late to get to the bottom of the unsolved mysteries and culpabilities of the events of that terrible day. But persuading people that a new investigation is absolutely essential is not going to be easy. Let me illustrate.

At a social event recently I tested out reactions to questions about 9/11 events on several highly educated people. One man identified himself as a professor of criminology at a local university. I couldn't resist asking him whether he viewed the 9/11 attacks as crimes. His immediate response: "No, it was an act of war." He indicated that he regarded crimes as smaller events. I went on to ask whether the murder of more than 3,000 people was not also a crime. He relented and finally agreed that it was a crime as well as an act of war, though the latter category would take precedence in any societal response. Apparently, it is less of a crime to commit mass murder than a single murder – even to a criminologist.

I then asked a well-known news reporter for our local newspaper what he thought about the 9/11 events. I mentioned my participation in the Toronto Hearings, and asked whether the local paper might be interested in doing a story on what came out of the Hearings. His reply was that it probably would have to be treated as a human interest rather than a news story. Was this an example of instant self-censorship by an otherwise open and respected journalist?

I asked another well-educated professional whether he would consider a look at the factual evidence and testimony given in Toronto. His response was, in effect, "No, my mind is made up." His view was that conspiracy theorists assemble isolated facts to compose a formulation already in their minds. "Elaborate theories don't hold up under close scrutiny. Nobody could put together the complex conspiracies that theorists put forward. I believe in chaos theory. Nothing so complex as 9/11 could be planned. No, I won't look at your facts or 'evidence.'" This is a man who has spent his life, as I have, as a professional city planner.

On another occasion, a friend who is a professional architect was asked to look at the photographs of the collapses of the three World Trade Center buildings. He refused and indicated that it was his firm belief, having seen videos of the collapses, that the buildings had come down just as one might have expected from the plane crash damage and ensuing fires. He was not going to jeopardize his mental images with new information.

The resistance of such educated people to looking at evidence was disappointing though not surprising. Once a mental stand is taken, there is a heavy price to revising an opinion about so traumatic an event as 9/11. Laurie Manwell has thoughtfully explained in her Toronto Hearings paper the real obstacles to getting people to take a second look, and the even greater obstacles to people's revision of a previously adopted conclusion about the events of that terrible day. "Cognitive dissonance" is a powerful barrier to reconsideration, even when faced with scientifically-based facts and robust alternative theories. The Nobel-winning psychologist Daniel Kahneman has identified and measured a related concept he calls "cognitive illusion," which is the result of quick, intuitive reactions to a threatening situation, probably an evolutionary residual built in to the species to ensure survival in situations of imminent attack.[363] This System 1 reaction, as Kahneman calls it, contrasts with System 2 cognition, based on analysis and rational thinking. System 2 cognition, Kahneman has shown, produces much more accurate conclusions and outcomes. But it comes at a price because thinking takes effort and time. System 1 – intuitive, immediate reaction – is far less reliable than System 2 but is easier to achieve quickly. Relying on System 1 reactions, many people have found that accepting the official explanations of 9/11 is less threatening, and easier to accept. The result is collective cognitive illusion, abetted by the imposed or self-imposed censorship of alternative analyses by the mainstream media.

Were Crimes Committed?

The federal and state authorities chose to categorize the events of 9/11 as acts of war, and by doing so have been able to avoid criminal procedures in courts of law. True, there have been trials of several accused "masterminds" in military tribunals, but these have lacked the rigor, thoroughness, and legality that would have prevailed in civilian criminal courts. The use of torture on accused accomplices further throws into doubt the validity of the confessions so secured.

The alleged perpetrators of the murders on 9/11 were presumed to have self-immolated in suicidal hijackings. So it was asserted that there was no need to conduct further criminal investigations concerning the circumstances and alleged perpetrators of the crimes of 9/11. This confusion served as an excuse to limit further criminal investigations.

One might think that an array of criminal investigations would have been an inevitable outcome of the murder of more than 3,000 innocent people, but this has not been the case. Nor have any criminal indictments emanated from the continuing deaths of area workers and first responders who have suffered mesothelioma cancer and other pulmonary illnesses, having erroneously been assured by the Environmental Protection Agency in the aftermath of the attacks that the air was safe to breathe. (It is anticipated that the death toll among this group will eventually exceed the number who died on 9/11.) We should simply note that there is no statute of limitations on the crime of murder, and that it is never too late to initiate new investigations on the basis of new evidence in capital cases.

Apart from the possibility of bringing criminal proceedings against those responsible for the planning and carrying out the murderous acts on September 11, there are two other categories of crimes for which investigations are needed and have not yet been initiated. The first category is official malfeasance or dereliction of duty resulting in death or injury that should have been prevented. The second category consists of acts intended to cover up or conceal crimes. To date no responsible officials, military or civilian, have been reprimanded, demoted, or punished for failure to perform their duties or fulfill their assigned responsibilities on September 11. Indeed, several of the key actors have been rewarded with promotions or awards despite evidence of having failed in their duty to protect the American people.

The possibility of cover-ups through outright lying in testimony to the Joint Congressional Hearings or the 9/11 Commission cannot be ruled out.[364] Omissions and skewing of evidence, or professionally unethical behavior by officials, researchers and contracted consultants lie in a gray area of the law, though the conscious act of concealing crimes is actionable. A new, honest investigation conducted with subpoena powers should be empanelled to look into whether such crimes might have been committed.

Possible Venues for Remedies

What venues might be available in which to seek truth and justice? Before criminal charges can be brought, the true facts underlying the events of September 11 must be established. A number of initiatives have been proposed for actions within the United States. These include the creation of a standing Congressional committee on the events and continuing impacts of the 9/11 attacks. A campaign has been started calling for write-in petitions to be sent to the White House to open a new investigation. In addition, the use of ballot referenda in selected states where it is legal to do so upon petition has been suggested by former Senator Mike Gravel. Senator Gravel is currently seeking funding to obtain the needed minimum number of signatures to get on the ballots of several states. These promising initiatives should continue to be pursued.

Regrettably, the three branches of the US national government have so far proved that they cannot be relied on to conduct independent investigations or to pursue effective civil or criminal proceedings. So it may be necessary to look elsewhere. We should keep in mind that citizens from ninety countries, in addition to the United States, were killed on September 11, 2001. Foreign nationals killed totaled 372, or about 12 percent of the 2,977 victims. So there is ample reason for the international community to look beyond American institutions for objective, independent investigations and international criminal proceedings, if warranted.

THE 9/11 TORONTO REPORT

The initial step might be to convene an independent international blue-ribbon panel to confirm or refute the physical and chemical findings which point to controlled demolitions. Investigations might also be placed in the hands of the National Academy of Science and/or the National Academy of Engineering.

There are approximately 2,200 National Academy of Science members and 400 foreign associates. Some 200 NAS members have received Nobel prizes. The NAS, headquartered in Washington, DC, was founded in the 1860s.

The National Academy of Engineering (NAE), founded in 1964, is a private, independent, nonprofit institution that provides engineering leadership in service to the nation. The mission of the NAE is to promote the technological welfare of the nation by marshaling the expertise and insights of eminent members of the engineering profession. In addition to its role as advisor to the federal government, the NAE also conducts independent studies to examine important topics in engineering and technology. The NAE has more than 2,000 peer-elected members and foreign associates, senior professionals in business, academia, and government who are among the world's most accomplished engineers. They provide the leadership and expertise for numerous projects focused on the relationships between engineering, technology, and the quality of life.

The academies declare that they are science-based and are politically independent. One would expect that the appointment of totally objective committees to examine and judge the evidence brought forward to date might be within the capacity and mandate of the academies. Foreign associate representation would add to the confidence the public might have in judgments emanating from these prestigious institutions. Should the academies be reluctant to take on such formidable tasks, an independent international scientific blue-ribbon panel to confirm or refute physical and chemical findings could be formed under the auspices of some respected institution acting and widely regarded as an honest broker.

Should independent investigations indicate that crimes may have been committed, according to US law, including both federal and State law, or applicable international law, as recognized by the UN Charter or the Charter of the Nuremberg Tribunal of 1950, grand juries should be empanelled to bring indictments and set in motion judicial proceedings in appropriate venues.

A US federal grand jury enquiry with subpoena powers would be the best place for proceedings to begin. State or local courts are less suitable given the wide scope of investigation, but should not be ruled out.

Since international crimes may have been committed, the jurisdiction of courts in other sovereign nations and the International Criminal Court (ICC) in the Hague are possible venues for investigations and prosecutions. Though the attacks took place on US soil, the involvement of foreign nationals and the gravity of international consequences appear to provide ample warrant for ICC jurisdiction. However, the United States has revoked its original signing of the Rome Statute of 2002 establishing the ICC, and so it is not bound by the provisions of the Treaty. (As of 2012 approximately 120 states are parties to the Statute of the Court.) Under the Treaty, international crimes can be investigated by the ICC only under one or more of the following conditions:

- where the person accused of committing a crime is a national of a state party (or where the person's state has accepted the jurisdiction of the Court);
- where the alleged crime was committed on the territory of a state party (or where the state on whose territory the crime was committed has accepted the jurisdiction of the Court); or
- where a situation is referred to the Court by the UN Security Council.

The first two conditions do not appear to be applicable to the September 11 situation and the third proviso would, unfortunately, in all likelihood be vetoed in the Security Council by the United States delegation. The stance of the United States government against widely accepted international law is particularly regrettable in light of the leadership of the US in establishing the Nuremberg Principles in 1950 at the end of the Second World War.[365] These principles are highly germane to possible crimes committed in connection with the September 11 attacks. It remains to be seen whether they can be invoked in any international venue.

An alternative to proceedings at the International Criminal Court might be to convene an unofficial, but prestigious tribunal similar to the Russell Tribunal which focused attention on the criminality (and irrationality) of the war in Vietnam. Though it lacked status, the Tribunal brought the attention of world opinion and the international community to bear on the tragedy unfolding in Southeast Asia, thereby helping to end the conflict there.

REFLECTIONS ON THE TORONTO HEARINGS

Costs (and benefits) that might be associated with a new, honest investigation

What costs and benefits might result from a new, authentic, objective, believable investigation? If it can be shown and a majority of people come to understand who planned and carried out the events of September 11, 2011, how would (or could) this understanding affect US society, politics and image in the world? The answer to these questions depends on what the independent investigation determines to be the facts. The investigation may conclude that the tragedy of 9/11 was indeed the result of 19 hijackers commandeering four jet airliners and occurred only through malfeasance or dereliction of duty on the part of those responsible for protecting the country, and that a cover-up was undertaken merely to conceal incompetence. The two dominant parties have taken the view to forget the past and simply move on. Reprimands would be unlikely and the public would lose confidence in governmental response and accountability.

Another scenario would be where the responsible authorities, both civilian and military, were found to have simply moved aside, passively but intentionally, enabling the attacks to occur as described in the official reports, despite being aware of their likelihood and timing. The result would be a further loss of trust in authority. But culpability and accountability would probably be difficult to prove.

A third scenario that might be found would be where American authorities secretly farmed out to third parties the planning and logistics of carrying out the attacks and building collapses, but keeping enough distance to maintain deniability. These third parties could be foreign intelligence services, or pseudo-business corporations formed specifically for the task, or a combination of the two. Such enterprises have been used in the past to carry out covert activities.

A fourth, and in my opinion least likely, scenario would be where a special, official unit was set up within the American intelligence and governing circles to carry out the attacks. This would be the most difficult to keep secret and insulated from traditional military and intelligence entities which might harbor honest whistle-blowers.

So the degree of involvement by previously trusted officials would determine the level of trauma that a revelation of inside complicity, passive or active, would induce in the American people. Could the body politic withstand serious revelations without severe damage to cherished American ideals and institutional beliefs?

On the other hand, would the failure to look at unpleasant realities openly and honestly be even more damaging to American society and institutions? It is difficult to say, but there have been examples of societies and nations facing up to internal dysfunction, trauma, and immoral practices, emerging from the painful process stronger and politically more free. The American Civil War was such a case, as was the less bloody termination of the Apartheid system in South Africa. Similarly, Soviet Communism bloodlessly collapsed as a result of internal contradictions and lies. Could the American system embrace a comparable, but equally turbulent catharsis? Given the manipulation of the media, information controls, and the capacity of the American people for self-delusion, it is an open question. A polarized country might simply become more polarized. But that is a risk worth taking. We have already lost so much of our freedom and so many of our rights in the wake of 9/11 that to fail to uncover the truth would be to encourage further deterioration of our protections and liberties.

The Toronto Hearings are just a beginning. It can be said of these Hearings what Philip Shenon said in his book, *The Commission, The Uncensored History of the 9/11 Investigation*: *"The full truth has not been told yet. It won't be told until there is an objective, independent investigation."*[366]

CHAPTER SIXTEEN

Strengths and Weaknesses of the Toronto 9/11 Hearings in Advancing the Case for a New Investigation

BY HERB JENKINS

THE PRIMARY STATED OBJECTIVE OF THE TORONTO 9/11 hearings was to marshal and assess the strongest evidence against the official account of September 11, 2001. In fact, however, the hearings attempted to do a lot more than that. Several witnesses argued that Washington is a secretive, deceptive war machine bent on global domination through preemptive wars of conquest. The largest set of witnesses presented evidence-based arguments to show that powerful people within this war machine either let the attacks go forward or manufactured them by their own hand. Many presenters supported the more radical alternative: the government engineered 9/11. The key to making that case was presented in papers that argued that controlled demolition destroyed the World Trade Center

Twin Towers and Building 7 under the cover of the impacts of the jetliners and the ensuing fires. All of these matters go beyond presenting purely negative evidence that the official account is false.

The central purpose of the hearings was to advance the case for a new investigation of 9/11. To fulfill that purpose, the hearings would have to change the perceptions of many Americans who have accepted the official account. The official account holds that the events of 9/11 were caused by a surprise attack from 19 Islamic terrorists who hijacked four jet liners and managed to fly two of them into the WTC and a third into the Pentagon. I believe that to change perceptions the hearings had to succeed at several levels. First, they needed to present convincing evidence against the official account. Second, they needed to make a credible case that the government had both a motive for making 9/11 happen through controlled demolition and the possibility of carrying out that plan.

It would be unreasonable to expect the hearings to go beyond circumstantial evidence of the government's hand. Not enough is known about what actually transpired on 9/11 to make an evidence-based argument about who did it and how they did it. But in the long run, only direct evidence of this kind, not just circumstantial evidence, may be needed to turn the tide of public perceptions.

In the discussion below, I try to assess the strengths and weaknesses of the case for Washington D.C. as a war machine, and the claim that on 9/11 controlled demolition was used to accomplish its ends. I also offer my views on whether it is likely that these arguments would be sufficiently persuasive to succeed in its central purpose of a new investigation. I raise a further question: would such an investigation be likely to succeed in unraveling the mysteries of 9/11? Finally, I suggest a way forward that does not rely on a new state-sponsored investigation.

Obstacles to changing perceptions of 9/11

I do not have sure knowledge of what is in the mind of most Americans when they think about 9/11. The six points that follow are educated guesses. If they are about right, they mean that changing perceptions of 9/11 will be an uphill battle.

1. They find the official account to be simple and coherent. The intent of Al Qaeda-sponsored terrorists, to kill Americans and destroy their property, is accepted as common knowledge. Their ability to penetrate American defenses appears to have been amply demonstrated by, among other instances, the 1993 basement truck bombing of the North Tower of the WTC, the concurrent 1998 bombings of US embassies in Tanzania and Kenya, and the 2000 bombing of the USS Cole in Yemen. The events of 9/11 are seen as another chapter in that history.

2. They see no rival theory of how 9/11 was brought about which answers the questions of who, why, and how it was done.

3. They do not believe that a number of highly placed government officials would have the depth of moral depravity required to deliberately cause the horrific deaths of so many Americans.

4. They believe that many people would have to be involved in orchestrating a government conspiracy on the order of

9/11. They do not think the perpetrators would risk eventual detection by whistle blowers or confessors.

5. They find it improbable that government perpetrators would have the detailed foreknowledge of what transpired on 9/11 in order to create credible false evidence that the attack was perpetrated by Al Qaeda terrorists, and to cover up their own treasonous actions or inactions.

6. They are aware of the enormous consequences for Americans' image of their nation's place in history should it turn out that the government had a hand in 9/11, which makes it especially hard to accept that proposition.

The hearings can be viewed as an attempt to overcome these obstacles to changing public perceptions.

The case for Washington as a secretive, deceptive war machine

This theme was pursued in papers given by Lance de-Haven Smith, "9/11 and State Crimes against Democracy," and by Peter Dale Scott, "9/11 and Deep State Politics." I include Laurie Manwell's paper, "In Denial of Democracy," with this set because it argues that the failure of many to examine with an open mind the evidence for state crimes against democracy can be understood in terms of cognitive processes which protect prior beliefs from being challenged by a rational evaluation of the evidence. Michel Chossudovsky gave a presentation at the hearings titled, "Global Consequences of 9/11," which also developed the theme of Washington as a war machine but which was not included in this volume.

STRENGTHS AND WEAKNESSES OF THE TORONTO 9/11 HEARINGS IN ADVANCING THE CASE...

These papers seek to develop a broad view of how we are governed that would make a government hand in 9/11 believable. They argue that the Washington war machine is fueled by the military-industrial complex famously cited by Eisenhower, together with increasingly powerful intelligence agencies, by the acquiescence, perhaps the leadership, of the highest elected government officials, and a Congress inclined to show more deference than vigilance in its oversight of a huge security apparatus. It is seen as a machine designed to bring about a world order advocated by the authors of the "Project for the New American Century." That project was to achieve American global dominance through overwhelming military power and pre-emptive wars. Among the tools used by the war machine are the control of information, undercover armed operations, and the suppression of dissent.

Lance de-Haven Smith's paper, "9/11 and State Crimes Against Democracy," argues that it is more appropriate to treat the possibility of a government hand in 9/11 as an example of a state crime against democracy (SCAD) than as a conspiracy theory. I agree. The significant feature of the case against the government is not that officials conspired in secret to do this thing. Rather, it is what they are suspected of conspiring to do. In de-Haven Smith's words, they were engaged in an example of concerted actions or inactions by government insiders intended to manipulate democratic processes and undermine popular sovereignty. One hopes that this new language might displace the brilliant sound bite used to dismiss out-of-hand the evidence-based arguments of 9/11 researchers: "They're conspiracy theories."

However that turns out, de-Haven Smith's term sets the stage for a comparative examination of 9/11 in the context of other suspected or generally accepted examples of SCADs in US history. In Table 1 of his essay, de-Haven Smith places the events of 9/11 among 19 other possible examples of SCADs. He rates the level of confirmation of state involvement in these examples from low to high. 9/11 gets a "medium" as do the assassinations of John F. Kennedy, Lee Harvey Oswald, and the attempted assassination of George Wallace.

I see a downside in the approach exemplified in Table 1. If one is not prepared to believe that the government had a hand in one or more of these other events, the case for government complicity in 9/11 may suffer collateral damage. The damage would take the form of deciding that the author is prone to see government criminality everywhere and thus his judgments on 9/11 complicity can't be trusted. The fact that de-Haven Smith does not claim a high degree of confirmation for many of his examples might reduce the collateral damage. I hope so because I see the approach taken in Table 1 as worthy of careful consideration when trying to come to a reasoned position on the case for Washington as a war machine.

Another downside is that the generalization from other SCADs to 9/11 is questionable. The scale of death and destruction on 9/11 was far greater, and the alleged role of the government agents much more heinous, than in the other examples. Moreover, only a few of the examples included by de-Haven Smith involve false flag attacks of the kind alleged to have occurred on 9/11. For these reasons one has to question the strength of the implication he wishes to draw from his analysis: if they could do those other things, they could do 9/11 as well.

STRENGTHS AND WEAKNESSES OF THE TORONTO 9/11 HEARINGS IN ADVANCING THE CASE...

Table 3 in de-Haven Smith's essay is entitled "The Coincidence Theory of 9/11." Contained in it are collected events (referred to as factors) pointing to the possibility that elements of the US government intended to allow, or to bring about, the death and destruction of 9/11. It provides a compact and, on its face, persuasive tabulation of the observations that support his thesis. The rival explanation to account for this entire set of events, he argues, is that they are, like the tosses of a fair coin, independent of one another. Their joint occurrence is no more than coincidence. If so, the probability of their joint occurrence is given by the product of their individual probabilities. Since there are some 50 events identified in Table 3, the probability of their joint occurrence as independent events, he rightly concludes, is astronomically small.

The opposition of the "intentional hypothesis" with a "coincidence hypothesis" is commonly made by 9/11 skeptics of the official account. But coincidence is not the only alternative explanation. Sets of 9/11 events could be related (not independent) for reasons other than an intention to allow them to happen or to make them happen. For example, the repeated failures of the air defense system to intercept hijacked jet liners could reflect systemic failures in the design of that system and/or in the training of operators to deal with this form of attack. To take another example, the repeated failures of various intelligence agencies to share their information on suspected terrorists operating in the US might be traced to their mutual distrust, their proprietary cultures, and their aggressive competition for power. These alternatives to coincidence theory also need to be assessed.

The general point is that the serious rival to the hypothesis of government intention behind the events surrounding 9/11 is not coincidence. The critical argument has to show that intention is a better hypothesis than others which also claim the events are related, but for other reasons. That has not been done in deHaven Smith's paper. Yet, it remains an important paper because it leads one to think about the possible role of government on 9/11 in an historical context of other known or suspected crimes against democracy. It invites one to connect the dots.

Michel Chossudovsky claimed in his presentation that Al Qaeda is a CIA asset, not an enemy bent on a jihad against America and the West. Al Qaeda, he said, has been co-opted by the CIA, to provide fabricated terrorist incidents as pretexts for US military interventions. An evidence-based argument for that claim would have to show that each of the successful and thwarted attacks which have in the past been traced to Al Qaeda were actually perpetrated by US intelligence agencies. To overturn the entire historical record on Al Qaeda would be a major undertaking. It is not surprising that in the absence of such an undertaking this view rests on assertions rather than evidence.

Peter Dale Scott in his paper, "9/11 and Deep State Politics," presents a narrative of complex relations among the FBI, the CIA with its special forces, and the Department of Defense with its own intelligence and special forces branches. Moreover, he points out, within the CIA, agents with special clearances develop liaison arrangements with foreign intelligence agents of Saudi Arabia, Pakistan, and Egypt. Only some CIA agents are cleared to be in on these arrangements.

STRENGTHS AND WEAKNESSES OF THE TORONTO 9/11 HEARINGS IN ADVANCING THE CASE...

Much of Scott's paper is based on Kevin Fenton's detective work reported in his book, *Disconnecting the Dots*. Using open sources, the book constructs an account of how intelligence agencies failed to protect the American people from mass murder on 9/11. Fenton concludes that the failures of US intelligence to share and act on information held by some of its agents on plans to hijack jetliners and use them as weapons was motivated by the intention of those agents to allow the 9/11 attacks to go forward. Scott, on the other hand, favors "a more benign" interpretation. The desire to maintain liaison with foreign intelligence agents, and to protect informants with inside knowledge of Al Qaeda's plans, could explain, he believes, the otherwise incredible dysfunctionality of US intelligence. Perhaps, he adds, as those terrorist plans matured, some agents with the more sinister motive of allowing the attacks to go forward, exploited this dysfunctionality.

Scott and Chossudovsky have conflicting interpretations of the CIA's relation to Al Qaeda. Scott treats Al Qaeda as an enemy, although one that is sometimes protected and often mismanaged by the CIA. He writes, for example, "The behavior of these two eventual hijackers (Khalid Al-Midhar and Nawaf al-Hazmi) was so unprofessional that, without this CIA protection from the "Alec Station Group," they would almost certainly have been detected and detained or deported, long before they boarded Flight 77 in Washington."

Scott's interpretation also differs from that of Kolar's in the matter of the hijackers. As shown by the above quote, Scott treats Al Qaeda hijackers as real – they boarded the jets. On the other hand, Jay Kolar in his presentation "The Alleged 9/11 Hijackers," concluded that "no evidence exists that any of the so-called 'hijackers' ever boarded planes that crashed on 9/11."

It is not surprising that conflicting interpretations emerge from efforts to penetrate the work of secret agencies by investigators who are forced to rely on third party reports that are often unverifiable. Nevertheless, it is unfortunate, in my view, that the hearings did not address these conflicts more directly.

Only time will tell whether efforts like this will succeed in persuading American citizens that they should seriously consider the possibility that their government has allowed elements of its intelligence, military, political and corporate sectors to orchestrate mass murder in order to further a policy of global domination through pre-emptive wars. I do, however, strongly endorse Scott's broad conclusion, which de-Haven Smith's paper also supports: "the history of espionage tells us that secret power, when operating in the sphere of illegal activities, becomes, time after time, antithetical to public democratic power."

Laurie Maxwell in her paper, "In Denial of Democracy," makes an extended argument that unconscious, irrational, thought processes help to explain the resistance of the American public to evidence that state crimes against democracy were committed on 9/11. Among such processes studied in the literature of cognitive psychology are dissonance reduction, and confirmation bias. When confronted with evidence that threatens a strongly held belief, we suffer cognitive dissonance. That leads us to protect the prior belief by dismissing the contradictory evidence, or selectively attending to just confirming evidence for our belief (confirmation bias), or by denigrating the source of the conflicting evidence. Cognitive processes of the kind she discusses distort, short circuit, or otherwise corrupt the more deliberate process of critical reasoning. Daniel Kahneman in his recent book, *Thinking, Fast and Slow*, identifies failures to think critically (a slow and effortful kind of thinking) as the tendency to believe that, what you see (or hear) is all there is (the fast and easy kind of thinking). In other words, we fail by not looking for, or seriously weighing, evidence that would go against what we believe from the outset.

The psychological literature treats these irrational tendencies as universal. They would afflict anyone who tries to reason their way to an understanding of 9/11 whether their initial belief was in the criminal acts of government, or those of Al Qaeda. These tendencies can only be held at bay by deliberately applying the art of critical thinking, as our best scientists have learned to do. The issue then becomes, is there a reason to think that those who question the official account of 9/11 are more likely to dig for other explanations than are those who believe in the official account? I think there may well be. If you accept the simple, coherent, and dominant official account of 9/11, there is little reason to look for or credit other explanations. But if you are a 9/11 skeptic, you have to dig for evidence that both challenges the official account and supports a rival account. You can hardly escape confronting opposing explanations. In my view, the work of the 9/11 skeptics who argued at these hearings that only controlled demolition could have brought down the WTC buildings exemplifies critical thinking.

On the other hand I have to say that the hearings as a whole would not get high marks for seeking out other explanations. None of the presenters tried to support the official account, nor sought to debunk the entire case against it. Although panelists were tasked with questioning the evidence presented, they were not in a position to make extended counter arguments. While one sidedness should not, in my view, discredit the arguments presented at the hearings, those arguments might have more impact if direct confrontations with those who hold opposing views had been part of the hearings.

Is the evidence for planted explosives sufficient to change public perceptions?

Forensic autopsies of the destruction of WTC buildings.

The two papers by Ryan, and those of Gage, MacQueen, Chandler, and Cole present many lines of converging evidence that the twin towers and building 7 were brought to the ground through controlled demolition. Griffin's on paper the inadequacies of the 9/11 Commission prefaces this core area of the hearings by recounting the many omissions and distortions in *The 9/11 Commission Report* on the subject of what caused the twin towers to collapse.

These papers present the strongest evidence against the official account, and the strongest circumstantial evidence for believing the US government had a hand in 9/11. Nothing would be gained by my rehearsing all of this evidence. Instead I will indicate in a summary fashion what I think has been accomplished and then go on to raise questions about what those accomplishments might portend for the long-term goal of mounting a real investigation.

The first accomplishment has been to present a convincing case that the previous investigations of 9/11 – those by FEMA, the 9/11 Commission, and by NIST – all failed to confront important facts that challenge the official account. I think it was demonstrated that those investigations were designed not to understand what actually happened, but rather to defend the official account, which they did by selective omissions and distortions of the evidence.

The second accomplishment is to have confronted directly each of several different versions espoused in these official investigations of why the buildings collapsed and to have shown them to be inadequate to the facts. They did this through a systematic compilation of eye witness accounts of explosions, through the discovery in the rubble of the buildings of the residue of an advanced, thermitic accelerate/explosive, nano-thermite, and through structural and dynamic analyses showing that the observed characteristics of the way the buildings collapsed can only be accommodated on the assumption that at one point the supporting steel columns and girders were blown apart. The case for controlled demolition has also been supported by experimental tests showing that thermite has the capacity to cut steel beams, and that other accounts of how they might have been weakened are not tenable. This effort has produced so many converging lines of evidence, that in my view, controlled demolition is now the strongest hypothesis for how these buildings were brought to the ground.

I know of no effort on the part of those who would support the official account to either refute or explain all the evidence for controlled demolition. They have not to my knowledge refuted the evidence for nano-thermite in the rubble nor offered an explanation of what it was doing there. They have not explained the corroborated evidence of molten steel prior to the collapse and subsequently in the rubble. They have not countered the evidence that although building fires do not melt steel, thermite can.

They have not made a serious attempt to construct a single hypothesis that could account both for the destruction of the twin towers after they were hit by the jetliners, and for the destruction of building 7, which was not hit.

Evidence for planted explosions at the Pentagon

Barbara Honegger, in her presentation "Eye Witnesses and Evidence of Explosions at the Pentagon," covered evidence to show that the damage to the Pentagon was caused by explosives, not the alleged impact of the Boeing 757 on AA's Flight 77. Three principal lines of evidence were put forth. Photographs were shown of clocks in the Pentagon stopped by the force of these explosions at least 7 minutes before the time of impact on which the official account finally settled. Photographs were also shown purportedly identifying (I cannot interpret them clearly) three separate areas of damage positioned in a way that could not have been caused by the impact of any single aircraft or missile. They also are said to show damage in an area further toward the inside ring of the Pentagon than the Boeing 757 could have reached. Finally, there is the testimony of April Gallop, a witness inside the Pentagon at the time, who described in detail a scene of damage not consistent with extensive jet-fuel fires inside the Pentagon. The official account alleges that such fires contributed to the partial collapse of this wedge of the Pentagon.

If Honegger's evidence stands up to independent scrutiny, it would go a long way toward establishing the use of explosives inside the Pentagon, thereby implicating the hand of the government.

The relevance of questioning the motivation for and feasibility of controlled demolition

Some will take this evidence from WTC and the Pentagon as conclusive. For them, whether or not one can imagine a believable motivation and a feasible way of carrying out controlled demolition is immaterial. The fact stands, the buildings were demolished by planted explosives. One 9/11 researcher put it to me this way: if you find a dead body with a fatal bullet wound through its head, you don't have to know what motivated someone to kill the person nor how they did it to know there has been a murder. But these hearings tried to go beyond a fatally wounded body to implicate the government in the murder. If one finds the evidence of that less than completely conclusive, then questions of why it would be done and how it could be done–of motivation and feasibility– are material. In what follows I ask those questions.

The need for specific foreknowledge of where the attacks would hit

Obviously, perpetrators would need foreknowledge of the attacks to set the explosives. Paul Zarembka's paper, "Evidence of Insider Trading before 9/11" adds to other indications in the 9/11 research literature that some did know the date on which the attacks would occur, the airlines involved, and perhaps even the buildings to be targeted. But the perpetrators would need to know more than that. They would need to know the locus of impacts in order to know where to put explosives in advance. In the case of the Pentagon, that knowledge would have to be quite specific as to the one wedge that was allegedly struck by the hijacked jet. In the case of the twin towers the perpetrators would want to know in advance that the impact locations would be such that damage from them could appear to eventually cause their complete collapse, and through collateral damage, that of building 7. Otherwise, the use of explosives could not be covered up. The hearings did not deal with the question of how alleged perpetrators could acquire reliable advanced information of this more specific kind.

Motivation and feasibility of a plan to use explosives to amplify the effect of anticipated terrorist attacks

One hypothetical motive for planted explosives takes the form of using them to amplify the death and destruction from terrorists attacks which the government perpetrators deliberately allowed to go forward, but did not manufacture. What might motivate perpetrators to carry out such a plan?

They would have to believe that the death and destruction resulting solely from the anticipated attack by jets would not be a sufficiently horrific demonstration of the threat to America from Islamic terrorists to mobilize public opinion and political will to enact legislation for an all-out war on terror. They would also have to think that more deaths and much greater destruction would be needed and could be supplied by detonating explosives under the cover of the jetliner attacks. It seems unlikely to me that sane people would make that bet and risk detection for such an uncertain gain.

Putting aside the question of motive, would such a plan have a reasonable chance for success? As noted above, the perpetrators would of course have to know the targets the terrorists planned to hit well enough in advance to set the explosives. They would have to bet on the success of the hijackers in getting through whatever security and air defense measures had not been co-opted. They would also have to bet on the ability of the hijacker pilots to hit their targets. That bet now seems a long shot especially in the case of the inexperienced and inept hijacker pilot, Hani Hanjour, who is alleged in the official account to have executed a very exacting maneuver to strike the Pentagon at ground level. As I noted previously, to use the impacts as a cover for explosives they would have to know quite precisely the location of the impact on the Pentagon while in the case of the twin towers they would have to bet that the impact locations would be such that the claim that they were sufficient to bring about their complete destruction would not be immediately dismissed by the public as absurd. I believe that most people would find both the motive and feasibility in this scenario doubtful.

Motive and feasibility of using explosives as part a plan to manufacture 9/11

Many 9/11 researchers believe that the government not merely allowed the attacks to go forward, they actually manufactured and controlled those attacks. That view implies that the jets were remotely controlled by the perpetrators. There may or may not have been hijackers aboard. Although the feasibility of such a plan was not the focus of any paper at the hearings, the matter is relevant to the central question I am addressing: is the case for planted explosives likely to be persuasive with the broader public?

The motive for taking over the control of the jets is relatively easy to imagine since, on the hypothesis that government agents made it happen, none of the events of 9/11 would have transpired were it not for the government's hand. There would be no pretext at all for a greatly enlarged, all-out war on terror. On this scenario there remains, however, the tenuous claim, shared by the previous scenario, that the perpetrators would believe that the horrific destruction and loss of life caused by flying the jets into their targets needed to be amplified by the added death and destruction made possible by the planted explosives.

What can be said about feasibility? Pilots, passengers, and hijackers, if they were actually aboard, could be put down remotely by discharging a nerve gas. The technical capacity to remotely control the flight paths through a GPS to autopilot linkage was apparently in place (see Aidan Monaghan's paper, "Plausibility of 9/11 Aircraft Attacks Generated by GPS-Guided Aircraft Autopilot Systems." *Journal of 9/11 studies* , vol. 23, 2008). Systems in these aircraft allow a high degree of precision of control, probably within 6 or 7 meters. With it, perpetrators could know the locations of the impacts in advance. They could hardly do that if hijackers were in control.

On the other hand, the feasibility of making it appear that Islamic terrorists, not government agents, were the perpetrators is problematical. It would require faking many lines of evidence. Kolar believes they would have to, and actually did, fake evidence that the hijackers boarded the planes. They would have to fake evidence of intercepted communications from terrorists to passengers. They would have to simulate conversations between certain passengers and their ground-based contacts. To do that it would be necessary to imitate the sounds of their voices (voice morphing). They would also have to know enough about certain passengers to make the content of their conversations pass for the real thing. They would have to put in place black box flight data recorders with faked data so that the evidence of remote control would be eliminated and it would appear that the jets were being flown by hijackers. Although 9/11 researchers have produced evidence suggestive of fakery, to manage all of it is a tall order.

In my view the hypothesis that the motive for using explosions to cause more death and destruction on 9/11 remains tenuous under the scenario that government agents made 9/11 happen. As well, the scenario raises some questions of feasibility that are problematical.

Does the evidence of nano-thermite in the rubble of the WTC buildings destroyed on 9/11 force the conclusion that government perpetrators used explosives?

The testimony by Niels Harrit titled "Incendiary/explosive residue in the WTC dust," reported research by him and his scientific colleagues that identified by means of spectrographic and other analyses the presence of a technically advanced incendiary/explosive, nano-thermite. For the sake of argument let us assume the truth of each of a set of propositions about this discovery. First, that the results of these tests are reliable; if carried out independently by other competent scientists they would be replicated. Second, the results are valid. This assumption is that unlike many medical tests for diseases, his tests do not admit of false positive results. Third, let us assume, as Harrit's tests have shown, that this chemical could not have been a by-product of the buildings' collapse from other causes. That leads to the assumption that nano-thermite was in some way applied to the steel framework of the buildings and used, perhaps together with other types of explosives, in the destruction of the buildings.

Even given these assumptions, is the case for the responsibility of US government agents in bringing about the complete demolition of buildings conclusive? Not completely, I think, because one would also have to believe that this substance could not have been procured, placed and detonated by perpetrators other than agents of the US government. It has been reported that in the US this technically advanced agent is only produced in military laboratories and is not commercially available. But that still does not rule out the possibility that it was stolen, or perhaps procured from outside the US, and put in place by perpetrators other than agents of the US.

Extraordinary claims require extraordinarily conclusive evidence. A prudent person might say that 9/11 research on thermitic materials in the rubble has made remarkable progress toward meeting that standard, but it is not yet there.

Access for placing explosives without detection

A frequently cited objection to the hypothesis of planted explosions is the belief that they could not be put in place without being detected by those charged with building security, or by the tenants of the buildings. Although no one has come forward with close estimates of the weight of explosives that would have to be used, it is said to be on the order of tons. Those familiar with demolition say that preparing the buildings would be a huge job requiring the work of many experienced workers over an extended period of time. Escaping detection would not be a simple matter.

Ideas have, however, been put forth on how it could have been done. Richard Gage and others have pointed out that an elevator company undertook a very extensive modernization of the ele-

STRENGTHS AND WEAKNESSES OF THE TORONTO 9/11 HEARINGS IN ADVANCING THE CASE...

vators in each of the twin towers requiring a large crew of workers for many months. This project might be used as a cover for demolition workers since access to the steel core columns could be gained from the shafts without detection from outside of them. Doubts have been cast on the legitimacy of the security corporation charged with the responsibility to protect the WTC complex of buildings by connecting its management to the family of George Bush. Although not presented at the hearings, Kevin Ryan has researched the tenants of the towers. He reveals ways they might benefit from a stepped up war on terror. He also traces a surprising network of connections between tenants and other corporations that could provide access to the wherewithal for demolition. He paints a picture of convergence between corporate and government interests to make 9/11 happen. (See the series of four papers by Ryan at: www.911Review.com. Parts one, two, and four appear under the common main title: "Demolition Access to the WTC Towers." Part three has the title: "Carlyle, Kissinger, SAIC and Halliburton: A 9/11 Convergence"). This strikes me as a line of research that should be pursued.

In the case of building 7, no one to my knowledge has claimed that elevator modernization might have provided access to core columns. It has been suggested, however, that the extensive rebuilding on the 23rd floor required by setting up Mayor Giuliani's Office of Emergency Management might provide a path to cover up access. It has also been suggested that some would benefit from the destruction of records held by such building tenants as the SEC, CIA, FBI, DoD, or the IRS, but no one has explained why it would be in the interest of any one of these agencies to cooperate with the rigging of the building for explosive destruction in order to destroy records. Those agencies appear to have no trouble destroying records without bringing down buildings. I suppose one should add the possibility that Larry Silverstein, the owner of Building 7, who stood to profit through insurance payouts from its destruction, might have been able to cover up such an operation.

I think that identifying several possible ways in which explosives could be placed without the perpetrators being apprehended does do something to counter the objection "they couldn't get away with it, and they wouldn't risk it." But again, we have nothing like direct evidence that one or more of these pathways were actually used. Moreover, each possibility implies a widening circle of people in the know and willing to be part of a criminal conspiracy, or to stand by while they see it being committed.

Baffling aspects of the demolition of WTC 7

The apparent demolition of WTC 7 has been declared the Achilles heel of the official account. It implies that perpetrators had foreknowledge of the attack on the twin towers, and the capability of using explosives to cause their complete destruction. But there are several baffling aspects of the demolition of WTC 7 which until they are resolved should make a prudent person hesitate to conclude that, by itself, the demolition of 7 by explosives is conclusive evidence that the towers were demolished in the same way.

Larry Silverstein, talking to an interviewer on a PBS program about what transpired in the late afternoon of 9/11, well after the north and south towers had collapsed, said: "I remember getting a call from the commander of the fire department telling me that they were not sure they were going to be able to control the fire. I said, we have had such a terrible loss of life, maybe the smartest

STRENGTHS AND WEAKNESSES OF THE TORONTO 9/11 HEARINGS IN ADVANCING THE CASE...

thing to do is to pull it, and they made the decision to pull it, and we watched the building come down." There seems to be little doubt that by "pull it," said to be a phrase commonly used in the trade to refer to demolition, Silverstein also meant, "demolish it." He later claimed that he meant by this phrase, "pull the firemen out." It has been pointed out that since the firemen were known to have been removed already when Silverstein said, "pull it," his later version makes no sense.

If Silverstein is recommending to the commander that he demolish the building that suggests that both Silverstein and the commander knew that WTC 7 was already rigged with explosives. So, do we conclude that the commander of the NYFD, who has just witnessed the death of many of his first responders in the towers allegedly because of their explosive demolition, was in on the plan to use controlled demolition at the WTC 7? Even more baffling is the question of why no one seems to have interviewed the commander to see what he says for himself about how he understood his telephone conversation with Silverstein and what he did as a result.

The alleged motive for government agents to have caused the twin towers to collapse completely through the use of pre-planted explosions is to create a stronger Pearl Harbor effect. I have commented that this putative motive seems tenuous. However that may be, it could hardly be a motive for demolishing WTC 7 late in the afternoon of 9/11. By that time the complete destruction of the twin towers has already caused almost 3,000 deaths, and two huge iconic buildings have been reduced to dust and rubble. Surely the destruction of a now empty 47 story structure was not needed to amplify a Pearl Harbor effect. Moreover, if that was intended by the perpetrators, why was the collapse of WTC 7 so little publicized that many Americans still do not know it happened? Finally, because building 7 was not hit by a jetliner, using explosives to demolish it runs the risk of exposing their use on the twin towers. The reality of that risk has been demonstrated at these hearings.

Another hypothesis for what the perpetrators planned for WTC 7 has been offered in the 9/11 literature. It was prompted by eye witness accounts of explosions within WTC 7 much earlier in the day, long before its eventual collapse. (See for example, Chandler, "A refutation of the official account."). Griffin, in his book *The Mysterious Collapse of World Trade Center 7*, at Appendix A, has offered the hypothesis that these explosions were part of a failed attempt by the perpetrators to demolish the building earlier in the day, at about the same time that the north tower was made to collapse. He goes on to suggest that people (fire fighters? demolition experts?) went back into the building to repair the demolition system which was then activated at 5:21 PM and finally succeeded in bringing the building down.

In any case, it now appears likely that a somewhat different set of perpetrators, with somewhat different motives, and different opportunities for planting explosions, are implicated in the case of the twin towers and building 7. That makes the argument that, if you accept the controlled demolition of WTC 7 you must also accept controlled demolition of the twin towers, less compelling.

STRENGTHS AND WEAKNESSES OF THE TORONTO 9/11
HEARINGS IN ADVANCING THE CASE...

Concluding comments on the strengths and weaknesses of the Toronto 9/11 Hearings in advancing the case for a new investigation

Despite the strength of multiple, converging lines of evidence that explosives were used in the three WTC buildings, and in the Pentagon, I have explained why, in my view, this circumstantial evidence of the government's hand will probably prove insufficient to bring about a ground swell of public opinion in favor of a real investigation of 9/11. I turn now to some concluding comments about the ability of the kind of material presented at the Toronto Hearings as a whole to achieve that goal.

There are many unknowns, blanks, and loose ends about 9/11 that stand in the way of developing a rival account strong enough to persuade the public and political leaders to make a real effort to uncover the truth. The present lack of consensus even among independent investigators after ten years on whether the damage to the Pentagon was caused from the outside or the inside is a striking example of one of the critical unknowns. We have no direct evidence filling in the blanks on how advanced explosives for demolition might have been procured, and put in place. We have reports that point to criminal acts by highly placed people which are left as loose ends. One of the important loose ends is testimony by Transportation Secretary, Norman Mineta, who said that he overheard an interchange between a young naval lieutenant and Vice President Dick Cheney in the Presidential Emergency Operations Center in the basement of the White House on the morning of 9/11. The lieutenant enters the room several times with reports of the position of an unidentified aircraft headed for the Pentagon. When it is only 10 miles out he asks Cheney: "Do the orders still stand?" To which Cheney abruptly replies: "Of course they still stand, have you heard anything to the contrary?" Mineta interpreted this as a reference to an order to shoot down aircraft entering the prohibited airspace around the Pentagon. But Griffin ("Anomalies of flights 77 and 93") argues that the only intelligible interpretation in the circumstances is that Cheney's order was to "stand down," to do nothing.

Knowing who is right is a critical piece of information for rival accounts of 9/11. The young naval lieutenant has been identified in Paul Rea's recent book, *Mounting Evidence: Why we Need a New Investigation into 9/11*, as Douglas F. Cochrane. He certainly knows what he meant by "the orders," as must a host of other military people. Yet here, as in other seemingly critical revelations about 9/11, the story ends without a resolution.

I am also troubled by the ever widening circle of agencies and individuals implicated as having taken part at some level on the hypothesis that 9/11 was manufactured under the leadership of government agents. Although the core group responsible for conceiving the plan might be small, the number who would have to cooperate in its execution, take an active part in the cover-up, or just keep quiet about what they came to know, is large. Included as suspects by one or more versions of this rival account are, of course, elected government officials in high places, agents within the CIA, the FBI, and the Department of Defense, officials in the North American Aerospace Defense Command, and in the North East Air Defense Command. Also implicated are pilots of interceptors who must have known the orders of engagement on which they were deployed, FAA flight controllers, airport security personnel in two major airports, the Commander of the New

STRENGTHS AND WEAKNESSES OF THE TORONTO 9/11 HEARINGS IN ADVANCING THE CASE...

York Fire Department, former Mayor Giuliani, and, of course, Larry Silverstein. They include demolition experts who would be needed to rig the buildings, and still others to procure the explosives. Implicated as well are scientists and others at NIST, and on the 9/11 Commission, who knew those reports were unscientific, personnel of United and American Airlines as might be needed to allow or enable the remote control of the Boeing jets, personnel actually operating the remote control system, personnel in the National Transportation Safety Board who were needed to create and put in place flight data recorders with faked data, experts in voice morphing to simulate conversations between passengers and their ground-based contacts, building-security personnel at the WTC buildings, some private tenants of the WTC buildings, corporations under contract to modernize the elevators in the twin towers, and some independent scientists producing analyses in support of the official account of the collapse of WTC buildings which they knew to be erroneous.

The wider the circle, the more difficult it is to accept the feasibility of successfully orchestrating such a complex, multifaceted operation and covering it up. It may even occur to some that a society which harbors so many corrupt influential leaders would be unlikely to conduct an authentic investigation of 9/11.

Former Senator Mike Gravel in his presentation, "An Actionable Plan for a Citizens' 9/11 Investigation Commission," believes there is no chance that Congress or the White House would lend their support for a new investigation of 9/11. He reaches that conclusion even though he praises the work of the 9/11 truth movement and believes there is an urgent need for a new investigation. That view is echoed in Representative Cynthia McKinney's account at the hearings of her failed efforts to get her fellow congressmen to even talk about 9/11.

Gravel, who has long advocated a greater role for direct democracy, is energetically working to use state ballot initiatives to establish a citizens' committee for a new investigation. I hope that this bold effort to go around the Federal government succeeds, but I have misgivings about how much such a commission might do to advance the uphill battle for public opinion on 9/11.

Gravel suggests that the appointment of committee members should be guided by activists of the 9/11 movement. If so, the work of the committee is likely to be seen by a large segment of the public as serving an ideological, political bias and discounted for that reason. Moreover, we have seen how difficult it is to get an accurate, in-depth reconstruction of what brought about 9/11. Could a commission, even with the power to subpoena and to take testimony under oath, be expected to accomplish what ten years of research on 9/11 has not as yet managed to do? Teams of lawyers would be on hand to protect witnesses from perjury or self incrimination, and government agencies from releasing information that might testify to their criminal actions.

I think that one of the major reasons research has not gone further toward finding the connective tissue for a rival account has been the destruction, confiscation or withholding of information by government agencies. Those efforts have blocked access to information which might break open the mysteries of 9/11.

There are, in fact, some notable examples of destruction or confiscation of evidence. The Defense Intelligence Agency destroyed files on "Able Danger," a project which tracked the activities of terrorists in the US who became alleged 9/11 hijackers. FAA managers destroyed tapes of FAA controllers recounting their communications with the hijacked jets. The SEC destroyed data on stock trades in the days leading up to 9/11. New York City officials had all but a few traces of the steel frameworks of all three buildings destroyed on 9/11 removed and shipped to China before they could be part of a forensic autopsy. The CIA destroyed records of the interrogation of Guantanamo detainees on whose testimony the 9/11 Commission relied. Tapes from private company video cameras which might contain definitive evidence of what caused the damage to the Pentagon were confiscated shortly after the attack.

Scores of requests for information under the Freedom of Information Act (FOIA) have been turned down. The FOIA law contains nine articles allowing for the exemption of documents on various grounds. One of those grounds exempts classified documents pertaining to national defense. By executive order in 2009, a requested document may be retroactively classified. Documents pertaining to the deliberative processes of the government may be exempt under "executive privilege." States have codified their own bases for the exempting documents which they hold.

In practice many agencies have interpreted the exemptions broadly to prevent disclosure. They often state without explanation, for example, that public safety would be jeopardized. Another frequent response is that, "No documents relevant to the information requested have been found," under circumstances which make that hard to believe. Aidan Monaghan, who has been tireless in his pursuit of information under FOIA, has come to believe that the FBI is seeking to exempt all documents relating to 9/11. He has recounted his requests on the Corbett Report (see Look for interview 211 on 08/16/2010, and for his blogs on).

Here are examples of specific FOIA requests denied. NIST has refused to release results for the application of its computer model for the initiation of collapse of WTC 7 on the grounds that to do so might jeopardize public safety. Structural drawings of all WTC buildings destroyed on 9/11 have been withheld on the grounds that they are "sensitive" buildings. Data pertaining to the Turner Construction Company's contract for repairs and maintenance to the twin towers, including steel columns in elevator shafts, have been denied.

Monaghan's requests for records pertaining to or establishing in-flight phone calls from United Airlines Flights 175 and 93, and American Flight 77, have been denied. Records of automated radio communications between ground based control centers and the aircraft involved in 9/11 have been withheld. These are potentially highly significant since they might reveal whether this system was used to fly pilotless jets into their targets. Also denied have been requests for data collected from the wreckage of Flights 77 and 93, including human remains, flight data recorders, and an audio copy of the cockpit voice recorder on Flight 93.

The wall of secrecy to which these examples testify is, I believe, one of the most formidable obstacles preventing 9/11 research from breaking through to a clear enough understanding of 9/11 and resolving the deep divide among Americans on how far their government can be trusted.

A way forward

I do not fault the Toronto hearings for not having presented direct evidence of who in the government perpetrated 911, and why and how they did it. Research on 9/11 has not yet made that possible. Given the way we are governed, those who might have been involved would have the power to keep that information secret. Despite the uphill battle to cut through the mysteries of 9/11, a convincing indictment of perpetrators through continued research, rather than a through new commission of investigation, may be the only way to turn the tide of public opinion. In addition to continuing with research which might eventually provide such an indictment, I believe those in the movement for the truth about 9/11 should get strongly behind a movement for open government.

In his campaign for President, Obama spoke often and eloquently of the need for an open government to restore trust. He promised one of the most transparent governments in history—a government that would allow "anyone to ensure that our business is the people's business." It was a theme to which many resonated, and for good reason. Those who saw the wars in Vietnam and Iraq as tragic mistakes of American policy know that government deception under the cloak of secrecy allowed these wars to happen. Had we known of the things much later revealed in the Pentagon papers, we might never have gone into Vietnam. Had we known that our intelligence agencies were lying about weapons of mass destruction and Al Qaeda in Iraq, that disastrous war might never have been pursued. The subversion of democratic process through secrecy has come at an enormous cost in lives lost or broken. I hope that a growing realization of that will motivate deep public support for the kind of sea change in government that Obama's vision held out, but which has yet to occur.

In common with all other Americans who care about democracy, those who research 9/11 have a vital interest in the success of a political movement for a government that would really strive to make its business the people's business. Without such a government it may not be possible to learn enough to ever understand the deeply troubling questions surrounding 9/11. Without a more open government, I see no way to repair the profound distrust of government that now cripples democracy in America.

CHAPTER SEVENTEEN

Remarks on the Toronto Hearings

BY RICHARD B. LEE

I WOULD LIKE TO SHARE A FEW PERSONAL REFLECTIONS ON the International Hearings into the Events of 9/11 held in Toronto, Canada. The hearings asked two important questions. Do the observed facts of 9/11 support the thesis that 19 Arab men directed by a man in a cave in Afghanistan pulled off the multiple catastrophic events that unfolded on that day? And if not, who did?

The Hearings have been extraordinarily effective in presenting carefully compiled scientific evidence that casts serious doubt on the veracity of the official story. The overwhelming burden of that evidence leads to the conclusion that the official story is based on false premises, and succeeds only by ignoring or distorting masses of contrary evidence.

Here we come to a crucial question: are we going to look at the science or are we going to be misdirected by media and political expediency? The laws of physics exist regardless of the political climate and are not subject to manipulation, by even the most sophisticated PR firms.

Whoever were the perpetrators of the terror acts of 9/11, they have been so successful in keeping attention focused on the official story, repeated endlessly, that the majority of the public accepts it without question. This includes even large segments of the public and public intellectuals who are strongly critical of US foreign and domestic policies in most other areas.

So my first reflection is the awareness of just how uphill is the battle faced by the advocates for 9/11 truth. In September of 2011, as the tenth anniversary approached, we witnessed the constant barrage of TV observances of 9/11. Even as the Toronto Hearings exposed 9/11 to scientific scrutiny and painstaking deconstruction, the public face of the "official" 9/11 narrative continued to roll along as a snowballing mass of myths hardening into dogma.

We have come to appreciate just how great is the psychological investment in these myths by the public, even by those who were and are otherwise highly critical of the Bush administration.

We can also pinpoint the methods used. One of several ways in which official media continue to shape the 9/11 story is to ridicule the 9/11 Truth Movement as "truthers" equating them with the right-wing "birthers" who maintain the absurd claim that President Obama was foreign-born.

Another even more potent weapon of the defenders of the official story is to label critics as "deniers" showing disrespect for the dead (with subtle linking to the anathema of Holocaust deniers). To the contrary, the 9/11 hearings were convened in a spirit of tremendous respect for the dead, by struggling to discover the real circumstances of their deaths.

And the 9-11 critics presenting at the Hearings are anything but fringe elements. They represent an array of respected and professionally credentialed expert witnesses: Example: the 1550 Architects and Engineers who have signed a statement calling for a new independent inquiry into 9/11. What led them to sign on? Simply put, they took a hard look at the data, and made unbiased evaluations of the evidence.

The organizers are to be commended for assembling such an impressive array of presenters, showing a healthy skepticism for received wisdom and a corresponding respect for basic science. Sadly, science has taken a beating in the last ten years; in the dubious conclusions reached by NIST researchers about WTC 1 and 2 building collapses and the many other anomalies and contradictions in the official story. However, the basic laws of physics form a bedrock of truth that even the most sophisticated political propaganda cannot ignore or sidestep.

There are many telling critiques of the official story, regarding such diverse topics as what actually struck the Pentagon, how did flight 93 crash into a Pennsylvania field, the failures of NORAD response, and why has the clear evidence of insider trading on relevant stocks in advance of 9/11 never been investigated.

Three Lines of Evidence

Three lines of evidence I found particularly persuasive are the following:

1) The collapse of the three (not two) towers

2) The molecular evidence in the dust of controlled demolition

3) The strange anomalies in the lives, identities, and actions of the hijackers

The Towers

I found convincing the evidence that in the case of the twin towers, the kinetic energy produced and the speed of their collapse was far in excess of what one would expect from a collapse caused solely by fires. Steel girders were thrown laterally hundreds of feet. It seems inescapable that fires alone could not have brought down the buildings. Added to this is the historical fact that prior to 9/11, no hi-rise steel framed building had **ever** collapsed due to fires. Also, I was struck by the well over 100 individual ground level witnesses who described hearing and seeing explosions in the minutes **before** the towers' collapse.

Building 7, which was not struck by an aircraft, nevertheless collapsed in free-fall at 5:20 PM on Sept. 11. There had been minimal damage to only a few floors of the building and the few fires that were burning had largely been put out. No remotely plausible explanation for WTC 7's collapse has been presented in the official narrative. However, the videos of the collapse looked to many professional engineers like a classic controlled demolition.

The Dust

The Hearings heard some startling new revelations. I feel that at least one area of evidence has been so thoroughly explored that we have drilled down close to bedrock: the brilliant work on the analysis of the twin towers post-collapse dust. Certain microscopic particles were found in the debris that are only produced at temperatures far in excess of jet fuel fires or any other combustible material in the towers. However they are common chemical byproducts of an incendiary and explosive material called thermite. Thermite can be used in the controlled demolition of a building. That, to my mind is the Rosetta Stone of the 9/11 mystery.

The Hijackers and the flights

There are many anomalies in the actions and identities of the putative hijackers. I will mention briefly five:

1. Key elements of the official narrative that identified the "hijackers" were claimed to come from in-flight cell phone calls. Yet sending and receiving cell-phone calls in aircraft at cruising altitudes was a physical impossibility with the technology current in 2001.

2. No four-digit hijacking code was sent from any of the four flights, yet in the time that it would take alleged hijackers to break into the cockpit the code could easily be sent.

3. Only two airport security camera footages were released as evidence of the hijacker's identity and this shows men in the terminal, not actually boarding any flight, and one of these shows clear evidence of doctoring.

4. All accounts of the hijackers from flight training schools attest that they were very inexperienced and unskilled in their flight lessons with single-engine aircraft, yet the official account has them skillfully piloting giant 757s and 767s with pinpoint accuracy. I found this point particularly important.

5. No names of the hijackers appear on any official passenger lists and a number of the alleged hijackers were apparently alive on Sept 12 and after. A bank was reported to have ordered the accounts frozen of one hijacker on Sept 19.

This leads to a conclusion that flies in the face of a central theme of the official narrative, that certain 19 Arab men hijacked four aircraft on 9/11. In the absence of the alleged evidence from cell-phone calls, airport camera footage, flight schools, and passenger lists presented above, is there any hard data that *any* of the 19 men actually boarded *any* of the four flights?

These lines of evidence and the many others outlined at the Hearings should provide ample grounds for thoughtful people to reconsider the received wisdom on the events of 9/11.

Follow-Up

Of the many lines of inquiry to be followed up, I will mention two. First, regarding the WTC Towers, in view of the catastrophic collapse of Towers 1, 2, and 7, how have building codes changed since 9/11 to correct the alleged design defects that brought the towers down according to the official account? If there has been no substantial change in building codes is that not a tacit admission that the circumstances of the three towers' collapse were not as presented in the official reports?

And in similar vein: The official story identifies dozens of government officials whose "mistakes" and "errors in judgment" caused the hijackings to succeed and who misplayed the events following. What became of these key government personnel in FAA, NORAD, FBI, FEMA, EPA, SEC and other agencies? How many were disciplined, demoted, or fired for their egregious incompetence? Alternately how many were commended and promoted after 9/11?

Conclusion

The task before the International Hearings on the Events of September 11, 2001 and the 9/11 Truth Movement is to overcome the inertia of the official story constantly reinforced by the mass media and hardening into dogma. At the hearings we four panelists were impressed by the seriousness of the witnesses, their willingness to submit their evidence to scientific scrutiny and evaluation, and their challenging the authors of the official story to refute the evidence presented.

Therefore we support the call for a full and independent public inquiry into 9/11 with subpoena powers. The events on that day led to two wars still ongoing, plus sharp restrictions on civil liberties, wiretapping, torture, rendition, and suspension of habeas corpus. The proponents of the official story will have ample opportunity to answer and refute evidence presented. Only this way can the 3000 victims of 9/11 be truly laid to rest and their memory honored.

Finally as a Torontonian, I am proud of the courage that Ryerson University showed in providing a site for these Hearings and pleased that the Hearings and what they stand for will be forever associated with my city.

CHAPTER EIGHTEEN

Report on the Toronto Hearings

BY FERDINANDO IMPOSIMATO

Introduction

THE TORONTO HEARINGS WERE HELD AT RYERSON UNIVERsity of Toronto, Canada, from 8 to 11 September 2011. The aim of the Hearings was to assess the historical truth of 9/11, according to the guidelines set forth at the outset of the Hearings by James Gourley, Director of the International Center for 9/11 Studies. He said the goal was to bring attention to the most substantial evidence accumulated over the past ten years, evidence that the 9/11 Commission Report and the various reports issued by the National Institute of Standards and Technology (NIST) failed to adequately address. This evidence demonstrates that there is a need for a new, independent and international investigation into the events of 9/11. The Hearings were not said to be a new investigation in themselves, but strove to "provide a succinct summary of the strongest evidence that a new investigation is immediately warranted and that the international community cannot abdicate this responsibility any longer." Gourley clarified that the Hearings would "be analogous to a legal proceeding that is known in the United States as a Grand Jury hearing."

Gourley also analogized the Hearings to a preliminary hearing or committal procedure under criminal law, where the common thread among all of these proceedings is that a prosecutor presents to an adjudicator his best evidence that the defendant committed the crime in question, often without the defendant or suspect present. Gourley stated that NIST and the 9/11 Commission members had been invited several times to participate in the Hearings, but they declined to do so.

The Hearings were not meant to establish whether there is enough evidence to convict or absolve employees or agents of the United States government, but to assess "whether there is a prima facie case that can be made against" one or more employees or agents. A prima facie case has been made when evidence that – unless rebutted – would be sufficient to prove a particular proposition or fact.

During the international Toronto Hearings, the panelists listened to impartial and independent witnesses, who have collected the best evidence that contradicts the official government version of events. Each witness presented opening statements of high level in different fields: engineering, chemistry, economics, history, political science, neuroscience, and each witness answered questions posed by the panel.

The evidence we must utilize in analyzing 9/11 includes not only direct evidence but also circumstantial evidence, i.e. logical evidence. A confession or first-hand witness testimony is an example of direct evidence, while logical evidence is indirect evidence, i.e. indirect testimony or the deduction of an unknown fact. For example, the possession of the weapon used in a crime is circumstantial evidence that can help prove the responsibility of the possessor of the weapon regarding that specific crime. The system of logic evidence was discussed by the Greek philosopher Aristotle, circa 450 BC, in the opera "The Organon".

In this report, I will utilize both direct and circumstantial evidence to analyze and discuss the events of 11 September 2001. I agree with what professor Lance de Haven-Smith presented regarding State Crimes Against Democracy. In his interesting, well-documented analysis, he uses circumstantial evidence, which sometimes can be stronger than direct evidence. This is true when that evidence is founded on the facts "true and first," according to the definition of Aristotle. If the circumstantial evidence is based on simple opinion or on wrong facts, the deduction is erroneous. But the facts that de Haven-Smith describes in Tables 2 and 3 are precise and true.

I will utilize all the statements of the Hearings witnesses and their scientific expertise, and focus on the relevant aspects of the evidence presented which deserves further investigations by the government prosecutors with subpoena power in the USA. I also recognize that there are many other evidence sources available which also support the case for further investigation in these areas.

The 9/11 attacks were crimes against humanity and, as with every crime, requires an intentional human behavior, active or omitting, which is the cause of the events. A finding that there is probable cause to believe that a particular suspect committed a given crime requires probable cause that the suspect intended to provoke the events. For example, the impacts of the airplanes could have arisen from human error. In that case, a crime might not have occurred for lack of a will to do harm.

On the other hand, it is possible that the events are the consequence of intentional human action. In this case, the likely culprits could be those who were responsible for the voluntary impact of the planes with the buildings, or those who placed explosive charges in the World Trade Center buildings before the attack. The United States Justice Department has a duty to establish the cause of the destruction of the three World Trade Center buildings, and who, if anyone, intended that outcome.

To date, many of the relevant facts of 9/11 have not been publicly examined or constructed by a prosecutor or an independent jury in one of the 50 US states. Instead, the official investigations have been conducted by various agencies of the Bush administration and by two commissions that were appointed by Congress. The 9/11 Commission was directed by Philip Zelikow, who was appointed by the Bush administration as a replacement for its first appointed director, Henry Kissinger, who was unacceptable to the leading organization of victims' families because of his suspected client relationships with members of the bin Laden family and his unwillingness to disclose his entire client list.

Under the Bush administration, Congress later charged NIST with determining the cause of the destruction of the three World Trade Center buildings. Congress charged the 9/11 Commission and Congressional Joint Inquiry to assess the actions of the terrorists and of the secret services. But these bodies – NIST, the 9/11 Commission, and the Joint Congressional Inquiry – gave incomplete and subjective accounts of the 9/11 events, and both of them concluded that no members of the United States government bore responsibility for failing to prevent the 9/11 attacks. It is impossible to accept the conclusions of these bodies, which are against the truth.

The NIST Reports

On November 20, 2005, the National Institute for Standards and Technology (NIST) published its "final report on the cause of collapse of the Twin Towers" and later another report on the cause of the collapse of WTC 7, a 47-story skyscraper that came down into its footprint at about 5:20 PM, in freefall for more than two seconds and near freefall throughout its collapse. It was not impacted by an airplane.

The NIST conclusions were as follows: The airplanes that struck each of the twin towers caused a breach and explosion in a gigantic fireball. The remaining jet fuel flowed onto the lower floors, sustaining the fires. The heat from the fires deformed the structures of the buildings, and both towers collapsed completely, from top to bottom. Very little of recognizable size remained, except some steel and aluminum fragments and the pulverized dust from the concrete floors. The collapses caused more than 90 percent of the casualties on 9/11, amounting to about 3000 people. WTC 7 collapsed in a way that was inconsistent with the common experience of engineers, and required NIST to assert a new theory of thermal expansion to give their explanation the appearance of a scientific justification.

The final NIST report set out by limiting the scope of its inquiry to the fall of the twin towers, maintaining that the impacts of the planes, one against each tower, together with the fires, had caused the fall of all three buildings, WTC 1, 2 and 7. All three buildings collapsed completely, although Building 7 was not hit, against any common experience and the lack of any similar past events. According to the common knowledge at the time, never had a steel skyscraper completely collapsed. The Twin Towers report, although giving ample evidence to the impact of the planes, the fires, the loss of human lives, does not analyze the real nature of the collapses. These had features similar to controlled explosions. This diagnosis has been given by the architect Richard Gage and by professional engineer Jon Cole, both of them highly experienced professionals, through convincing tests, scientific proofs and visual testimonies of people absolutely above suspicion, such as firemen and victims.

The authoritative theologian David Ray Griffin, one of the most significant witnesses heard at the Toronto Hearings, described very precisely and in detail why the hypothesis of controlled demolition should be taken into consideration. The buildings fell down straight, nearly in freefall acceleration. The ruins contained spots that were red-hot for months. Various witnesses heard bursts of explosions. Nearly all of the concrete of these big structures was reduced to extremely thin powder. Large amounts of this powder, together with steel beams, were thrown horizontally at least one hundred meters from the buildings. Many beams and columns fell down in sections around ten meters long.

The WTC 7's 47 floors collapsed late in the afternoon of September 11, 2001. According to NIST, the collapse of the third tower was due to the fires provoked by the collapse of the twin towers.

On the contrary, with regard to such thesis, chemist and independent researcher Kevin Ryan demonstrated that NIST gave contradictory versions of the events, and of the collapse of the third tower. NIST declared in a preliminary report that WTC 7 had been destroyed because of the fires provoked by diesel fuel stored in the building for emergency power, while in the following report declared that the fuel was not the reason for the collapse of WTC 7.

Similarly, Syvaray Shyam Sunder, the lead NIST investigator, declared early on that WTC 7 came down because of the building had been "excavated" from the debris of the Twin Towers. This claim was contradicted from the fact, noted by Ryan, that the spread of the debris in Ground Zero was asymmetric, and the other buildings close to the Twin Towers had nearly no damage. The NIST thesis is also inconsistent because the spread of the debris should have caused an asymmetric collapse, not a symmetric collapse at free fall speed.

Other relevant and appropriate comments of Kevin Ryan towards the NIST report were concerning the "thermal expansion" of the structural steel, which allegedly caused the collapse of the 13th floor, starting a chain reaction of collapses of other floors.

After having declared that WTC 7 fell down because of the fires provoked by the diesel fuel and from the debris, NIST departed from this account and gave as the reason for the collapse, rapid thermal expansion.

According to the NIST reports, the investigations were conducted over three years. The expert Kevin Ryan, on the contrary, said that NIST began its investigation on the WTC in August 2002 and wrote the first report regarding the WTC 7 in June 2004. The first suspicion that arises is that the NIST report 2004, before its publication, was vetted by the Bush administration, because the Bush administration controlled the Department of Commerce, which oversees NIST. That is the first handicap to the impartiality and credibility of the NIST report.

It appears strange that NIST, besides not conducting any scientific experimentation to support its report on WTC 7 as requested by external experts, did not question the eyewitnesses who had seen the collapse and perceived the repeated explosions before the buildings collapse. Several citizens, policemen and firemen were able to describe the circumstances of the three buildings' destruction.

At the Toronto Hearings, Kevin Ryan noted that when the Twin Towers fell, they appeared to explode, starting from the top down. He said that high-velocity bursts could be seen 30 floors below the collapse front, that debris appeared to shoot away from the building, and the concrete floors turned to dust. This, he said, would not happen if the building was being crushed downward after being softened or weakened from fire.

These are only some of several precise observations made by expert Kevin Ryan that appear clear and convincing to me.

Additional comments regarding the NIST version came from David Chandler, physics instructor and expert witness at the Hearings. When on August 2008 NIST circulated the first version of its report on WTC 7, NIST declared that a 17-floor segment of the building fell down in a time 40% longer than the time calculated for free fall and as such, NIST's explanation of the event was "consistent with physical principles."

REPORT ON THE TORONTO HEARINGS

According to NIST the collapse took place in three distinct phases. During his testimony, Chandler pointed out that many available videos show that for around two and half seconds the acceleration of the building could not be distinguished from free fall.

NIST was obliged to agree on such an empirical fact, stressed by Chandler, and understandable by everybody, that the main portion of the collapse took place in six and half seconds. After the comments by Chandler in November 2008, NIST in its final report on Building 7 surprisingly admitted the fact of free fall. Its earlier failure to do so is proof of, at a minimum, poor skill on the part of NIST investigators.

At this point Chandler noted, "free fall can happen only if the resistance to the movement is zero." And this can happen only in front of a controlled demolition due to explosive devices. This thesis was presented by Chandler during the Hearings, thus confirming the absolute inadequacy of NIST's investigations.

As a matter of fact, the final NIST reports do not explain how it is possible that three modern steel hi-rise buildings fell down completely from fire, again absolutely lacking past examples of such type. Never before had a steel skyscraper collapsed totally if not because of controlled demolitions due to explosives devices. The NIST report, although devoting a lot of space to the impact of the planes, to the fires, to the loss of the human lives, does not try to explain the nature of collapse showing so many characteristics of controlled demolition: the explosions, the powder, the perfectly vertical fall, the nearly free fall acceleration. An exception to the silence of NIST can be seen in two lines where NIST presumes to answer the comments made to the draft of the reports.

NIST avoids these problems declaring them out of the scope of the investigations, claiming merely that "global collapse was inevitable" after the start of the collapse.

In conclusion, the NIST investigation, because of the clear contradictions and the implicitly admitted mistakes, does not persuasively demonstrate at all that the three towers fell down because of the impacts of the planes and the fires. Other factors, such as bombs and/or incendiary devices, seem to be required to explain the observed facts.

The appearance of controlled demolition not only casts doubt on the official account of how the buildings fell, it raises obvious questions about possible official foreknowledge and complicity (because of the extensive engineering effort and access to secure buildings required). The crucial issue that professor Lance deHaven-Smith identified is the following: "These doubts and questions are compounded by the actions of US governing authorities in the aftermath of 9/11: immediately invading Afghanistan, adopting an official policy of preventive war, and manipulating intelligence to justify the invasion and occupation of Iraq. These actions are prima facie evidence of a pre-existing agenda to contrive a pretext for waging wars of aggression in the Middle East to gain control of diminishing energy supplies." This is a perfect use of logical evidence, which is admissible in a judicial system, and I agree with this theory.

The information presented and conclusions reached by expert witnesses at Toronto Hearings Witnesses are more valid and probable than the information and conclusions set forth by NIST. The Toronto Hearings experts are independent and impartial, unlike NIST experts. They gave both the empirical and documentary evidence that three buildings were destroyed by airplane impact and probably by other causes, such as pre-planted explosives.

The attack on the Pentagon and the lack of proper investigation

The NIST, a non-independent agency incapable of reconstructing the dynamics of the building collapses, did not analyze the attack against the Pentagon. Nevertheless there are several anomalies and omissions in the official position on what happened at the Pentagon as expressed in the 9/11 Commission Report.

First of all, it appears impossible that the greatest military power of the entire world remained ineffective for more than an hour, ignoring the presence of rogue airplanes inside its airspace. The 9/11 Commission said that until 9:36 am, one or two minutes before Pentagon was struck, nobody knew that an airplane was directed towards Washington. On the contrary, Secretary of Transportation Norman Mineta testified before the 9/11 Commission about a conversation between Vice President Cheney and others in the Presidential Emergency Operating Center of the White House about the jetliner heading towards the Pentagon at least ten minutes prior to the crash. This testimony was not discussed in the 9/11 Commission Report. The Commission also failed to consider that for AA77, piloted by Hani Hanjour, to strike the Pentagon at the location it did, would have executed a spiral descent that would have been very difficult for an inexperienced pilot, and Hanjour was consistently described by his flight instructors as a bad pilot.

Recommendations

The omissions of relevant evidence in the NIST investigation and the investigation of the Pentagon, their contradictions and the lack of independence and impartiality, as a body controlled by the Bush administration, requires an impartial, independent scientific investigation group, whose membership could be decided by a state prosecutor or by a jury, executed by an independent group of technical experts. The group's task would be to determine the real technical cause of the destruction of the three WTC skyscrapers and part of the Pentagon, including the reasons for their collapse and dismemberment. The possibility of controlled demolition would have to be explicitly investigated by such a group.

By the rules of common law, according to the most accepted doctrine, where specific scientific competence is needed, a judge and jury cannot rely on just their personal scientific knowledge, which may be inadequate for the analysis required. In this case, expert opinions must be accepted by the judge in order to ascertain the truth and everything must be done according to due process of law. None of the official reports emerged from actual criminal investigations.

Evidence regarding events that occurred before September 11, 2001

Witnesses at the Toronto Hearings presented several facts that, through appropriate investigations and expertise, can become legal evidence presented before a grand jury. Some of these elements prove the criminal responsibility of persons different from the material executors of the attacks, or officials who, as members of governmental institutions, refrained from acting to prevent the terrorist attacks. The Panel will bring its attention to and indicate the evidence that deserves further investigation by state prosecutors.

Research by historians, scientists, and witnesses, inquiries by courageous reporters on the signs ignored by the US government, and on the insider trading that happened just before 9/11, and other reliable information support an account of 9/11 that is quite different from the official version. The truth will allow us to see over the deviations, the inert behavior, and the conspiracy of silence often used to cover up official government complicity.

Insider trading: CIA and FBI involvement

The presentation by experts of the evidence of insider trading executed before 9/11 make it very likely that the CIA and FBI knew in advance the date and place of the attack, and which two airlines would be affected. The evidence of insider trading as fact is founded mainly on the evidence presented by Paul Zarembka and Kevin Ryan. First of all Zarembka, professor of economics at the State University of New York Buffalo, covered several scientific studies proving the high probability of insider trading before the 9/11 attacks. He stressed that several suspicious financial transactions had been concluded by unknown people shortly before the attacks.

Professor Zarembka addressed evidence of insider trading before September 11, sometimes referred to by the broader phrase *informed* trading. He also mentioned certain open questions about financial issues surrounding September 11 that otherwise deserve investigations, including large increases in the M1 money supply in the United States reported for July and August 2001, huge financial transactions reported to have taken place at computers at the World Trade Center minutes before the attacks, selling short (as opposed to shorting with options), the disappearance of gold and securities from the World Trade Center, the specific financial firms in the World Trade Center directly hit by planes, the financial investigations sabotaged by the WTC or Pentagon attacks, and the insurance payoffs to the owner of destroyed buildings, particularly Larry Silverstein.

Professor Zarembka stressed that the 9/11 Commission stated that it found no evidence of insider trading before the attacks, and that the SEC lied in response to a FOIA request for supporting documentation by stating that their records had been destroyed. However, on January 14, 2009, several documents, including two SEC memos, were made public. One of these memos identified a specific options trader who recommended shorting American Airlines stock, and an unidentified institutional investor who did actually sell short United Airlines stock. Another of the memos showed that the SEC did not investigate insider trading in stock indexes, indicating that the US government's investigation was not as thorough as it led the public to believe.

Professor Zarembka also discussed several academic studies that identified several categories of pre-9/11 transactions that were almost certainly examples of informed trading. Two of the studies have been peer-reviewed and published in established journals, and one has been submitted for peer review.

There is strong circumstantial evidence, founded in fact, that insider trading happened prior to and in connection with September 11, 2001. The evidence consists in the same operations, objectively demonstrated, that have been done between September 6 and 10. Some relevant information was hidden by the 9/11

Commission and US government, but we do not know who was responsible for these operations because of the lack of needed investigations, as admitted by the Department of Justice prosecutor Ken Breen in one of the SEC memos. Further circumstantial evidence against Bush and the FBI director is that the FBI and 9/11 Commission, which investigated insider trading, did not adequately address the evidence of it.

There is precise circumstantial evidence that (a) the crime of insider trading was committed with participation of institutional investors, as CIA and FBI, (b) the 9/11 Commission intentionally and fraudulently hid the evidence to provide cover for the institutional and politically responsible parties, (c) the US Justice Department acted against the law and the truth in order to cover high governmental responsibility (d) more important, the US government could have prevented the 9/11 crimes against humanity, but did not want do that, in violation of the duty to prevent the crime.

The scientific and documentary analysis made by Professor Zarembka has been confirmed by the logical considerations of Kevin Ryan. A confirmation comes also from German Central Bank President, Ernst Welteke, who said his bank conducted a study that strongly indicated "terrorism insider trading" associated with 9/11. Professor Zarembka stated that the researchers he cited had found "almost irrefutable proof of insider trading."

The 9/11 Commission and FBI involuntarily gave us a confirmation of insider trading when they affirmed that the originator of the financial transactions suspected of insider trading is not connected with terrorists and Al Qaeda. To the 9/11 Commission, this fact meant that insider trading did not occur. I agree with the fact that no ties have been found between the people who purchased the shares and Al Qaeda terrorists. Nevertheless, that proves the involvement in insider trading of people outside of terrorism and Al Qaeda, but does not exclude that these people were aware of the 9/11 attacks, as I am convinced. And that they could have helped prevent the attack, but preferred instead to gain illicit money at the cost of thousands of lives. So the insider trading must be attributed to those who, inside governmental institutions, were informed of the 9/11 attacks, starting from the upper levels of the CIA and FBI and from President George W. Bush's administration. These people likely used some other people for the transactions. The issue of insider trading before the 9/11 attacks deserves further attention by state and federal prosecutors.

CIA involvement in the 9/11 attacks: The testimony of Peter Dale Scott

Professor Peter Dale Scott is an indirect, documentary witness; he presented several pieces of circumstantial evidence about the CIA's involvement in 9/11-related events. He described "How the CIA Withheld Key Information from the FBI, Thus Allowing 9/11 to Happen." His research presentation constitutes evidence that confirms and integrates the statements of Richard Clarke, who is a direct witness of some facts regarding actions taken by CIA and FBI figures before 9/11.

Prof. Scott is an important witness, because he brings into sharp relief whether top 9/11 investigators exhibited administrative incompetence or deliberate deception. He concludes that there was "organized mendacity." This mendacity has been used to protect some important figures, people highly placed in the

Bush administration, whose important roles we already know played in the 9/11 tragedy. "These figures include President Bush, Vice-President Cheney, NORAD General Richard Myers, and CIA Director Tenet. They include also President Clinton's National Security Adviser, Samuel "Sandy" Berger, who prior to testifying on these matters, went to the National Archives and removed, and presumably destroyed, key relevant documents." Scott cites, among other books, Kevin Fenton's *Disconnecting the Dots: How 9/11 Was Allowed to Happen* (Walterville, OR: Trine Day, 2011) and John Farmer's *The Ground Truth: The Untold Story of America Under Attack on 9/11* (New York: NY: Riverhead Trade (Penguin), 2009).

Scott stressed that "the most important truths still remain unknown, in large part because many of the most important documents are still either unreleased or heavily redacted; the efforts at cover-up continue, if anything more aggressively than before."

Scott's analysis confirms the relevant statements of Richard Clarke that the withholding of numerous relevant pieces of information from authorities tracking the alleged terrorists, both pre-and post 9/11, were the work of relatively few people. He bases his reconstruction of 9/11 events on earlier important books by James Bamford, Lawrence Wright, Peter Lance, Philip Shenon, and Fenton, that "demonstrate beyond a shadow of a doubt that there was a systematic CIA pattern of withholding important information from the FBI, even when the FBI would normally be entitled to it." Even more brilliantly, he shows that the withholding of information has been systematically sustained through four successive post-9/11 investigations: those of the Congressional Inquiry chaired by Senators Bob Graham and Richard Shelby (still partly withheld), the 9/11 Commission, the Department of

Justice Inspector General, and the CIA Inspector General. There is a formidable confirmation to Richard Clarke's interview that is relevant because Clarke indicated some CIA involvement in that Tom Wilshire and Richard Blee were likely involved in the 9/11 plot.

Most importantly, Scott shows that the numerous withholdings, both pre- and post-9/11, were the work of relatively few people. The withholding of information from the FBI was principally the work of what he calls the "Alec Station group" – a group within but not identical with the Alec Station Unit, consisting largely of CIA personnel in Virginia, led by Michael Scheuer, though there were a few FBI people there as well. Key figures in this group were CIA officer Tom Wilshire (discussed in the 9/11 Commission Report as "John"), and his immediate superior at Alec Station, Richard Blee.

I agree with Professor Scott that the numerous withholdings, both pre- and post 9/11, were the work of relatively few people, including Tom Wilshire and Richard Blee, which is an important contribution to the historical truth and strong evidence of will on the part of US government officials to cause the 9/11 crime against humanity.

Recommendations

The above facts show a strong willingness on the part of persons at the highest FBI and CIA levels in Washington not to prevent the 9/11 attack, but rather favoring it. An independent investigation is needed with subpoena power to determine the level of involvement and culpability on the part of CIA and FBI personnel, including Blee and Wilshire.

REPORT ON THE TORONTO HEARINGS

What was the real motive for the 9/11 attack?

I find no flaws in the analysis by David Ray Griffin and Michel Chossudovsky of the motive of the crimes of 9/11. Their analyses clearly point to the conclusion that the 9/11 events pursued a precise end: "justify" the wars against Afghanistan and Iraq.

According to Chossudovsky, the 9/11 attacks had been used as a war pretext incident in which the over-twenty-year history of the CIA and creating and supporting the terror network now known as Al Qaeda has been shoved to the background. The fact that successive US governments since the Soviet-Afghan war have supported and abetted the Islamic terror network is no longer mentioned for obvious reasons. It might break the consensus regarding al Qaeda as the sworn enemy of America, which is a crucial building block of the entire National Security doctrine.

A courageous Senator Mike Gravel, one of the few US politicians who seems dedicated to revealing the truth about 9/11, gave a very interesting analysis about the motive behind the 9/11 attacks. He deplored President Barack Obama's announcement that he would "look forward, not back." Senator Gravel also stated:

> The tenth anniversary of 9/11 also reminds us of the horrors that resulted from the government's official 9/11 story. In addition to the interminable wars in Afghanistan and in Iraq, and the war on terror, the official line also conveniently set the stage for the Patriot Act that abridged so many of our liberties and civil rights. It also set the stage for a long list of other abuses such as egregious torture of "terror suspects" in the name of the national security. The U.S. Government's investigation that culminated in the 9/11 Commission

THE 9/11 TORONTO REPORT

Report purported to set the record straight about the perpetrators of terrorism on our soil and the mistakes made by those whose sacred task is to defend our shores. But this 2004 report has since been called in to question by a very long list of credible voices, not only within the United States but throughout the world.

The chairman of the Commission, Governor Thomas Kean, admitted failure: "We think the Commission, in many ways, was set up to fail. Because we had not enough money, we didn't have enough time, and we (were) appointed by the most partisan people in Washington."

Sen. Gravel also noted the comments of Commission co-Chair Congressman Lee Hamilton: "I don't believe for a minute we got everything right... The commission was set up to fail... People should keep asking questions about 9/11." Senator Max Cleland resigned from the Commission, stating: "It is a national scandal". John Farmer, a former New Jersey attorney general, who as general counsel helped lead the inquiry, said "At some level of the government, at some point in time... there was an agreement not to tell the truth about what happened... I was shocked at how different the truth was from the way it was described... The tapes [released by the military] told a radically different story from what had been told to us and the public for two years.... This is not true. There were interviews made of the FAA's New York center the night of 9/11. Those tapes were destroyed. Tapes of CIA interrogations were also destroyed. The story of 9/11 itself, to put it mildly, was distorted and was completely different from the way things happened."

This analysis by Senator Mike Gravel confirms that it is impossible to trust in the investigative bodies under the control of the US government, as it was a mistake to trust the NIST and the same agencies responsible of the deviation from the truth. The media also supported this strategy of disinformation to manipulate public opinion. Thus it is important to search for the historical truth based on trust in the US judiciary system, independent and impartial, in order to prevent the same people responsible for twisting the truth so thoroughly up to this point from repeating other "pre-emptive" wars. We have to charge those responsible for the worldwide "strategy of tension," which if unchecked could lead to unimaginably greater destruction and death than we have even yet seen.

The possible International Commission on 9/11 events: The International Criminal Court

The Statute of the International Criminal Court is a means to punish the responsible author of these crimes. The public opinion is not available to permit that, under the pretext of the fight against terrorism, somebody commits unpunished crimes against humanities against the civil people. This need is the basis of the ICC.

A) The principles of the International Criminal Court

The Statute, i.e. the primary legislative instrument determining the purpose, structure and functioning of the International Criminal Court, sets out the principles on which the Court's judicial work is predicated. The principles in question relate to the independence of its judges, cooperation between the Court and party

States, the legislative underpinnings of the new function of international justice, and the automatism of judicial action.

The International Criminal Court was set up as, in the words of the Statute, "a permanent institution [that] shall have the power to exercise its jurisdiction over persons for the most serious crimes of international concern." The Court was established at The Hague in the Netherlands, and its bodies consist of the Presidency, the Pre-Trial, Trial and Appeals Divisions, the Office of the Prosecutor and the Registry.

The Court is composed of 18 judges deemed to possess the qualifications that their respective countries require for appointment to the highest judicial offices. The judges of the Court are elected for 9 years by the Assembly of States Parties with a view to realizing equal representation of diverse legal systems, equitable geographical representation and a fair division of sexes. The judges must have established competence in criminal law and procedure or in international humanitarian law and the law of human rights. Similar requirements are expected of the Prosecutor and the Deputy Prosecutor, who must also have specific competence in criminal investigation and the prosecution of criminal cases.

A key feature of the Statute of the Court is its inclusion of the most significant and generally accepted principles of criminal law and procedure. Specifically, the Statute enshrines the principles of: personal criminal responsibility; nullum crimen sine lege; the non-retroactivity of criminal law; ne bis in idem; due process (respect for natural justice); the right of the defendant to confront witnesses; and the right to a fair trial.

B) Crimes coming under the jurisdiction of the Court

The Court may judge only crimes committed after the coming into force of the Statute. The jurisdiction of the Court refers above all to the so-called "core crimes," viz., genocide, crimes against humanity and war crimes. The Court may also exercise its jurisdictional powers in relation to the crime of aggression but, as noted above, may not do so until after the adoption of a provision that, pursuant to the relevant provisions of the Charter of the United Nations, defines the crime and sets out the conditions under which it may be prosecuted.[367]

The crime of genocide is defined as in the United Nations Convention of 1948. Crimes against humanity refer to several different types of criminal acts committed as part of a widespread or systematic attack against civilian populations. War crimes are assigned to the jurisdiction of the Court, especially when committed as part of a plan or policy, and the related illegal acts are determined with reference to the Geneva Convention of 1949 and to the rules and appropriate practices allowed in armed conflicts. War crimes also include acts committed in internal armed conflicts ("armed conflicts not of an international character"), with the exception of riots and isolated acts of violence.[368]

The Court has jurisdiction also in relation to offences against the administration of justice such as giving false testimony before the Court itself, corruptly influencing witnesses, knowingly presenting false evidence, intimidating or retaliating against Court officials, and soliciting or accepting bribes from Court officials.

C) *Limitations of the jurisdiction of the Court*

One of the fundamental principles enshrined by the Statute is the complementarity[369] of the jurisdiction of the International Criminal Court with respect to party States. On the basis of this principle, party States undertake, above all, to include the crimes as set forth in article 5 of the Statute in their respective national judicial systems. The Court may take action in regard to one of the crimes indicated in the Statute only if the State with primary jurisdiction fails to prosecute or does so in a negligent manner.

Article 20 of the Statute enshrines the fundamental rule of ne bis in idem (double jeopardy) for crimes prosecuted by the Court, but allows exceptions to the rule in cases of competing jurisdiction by an inefficient national judicial system.

One of the issues that was most discussed during the Rome conference concerned the jurisdictional reach of the Court – that is to say, how to specify the criteria used to relate crimes that are defined as such in the Statute with the attribution of legal cognizance over the same. Unlike the International Criminal Tribunal for the former Yugoslavia and the International Criminal Tribunal for Rwanda, both of which were set up as a result of a resolution adopted by the United Nations Security Council, the International Criminal Court was established by international treaty to which only the party States are bound. At the same time, the Statute assigns a very specific role to the Security Council for the prosecution of crimes that fall within the remit of the Court and, by the terms of Chapter 7 of the United Nations Charter, are deemed to constitute a threat to international peace and security.

It was thus intended that the Court would exercise jurisdiction for crimes falling within its remit when the crimes took place in the territory of a State that is party to the Statute or in a State that, on the basis of a special agreement, had accepted the jurisdiction of the Court, *or else when the author of the crime is a national of one of the party States.*

These criteria shall not be deemed binding – and the jurisdiction of the Court shall therefore not be subject to the foregoing limitations – in cases in which the United Nations Security Council submits to the Court Prosecutor one or more acts defined as crimes by article 5 of the Statute and constituting a threat to international peace and security.[370]

Another constraint on the Court's jurisdiction consists of the transitional provision introduced by article 124 of the Statute (which provides for the so-called "opt-out" clause). The article enables a State, on becoming party to the Treaty, to declare that for a period of 7 years after the entry into force of the Statute for the State concerned, it will not accept the jurisdiction of the Court with respect to war crimes committed by its nationals or on its territory.

A further jurisdictional limit to the Court derives from the provisions of article 16 of the Statute, which accords the United Nations Security Council the faculty to adopt a resolution requesting a one-year deferral of investigations or prosecution, and the faculty also to renew the request.

The possible Jurisdiction of ICC on the 9/11 facts

In case of inert behavior of the State, which has the duty to punish the culprits, it is possible to access the International Criminal Court, which has jurisdiction complementary to national criminal jurisdictions.

THE 9/11 TORONTO REPORT

In 9/11, we have: 1) Crimes against humanity committed as part of the widespread attack directed against the USA and civilians of other States; and 2) The case has not been investigated or prosecuted by the USA or any other country that has jurisdiction over it.

The only possibility to have justice is to submit the best evidence concerning the involvement in 9/11 of specific individuals to the ICC Prosecutor and ask him to investigate according the articles 12, 13, 15 and 17 letters a and b of the Statute of ICC, recalling also the following preamble of the Statute of ICC: "recognizing that such grave crimes threaten the peace, security and the well being of the world; affirming that the most serious crimes of concern to the international community as a whole must not go unpunished and that their effective prosecution must be ensured by taking measures at the national level and by enhancing international cooperation. Determined to put an end to impunity for the perpetrators of these crimes and thus to contribute to the prosecution of such crimes; recalling that the duty of every State to exercise its criminal Jurisdiction over those responsible for international crimes."

Appendix

Introduction Endnotes

[1] The National Commission on Terrorist Attacks Upon the United States, popularly known as the 9/11 Commission, convened from November 2002 to August 2004. It was the official investigative body tasked with providing the fullest possible account of the events of 9/11, and was formed as a response to 9/11 victim family members calling for an investigation. Many victims' family members and independent experts viewed the 9/11 Commission as having major conflicts of interest consid-ered the Commission's final report to contain many contradic-tions, omissions, and distortions of facts.

Since the 9/11 Commission, many attempts were made, some with the support of 9/11 victim family members, to call for a new and independent investigation. In recognizing that no state judicial or administrative branch appeared likely re-spond, discussions between several concerned citizens began in March of 2011 about the need for hearings organized by citi-zens for the 10th anniversary of 9/11. A steering committee was formed, consisting of James Gourley, Kevin Ryan, Graeme MacQueen, Laurie Manwell, and Adnan Zuberi. The steering committee agreed to name the event "The Toronto Hearings: The International Hearings into the Events of September 11, 2001" and set forth the goal of providing a professional exposi-tion and evaluation of the significant body of evidence that had been compiled over the previous ten years that contradicts the official narrative of 9/11.

The steering committee, along with an advisory committee, se-lected expert witnesses who have served or currently serve in industry, academia and government to present evidence to an esteemed panel, which would evaluate the expert witnesses and their testimony. The advisory committee included Elizabeth Woodworth, Carol Brouillet, Janice Matthews, Cheryl Curtiss, Barrie Zwicker and Daniel LeBlanc.

THE 9/11 TORONTO REPORT

A number of prominent individuals also lent their credibility and support to the Toronto Hearings by becoming patrons. The patrons of the Toronto Hearings included Bob McIlvaine, father of Bobby McIlvaine (died in WTC 1); John McMurtry, University Professor Emeritus of Philosophy at the University of Guelph and Fellow of Royal Society of Canada; William Pep-per, a barrister and human rights lawyer; Adolfo Perez Esquiv-el, Nobel Peace Laureate; Lynn Margulis (deceased), Distin-guished Professor of Geosciences at the University of Massa-chusetts and Fellow of the National Academy of Sciences; Alvin Lee, former President and Vice-Chancellor of McMaster Uni-versity; Guilietto Chiesa, former Member of the European Parliament; Val Scott, founding member of the New Democratic Party; and Bryant Brown, a former CEO of one of Canada's best managed businesses.

Chapter 2 Endnotes

[2] "Bush asks Daschle to Limit Sept. 11 Probes," CNN, January 29, 2002 (http://articles.cnn.com/2002-01-29/politics/inv.terror.probe_1_daschle-house-and-senate-intelligence-intelligence-committee?_s=PM:ALLPOLITICS).

[3] John Haag, "Access Denied" to Joint Inquiry on 9-11 by Bush Administration," BuzzFlash, July 29, 2003 (ash.com/contributors/03/07/29_denied.html).

[4] "The Kissinger Commission," New York Times, November 29, 2002 (http://www.nytimes.com/2002/11/29/opinion/the-kissinger-commission.html).

[5] See Peter Dale Scott, The Road to 9/11: Wealth, Empire, and the Future of America (Berkeley, University of California: 2007), 101, 106-07).

[6] Philip Shenon, The Commission: The Uncensored History of the 9/11 Investigation (Twelve, 2008), 33.

[7] John King, "Starr Investigation Costs Just Shy of $30 Million," April 1, 1998 (http://www.cnn.com/ALLPOLITICS/1998/04/01/starr.costs/).

[8] Timothy J. Burger, "9-11 Commission Funding Woes," Time, March 26, 2003 (http://www.time.com/time/nation/article/0,8599,437267,00.html).

[9] Philip Shenon, "9/11 Commission Could Subpoena Oval Office Files," New York Times, October 26, 2003 (http://www.nytimes.com/2003/10/26/national/26KEAN.html).

[10] Associated Press, December 27, 2003; David Corn, "Probing 9/11," Nation, 277/1 (July 7, 2003): 14-18, at 16; Paul Sperry, "Is Fix in at 9/11 Commission?" AntiWar.com, 31 March 2004 (http://antiwar.com/sperry/?articleid=2209); Emad Mekay, "Iraq Was Invaded 'to Protect Israel'–US Official," Asia Times, March 31, 2004 (www.atimes.com/atimes/Front_Page/FC31Aa01.html).

[11] James Mann, Rise of the Vulcans: The History of Bush's War Cabinet (New York: Viking, 2004), 316.

[12] David Ray Griffin, "Neocon Imperialism, 9/11, and the Attacks on Afghanistan and Iraq," Information Clearing House, February 27, 2007 (http://www.informationclearinghouse.info/article17194.htm).

[13] National Security Strategy of the United States (NSS 2002), 6, 15.

APPENDIX

[14] In *America Alone: The Neo-Conservatives and the Global Order* (Cambridge: Cambridge University Press, 2004), Stefan Halper and Jonathan Clarke wrote: "Never before had any president set out a formal national strategy *doctrine* that included preemption" (142).

[15] Shenon, *The Commission*, 170.

[16] Shenon, *The Commission*, 69-70, 86.

[17] Ibid., 390.

[18] Ernest May, "When Government Writes History: A Memoir of the 9/11 Commission," *New Republic*, May 23, 2005; cited in Bryan Sacks, "Making History: The Compromised 9-11 Commission," in Zarembka, ed., *The Hidden History of 9-11*, 223-60, at 258n10.

[19] Shenon, *The Commission*, 321.

[20] Thomas H. Kean and Lee H. Hamilton, with Benjamin Rhodes, *Without Precedent: The Inside Story of the 9/11 Commission* (New York: Alfred A. Knopf, 2006), 116. Kean and Hamilton evidently did not realize that this report undermined their claim that the 9/11 Commission, unlike conspiracy theorists, started with the relevant facts, not with a conclusion, so the Commissioners "were not setting out to advocate one theory or interpretation of 9/11 versus another" (ibid., 269-70).

[21] Philip Shenon, *The Commission: The Uncensored History of the 9/11 Investigation* (New York: Twelve, 2008), 388-89.

[22] Ibid.

[23] Statement of the Family Steering Committee for The 9/11 Independent Commission, March 20, 2004 (www.911independentcommission.org/mar202004.html).

[24] Shenon, *The Commission*, 106-07, 171-76

[25] Sara Kugler, "Families: 9/11 Panel Failing at Mission," Associated Press, May 19, 2004 (http://911citizenswatch.org/?s=testifying&paged=3).

[26] Benjamin Demott, "Whitewash as Public Service: How The 9/11 Commission Report Defrauds the Nation," Harper's, October 2004.

[27] "9/11: Press for Truth," 2006 (http://video.google.com/videoplay?docid=5589099104255077250).

[28] "Open Letter: National Security Experts Speak Out: 9/11 Commission Falls Short," 9/11 Citizens Watch, September 16, 2004 (http://911citizenswatch.org/?p=401).

[29] *The 9/11 Commission Report: Final Report of the National Commission on Terrorist Attacks upon the United States*, Authorized Edition (New York: W. W. Norton, 2004), xvi.

[30] Nicolas Marmie, "Saudi Man Alive in Morocco," Associated Press, September 22, 2001.

[31] "Panoply of the Absurd," *Der Spiegel*, September 8, 2003 (http://www.spiegel.de/international/spiegel/0,1518,265160,00.html). That it was *Der Spiegel*'s story that was absurd is shown in Jay Kolar's "Afterword" to "What We Now Know about the Alleged 9-11 Hijackers," which is in the paperback edition of Paul Zarembka, ed., *The Hidden History of 9-11-2001* (New York: Seven Stories, 2008). As Kolar also shows, the BBC later adopted the same view as *Der Spiegel*.

THE 9/11 TORONTO REPORT

[32] David Bamford, "Hijack 'Suspect' Alive in Morocco," BBC, September 22, 2001 (http://news.bbc.co.uk/1/hi/world/middle_east/1558669.stm).

[33] *The 9/11 Commission Report*, 5 (henceforth cited as 9/11CR).

[34] 9/11CR 1.

[35] 9/11CR 451n1; FBI Director Robert S. Mueller III, "Statement for the Record," Joint Intelligence Committee Inquiry, September 26, 2002 (http://www.fas.org/irp/congress/2002_hr/092602mueller.html).

[36] Mueller, "Statement for the Record"; "Portland Police Eye Local Ties," Associated Press, *Portsmouth Herald*, September 14, 2001 (http://archive.seacoastonline.com/2001news/9_14maine2.htm).

[37] "America Under Attack: How Could It Happen?" CNN, September 12, 2001, 8:00 PM (http://transcripts.cnn.com/TRANSCRIPTS/0109/12/se.60.html); "Two Brothers among Hijackers," CNN, September 13, 2001 (http://english.peopledaily.com.cn/200109/13/eng20010913_80131.html). This second story is no longer present on the CNN website.

[38] "Two Brothers"; "Hijack Suspect Detained, Cooperating with FBI," CNN, September 13, 2001(http://transcripts.cnn.com/TRANSCRIPTS/0109/13/ltm.01.html).

[39] "Feds Think They've Identified Some Hijackers," CNN, September 13, 2001 (http://edition.cnn.com/2001/US/09/12/investigation.terrorism/).

[40] I have told this story in "Where Did Authorities Find Atta's Treasure Trove of Information?" which is Chapter 16 of my *9/11 Contradictions*.

[41] Kevin Fagan, "Agents of Terror Leave Their Mark on Sin City," *San Francisco Chronicle*, October 4, 2001 (http://sfgate.com/cgi-bin/article.cgi?file=/chronicle/archive/2001/10/04/MN102970.DTL); David Wedge, "Terrorists Partied with Hooker at Hub-Area Hotel," *Boston Herald*, October 10, 2001 (http://s3.amazonaws.com/911timeline/2001/bostonherald101001.html).

[42] "Terrorist Stag Parties," *Wall Street Journal*, October 10, 2001 (http://www.opinionjournal.com/best/?id=95001298).

[43] See Daniel Hopsicker, *Welcome to Terrorland: Mohamed Atta and the 9/11 Cover-up in Florida* (Eugene: MacCowPress, 2004). These details from Hopsicker's book are summarized in his "Top Ten things You Never Knew about Mohamed Atta," Mad Cow Morning News, June 7, 2004 (www.madcowprod.com/index60.html), and in an interview in the Guerrilla News Forum, June 17, 2004 (www.guerrillanews.com/intelligence/doc4660.html), summarized in *The New Pearl Harbor*, 2nd ed., 243n1.

[44] 9/11CR 160. The text says: "When Atta arrived in Germany, he appeared religious, but not fanatically so. This would change."

[45] "Professor Dittmar Machule," interviewed by Liz Jackson, A Mission to Die For, Four Corners, October 18, 2001 (http://www.abc.net.au/4corners/atta/interviews/machule.htm).

[46] Ibid.

APPENDIX

[47] Thomas Tobin, "Florida: Terror's Launching Pad," *St. Petersburg Times*, September 1, 2002 (http://www.sptimes.com/2002/09/01/911/Florida__terror_s_lau.shtml); Elaine Allen-Emrich, "Hurt for Terrorists Reaches North Port," *Charlotte Sun-Herald*, September 14, 2001 (available at http://www.madcowprod.com/keller.htm).

[48] "9/11: Truth, Lies and Conspiracy: Interview: Lee Hamilton," CBC News, August 21, 2006, interview by Evan Solomon (http://www.cbc.ca/sunday/911hamilton.html).

[49] 9/11CR 40.

[50] The National Commission on Terrorist Attacks upon the United States, May 23, 2003, Panel 1.

[51] See Griffin, *The 9/11 Commission Report: Omissions and Distortions*, 220. The Mineta testimony is available on video at 911Truth.org (http://www.911truth.org/article.php?story=20050724164122860).

[52] Clarke, *Against All Enemies*, 7-8.

[53] 9/11CR 41.

[54] The Project for the New American Century, *Rebuilding America's Defenses: Strategy, Forces and Resources for a New Century*, September 2000 (www.newamericancentury.org), 51.

[55] See Griffin, *The 9/11 Commission: Omissions and Distortions*, 122-25.

[56] Jean-Charles Brisard and Guillaume Dasqui, *Forbidden Truth: U.S.–Taliban Secret Oil Diplomacy and the Failed Hunt for Bin Laden* (New York: Nation Books/Thunder's Mouth Press, 2002), and NPH 91; George Arney, "U.S. 'Planned Attack on Taleban'," BBC News, September 18, 2001.

[57] Griffin, *The 9/11 Commission: Omissions and Distortions*, 129-31.

[58] Ibid., 131-32.

[59] 9/11 Commission Hearing, March 23, 2004 (http://www.washingtonpost.com/wp-dyn/articles/A17798-2004Mar23.html).

[60] Richard A. Clarke, *Against All Enemies: Inside America's War on Terror* (New York: Free Press, 2004), 3, 7-9.

[61] "Interview: General Richard B. Myers," Armed Forces Radio and Television Services, October 17, 2001 (http://web.archive.org/web/20011118060728/http://www.dtic.mil/jcs/chairman/AFRTS_Interview.htm); 9/11CR 463n199; and 9/11CR 38.

[62] Clarke, *Against All Enemies*, 3-9, 12.

Chapter 3 Endnotes

[63] Jones SE, Legge FM, Ryan KR, Szamboti AF, Gourley JR (2008b) Fourteen points of agreement with official government reports on the World Trade Center destruction, The Open Civil Eng J 2(1):35–40. doi:10.2174/1874149500802010035.

[64] See NIST WTC report NCSTAR 1, figure 6-36

[65] Seattle Times, February 27, 1993

THE 9/11 TORONTO REPORT

[66] Quote from James Verhalen, chairman of the company that manufactured the fireproofing, United States Mineral Products, in the New York Times, December 14, 2001.
[67] New York Times, April 15, 2002.
[68] Personal email from Loring Knoblauch, CEO of UL, to Kevin Ryan, December 2003.
[69] Engineering News-Record, 1964.
[70] Ibid.
[71] NIST WTC report NCSTAR 1-6A, Appendix C.
[72] Tomasz Wierzbicki et al, "Aircraft Impact Damage," Massachusetts Institute of Technology.
[73] NIST Progress Report, May 2003.
[74] Ibid.
[75] S. Sunder, W. Grosshandler, H. S. Lew, et al. "National Institute of Standards and Technology (NIST) federal building and fire safety investigation of the World Trade Center disaster, answers to frequently asked questions," Gaithersburg, MD: National Institute of Standards and Technology, August 30, 2006. [Online]. Available: http://wtc.nist.gov.
[76] NIST WTC report NCSTAR 1-6B, figure 3-11.
[77] NIST WTC reports NCSTAR 1-6D and NCSTAR 1-6E.
[78] NIST WTC report NCSTAR 1-6, p115.
[79] Hart, Multi-Storey Buildings in Steel, Halsted Press.
[80] Shyam Sunder to New York Magazine, 2006.
[81] Shyam Sunder to Associated Press, 2008.
[82] NIST WTC report NCSTAR 1A, pages 21 to 22.
[83] John J. Salvarinas, Seven World Trade Center, New York, Fabrication and Construction Aspects, Canadian Structural Engineering 1 Conference, 1986.
[84] Letter from David Proe and Ian Thomas, professional research fellow and director respectively, Victoria University, to NIST during the public comment period, available at http://wtc.nist.gov.
[85] NIST WTC report NCSTAR 1-9, table 8-2.
[86] NIST WTC report NCSTAR 1-9, pp. 349 to 352.
[87] NIST WTC report NCSTAR 1-9, p 344.
[88] NIST WTC report NCSTAR 1A, p 7
[89] NIST WTC report NCSTAR 1A, p 7 (also see NCSTAR 1-9, table 8-1, p 340).
[90] See exchange between NIST advisor Charles Thornton and Shyam Sunder from the December 2007 advisory committee, http://wtc.nist.gov.
[91] See NIST's 2004 interim report, figure L-24b.
[92] NIST WTC report NCSTAR 1-9, figures 3-6 and 5-136.
[93] NIST WTC report NCSTAR 1-9, p 378.
[94] NIST WTC report NCSTAR 1-9, figure 12-69.

APPENDIX

Chapter 4 References

Arrows, F. & Fetzer, J. (2004). *American assassination: The strange death of Senator Paul Wellstone*. Brooklyn: Vox Pop.

Ahmed, N.F. (2005). *The war on truth: 9/11, disinformation, and the anatomy of terrorism*. Northampton, MA: Olive Branch Press.

Bacevich, A. J. (2005). *The new American militarism: How Americans are seduced by war*. Oxford: Oxford University Press.

Barstow, D. (2008). Message machine: Behind analysts, the Pentagon's hidden hand. *New York Times*, April 20, p.1.

Barstow, D. & Van Natta Jr., D. (2001). How Bush took Florida: Mining the overseas absentee vote. *New York Times*. July 15.

Beard, C.A., & Beard, M.R. (1927). *The rise of American civilization*. New York: The MacMillan Company.

Bernstein, C. & Woodward, B. (1974). *All the president's men*. New York: Simon and Schuster.

Black, W. K..(2005). *The best way to rob a bank is to own one*. Austin: University of Texas Press.

Blum, W. K. (2004). *Killing hope: U.S. military and C.I.A interventions since World War II*. Monroe, ME: Common Courage Press.

Bowen, R.S. (1991). *The immaculate deception: The Bush crime family exposed*. Chicago: Global Insights.

Broad, W. J., Johnston, D., Miller, J., & Zielbauer, P. (2001). Anthrax probe hampered by FBI blunders. *New York Times*, November 9.

Calavita, K., Pontell, H., & Tillman, R. (1999). *Big money crime: Fraud and politics in the savings and loan crisis*.

Clarke, R. A. (2004). *Against all enemies: Inside America's war on terror*. New York: The Free Press.

Dahl, R. & Lindblom, C. E. (1976). *Politics, Economics, and Welfare*. New Haven: Yale, 1946.

Dean, J. W. (2004). *Worse than Watergate: The secret presidency of George W. Bush*. New York: Little, Brown and Company.

Dean, J. W. (2007). *Broken government: How Republican rule destroyed the legislative, executive, and judicial branches*. New York: Viking.

deHaven-Smith, L. (2005). *The Battle for Florida*. Gainesville: University Press of Florida.

deHaven-Smith, L. (2006). "When political crimes are inside jobs: Detecting State Crimes Against Democracy," *Administrative Theory & Praxis*, Vol. 28: No. 3. (September), pp. 330-355.

deHaven-Smith, L., 2010. Beyond conspiracy theory: Patterns of high crime in American government. American Behavioral Scientist, 53 6), 795-825.

deHaven-Smith, L. and Witt, M., 2009. Preventing state crimes against democracy. *Administration & Society*, 41(5), 527-550.

Douglass, J. W. (2003). Interview with Donald Wilson, in DiEugenio, J. and Pease, L., Eds., *The Assassinations* (479-491). Los Angeles: Feral House.

THE 9/11 TORONTO REPORT

Douglass, J. W. (2008). *JFK and the unspeakable: Why he died and why it matters.* Maryknoll, NY: Orbis Books.

Eisenhower (1961). Farewell Address, available online from the Dwight D. Eisenhower Presidential Library and Museum at http://www.eisenhower.archives.gov/.

Ellsberg, D. (2002). *Secrets: A memoir of Vietnam and the pentagon papers.* London: Penguin Press.

Fetzer, J. H. (2000). Smoking guns and the death of JFK. In J. H. Fetzer (Ed.). *Murder in Dealey Plaza: What we know that we didn't know then about the death of JFK* (pp.1-16). Chicago: Catfeet Press.

Fisher, L. (2004). The way we go to war: The Iraq Resolution, in Gregg, G.L. and Rozell, M.J., eds., *Considering the Bush Presidency* (107-124). New York: Oxford University Press.

Ford, G. R. (1974). Proclamation 4311, granting a pardon to Richard Nixon. Available online at the Gerald R. Ford Presidential Library and Museum, at http://www.ford.utexas.edu/.

Frost, D. (1977). The third Nixon-Frost interview. *New York Times*, May 20, p. A16.

Garrison, J. (1988). *On the trail of the assassins: My investigation and prosecution of the murder of President Kennedy.* New York: Sheridan Square Press.

Goldsmith, J. (2007). *The terror presidency: Law and judgment inside the Bush Administration.* New York: W.W. Norton.

Goodman, M.A. (2008). *The failure of intelligence: The decline and fall of the CIA.* New York: Rowman and Littlefield.

Gray, L. P. (2008). *In Nixon's web: A year in the crosshairs of Watergate.* New York: Henry Holt.

Greenwald, G. (2007). *A tragic legacy: How a good vs. evil mentality destroyed the Bush presidency.* New York: Crown Publishing.

Griffin, D. R. (2004). *The new Pearl Harbor: Disturbing questions about the Bush administration and 9/11.* Northampton, Massachusetts: Olive Branch Press.

Griffin, D. R. (2005). *The 9/11 Commission report: Omissions and Distortions.* Northampton, Massachusetts: Olive Branch Press.

Griffin, R. P. (1950). Constitutional law: Corporations: Artificial 'persons' and the Fourteenth Amendment. *Michigan Law Review*, 48(7), 983-993.

Groden, R. J. (1993). *The Killing of a president: The complete photographic record of the JFK assassination, the conspiracy, and the cover-up.* New York: Penguin Books USA.

Haldeman, H. R. (1978). *The ends of power*, New York: Times Books.

Hall, M. (2005). Ridge reveals clashes on alerts. *USA Today*, May 10.

Hedegaard, E. (2007). The Last Confession of E. Howard Hunt, *Rolling Stone Magazine*, April 5, 2007.

Hedges, C. (2008). *American fascists: The Christian right and the war on America*, London: Vintage Books.

Hellinger, D. (2003). Paranoia, conspiracy and hegemony in American politics. In H.G. West H.G. & T. Sanders (Eds.), *Transparency and conspiracy: Ethnographies of suspicion in the new world order* (pp. 204-232): Durham: Duke University Press.

APPENDIX

Hoover, J. E, (1958). *Masters of deceit: The story of Communism in America and how to fight it.* New York: Henry Holt.

Horne, D. P. (2000). Evidence of a government cover-up: Two different brain specimens in President Kennedy's autopsy. In J. H. Fetzer (Ed.). *Murder in Dealey Plaza: What we know now that we didn't know then about the death of JFK* (pp. 299-310). Chicago: Catfeet Press.

Horton, S. (2007). Political profiling: The smoking gun. *Harpers.* April 13.

Hufschmid, E. (2002). *Painful questions: An analysis of the September 11th attack.* Goleta, CA: Endpoint Software.

Hunt, E. H. (1973). *Give us this day: The inside story of the CIA and the Bay of Pigs invasion … by one of its key organizers.* New Rochelle: Arlington House.

Hunt, E. H. (1974). *Undercover: Memoirs of an American secret agent.* New York: G. P. Putnam's Sons.

Isikoff, M. & Corn, D. (2006). *Hubris: The inside story of spin, scandal, and the selling of the Iraq War.* New York: Crown Publishers.

Johnson, C. (2004). *The sorrows of empire: Militarism, secrecy, and the end of the republic.* New York: Henry Holt.

Johnson, H. (2005). *The age of anxiety: McCarthyism to terrorism.* New York: Harcourt.

Johnson, L. (2004). Congressional supervision of America's secret agencies: The experience and legacy of the Church Commission. *Public Administration Review,* 64(1), 3-14.

Klein, N. (2007). *The shock doctrine: The rise of disaster capitalism.* New York: Allen Lane/Penguin Books.

Kornbluh, P. & Byrne, M. (Eds.)(1993). *The Iran-Contra scandal: The classified history.* New York: The New Press.

Kutler, S.I. (1990). *The wars of Watergate: The last crisis of Richard Nixon.* New York: W.W. Norton.

Lane, M. (1966). *Rush to judgment: A critique of the Warren Commission's inquiry into the murders of President John F. Kennedy, Officer J.D. Tippit, and Lee Harvey Oswald.* New York: Holt, Rinehart, and Winston.

Liddy, G.G. (1980). *Will: The autobiography of G. Gordon Liddy.* New York: St. Martin's Press.

Lowi, T. (1969). *The end of liberalism.* New York: Norton.

Mayer, J. (2008). *The dark side: The inside story of how the war on terror turned into a war on American ideals.* New York: Doubleday.

Marcus, G.E. (ed) (1999), *Paranoia within reason: A casebook on conspiracy as explanation.* Chicago: University of Chicago Press.

Marks, J. (1979). *The search for the Manchurian candidate: The CIA and mind control.* New York: W.W. Norton.

Marrs, J. (2006). *The terror conspiracy: Deception, 9/11 and the loss of liberty.* New York: Disinformation.

McCool, D. (1998). The subsystem family of concepts: A critique and a proposal. *Political Research Quarterly,* Vol. 51, No. 2 (June), pp. 551-570.

THE 9/11 TORONTO REPORT

McCord, J. W., Jr. (1974). *A Piece of Tape: The Watergate Story, Fact and Fiction*. Rockville, Maryland: Washington Media Services.

Miller, A. (Ed.). (2005). *What went wrong in Ohio: The Conyers' report on the 2004 presidential election*. Chicago: Academy Publishers.

Morgan, R. & Henshall, I. (2005). *9/11 revealed: The unanswered questions*. New York: Carroll & Graff Publishers.

Munson, R. (2005). *From Edison to Enron: The business of power and what it means for the future of electricity*. Westport, Connecticut: Praeger.

The 9-11 Commission report. New York: W.W. Norton.

Parish, J. & Parker, M. (2001), *The age of anxiety: Conspiracy theory and the human sciences*. Oxford: Blackwell Publishers.

Parry, R. (1993). *Trick or treason: The October surprise mystery*. New York: Sheridan Square Press, Inc.

Paul, D. & Hoffman, J. (2004). *Waking up from our nightmare: The 9/11/01 crimes in New York City*. San Francisco: Irresistible/Revolutionary.

Pease, L. (2003), *The RFK plot: Parts I and II*. In J. DiEugeio & L. Pease (Eds.). *The assassinations: Probe magazine on JFK, MLK, RFK, and Malcolm X* (pp. 536-570). Los Angeles: Feral House.

Rich, F. (2006). *The greatest story ever sold*. New York: Penguin.

Rich, F. (2007). *When the Vice President does it, that means it's not illegal*. New York Times, July 1.

Rogow, A.A. & Lasswell, H.D. (1963). *Power, Corruption, and Lies*. Englewood Cliffs, NJ: Prentice Hall.

Ruppert, M.C. (2004). *Crossing the Rubicon: The decline of the American Empire at the end of the Age of Oil*. Gabriola Island, BC: New Society Publishers.

Ryan, K.R., Gourley, J.R., & Jones, S.E. (2008). "Environmental anomalies at the World Trade Center: Evidence for energetic materials." *The Environmentalist*, DOI 10.1007/s10669-008-9182-4, available online at http://www.springerlink.com/content/f67q6272583h86n4/fulltext.pdf.

Sanders, T. & West, H.G. (2003). *Power revealed and concealed in the new world order*. In H.G. West H.G. & T. Sanders, Eds. *Transparency and conspiracy: Ethnographies of suspicion in the new world order* (pp.1-37): Durham: Duke University Press.

Savage, C. (2007). *Takeover: The return of the imperial presidency and the subversion of American democracy*. New York: Little, Brown and Company.

Scahill, J. (2007). *Blackwater: The rise of the world's most powerful mercenary army*. London: Serpent's Tail.

Scott, P. D. (1993). *Deep politics and the death of JFK*. Berkley, CA: University of California Press.

Shenon, P. (2008). *The commission: The uncensored history of the 9/11 investigation*. New York: Twelve.

Shorrock, T. (2008). *Spies for hire: The secret world of intelligence outsourcing*. New York: Simon & Schuster.

APPENDIX

Sick, G. (1991). *October surprise: America's hostages in Iran and the election of Ronald Reagan*. New York: Random House.

Summers, A. (2000). *The arrogance of power: The secret world of Richard Nixon*. New York: Viking.

Suskind, R. (2006). *The one percent doctrine: Deep inside America's pursuit of its enemies since 9/11*. New York: Simon and Schuster.

Talbot, D. (2007). *Brothers: The hidden history of the Kennedy years*. New York: Free Press.

Tarpley, W. G. (2005). *9/11 synthetic terror*. Joshua Tree, California: Progressive Press.

Thomas, E. & Hosenball, M. (2001). "Bush: 'We are at war'," *Newsweek*. September 24 issue.

Walsh, L. E. (1997). *Firewall: The Iran-Contra conspiracy and cover-up*. New York: W.W. Norton and Company.

Webb, G. (1998). *Dark alliance: The CIA, the Contras, and the crack cocaine explosion*. New York: Seven Stories Press.

Weiner, T. (2007). *Legacy of ashes: History of the CIA*. New York: Doubleday.

Weldon, C. (2005). *Countdown to terror*. Washington, D.C.: Regnery.

Weldon, D. (2000). The Kennedy limousine: Dallas 1963. In J. H. Fetzer (Ed.). *Murder in Dealey Plaza: What we know now that we didn't know then about the death of JFK* (pp. 129-158). Chicago: Catfeet Press.

Wheeler, M. (2007). *Anatomy of deceit: How the Bush administration used the media to sell the Iraq War and out a Spy*. Berkeley: Vaster Books.

White, R. F. (1998). Apologists and critics of the lone gunman theory: Assassination science and experts in post-modern America. In J. H. Fetzer (Ed.). *Assassination science: Experts speak out on the death of JFK* (pp. 377-413). Chicago: Catfeet Press.

Wilford, H. (2008). *The mighty Wurlitzer: How the CIA played America*. Cambridge: Harvard University Press.

Wise, D. (1976). *The American police state: The government against the people*. New York: Vintage Books.

Wise, D. and Ross, T.B. (1964). *The invisible government*. New York: Random House.

Wolin, S. (2008). *Democracy Incorporated: Managed democracy and the specter of inverted totalitarianism*. Princeton: Princeton University Press.

Woodward, B. (2006). "Closing the chapter on Watergate wasn't done lightly." *Washington Post*, December 28, p. A5.

Chapter 5 Endnotes

[95] John Farmer, *The Ground Truth*, 288; quoted in Anthony Summers and Robbyn Swan, *The Eleventh Day*, 147.

[9] Summers, 383-84; cf. Farmer, 41. Although a Democrat, Berger was subsequently protected by the Republican Bush Administration from having to testify to Congress about his behavior (a condition of his plea bargain).

THE 9/11 TORONTO REPORT

[97] Summers, 334.

[98] Fenton, 72-79. Grewe subsequently left government to work at the Mitre Corp., a private firm doing CIA contract work with the CIA and another private firm, Ptech. Questions about Ptech and Mitre Corp's work on FAA-NORAD interoperability systems were raised in 9/11 testimony presented some years ago by Indira Singh; see Scott, *Road to 9/11*, 175.

[99] Fenton, 78. Kirsten Wilhelm of the National Archives told Fenton (p. 78) that "It appears Barbara Grewe conducted the interviews with 'John' [Wilshire] and Jane [Corsi]," another key figure. Wilhelm could find no "memorandum for the record" (MFR) for the Wilshire interview, which Fenton understandably calls "about the most important interview the Commission conducted" (p. 79). Summers, also citing correspondence with Kirsten Wilhelm, disagrees, saying that the report of Wilshire's interview exists, but "is redacted in its entirety" (Summers, 381, cf. 552). This is an important point to be focused on in future investigations.

[100] Fenton, 225ss.

[101] Fenton, 38; citing *9/11 Report*, 181-82.

[102] Fenton, 42-45; summarizing Justice Department IG Report, 239-42; cf. Wright, 311-12.

[103] Fenton, 50; summarizing Justice Department IG Report, 242-43; cf. Wright, 311.

[104] Fenton, 45.

[105] Fenton, 383-86.

[106] Fenton, 48. Cf. Lawrence Wright, "The Agent," *New Yorker*, July 10 and 17, 2006, 68; quoted approvingly in Peter Dale Scott, *American War Machine*, 199.

[107] Fenton, 371, cf. 95.

[108] Fenton, 239-42, 310-22. Fenton notes that Corsi worked at FBI HQ, which coordinated "liaisons with foreign services" (Fenton, 313).

[109] Fenton, 310.

[110] At first I suspected, as have others, that the two men were Saudi double agents. Another real possibility is that they were sent as designated targets, to be surveilled by the Saudis and the Americans separately or together.

[111] Summers, 396

[112] *9/11 Report*, 184.

[113] Steve Coll, *Ghost Wars*, 456-57.

[114] Thomas E. Ricks and Susan B. Glasser, *Washington Post*, October 14, 2001, http://www.washingtonpost.com/ac2/wp-dyn/A55834-2001Oct13.

[115] I myself acquired a special, higher-than-top-secret clearance to access intelligence from NATO, a relatively overt and straightforward liaison.

[116] John Berger, *Ali Mohamed*, 20 (Cloonan); *9/11 Report*, 261 (PDB). Cf. John Berger, "Mohamed was one of the primary sources for the infamous August 6, 2001, presidential daily brief (PDB)" (Scott, *Road to 9/11*, 158).

[117] James Risen, *New York Times*, October 31, 1998; in Scott, *Road to 9/11*, 346-47.

[118] *Raleigh News and Observer*, November 13, 2001; in Scott, *Road to 9/11*, 347.

APPENDIX

[119] Dana Priest and William M. Arkin, "'Top Secret America': A look at the military's Joint Special Operations Command," *Washington Post*, September 2, 2011, http://www.washingtonpost.com/world/national-security/top-secret-america-a-look-at-the-militarys-joint-special-operations-command/2011/08/30/gIQAvYuAxJ_story.html.

[120] Fenton, 168-69; Summers, 371, 550.

[121] Fenton, 313.

[122] Scott, *American War Machine*, 161; Scott, *Road to 9/11*, 62-63.

[123] Ahmed Rashid, *Taliban*, 129.

[124] John Prados, *Safe for Democracy*, 489; discussion in Scott, *American War Machine*, 12-13.

[125] Fenton, 104.

[126] Summers, 397.

[127] Joseph J. and Susan B. Trento, in Summers, 399.

[128] Wright, 161; in Summers, 216.

[129] Ralph Blumenthal, "Tapes Depict Proposal to Thwart Bomb Used in Trade Center Blast," *New York Times*, October 28, 1993, emphasis added. The next day, the *Times* published a modest correction: "Transcripts of tapes made secretly by an informant, Emad A. Salem, quote him as saying he warned the Government that a bomb was being built. But the transcripts do not make clear the extent to which the Federal authorities knew that the target was the World Trade Center."

[130] Scott, *Road to 9/11*, 145.

[131] Peter Dale Scott, "Bosnia, Kosovo, and Now Libya: The Human Costs of Washington's On-Going Collusion with Terrorists," Asian-Pacific Journal: Japan Focus, July 29, 2011, http://japanfocus.org/-Peter_Dale-Scott/3578. Evan Kohlmann has described how a Zagreb office in support of the Saudi-backed jihad in Bosnia received "all orders and funding directly from the main United States office of Al-Kifah on Atlantic Avenue controlled by Shaykh Omar Abdel Rahman" (Evan Kohlmann, Al-Qaida's Jihad in Europe, 39-41; citing Steve Coll and Steve LeVine, "Global Network Provides Money, Haven," *Washington Post*, August 3, 1993).

[132] Scott, *Road to 9/11*, 151-59.

[133] Fenton, 310.

[134] Fenton, 371, cf. 95.

[135] Joint Chiefs of Staff, "Courses of Action Related to Cuba (Case II)," in Scott, *American War Machine*, 196.

[136] Washington Post, September 30, 2001; in Summers, 293; cf. 9/11 Report, 221-22.

[137] Fenton, 360-61, 385.

[138] Scott, American War Machine, 201.

[139] Scott, American War Machine, 200-02.

[140] Clarke, 30-33; Summers, 175-76; James Bamford, A Pretext for War, 287.

[141] Thomas E. Ricks and Susan B. Glasser, Washington Post, October 14, 2001, http://www.washingtonpost.com/ac2/wp-dyn/A55834-2001Oct13.

[142] Coll, 467-69.
[143] Coll, 534-36.
[144] Coll, 558.
[145] Coll, 573-74.
[146] Fenton, 108.
[147] Fenton, 110-14.
[148] George Tenet, At the Center of the Storm, 255.
[149] Jeremy Scahill, "Shhhhhh! JSOC is Hiring Interrogators and Covert Operatives for 'Special Access Programs,'" *Nation*, August 25, 2010, http://www.thenation.com/blog/154133/shhhhhh-jsoc-hiring-interrogators-and-covert-operatives-special-access-programs.
[150] Fenton, 127-30; Summers, 387-88.
[151] Jason Vest, "Implausible Denial II," *Nation*, May 31, 2004, http://www.thenation.com/article/implausible-denial-ii.
[152] Peter Dale Scott, "Is the State of Emergency Superseding our Constitution? Continuity of Government Planning, War and American Society," November 28, 2010, http://1/japanfocus.org/-Peter_Dale-Scott/3448.

Chapter 6 References

Arvedlund, Erin E. (2001), "Follow the Money: Terrorist conspirators could have profited more from fall of entire market than single stocks", *Barron's*, October 8.

Chesney, Marc (2010), Remo Crameri, and Loriano Mancini, "Detecting Informed Trading Activities in the Options Markets", April 15, 2010, at SSRN: http://ssrn.com/abstract=1522157.

Gaffney, Mark H. (2011), "Black 9/11: A Walk on the Dark Side" (Second in a series), *Foreign Policy Journal*, March 2, at www.foreignpolicyjournal.com/2011/03/02/black-911-a-walk-on-the-dark-side-2/0/, accessed August 5, 2011.

Griffin, David R. (2005), *The 9/11 Commission Report: Omissions and Distortions*, Northampton, MA: Interlink.

Kay, Jonathan (2011), *Among the Truthers*, Toronto: HarperCollins.

Poteshman, Allen M. (2006), "Unusual Option Market Activity and the Terrorist Attacks of September 11, 2001", *Journal of Business*, Vol. 79, pp. 1703-1726.

Ryan, Kevin (2010), "Evidence for Informed Trading on the Attacks of September 11", *Foreign Policy Journal*, November 18, at www.foreignpolicyjournal.com/2010/11/18/evidence-for-informed-trading-on-the-attacks-of-september-11/, accessed August 5, 2011.

Wong, Wing-Keung, Howard E. Thompson, and Kweehong The (2011), "Was there Abnormal Trading in the S&P 500 Index Options Prior to the September 11 Attacks?", *Multinational Finance Journal*, Vol. 15, no. 1/2, pp. 1–46 at http://mfs.rutgers.edu/MFJ/Articles-pdf/V15N12p1.pdf.

APPENDIX

Zarembka, Paul (2008), "Initiation of the 9-11 Operation, with Evidence of Insider Trading Beforehand", *The Hidden History of 9-11*, P. Zarembka, editor, New York: Seven Stories Press, 2nd edition, pp. 47-74 (1st edition, Amsterdam: Elsevier Press, 2006).

Chapter 6 Endnotes

[153] Zarembka, Paul (2008), "Initiation of the 9-11 Operation, with Evidence of Insider Trading Beforehand", *The Hidden History of 9-11*, P. Zarembka, editor, New York: Seven Stories Press, 2nd edition, pp. 64-66, 69-71 (1st edition, Amsterdam: Elsevier Press, 2006).

[154] www.9-11commission.gov/report/911Report.pdf, p. 499, fn. 130

[155] http://maxkeiser.com/wp-content/uploads/2010/06/FOIAresponseGIF1.gif

[156] The January 14, 2009 date was reported to this author on July 25, 2011 by Kristen Wilhelm of the Center for Legislative Archives as follows: "The 9/11 Commission's Joseph Cella Memoranda for the Record were scanned and uploaded to the NARA Archival Research Catalog for the opening of the 9/11 Commission records on Jan. 14, 2009." See also the NARA prior notice of the general opening at www.archives.gov/press/press-releases/2009/nr09-41.html. It may be of some interest that attention was drawn to this release on the very day of January 14 (see the January 15 posting at http://screwloosechange.blogspot.com/2009/01/more-on-911-put-options.html, and its link to postings on January 14 at http://forums.randi.org/showthread.php?t=132904&page=2, both accessed August 12, 2011. Thanks are offered to "lapman" and "Mike W" – the latter being presumably Mike Williams given his later reference to this release). Williams receives further attention in the course of this article.

[157] http://media.nara.gov/9-11/MFR/t-0148-911MFR-00138.pdf. Another 75 trade is also cited for another contract not in contention.

[158] http://media.nara.gov/9-11/MFR/t-0148-911MFR-00139.pdf (p. 14)

[159] http://media.nara.gov/9-11/MFR/t-0148-911MFR-00074.pdf

[160] Poteshman, Allen M. (2006), "Unusual Option Market Activity and the Terrorist Attacks of September 11, 2001", *Journal of Business*, Vol. 79, pp. 1703-1726.

[161] *See e.g.*, Griffin, David R. (2005), *The 9/11 Commission Report: Omissions and Distortions*, Northampton, MA: Interlink, pp. 52-57; Zarembka, pp. 67-69.

[162] Poteshman, 2006, pp. 1711-12.

[163] Poteshman, 2006, pp. 1720, Table 4.

[164] Poteshman, 2006, pp. 1716.

[165] Wong, Wing-Keung, Howard E. Thompson, and Kweehong The (2011), "Was there Abnormal Trading in the S&P 500 Index Options Prior to the September 11 Attacks?", *Multinational Finance Journal*, Vol. 15, no. 1/2, pp. 1–46 at http://mfs.rutgers.edu/MFJ/Articles-pdf/V15N12p1.pdf.

[166] Wong, 2011, p.44.

[167] Poteshman, 2006, p. 1723.

168 Chesney, Marc (2010), Remo Crameri, and Loriano Mancini, "Detecting Informed Trading Activities in the Options Markets", April 15, 2010, at SSRN: http://ssrn.com/abstract=1522157.

169 "The main motivation for considering increments in open interests is the following. Large volumes do not necessarily imply that large buy orders are executed because the same put option could be traded several times during the day. In contrast large increments in open interest are originated by large buy orders. These increments also imply that other long investors are unwilling to close their positions forcing the market maker to issue new put options." (Chesney, et al., pp. 8-9).

170 In order to abstract from intraday speculation, they compare daily changes in open interest to the reported volumes of transactions (the difference between the two should be small). In other words, purchases are too dominant, with sales or exercises of options small.

171 This calculation could seem to suggest 103 times in eight and one-quarter years beginning in January 1998. But the AMR stock price fell considerably from April 2002 to a low of $1.25 within one year thereafter, implying much higher volumes than required for similar dollar option positions.

172 Actually, AMR closed at $17.90 on both September 21 and 27 before the October 20 option expiration; the $18.00 on September 17 was not quite the lowest. However, presumably the option price was the highest on September 17.

173 Let Gt be the cumulative gains achieved through the exercises of the selected option in the shortest time available from the day of the calculated maximum up to ten trading days thereafter. Chesney's third criterion is then offered as a pair of conditions for the option trade in question, that is,

$$rtmax \geq q0.90(rtmax)$$
and
$$Gt \geq q0.98(Gt).$$

The quantiles at day t for the rtmax and Gt distributions – q0.90(rtmax) and q0.98(Gt) – are computed using the preceding two years of data. These criteria are the quantiles for the top 10% of initial profiting and top 2% of total gains.

174 Chesney, et al., 2010, p. 35, Table 2 and p. 38, Table 4

175 See http://community.seattletimes.nwsource.com/archive/?date=20010908&slug=boeing08, accessed August 20, 2011.

176 This recommendation was for the put-option contract with a $30 strike price to expire on October 20, 2001. It read as follows:

> September 9, 2001
>
> Vol. 12, No. 28
>
> Stocks Skid On A Jump In The Jobless Rate. This Week, We Take To The Air
>
> This past week, stocks were pressed to the downside – with the highlight being Friday's blue chip decline. Wall Street was surprised by a spike, to a four-year high, in the jobless rate. And the market took its lumps. This week, I see opportunity for you to have fun and profit with an airline play. So, without further ado, here's…

APPENDIX

This Week's Option Recommendation

Buy the AMR October $30 put for $170 [100 shares for $1.70 per share], or less, good this week.

Shares of AMR Corp. trade on the New York Stock Exchange under the symbol "AMR". The symbol for this option reco is "AMRVF". American Airlines closed the week at $30.15. The 52-week range for AMR is $27.62-$43.93. My downside price target is $22-$26.

The major airline is under pressure. At $25, each $30 put would have $500 of intrinsic value. If AMR is at or above $30 on the third Friday in October, your option will expire worthless. That is your risk. Set your stop-loss at $100, to preserve capital, in case my expectations go awry.

That's buy the AMR October $30 put for $170, or less, good this week.

– www.911myths.com/index.php/Put_Options#Options_Hotline, accessed 719/2011.

[177] Kay, Jonathan (2011), Among the Truthers, Toronto: HarperCollins.

[178] www.911myths.com/index.php/Put_Options#Boeing, accessed August 4, 2011.

[179] Within the same discussion, Williams cites many reports of put-option volumes without those using accurate data. Some reported data are about double the actual levels, presumably due to author errors in understanding optionmetric data which considers the buy and sell sides of one transaction to be distinct. It is preferable to focus on those who argue for insider trading using correct data.

Chapter 7 Endnotes

[180] "NORAD's Response Times," North American Aerospace Defense Command, September 18, 2001 (www.standdown.net/noradseptember182001pressrelease.htm).

[181] Thomas H. Kean and Lee H. Hamilton, with Benjamin Rhodes, *Without Precedent: The Inside Story of the 9/11 Commission* (New York: Alfred A. Knopf, 2006), 259. Kean and Hamilton wrote: "… how they had failed to shot down at least one of the planes." The context shows, however, that they had in mind American 77 (along with United 93).

[182] "FAA Clarification Memo to 9/11 Independent Commission," May 22, 2003 (http://www.911truth.org/article.php?story=2004081200421797).

[183] Kean and Hamilton, *Without Precedent*, 259.

[184] 9/11 Commission Hearing, May 23, 2003 (http://www.9-11commission.gov/archive/hearing2/9-11Commission_Hearing_2003-05-23.htm).

[185] *The 9/11 Commission Report*, 2004 (www.9-11commission.gov/report/911Report.pdf), henceforth 9/11CR, 34.

[186] 9/11CR 34.

[187] Ibid.

[188] 9/11 Commission Hearing, May 23, 2003 (http://www.9-11commission.gov/archive/hearing2/9-11Commission_Hearing_2003-05-23.htm).

THE 9/11 TORONTO REPORT

[189] Matthew Wald, "Pentagon Tracked Deadly Jet but Found No Way to Stop It," *New York Times*, September 15, 2001 (http://www.attackonamerica.net/pentagontracked deadlyjet.html).

[190] 9/11CR 24.

[191] 9/11 Commission Hearing, May 23, 2003.

[192] 9/11 Commission Hearing, June 17, 2004.

[193] Philip Shenon, *The Commission*, 205.

[194] Ibid., 208.

[195] Michael Bronner, "9/11 Live: The NORAD Tapes," *Vanity Fair*, August 2006: 262-285, 264. For my discussion of Bronner's essay and my reasons to believe the tapes to have been doctored, see the first chapter of my book, *Debunking 9/1 Debunking: An Answer to Popular Mechanics and Other Defenders of the Official Conspiracy Theory* (Northampton: Olive Branch [Interlink Books], 2006), entitled "9/11 Live or Distorted: Do the NORAD Tapes Verify *The 9/11 Commission Report?*"

[196] Frank Legge, "What Hit the Pentagon? Misinformation and its Effect on the Credibility of 9/11 Truth," *Journal of 9/11 Studies*, February 15, 2010 (http://www.journalof911studies.com/volume/2009/WhatHitPentagonDrLeggeAug.pdf).

[197] David Chandler and Jon Cole, "Joint Statement on the Pentagon: David Chandler and Jon Cole," 911Blogger, January 7, 2011 (http://911blogger.com/news/2011-01-01/joint-statement-pentagon-david-chandler-and-jon-cole).

[198] Legge, "What Hit the Pentagon?"

[199] Chandler and Cole, "Joint Statement on the Pentagon."

[200] 9/11CR 40.

[201] Clarke, *Against All Enemies* (Free Press, 2004), 1-4.

[202] "9/11: Interviews by Peter Jennings," ABC News, September 11, 2002 (http://s3.amazon-aws.com/911timeline/2002/abcnews091102.html); "Sept. 11's Moments of Crisis: Part 2: Scramble," ABC News, September 14, 2002 (http://enigma911.110mb.com/cache/abcnews/sept11_moments_2.html).

[203] See Gregor Holland, "The Mineta Testimony: 9/11 Commission Exposed," 911truthmovement.org, 1 November 2005 (http://www.911truthmovement.org/archives/2005/11/post.php).

[204] Chandler and Cole, "Joint Statement on the Pentagon."

[205] Legge, "What Hit the Pentagon?"

[206] Jim Yardley, "A Trainee Noted for Incompetence," *New York Times*, May 4, 2002 (http://newsmine.org/content.php?ol=9-11/suspects/flying-skills/pilot-trainee-noted-for-incompetence.txt).

[207] Marc Fisher and Don Phillips, "On Flight 77: 'Our Plane Is Being Hijacked,'" *Washington Post*, September 12, 2001 (http://www.washingtonpost.com/ac2/wp-dyn?pagename=article&node=&contentId=A14365-2001Sep11).

[208] Steve Fainaru and Alia Ibrahim, "Mysterious Trip to Flight 77 Cockpit," *Washington Post*, September 10, 2002 (http://www.washingtonpost.com/wp-dyn/content/article/2007/08/13/AR2007081300752_pf.html).

APPENDIX

[209] Legge, "What Hit the Pentagon?"

[210] Chandler and Cole, "Joint Statement on the Pentagon."

[211] Alan Miller, "U.S. Navy 'Top Gun' Pilot Questions 911 Pentagon Story," OpEdNews.com, September 6, 2007 (http://www.rense.com/general78/pent.htm).

[212] Legge, "What Hit the Pentagon?"

[213] Chandler and Cole, "Joint Statement on the Pentagon."

[214] "The Pentagon," GlobalSecurity.org (http://www.globalsecurity.org/military/facility/pentagon.htm).

[215] "Interview with Theodore Olsen [sic]," *9/11 Commission, FBI Source Documents, Chronological, September 11*, 2001Intelfiles.com, March 14, 2008 (http://intelfiles.egoplex.com:80/2008/03/911-commission-fbi-source-documents.html).

[216] "America's New War: Recovering from Tragedy," Larry King Live, CNN, September 14, 2001 (http://edition.cnn.com/TRANSCRIPTS/0109/14/lkl.00.html)

[217] United States v. Zacarias Moussaoui, Exhibit Number P200054 (http://www.vaed.uscourts.gov/notable-cases/moussaoui/exhibits/prosecution/flights/P200054.html). These documents can be more easily viewed in an article by Jim Hoffman, "Detailed Account of Phone Calls from September 11th Flights" (http://911research.wtc7.net/planes/evidence/calldetail.html).

[218] "T7 B12 Flight 93 Calls- General Fdr- 5-20-04 DOJ Briefing on Cell and Phone Calls From AA 77 408," Federal Bureau of Investigation, May 20, 2004 (http://www.scribd.com/doc/18886083/T7-B12-Flight-93-Calls-General-Fdr-52004-DOJ-Briefing-on-Cell-and-Phone-Calls-From-AA-77-408).

[219] See "Barbara Olson" under "Flight 77" in Hoffman, "Detailed Account of Phone Calls from September 11th Flights" (http://911research.wtc7.net/planes/evidence/calldetail.html).

[220] This exception is "9/11: The Unofficial Story," November 27, 2009, produced by the Canadian Broadcasting Corporation's *Fifth Estate* (http://www.cbc.ca/fifth/2009-2010/the_unofficial_story); also available on You Tube (http://www.youtube.com/user/SaveOurSovereignty3#p/u/3/8SK1PWIGs48).

[221] "Interview with Deena Lynne Burnett," Federal Bureau of Investigation, September 11, 2001 (http://intelfiles.egoplex.com/2001-09-11-FBI-FD302-deena-lynne-burnett.pdf).

[222] Ibid.

[223] Deena L. Burnett (with Anthony F. Giombetti), *Fighting Back: Living Life Beyond Ourselves* (Longwood, Florida: Advantage Inspirational Books, 2006), 61.

[224] Thomas Burnett, Jr., United Airlines Flight #93 Telephone Calls (http://911research.wtc7.net/planes/evidence/docs/exhibit/ThomasBurnett.png). According to this report, Burnett placed two calls from row 24 ABC and one call from row 25 ABC (although he had been assigned a seat in row 4).

[225] See David Ray Griffin, *9/11 Ten Years Later: When State Crimes Against Democracy Succeed* (Olive Branch [Interlink Books] 2011), Ch. 5, "Phone Calls from the 9/11 Planes: How They Fooled America."

THE 9/11 TORONTO REPORT

[226] 9/11 Commission Hearing, May 23, 2007 (http://www.9-11commission.gov/archive/hearing2/9-11Commission_Hearing_2003-05-23.htm).

[227] 9/11CR 38.

[228] 9/11CR 28-30. See the discussion in my *9/11 Contradictions: An Open Letter to Congress and the Press* (Northampton: Olive Branch [Interlink Books], 2008), 11 – 13.

[229] Clarke, *Against All Enemies*, 7.

[230] "9/11: Interviews by Peter Jennings," ABC News, September 11, 2002 (s3.amazonaws.com/911timeline/2002/abcnews091102.html).

[231] Ibid.

[232] "Conversation With Major General Larry Arnold, Commander, 1st Air Force, Tyndall AFB, Florida," *Code One: An Airpower Projection Magazine*, January 2002 (http://www.codeonemagazine.com/archives/2002/articles/jan_02/defense).

[233] 9/11 Commission Hearing, May 23, 2003.

[234] Kevin Dennehy, "I Thought It Was the Start of World War III," *Cape Cod Times*, August 21, 2002 (http://911research.wtc7.net/cache/planes/analysis/norad/capecodtimes082102_ithought.html).

[235] General Myers Confirmation Hearing, Senate Armed Services Committee, September 13, 2001 (http://emperors-clothes.com/9-11backups/mycon.htm).

[236] Ibid.

[237] Jonathan Silver, "NORAD Denies Military Shot Down Flight 93," *Pittsburgh Post-Gazette*, September 14, 2001 (http://www.post-gazette.com/headlines/20010914norad0914p3.asp).

[238] Richard Wallace, "What Did Happen to Flight 93?" *Daily Mirror*, September 12, 2002 (http://911research.wtc7.net/cache/planes/evidence/mirror_whatdidhappen.html).

[239] 9/11CR 37.

[240] Clarke, *Against All Enemies*, 7-8.

[241] Sylvia Adcock, Brian Donovan and Craig Gordon, "Air Attack on Pentagon Indicates Weaknesses," *Newsday*, September 23, 2001 (http://s3.amazonaws.com/911timeline/2001/newsday092301.html).

[242] Chitra Ragavan and Mark Mazzetti, "Pieces of the Puzzle: A Top-Secret Conference Call on September 11 Could Shed New Light on the Terrorist Attacks," *U.S. News and World Report*, August 31, 2003 (http://www.usnews.com/usnews/news/articles/030908/8sept11.htm).

[243] "9/11: Interviews by Peter Jennings," ABC News, September 11, 2002 (s3.amazonaws.com/911timeline/2002/abcnews091102.html).

[244] Albert McKeon, "FAA Worker Says Hijacked Airliners Pilots Almost Collided Before Striking World Trade Center," *Telegraph* (Nashua), September 13, 2001 (http://www.freerepublic.com/focus/f-news/587567/posts).

[245] "Deputy Secretary Wolfowitz Interview with PBS NewsHour," PBS, September 14, 2001 (http://www.defenselink.mil/transcripts/transcript.aspx?transcriptid=1882).

[246] "Feds Would Have Shot Down Pa. Jet," CBS News, September 16, 2001 (http://www.cbsnews.com/stories/2001/09/12/archive/main311011.shtml).

APPENDIX

[247] Dave Foster, "UST Grad Guides Bombers in War," *Aquin*, December 4, 2002 (http://www.stthomas.edu/aquin/archive/041202/anaconda.html); Matthew L. Wald with Kevin Sack, "'We Have Some Planes,' Hijacker Told Controller," *New York Times*, October 16, 2001 (http://s3.amazonaws.com/911timeline/2001/nyt101601.html); William B. Scott, "Exercise Jump-Starts Response to Attacks," Aviation Week & Space Technology, June 3 2002 (http://web.archive.org/web/20020917072642/http://www.aviationnow.com/content/publication/awst/20020603/avi_stor.htm); Pamela S. Freni, *Ground Stop: An Inside Look at the Federal Aviation Administration on September 11, 2001* (Lincoln, NE: iUniverse, 2003), 41.

[248] Newseum, *Running Toward Danger* (Lanham: Rowman & Littlefield, 2002), 148.

[249] Ibid., 149.

[250] Debra Erdley, "Crash Debris Found 8 Miles Away," *Pittsburgh Tribune-Review*, September 14, 2001 (http://www.pittsburghlive.com/x/pittsburghtrib/s_12967.html).

[251] Erdley, "Crash Debris Found 8 Miles Away"; Bill Heltzel and Tom Gibb, "2 Planes Had No Part in Crash of Flight 93," *Pittsburgh Post-Gazette*, September 16, 2001 (http://www.post-gazette.com/headlines/20010916otherjetnat5p5.asp); Richard Wallace, "What Did Happen to Flight 93?" *Daily Mirror*, September 12, 2002 (http://911research.wtc7.net/cache/planes/evidence/mirror_whatdidhappen.html).

[252] On the remaining fuel, see John O'Callaghan and Daniel Bower, "Study of Autopilot, Navigation Equipment, and Fuel Consumption Activity Based on United Airlines Flight 93 and American Airlines Flight 77 Digital Flight Data Recorder Information," National Transportation Safety Board, February 13, 2002 (http://www.scribd.com/doc/31594959/9-11-NTSB-Autopilot-Study-Flight-AA77-UA93). On the lack of contamination, see "Environmental Restoration begins at Somerset Site," WTAE-TV, October 2, 2001 (http://html.thepittsburghchannel.com/pit/news/stories/news-100064120011002-151006.html), and "Latest Somerset Crash Site Findings May Yield Added IDs," *Pittsburgh Post-Gazette*, October 3, 2001 (http://www.postgazette.com/headlines/20011003crash1003p3.asp).

[253] "America Under Attack: FBI and State Police Cordon Off Debris Area Six to Eight Miles from Crater Where Plane Went Down," CNN, September 13, 2001 (http://transcripts.cnn.com/TRANSCRIPTS/0109/13/bn.01.html).

[254] "Homes, Neighbors Rattled by Crash," *Pittsburgh Tribune-Review*, September 12, 2001 (http://www.pittsburghlive.com/x/pittsburghtrib/s_12942.html); Robin Acton and Richard Gazarik, "Human Remains Recovered in Somerset," *Pittsburgh Tribune-Review*, September 13, 2001 (http://www.pittsburghlive.com/x/pittsburghtrib/s_47536.html); Richard Gazarik and Robin Acton, "Black Box Recovered at Shanksville Site," *Pittsburgh Tribune-Review*, September 14, 2001 (http://www.pittsburghlive.com/x/pittsburghtrib/s_12969.html).

THE 9/11 TORONTO REPORT

Chapter 8 Endnotes

[255] The importance of eyewitnesses in criminal investigation is affirmed in such publications as: Charles Regini, "The Cold Case Concept," *FBI Law Enforcement Bulletin*, Aug. 1997; Charles Welford and James Cronin, "Clearing up Homicide Clearance Rates," *National Institute of Justice Journal*, April, 2000; and Vivian Lord, "Implementing a Cold Case Homicide Unit: A Challenging Task," *FBI Law Enforcement Bulletin*, Feb. 2005. Among social scientists an attack against na ve acceptance of eyewitness evidence (and especially against a na ve view of human memory) was led some time ago by Harvard's Elizabeth Loftus. See, for example, her *Eyewitness Testimony* (Cambridge, Mass.: Harvard Univ. Press, 1979). But Loftus did not claim to have made eyewitnesses unnecessary. As she said in a book co-authored with James Doyle in 1997, "Despite the inaccuracies of eyewitness testimony and the misconceptions of jurors, the legal system can neither afford to exclude eyewitness testimony legally nor ignore it. Sometimes it is the only evidence available, and it is often correct." *Eyewitness Testimony: Civil and Criminal*. Lexis Law Publishing, Charlotteville, 3rd ed., p. 7.

[256] *NFPA 921: Guide for Fire and Explosion Investigations.* NFPA publication. Massachusetts, USA., 2004. Section 21.16.

[257] "Explosive Testimony: Revelations about the Twin Towers in the 9/11 Oral Histories." January 26, 2006. Available online at: http://www.911truth.org/article.php?story=20060118104223192

[258] Graeme MacQueen, "118 Witnesses: the Firefighters' Testimony to Explosions in the Twin Towers." *Journal of 9/11 Studies*, 2006, p. 47. Available online at: http://www.journalof911studies.com/articles/Article_5_118Witnesses_WorldTradeCenter.pdf

[259] "Explosive Testimony: Revelations about the Twin Towers in the 9/11 Oral Histories." January 26, 2006. Available online at: http://www.911truth.org/article.php?story=20060118104223192

[260] Graeme MacQueen, "118 Witnesses: the Firefighters' Testimony to Explosions in the Twin Towers." *Journal of 9/11 Studies*, 2006, p. 47. Available online at: http://www.journalof911studies.com/articles/Article_5_118Witnesses_WorldTradeCenter.pdf

[261] A lengthy and important video clip showing Burkett fleeing from both collapses can be found here: http://www.youtube.com/watch?v=rBO2rlo_QbQ

[262] http://www.archive.org/details/cnn200109111421-1503

[263] http://www.youtube.com/watch?v=Mv6LfwLeRxo

[264] http://www.youtube.com/watch?v=-npAbNl2ihY. Jack Kelley eventually had to resign from USA Today in disgrace. http://www.usatoday.com/news/2004-04-22-report-one_x.htm

[265] http://www.youtube.com/watch?v=4VBUOo2isRM

[266] The clip from the Naudet film is available online at: http://www.youtube.com/watch?v=jODfN8oZWe0.

[267] The Lemos interview is available online at http://www.youtube.com/watch?v=Z4AcOsaz0LI

[268] Note that Bussey has been given a structural failure hypothesis within which, in the full article, he situates his experience, apparently not realizing that his description of what he actually saw is incompatible with that hypothesis.

APPENDIX

[269] A well known video clip, shown on network television on 9/11 and variously magnified and analyzed, is available online at: http://www.youtube.com/watch?v=kZKOKv0q8I8.

[270] Taylor & Francis. Boca Raton, 2006. This book is part of the series, *Practical Aspects of Criminal and Forensic Investigation*.

[271] Susan Hagen and Mary Caroub, *Women at Ground Zero: Stories of Courage and Compassion*. Alpha, 2002.

[272] The reports submitted by PAPD officers were released along with other materials in August, 2003 after The *New York Times* sued the city of New York to make them public. See Kevin Flynn and Jim Dwyer, "The Port Authority Files: Voices; Officers' Sept. 11 Accounts: Catastrophe in the Details." *New York Times*, August 30, 2003. The PAPD reports in their entirety were posted in 2003 by The Memory Hole and, although this site was hacked in 2009, the documents are available online at: http://adam.pra.to/public/mir/www.thememoryhole.org/911/pa-transcripts/

[273] This is what we expect. The tendency of people to adjust their memories in this way has been noted by social scientists researching eyewitness recollection. See Loftus and Doyle, p. 54: "The 'contamination' of recollection can occur through witnesses talking to other witnesses, through questions asked by authorities, by media accounts." And in the same volume (p. 98): "it has been shown that highly credible people can manipulate others more readily. They can persuade others, they can change attitudes, and they can influence the behavior or others in countless ways."

[274] *The 9/11 Commission Report: Final Report of the National Commission on Terrorist Attacks Upon the United States* (New York: W. W. Norton, 2004), p. 306.

[275] *NIST NCSTAR 1: Final Report on the Collapse of the World Trade Center Towers*. National Institute of Standards and Technology. Sept. 2005, p. xxix.

[276] NIST final report on the Towers, Chapter 7, p. 155 ff.

[277] NIST final report on the Towers, p. 157.

[278] NIST final report on the Towers, pp. xxxvii and 143.

Chapter 9 Endnotes

[279] Interview with Danny Jowenko: http://www.youtube.com/watch?v=877gr6xtQIc

[280] FEMA, "World Trade Center Building Performance Study", available at http://www.fema.gov/library/viewRecord.do?id=1728.

[281] NIST estimates 443 mph for AA11 (WTC 1) and 542 mph for UAL 175 (WTC 2) in NIST NCSTAR 1-2, p. 165.

[282] Chandler, David, "High Speed Massive Projectiles from the WTC on 9/11", available at http://911speakout.org/?page_id=8

[283] NIST's "Probable Collapse Sequence" is outlined in NIST NCSTAR 1A, p. 21.

[284] Sarns, Chris, "A Compilation of Research By Chris Sarns on World Trade Center 7's Mysterious Collapse", available at http://truthphalanx.com/chris_sarns/

[285] The discovery was announced in a blog post at http://911blogger.com/node/6400 submitted by 911veritas on Sat, 02/24/2007 – 1:15pm. The erroneous report was

THE 9/11 TORONTO REPORT

discovered while searching an archive of 9/11 first day news coverage. WTC 7 is reported to have collapsed while it is still visible in the background.

[286] In a news report available at http://www.youtube.com/watch?v=f_sNl7l6tOU, CNN reporter Allan Dodds Frank describes the collapse of a building, approximately 50 stories tall, at 10:45 am. No such building collapsed at that time, but the description fits WTC 7 which collapsed much later that day.

[287] NIST FOIA release: footage labeled "CBS-Net Dub5 09" taken by "Camera 3" has a definite boom a few seconds before the collapse of the East Penthouse. Available at http://www.youtube.com/watch?v=0j8XN3iKLak

[288] Chandler, David, "WTC7 in Freefall–No Longer Controversial", available at http://www.youtube.com/watch?v=rVCDpL4Ax7I

[289] NIST NCSTAR 1A, p. xxviii.

[290] NIST NCSTAR 1A for public comment, p. 41.

[291] Hammond, Jeremy R., "Video Analysis of NIST's Claim of a 5.4 s Collapse Time Over 18 Stories for WTC 7", *Foreign Policy Journal*, July 11, 2011.

[292] Chandler, David, "WTC7: NIST Finally Admits Freefall (Part I)" available at http://www.youtube.com/watch?v=eDvNS9iMjzA

[293] NIST NCSTAR 1-9 and NCSTAR 1A.

[294] NIST NCSTAR 1A p. 45.

Chapter 10 Endnotes

[295] Jones SE, Farrer J, Jenkins GS, et al. Extremely high temperatures during the World Trade Center destruction. J 9/11 Studies 2008; 19: 1-11. [Accessed February 7, 2009]. Available from: http://www.journalof911studies.com/articles/WTCHighTemp2.pdf

[296] Ryan KR, Gourley JR, Jones SE. Environmental anomalies at the World Trade Center: evidence for energetic materials. Environmentalist 2009; 29(1):56-63. [Accessed February 7, 2009]. Available from: http://www.springerlink.com/content/f67q6272583h86n4/

[297] Presentation by Leslie Robertson, http://www.youtube.com/watch?v=rjmHqES_lto

[298] Structural Fire Protection, ASCE Manuals and Reports on Engineering Practice no. 78, 1992, p 172

[299] Kevin R. Ryan, Metallic Microspheres in WTC Dust, OpEd News, January 6, 2008, Available: http://www.opednews.com/articles/life_a_kevin_ry_080106_metallic_microsphere.htm

[300] Paul J. Lioy, Dust: the inside story of its role in the September 11th aftermath, p 219

[301] RJ Lee Group, WTC Dust Signature Report, December, 2003.

[302] Ibid.

[303] Ibid.

[304] Federal Emergency Management Agency (FEMA), World Trade Center building performance study: Preliminary observations, and recommendations, Report FEMA 403. Washington, D.C.: Federal Emergency Management Agency, May 2002.

APPENDIX

[305] James Glanz and Eric Lipton, A Search for Clues In Towers' Collapse; Engineers Volunteer to Examine Steel Debris Taken to Scrapyards, The New York Times, February 2, 2002.

[306] Eric Lipton and Andrew C. Revkin, A NATION CHALLENGED: THE FIREFIGHTERS; With Water and Sweat, Fighting the Most Stubborn Fire, The New York Times, November 19, 2001.

[307] Garrett L, Full effects of WTC pollution may never be known. Newsday, 14 September 2003.

[308] Kidder M, Britt PF, Zhang Z et al, Pore size effects in the pyrolysis of 1,3-Diphenylpropane confined in mesoporous silicas. Chem Commun (Camb) 2003:2804–2805. doi:10.1039/b310405b.

[309] Cahill TA, Shackelford CJ, Meier M et al, Very fine aerosols from the World Trade Center collapse piles: anaerobic incineration. http://e-reports-ext.llnl.gov/pdf/305393.pdf. Accessed 16 Feb 2008

[310] Jim Hoffman, The North Tower's Dust Cloud: Analysis of Energy Requirements for the Expansion of the Dust Cloud Following the Collapse of 1 World Trade Center, 911Research.wtc7.net, October 16, 2003

Chapter 11 Endnotes

[311] Questions and Answers about the NIST WTC Towers Investigation, response to question 8, 4th paragraph. Available at http://www.nist.gov/el/disasterstudies/wtc/faqs_wtctowers.cfm

[312] http://www.youtube.com/watch?v=5d5iIoCiI8g

[313] "Skyride Tower Felled by Melting Steel Legs," *Popular Mechanics*. Nov. 1935. p. 657.

Chapter 12 Endnotes

[314] S R Badger, K P Rickabaugh, M S Potter, B E Scheetz, H R Bhattacharjee and R J Lee (2004). World Trade Center Particulate Contamination Signature. Microscopy and Microanalysis, 10 (Suppl. 02), pp. 948-949 doi:10.1017/S1431927604887452.

[315] Heather A. Lowers and Gregory P. Meeker (2005). Particle Atlas of World Trade Center Dust. (Online report available USGS website: http://pubs.usgs.gov/of/2005/1165/508OF05-1165.html#heading08).

[316] Niels H. Harrit, et al. "Active Thermitic Material Discovered in Dust from the 9/11 World Trade Center Catastrophe," The Open Chemical Physics Journal, Vol 2, 2009, (DOI: 10.2174/1874412500902010007).

[317] John Gartner (2005). "Military Reloads with Nanotech." MIT Technology Review. (Available at: http://www.technologyreview.com/NanoTech/14105/?a=f).

[318] AMPTIAC Quarterly (2002), Special Issue, "DOD Researchers Provide A Look Inside Nanotechnology." (available at http://ammtiac.alionscience.com/pdf/AMPQ6_1.pdf).

[319] B. J. Clapsaddle, L. Zhao, D. Prentice, M. L. Pantoya, A. E. Gash, J. H. Satcher Jr., K. J. Shea, R. L. Simpson (2005). "Formulation and Performance of Novel Energetic

Nanocomposites and Gas Generators Prepared by Sol-Gel Methods." Lawrence Livermore National Laboratory Publication.
(Available at https://e-reports-ext.llnl.gov/pdf/318263.pdf).

[320] Further suggested reading: Jim Hoffman, "Explosives Found in World Trade Center Dust" (available at http://911research.wtc7.net/essays/thermite/explosive_residues.html) and "Wake Up and Smell the Aluminothermic Nanocomposite Explosives" (available at http://911research.wtc7.net/essays/thermite/explosives_evidence_timeline.html).

Chapter 13 Endnotes

[321] "The official [FBI] investigation, known as 'OKBOMB'...", Wikipedia, Oklahoma City Bombing entry, paragraph 3, http://en.wikipedia.org/wiki/OKBomb.

[322] "The Terrorist Hunter," *Time* magazine, May 9, 2011, p. 27; and "Bush: 'We're at War'", *Newsweek*, Sept. 24, 2001,
http://www.ratical.org/ratville/JFK/JohnJudge/linkscopy/GWBwereAtWar.html.

[323] "9/11 Investigation: PENTTBOM," FBI website, http://www.fbi.gov/about-us/history/famous-cases/9-11-investigation.

[324] Communication with the author by Monica Gabrielle. In her videotaped testimony to the Toronto Hearings, another Jersey Girl, Lori van Auken, mentioned that other FBI briefers told the Jersey Girls that the agency's code name for the 9/11 investigation ends in BOM[B] because the plot included planes being used as bombs.

[325] "Pentagon Attack Came Minutes After Rumsfeld Predicted 'There Will Be Another Event,'" by Robert Burns, Associated Press, Sept. 11, 2001, 5:58 p.m. EDT.

[326] 9/11 Commission staff report on Team 8 interview with Navy Capt. Charles Joseph Leidig, http://cryptome.org/nara/dod/dod-04-0429.pdf.

[327] *Pentagon 9/11*, Alfred Goldberg et al., Washington, D.C., Office of the Secretary of Defense, 2007, p. 31.

[328] Army Lt. Col. Victor Correa entry, compilation of witness accounts by Eric Bart, http://web.archive.org/web/20040501101751/http://eric-bart.net/iwpb/witness.html.

[329] "9/11 Pentagon Victims Recall Their Journey of Survival," by Christie Vanover, INCOM, *Fort Riley Post*, Sept. 5, 2002, http://www.army.mil/article/27202.

[330] *Frederick (Md.) News-Post*, Sept. 7, 2011.

[331] Lt. Col. Brian Birdwell interview excerpt in *Then Came the Fire: Personal Accounts from the Pentagon – 11 September 2001*, by Stephen J. Lofgren, General Editor, Center of Military History, United States Army, Washington, D.C., Sept. 2011, pp. 72-73,
http://www.scribd.com/doc/65563423/THEN-CAME-THE-FIRE-PERSONAL-ACCOUNTS-FROM-THE-PENTAGON-11-SEPTEMBER-2001.

[332] Terry Morin quote, "9/11 and the Pentagon Attack: What Eyewitnesses Described," No. 640, Arabesque, April 2 2007, http://arabesque911.blogspot.com/2007/04/911-and-pentagon-attack-what.html.

[333] "The Works of Humankind: A Dispatch by Don Perkal,"
http://www.mcsweeneys.net/2001/09/19perkal.html; and
http://911research.wtc7.net/pentagon/evidence/witnesses/explosive.html.

APPENDIX

[334] Gilah Goldsmith quote, compilation of witness accounts by Eric Bart, http://web.archive.org/web/20040501101751/http://eric-bart.net/iwpb/witness.html.

[335] Two-hour videotaped under-oath testimony interview of April Gallop by the author, Irvine, Calif., March 2007, submitted in evidence to these Toronto Hearings, to Prof. Graeme MacQueen. This testimony formed a basis for a lawsuit Gallop brought against Secretary of Defense Donald Rumsfeld, then Acting Chmn. of the Joint Chiefs of Staff Gen. Richard Myers, and Vice President Dick Cheney. See also video of keynote Gallop's keynote address to Freedom Law Center conference, March 2007, Irvine, CA, http://www.youtube.com/watch?v=5U5hOyZlrcY&feature=gv.

[336] TruTV, "Conspiracy Theory" episode on the Pentagon attack with Jesse Ventura, aired Dec. 17, 2010, http://www.youtube.com/watch?v=TrZ14NRbT-s.

[337] In the Qs and As following her keynote address to the Freedom Law Center conference (see Note 15), April Gallop states, "I know my watch stopped at 9:30. The watch that I had on stopped at 9:30," at 30:31 3 :13 min. in http://www.youtube.com/watch?v=5U5hOyZlrcY&feature=gv.

[338] *September 11: An Oral History,* by Dean E. Murphy, New York, Doubleday, 2002, p. 212.

[339] The photo on the right of a Navy/Marine Corps wall clock stopped at 9:31:40 was posted on an official Navy web site http://www.news.navy.mil/view_single.asp?id=2480Pentagonclock_BBC. The electric Skillcraft wall clock on the left stopped at 9:32:30 is from the Pentagon helipad firehouse outside the west wall and is in the official 9/11 exhibit at the Smithsonian Institution National Museum of American History, http://americanhistory.si.edu/september11/collection/record.asp?ID=19. Heliport firefighters Alan Wallace and Mark Skipper raced out of the way of an incoming white plane with two horizontal stripes on its fuselage that exploded into a fireball at or near the heliport, stopping the heliport clock at 9:32:30. This plane is the source of what one witness called "millions" of pieces of small confetti-like wreckage in the vicinity of the helipad 100 feet and more north of the official story alleged impact point, and cannot be Flight 77, as the fuselage of of American Airlines planes are a silvery polished aluminum, not white.

[340] "'Concrete Autopsy' Helps Strengthen Pentagon," by Kerry Hall, *National Geographic Today,* July 9, 2002, http://news.nationalgeographic.com/news/2002/07/0709_020708_TVpentagon.html.

[341] "It is impossible that jet fuel [fires] raised the temperature of this floor more than 495 degrees F.," "Jet Fuel: How Hot Did It Heat the World Trade Center?" http://911research.wtc7.net/mirrors/guardian2/wtc/how-hot.htm.

[342] Department of Defense News Briefing, Sept. 15, 2001, segment with Terry Mitchell of ASDPA audio visual, defenselink.mil/news/Sep2001/t09152001_t915evey.html; reported with commentary in *Pentagate* by Thierry Meyssan, Carnot Publishing, p. 18.

[343] Jacqueline Augustino, FEMA photos, http://www.photolibrary.fema.gov/photolibrary/photo_details.do?id=4958.

[344] "Pentagon 9/11 Flight 'Black Box' Data File Created Before Actual 'Black Box' was Recovered," http://911blogger.com/news/2008-05-18/pentagon-911-flight-black-box-data-file-created-actual-black-box-was-recovered, by Aidan Monaghan.

THE 9/11 TORONTO REPORT

[345] "Flight Data Expert [Dennis Cimino] Confirmation: No Evidence Linking FDR Data to American 77," Pilots for 9/11 Truth, http://pilotsfor911truth.org/Dennis-Cimino-AA77-FDR.html. See also the presentation by Cimino at the Vancouver 9/11 Hearings, 2012, video at http://www.youtube.com/watch?v=mmGi5YeQ_Bw.

[346] Author's interview of Sept. 4, 2004 with former Acting Principal Deputy Assistant Secretary of Defense for Special Operations and Low-Intensity Conflict Robert Andrews, and article based on this interview published on the website of the Naval Postgraduate School (no longer online), "Special Operations Policy Expert and Veteran Robert Andrews Gives Distinguished Guest Lectures at NPS." See also author's California Jurat with Affiant Statement signed by Barbara Honegger and Notary Public Kelly Harlow of Monterey, Calif., May 25, 2011, which has been provided to the Toronto Hearing Panelists and organizers.

[347] Transcript of the first Pentagon press briefing of Sept. 11, 2001, c. 10:00 a.m., subsequently removed from the Department of Defense website. In *9/11: The Big Lie*, p. 13 footnote 1, Thierry Meyssan notes that as of 2002, it could be accessed via the Yale University website at http://www.yale.edu/lawweb/avalon/sept_11/dod_brief03.htm.

[348] *Firefight: Inside the Battle to Save the Pentagon on 9/11*, by Patrick Creed and Rick Newman, Presidio Press, pp. 276-277, 2008, also reported that Rumsfeld went to a conference room in the Executive Support Center where he joined a secure video teleconference with Vice President Dick Cheney and other officials.

[349] Lt. Col. Victor Correa interview excerpt in *Then Came the Fire: Personal Accounts from the Pentagon – 11 September 2001*, by Stephen J. Lofgren, General Editor, Center of Military History, United States Army, Washington, D.C., Sept. 2011, p. 64, http://www.scribd.com/doc/65563423/THEN-CAME-THE-FIRE-PERSONAL-ACCOUNTS-FROM-THE-PENTAGON-11-SEPTEMBER-2001.

[350] WashingtonPost.com, Sept. 11, 2001.

[351] "The Targeted Ones", *The Washington Post*, from U.S. Navy, Navy personnel and Depot. Defense sources, http://4.bp.blogspot.com/_j1WCY4T_2yI/SSJjfSvi0LI/AAAAAAAAEzI/OS7hJJYawTY/s1600-h/PENTAG~1.GIF. There is precedent for the government targeting its own intelligence personnel in a terrorist attack. Following the bombing of Pan Am Flight 103 over Lockerbie, Scotland, Pan American Airlines sued the U.S. government claiming federal authorities knew intelligence officers were on board, had prior knowledge of the impending attack, and had not attempted to prevent it, http://en.wikipedia.org/wiki/Pan_Am_Flight_103.

[352] "Survivor of Pentagon Attack Has Positive Attitude," by Sarah Zablotsky, *Pittsburgh Post-Gazette*, June 11, 2006, http://www.post-gazette.com/neigh_south/20030611s19kevin0611p6.asp.

[353] *CHIPS* magazine, Spring/June 2003 issue.

[354] "The Last Watch," by Richard Leiby, *Washington Post*, Jan. 20, 2002.

[355] Rear Admiral Jeffrey Hathaway bio information, History Commons, http://www.historycommons.org/context.jsp?item=complete_911_timeline_3229#complete_911_timeline_3229.

APPENDIX

[356] "The Pentagon Attack Papers," by Barbara Honegger, appendix to The Terror Conspiracy (first ed.) and The Terror Conspiracy Revisited (second ed.), by Jim Marrs; more recent online edition at www.sd911truth.org.

[357] E.P. Heidner, "Collateral Damage: U.S. Covert Operations and the Terrorist Attacks of September 11, 2001," http://www.scribd.com/doc/9442970/Collateral-Damage-US-Covert-Operations-and-the-Terrorist-Attacks-on-September-11-200128062008 or http://www.wanttoknow.info/911/Collateral-Damage-911-black_eagle_fund_trust.pdf.

[358] *Pentagon 9/11*, Alfred Goldberg, et al., Washington, D.C., U.S. Government Printing Office, 2007, p. 119, ISBN 978-0-16-078328-9.

[359] Interview with Pentagon renovation construction worker Terry Cohen, NBC Channel 4 News, Sept. 11, 2001,

http://letsrollforums.com/miltary-testimony-huge-explosion-t19067.html, scroll to third video screen.

[360] "Local Washington DC Affiliate Captures 2nd Powerful Pentagon Explosion on 9/11," video at http://www.youtube.com/watch?v=6ykfKS8Rbls. The anchor asks the reporter on site at the Pentagon if she saw anything overhead that could have been the cause of the second explosion, and she answers no, making it clear that it was an internal explosion.

[361] Cheney made this reference that the presidency should be imperial and have the powers of a monarchy in the dissenting minority report he commissioned as ranking House Republican on the Congressional Joint House-Senate Iran-Contra Committee that was published along with the majority report. It referred to his Nixonian opinion that the Reagan-Bush Sr. Administration's sending of arms to the Nicaraguan Contras in direct violation of federal law, the Boland Amendment, should not be considered illegal because the President had authorized it and because the president has the final word in everything relating to foreign policy. When asked by a reporter in 2005 to explain his expansive views about presidential power, Cheney replied, "…go look at the minority views that were filed with the Iran-contra committee."

Chapter 14 References

Altemeyer, B. (1996). The authoritarian specter. Cambridge, MA: Harvard University Press.

Ambady, N., & Rosenthal, R. (1992). Thin slices of expressive behavior as predictors of interpersonal consequences: A meta-analysis. Psychological Bulletin, 111, 256-274.

Asch, S. E. (1946). Forming impressions of personality. Journal of Abnormal and Social Psychology, 41, 258-290.

Bandura, A. (1999). Moral disengagement in the perpetration of inhumanities. Personality and Social Psychology Review, 3, 193-209.

Barber, B. R. (2003). Fear's empire: War, terrorism, and democracy. New York: Norton.

Bargh, J. A., & Chartrand, T. L. (1999). The unbearable automaticity of being. American Psychologist, 54, 462-479.

Baumeister, R. F. (1997). Evil: Inside human violence and cruelty. New York: Freeman.

THE 9/11 TORONTO REPORT

Baumeister, R. F., & Vohs, K. D. (2001). Narcissism as an addiction to esteem. Psychological Inquiry, 12, 206-210.

Bengston, J. K., & Marshik, T. T. (2007). An ecological study of intersubjectivity and the opening of closed minds. Journal of Educational Psychology, 99, 1-11.

Bodenhausen, G., Sheppard, L., & Kramer, G. (1994). Negative affect and social judgment: The different impact of anger and sadness. European Journal of Social Psychology, 24, 45-62.

Brehm, J. W. (1966). A theory of psychological reactance. New York: Academic Press.

Bugental, J. F. T., & McBeath, B. (1995). Depth existential therapy: Evolution since World War II. In B. Bongar & L. E. Beutler (Eds.), Comprehensive textbook of psychotherapy: Theory and practice. Oxford textbooks in clinical psychology (pp. 111-122). New York: Oxford University Press.

Carlson, N. R. (1994). Physiology of behavior (5th ed.). Boston: Allyn & Bacon.

Carson, R. C., Butcher, J. N., & Mineka, S. (1996). Abnormal psychology and modern life (10th ed.). New York: HarperCollins.

Castano, E. (2004). In case of death, cling to the ingroup. European Journal of Social Psychology, 34, 375-384.

Chanley, V. A. (2002). Trust in government in the aftermath of 9/11: Determinants and consequences. Political Psychology, 23, 469-483.

Cho, J., Boyle, M. P., Keum, H., Shevy, M. D., McLeod, D. M., Shah, D. V., et al. (2003). Media, terrorism, and emotionality: Emotional differences in media content and public Reactions to the September 11th terrorist attacks. Journal of Broadcasting and Electronic Media, 47, 309-327.

Chomsky, N. (2004). On historical amnesia, foreign policy, and Iraq. Retrieved December 1, 2009, from http://www.chomsky.info/interviews/20040217.htm

Coady, D. (2003). Conspiracy theories and official stories. International Journal of Applied Philosophy, 17, 197-209.

Edwards, J. (2004). After the fall. Discourse and Society, 15, 155-84.

Elliot, A. J. & Fryer, J. W. (2008). The goal construct in psychology. In J. Y. Shah & W. L. Gardner (Eds.), Handbook of motivation science (pp. 235-250). New York: Guilford.

Elliott, R., & Greenberg, L. S. (1995). Experiential therapy in practice: The process-experiential approach. In B. Bongar & L. E. Beutler (Eds.), Comprehensive textbook of psychotherapy: Theory and practice. Oxford textbooks in clinical psychology (pp. 123- 139). New York: Oxford University Press.

Embry, D. D. (2007). Psychological weapons of mass disruption through vicarious classical conditioning. In B. Bongar, L. M. Brown, L. E. Beutler, J. N. Breckenridge, & P. G. Zimbardo (Eds.), Psychology of terrorism (pp. 164-174). New York: Oxford University Press.

Falomir-Pichastor, J. M., Staerkl, C., Depuiset, M. A., & Butera, F. (2005). Democracy justifies the means: Political group structure moderates the perceived legitimacy of intergroup aggression. Personality and Social Psychology Bulletin, 31, 1683-1695.

Festinger, N. T. (1957). A theory of cognitive dissonance. Stanford, CA: Stanford University Press.

APPENDIX

Frankl, V. E. (1963). Man's search for meaning. Markham, ON: Simon & Schuster. (Original work published 1939)

Gable, S. L., & Strachman, A. (2008). Approaching social rewards and avoiding social punishments: Appetitive and aversive social motivation. In J. Y. Shah & W. L. Gardner (Eds.), Handbook of motivation science (pp. 561-575). New York: Guilford.

Gershuny, B., & Thayer, J. (1999). Relations among psychological trauma, dissociative phenomena, and trauma-related distress: A review and integration. Clinical Psychology Review, 19, 631-657.

Goodwin, S., & Devos, T. (2002, October). American identity under siege: National and racial identities in the wake of the September 11th attack. Paper presented at the annual meeting of the Society for Experimental Social Psychology, Columbus, OH.

Graber, D. (2004). Mediated politics and citizenship in the twenty-first century. Annual Review of Psychology, 55, 545-571.

Greenberg, J., Pyszczynski, T., Solomon, S., Rosenblatt, A., Veeder, M., Kirkland, S., et al. (1990). Evidence for terror management theory II: The effects of mortal salience on Reactions to those who threaten of bolster the cultural worldview. Journal of Personality And Social Psychology, 58, 308-318.

Greenberg, J., Solomon, S., & Arndt, J. (2008). A basic but uniquely human motivation: Terror management. In J. Y. Shah & W. L. Gardner (Eds.), Handbook of motivation science (pp. 114-134). New York: Guilford.

Greenberg, J., Solomon, S., & Pyszczynski, T. (1997). Terror management theory of self-esteem and cultural worldviews: Empirical assessments and conceptual refinements. In M. Zanna (Ed.), Advances in experimental social psychology (Vol. 30). San Diego, CA: Academic Press.

Greenberg, M., Craighill, P., & Greenberg, A. (2004). Trying to understand behavioral responses to terrorism: Personal civil liberties, environmental hazards, and U.S. resident reactions to the September 11, 2001 attacks. Human Ecology Review, 11, 165-176.

Haji, R. & McGregor, I. (2002, June). Compensatory zeal and extremism about Canada and Islam: Responses to uncertainty and self-worth threats. Poster presented at the annual Meeting of the Society for the Psychological Study of Social Issues, Toronto, Canada.

Harmon-Jones, E., & Harmon-Jones, C. (2008). Cognitive dissonance theory: An update with a focus on the action-based model. In J. Y. Shah & W. L. Gardner (Eds.), Handbook of motivation science (pp. 71-83). New York: Guilford.

Herman, E., & Chomsky, N. (1989). Manufacturing consent. New York: Pantheon.

Herman, J. (1997). Trauma and recovery. New York: Basic Books.

Husting, G., & Orr, M. (2007). Dangerous machinery: "Conspiracy theorist" as a transpersonal strategy of exclusion. Symbolic Interaction, 30, 127-150.

Jackson, O. A. (2008). The impact of the 9/11 terrorist attacks on the U.S. economy. Journal of 9/11 Studies, 20, 1-27.

Janoff-Bulman, R. (1992). Shattered assumptions: Towards a new psychology of trauma. New York: Free Press.

Johnson, C. (1966). Revolutionary change. Boston: Little, Brown.

Jost, J. T., Banaji, M. R., & Nosek, B. A. (2004). A decade of social justification theory: Accumulated evidence of conscious and unconscious bolstering of the status quo. Political Psychology, 25, 881-919.

Jost, J. T., Pietrzak, J., Liviatan, I., Mandisodza, A. N., & Napier, J. L. (2008). System Justification as conscious and nonconscious goal pursuit. In J. Y. Shah & W. L. Gardner (Eds.), Handbook of motivation science (pp. 591-605). New York: Guilford.

Jung, C. G. (1956). Symbols of transformation (Collected Works Vol. 5). Princeton, NJ: Princeton University Press. (Original work published 1911 as The Psychology of the Unconscious).

Kelley, H. H. (1950). The warm-cold variable in first impressions of persons. Journal of Personality, 18, 431-439.

Klofstad, C. A. (2007). Talk leads to recruitment: How discussions about politics and current events increase civic participation. Political Research Quarterly, 60, 180-191.

Kosloff, S., Solomon, S., Greenberg, J., Cohen, F., Gershuny, B., Routledge, C., et al. (2006). Fatal distraction: The impact of mortal salience on dissociative responses to 9/11 and subsequent anxiety sensitivity. Basic and Applied Social Psychology, 28, 349-356.

Kruglanski, A. W. (1989). Lay epistemics and human knowledge: Cognitive and motivational bases. New York: Plenum.

Kruglanski, A. W., & Young Chun, W. (2008). Motivated closed-mindedness and its social consequences. In J. Y. Shah & W. L. Gardner (Eds.), Handbook of motivation science (pp. 84-99). New York: Guilford.

Landau, M. J., Solomon, S., Greenberg, J., Cohen, F., Pyszczynski, T., Arndt, J., et al. (2004). Deliver us from evil: The effects of mortality salience and reminders of 9/11 on support for President George W. Bush. Personality and Social Psychology Bulletin, 30, 1136-1150.

Lasswell, H.D. (1937). Sino-Japanese crisis: The garrison state versus the civilian state. The China Quarterly, 11, 643-649.

Lasswell, H.D. (1941). The garrison state. The American Journal of Sociology, 46, 455-468.

Lasswell, H.D. (1950). The universal peril: Perpetual crisis and the garrison-prison state. In L. Bryson, L. Finkelstein, & R.M. MacIver (Eds.). Perspectives on a troubled decade: Science, philosophy, and religion (pp. 325-327). New York: Harper.

Lazarus, R. S. (1991). Emotion and adaptation. New York: Oxford University Press.

Manwell, L. A. (2007a). Faulty towers of belief: Part I. Demolishing the iconic psychological barriers to 9/11 truth. Journal of 9/11 Studies, 12, 1-55.

Manwell, L. A. (2007b). Faulty towers of belief: Part II: Rebuilding the road to freedom of reason. Journal of 9/11 Studies, 14, 1-64.

McClosky, H. (1964). Consensus and ideology in American politics. American Political Science Review, 58, 361-382.

McDermott, R., & Zimbardo, P.G. (2007). The psychology of terrorist alerts. In B. Bongar, L. M. Brown, L. E. Beutler, J. N. Breckenridge, & P. G. Zimbardo (Eds.), Psychology of terrorism (pp. 357-372). New York: Oxford University Press.

McGregor, H. A., Lieberman, J. D., Greenberg, J., Solomon, S., Arndt, J., Simon, L., et al. (1998). Terror management and aggression: Evidence that mortality salience motivates aggression against world-view threatening others. Journal of Personality and Social Psychology, 74, 590-605.

McGregor, I. (2006). Zeal appeal: The allure of moral extremes. Basic and Applied Social Psychology, 28, 343-348.

McGregor, I., & Jordan, C. H. (2007). The mask of zeal: Low implicit self-esteem, threat, and defensive extremism. Self and Identity, 6, 223-237.

McGregor, I., Nail, P. R., Marigold, D. C., & Kang, S.-J. (2005). Defensive pride and consensus: Strength in imaginary numbers. Journal of Personality and Social Psychology, 89, 978-996.

McGregor, I., Zanna, M. P., Holmes, J. G., & Spencer, S. J. (2001). Compensatory conviction in the face of personal uncertainty: Going to extremes and being oneself. Journal of Personality and Social Psychology, 80, 472-488.

Moore, D. W. (2001). Bush support rides the wave of anti-terrorism: Ratings on job performance, personal characteristics soar [Poll analyses, Gallup Organization]. Available from http://www.gallup.com/poll/4975/Bush-Support-Rides-Wave-AntiTerrorism.aspx

Nunn, C. Z., Crockett, H. J., & Williams, J. A. (1978). Tolerance for nonconformity. San Francisco: Jossey-Bass.

Peck, M. S. (1983). People of the lie: The hope for healing human evil. New York: Simon & Schuster.

Petrocelli, J. V., Tormala, Z. L., & Rucker, D. D. (2007). Unpacking attitude certainty: Attitude clarity and attitude correctness. Journal of Personality and Social Psychology, 92, 30-41.

Pilger, J. (2004). The case for civil disobedience. In D. Miller (Ed.), Tell me lies: Propaganda and media distortion in the attack on Iraq (pp. 23-28). Ann Arbor, MI: Pluto.

Prothro, J. W., & Grigg, C. M. (1960). Fundamental principles of democracy: Bases of agreement and disagreement. Journal of Politics, 22, 276-294.

Pyszczynski, T., Abdollahi, A., Solomon, S., Greenberg, J., Cohen, F., & Weise, D. (2006). Mortality salience, martyrdom, and military might: The great Satan versus the axis of evil. Personality and Social Psychology Bulletin, 32, 525-537.

Pyszczynski, T., Solomon, S., & Greenberg, J. (2003). In the wake of 9/11: The psychology of terror. Washington, DC: American Psychological Association.

Pyszczynski, T., Wicklund, R. A., Floresku, S., Gauch, G., Koch, H., Solomon, S., et al. (1996). Whistling in the dark: Exaggerated estimates of social consensus in response to incidental reminders of mortality. Psychological Science, 7, 332-336.

Reed, A., II, & Aquino, K. F. (2003). Moral identity and the expanding circle of moral regard toward out-groups. Journal of Personality and Social Psychology, 84, 1270-1286.

Robbins, R. W., & Beer, J. S. (2001). Positive illusions about the self: Short-term benefits and long-term costs. Journal of Personality and Social Psychology, 80, 340-352.

Rosenthal, R., & Rubin, D. B. (1978). Interpersonal expectancy effects: The first 345 studies. Behavioral and Brain Sciences, 3, 377-415.

THE 9/11 TORONTO REPORT

Ross, L., & Ward, A. (1995). Psychological barriers to dispute resolution. In M. Zanna (Ed.), Advances in experimental social psychology (Vol. 27, pp. 255-303). San Diego, CA: Academic Press.

Ross, L., & Ward, A. (1996). Na ve realism in everyday and everyday life: Implications for social conflict and misunderstanding. In T. Brown, E. S. Reed, & E. Turiel (Eds.), Values and knowledge. The Jean Piaget symposium series (pp. 103-135). San Diego, CA: Academic Press.

Roth, K. (2008). Despots masquerading as democrats: World Report 2008, Human Rights Watch. Available from http://hrw.org/wr2k8/introduction/index.htm

Simons, H. (1994). "Going meta": Definition and political applications. Quarterly Journal of Speech, 80, 468-481.

Small, D. A., Lerner, J. S., & Fischhoff, B. (2006). Emotion priming and attributions for terrorism: Americans' reactions in a national field experiment. Political Psychology, 27, 289-298.

Snow, N., & Taylor, P. M. (2006). The revival of the propaganda state: US propaganda at home and abroad since 9/11. International Communication Gazette, 68, 389-407.

Stouffer, S. A. (1955). Communism, conformity, and civil liberties. New York: Doubleday.

Stout, M. (2005). The sociopath next door. New York: Broadway.

Stroessner, S. J., & Scholer, A. A. (2008). Making things better and worse: Multiple motives in stereotyping and prejudice. In J. Y. Shah & W. L. Gardner (Eds.), Handbook of motivation science (pp. 576-590). New York: Guilford.

Sullivan, J. L., & Transue, J. E. (1999). The psychological underpinnings of democracy: A selective review of research on political tolerance, interpersonal trust, and social capital. Annual Review of Psychology, 50, 625-650.

Sullivan, J. L., Walsh, P., Shamir, M., Barnum, D. G., & Gibson, J. L. (1993). Why politicians are more tolerant: Selective recruitment and socialization among political elites in Britain, Israel, New Zealand, and the United States. British Journal of Political Science, 23, 51-76.

Thompson, S. C., & Schlehofer, M. M. (2008). The many sides of control motivation: Motives for high, low, and illusory control. In J. Y. Shah & W. L. Gardner (Eds.), Handbook of motivation science (pp. 41-56). New York: Guilford.

Tocqueville, A. de. (1945). Democracy in America (Vol. 1 and II). New York: Random House. (Original work published 1835 and 1940)

Tormala, Z. L., DeSensi, V. L., & Petty, R. E. (2007). Resisting persuasion by illegitimate means: A metacognitive perspective on minority influence. Personality and Social Psychology Bulletin, 33, 354-367.

Weaver, K., Garcia, S. M., Schwarz, N., & Miller, D. T. (2007). Inferring the popularity of an opinion from its familiarity: A repetitive voice can sound like a chorus. Journal of Personality and Social Psychology, 92, 821-833.

Widmeyer, W.N., & Loy, J.W. (1988). When you're hot, you're hot! Warm-cold effects in first impressions of persons and teaching effectiveness. *Journal of Educational Psychology*, 80, 11-121.

APPENDIX

Wood, W., Lundgren, S., Ouellette, J. A., Busceme, S., & Blackstone, T. (1994). Minority influence: A meta-analytic review of social influence processes. Psychological Bulletin, 115, 323-345.

Worchel, S., & Brehm, J. W. (1971). Direct and implied social restoration of freedom. Journal of Personality and Social Psychology, 18, 294-304.

Zimbardo, P. (2008). The Lucifer effect: Understanding how good people turn evil. New York: Random House.

Zuckerman, A. S. (2004). Returning to the social logic of politics. In A. S. Zuckerman (Ed.), The social logic of politics: Personal networks as contexts for political behavior (pp. 3-20). Philadelphia: Temple University Press.

Chapter 15 Endnotes

[362] To appreciate just how inadequate the families found the official 9/11 Commission Report, see: *Questions to the 9/11 Commission with ratings in its performance in providing Answers*, compiled by Mindy Kleinberg and Laurie Van Auken, Members of the Family Steering Committee for the 9/11 Independent Commission, 2004.

[363] Kahneman, Daniel. *Thinking, Fast and Slow*. New York: Farrah, Straus and Giroux, 2011.

[364] John Farmer, chief Counsel to the 9/11 Commission in his book, *The Ground Truth*, concluded that high-level witnesses from both NORAD and the FAA lied in their testimony to the Commission. And we should note that omission of pertinent evidence, available but unsought or withheld, constitutes a form of cover-up. John Farmer. *The Ground Truth: The Untold Story of America Under Attack on 9/11*. New York: Riverhead Books, 2009.

[365] *Principles of International Law Recognized in the Charter of the Nuremberg Tribunal and in the Judgment of the Tribunal*. Adopted by the International Law Commission of the United Nations, 1950.

Principle I

Any person who commits an act which constitutes a crime under international law is responsible therefor and liable to punishment.

Principle II

The fact that internal law does not impose a penalty for an act which constitutes a crime under international law does not relieve the person who committed the act from responsibility under international law.

Principle III

The fact that a person who committed an act which constitutes a crime under international law acted as Head of State or responsible Government official does not relieve him from responsibility under international law.

Principle IV

The fact that a person acted pursuant to order of his Government or of a superior does not relieve him from responsibility under international law, provided a moral choice was in fact possible to him.

Principle V

Any person charged with a crime under international law has the right to a fair trial on the facts and law.

Principle VI

The crimes hereinafter set out are punishable as crimes under; international law:

a. **Crimes against peace:**
   i. Planning, preparation, initiation or waging of a war of aggression or a war in violation of international treaties, agreements or assurances;
   ii. Participation in a common plan or conspiracy for the accomplishment of any of the acts mentioned under (i).

b. **War crimes:** Violations of the laws or customs of war which include, but are not limited to, murder, ill-treatment or deportation to slave-labor or for any other purpose of civilian population of or in occupied territory, murder or ill treatment of prisoners of war, of persons on the seas, killing of hostages, plunder of public or private property, wanton destruction of cities, towns, or villages, or devastation not justified by military necessity.

c. **Crimes against humanity:** Murder, extermination, enslavement, deportation and other inhuman acts done against any civilian population, or persecutions on political, racial or religious grounds, when such acts are done or such persecutions are carried on in execution of or in connection with any crime against peace or any war crime.

Principle VII

Complicity in the commission of a crime against peace, a war crime, or a crime against humanity as set forth in Principles VI is a crime under international law.

Source: http://deoxy.org/wc-nurem.htm

[366] Philip Shenon. *The Commission, The Uncensored History of the 9/11 Investigation.* New York: Twelve- Hachette Book Group, 2008.

Chapter 18 Endnotes

[367] Article 5 paragraph 1 of the Statute specifies that the jurisdiction of the Court is limited to the following crimes:

(a) The crime of genocide; (b) Crimes against humanity; (c) War crimes; (d) The crime of aggression. The second paragraph of the same article declares: "The Court shall exercise jurisdiction over the crime of aggression once a provision is adopted in accordance with articles 121 and 123 defining the crime and setting out the conditions under which the Court shall exercise jurisdiction with respect to this crime. Such a provision shall be consistent with the relevant provisions of the Charter of the United Nations."

APPENDIX

[368] See articles 6, 7 and 8 of the Statute.
[369] See articles 1, 17 and 20 of the Statute.
[370] See articles 12 and 13 of the Statute.